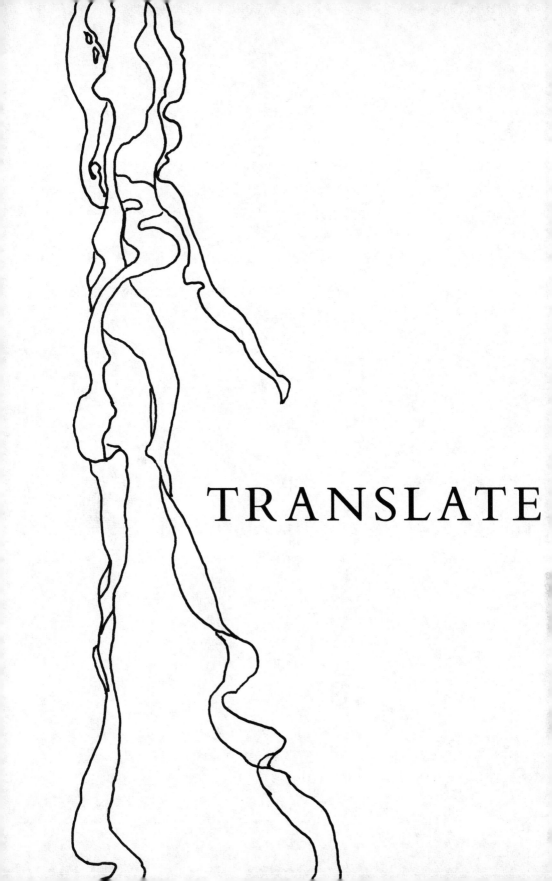

TRANSLATE

CLAIRE DOUGLAS

THIS DARKNESS

The Life of Christiana Morgan

SIMON & SCHUSTER
NEW YORK • LONDON • TORONTO • SYDNEY • TOKYO • SINGAPORE

SIMON & SCHUSTER
Simon & Schuster Building
Rockefeller Center
1230 Avenue of the Americas
New York, New York 10020

10 9 8 7 6 5 4 3 2 1

Library of Congress Cataloging-in-Publication Data

Douglas, Claire.
    Translate this darkness : the life of Christiana Morgan / Claire Douglas.
        p.   cm.
    Includes bibliographical references and index
    1. Morgan, Christiana.   2. Psychologists—United States—Biography.   3. Women
and psychoanalysis—United States   I. Title.
BF109.M674D68   1993
150'.92—dc20
[B]   93-13229   CIP
ISBN: 0-671-70378-1

Quotations from Christiana Morgan's letters and papers are used by permission of Hallee
Morgan, Caroline Murray, Edwin S. Shneidmann, and the Francis A. Countway Library
of Medicine, Harvard Medical School, Harvard University; Harvard University Archives,
Pusey Library, Harvard University; Henry A. Murray Research Center, Radcliffe Col-
lege. Quotations from Henry A. Murray's letters and papers are used by permission of
Caroline Murray, Edwin S. Shneidmann, and the Francis A. Countway Library of
Medicine, Harvard Medical School, Harvard University; Harvard University Archives,
Pusey Library, Harvard University; Henry A. Murray Research Center, Radcliffe Col-
lege. Quotations from Josephine R. Murray's diary by permission of Josephine L. Murray.
Quotations from Lewis Mumford's correspondence by permission of Sophie Mumford, the
Van Pelt Library, and Harcourt Brace Jovanovich for quotations from Lewis Mumford's
letters in My Work and Days: A Personal Chronicle (New York: Harcourt Brace
Jovanovich, 1979. Quotations from Robert Edmond Jones's letters from Hallee Morgan.
Quotations from C. G. Jung's Collected Works, Gerhard Adler, ed., C. G. Jung Letters
(1927), and The Visions Seminars, edited by Claire Douglas, all Princeton: Princeton
University Press; one letter through permission of the heirs of C. G. Jung, c/o Frau G.
Niedieck, Niedieck Linder AG. Parts of Chapter 9 appeared in another form in the San
Francisco Jung Institute Library Journal (1989).

for Lynn, Hallee, Josie, and Nina

Contents

PART TWO
WONA AND MANSOL
· 143 ·

Women have been in darkness for centuries. They don't know themselves. Or only poorly. And when women write, they translate this darkness. Men don't translate. They begin from a theoretical platform, already in place, already elaborated. The writing of women is really translating from the unknown, like a new way of communicating, rather than an already formed language.

MARGUERITE DURAS,
"Smothered Creativity"

Introduction

In 1927, the year in which she would turn thirty, Christiana Morgan received a letter from her former analyst, Carl Gustav Jung.

My dear Christiana Morgan,
Don't think you are forgotten. You would be far from the truth. . . . Let me thank you most sincerely for your pictures and the text. I went through the pictures, but not yet through the text. . . . Your material is most valuable to me. I often think of working through it, because it seems to me as if it were a most beautiful example of the original initiation process.

In early December your face haunted me for a while. I should have written then but there was a question of time.

Thank you for everything. *"Don't blame me!"* You are always a living reality to me whereas other former patients fade away into oblivion, becoming unreal shadows in

Hades. You are keeping on living. There seems to be some sort of living connection (but I should have said that long ago I suppose). You probably need a confirmation from my side of the ocean just as well. . . . But my dear, dear (!!) Christiana Morgan, you are just a bit of a marvel to me. Now don't laugh, there is nothing to laugh about. You were quite right in scolding me.

Yours affectionately. C.G.

Jung did "work through" Morgan's pictures and texts, making them the centerpiece of a four-year series of seminars. She affected others in similarly dramatic ways. The English philosopher Alfred North Whitehead commented to Morgan after seeing a sculpture of her: "Good heavens! What have you inspired? Woman becoming, woman moving out of darkness into light. The most magnificent statue of a woman I have ever seen." The critic Lewis Mumford called her one of the three great minds he had met at Harvard. And Henry A. Murray, one of America's most charismatic psychologists, cried when, past ninety, he remembered her. "She illumined my life," he said. His relationship with her, he admitted, was "the real story of my life."

Who was this woman? Aside from creating the fantasies and paintings Jung mined for his own use, Morgan worked as a lay analyst and as a research associate at Harvard's Psychological Clinic, where she was also a renowned interviewer and the coauthor with Henry Murray of early personality theory and of the Thematic Apperception Test. Her patients, lovers, and friends have recalled her beauty and her style; they have noted her creativity as well as her capacity to listen, elucidate, and yet remain profoundly and independently her own self. However, while Jung, Whitehead, Mumford, and maybe even Henry Murray still have a place in the world's canon, Morgan is forgotten. She remains at most a footnote in other people's history. How and why this happened is the subject of this book, as is the story of her Romantic love.

In the early twentieth century, both Freud and Jung had turned to their patients and to the women around them for help in formulating a psychology of women. In the circle of women around Freud and Jung, there were a few special individuals with a beguiling combination of vibrancy, charm, quick intuitive thinking, a deep interest in the world of ideas, and a capacity for exciting and inspiring the men in their lives. These women tended to manifest a problematical creativity of their own, which penetrated the uncon-

12

scious and explored its realms to a depth that fascinated both Freud and Jung. The women were able to form bridges between their own creative energies and the creativity at times latent in their analysts. However, instead of cultivating this creativity for their own benefit, the women were encouraged to project it onto a series of numinous men and to subordinate their own talents in order to advance the men's work. Each poured her talents and energy into the career of a male analyst who took her as a companion. Recently some of these women—Lou Andreas-Salomé, Anaïs Nin, Ruth Mack Brunswick, Beata (Tola) Rank, Toni Wolff, Sabina Spielrein, and Christiana Morgan—have found a degree of recognition, but all lack a comprehensive and empathic analysis of their struggle as creative women at the center of their own stories.

13

These women enjoyed a closeness to their mentors that men were rarely allowed. This right of access may have been due to their talents or even their beauty, but it may also have occurred because, as women, they were not considered rivals. The other side of this easy closeness was that they were seldom taken seriously. They were never "chosen" in the same way that Freud, Jung, or Murray chose their spiritual sons. Instead the women became, for a time, part of their great man's entourage, serving as patients, students, helpers, and sometimes, lovers. Each ended up far healthier than she had begun, but far less so than she could have been, had her era, her doctor, and she herself accorded her the full expression of her gifts.

Christiana Morgan is perhaps the least known of these women. Jung took Morgan's visions and imposed on them his own conceptual scheme, but Morgan herself vanished under the veil of his interpretation of her reality. Jung and Freud held title to psychology's words then, and what they wrote about the feminine soon became accepted truths. As the scholar Mary Belenky has explained it:

> Conceptions of knowledge and truth that are accepted and articulated today have been shaped throughout history by the male-dominated majority culture. Drawing on their own perspectives and visions, men have constructed the prevailing theories, written history, and set values that have become the guiding principles for men and women alike.

Women's words were acceptable only if they didn't stray too far. Beyond that was the deeply entrenched idea that women existed to serve men and could realize themselves only through their relationships to men.

14   Morgan spent her childhood as an independent, upper-class, post-Jamesian girl in a turn-of-the-century New England family that was part of the small, interrelated, and intertwined group of Boston "Brahmins." An intelligent, large-minded, and headstrong girl, Morgan received only a smattering of education and was prohibited, restricted, or mocked for wanting a larger, more vigorous life. She accomplished relatively little that people recognized as hers, lending herself, rather, to forwarding other people's success. Her own remarkable imaginative quest inspired Carl Jung and opened the Harvard Psychological Clinic to a new way of measuring creativity. Her notions helped mold a third force in American psychology, which focused on respect for the individual and on a personality's development over time.

Not only did Morgan give others a way to explain themselves through imagery; she also, quite self-consciously, "composed herself," to use Mary Bateson's term. This biography examines her tools, her environment, her composition, and, ultimately, her myth. She championed the body, the erotic, and the darkly feminine against American puritanism and flouted bourgeois convention by resolutely taking up an unconventional life. Yet the life she chose, as well as her beauty and her delight in masculine approval, kept many from taking her seriously. Boston, the First World War, the cultural and political ferment of the time, the teachings of Jung, and general views of gender, all patterned her experience, as did the prevailing Romanticism of her time, whose rigorously restrictive script for women claimed tragedy, mental illness, alcoholism, and suicide as the price for female creativity. Much that she could have been was sacrificed to the choices she made, yet much more could have flowered in no other way.

The symbolic meaning that Morgan attached to her own life and work is not the meaning I extract. She accepted, at least externally, a male definition of her role, although she sought a way out of its confinement through sexual experimentation. She learned from an early age to exert her power through the men in her life. As her contemporary Simone de Beauvoir wrote: "It is possible for women to use men as an instrument and perform masculine functions through [their] agency; the favorite mistresses of men of authority have always shared, through their powerful lovers, in the government of the world." In this way, Morgan gave her visions to Jung and worked almost invisibly as one of Murray's colleagues at Harvard. Morgan's ambivalence toward her own gifts makes it extremely difficult to assess her written work, because beyond the few articles or books that bear her name, most of her contributions to psychology rest unsigned and unattributable, jumbled among Henry Murray's unsorted papers in three libraries. Recovering Morgan's work challenges a biographer, because Morgan gave her ideas so freely to others. She did not take her creative work as seriously as she would have done had she been a man or had she been born a generation or two later, when the curriculum vitae became acknowledged as the sine qua non of academic advancement. Indeed, Morgan's uninterest in claiming or promoting her work only added to the prevalent attitude in the thirties, forties, and fifties: that women's work was supposed to be ignored or subsumed under that of the more assertive and credentialed male who claimed it as if by divine right. In going over the Psychological Clinic's files, I found her handwritten notes and research strewn through almost every project Murray undertook.

The fullness of what Morgan had to say has been lost or changed as it filtered through the masculine perspectives, needs, and prejudices of her time. This biography attempts to set prevailing theories aside and retranslate Christiana Morgan's life. It is an effort to tell her story anew, viewing her not as a competitor to the men in her life but as the extraordinary woman she was, given the particular time, place, and circumstances to which she was born. Morgan led a life that was of her time, yet she also was a visionary and an experimenter, who lived a paradoxically revolutionary life within the accepted context of the old. Her lifelong struggle to find a way to put all her talents to use thrust her into a conflict between what she knew she felt and what her culture, as well as Jung, told her she should be feeling. I believe that Morgan's life has much to say today to women who are engaged in a similar struggle. Her particular battle is an important landmark in our understanding of women's historical and psychological development.

The subtext of this biography concerns male and female relationships and what befalls a woman who strives to create a life of her own while remaining in thrall to the idea of Romantic love. Christiana Morgan was a powerful woman who never felt at ease with her strength. She was also a wounded woman whose early experiences left her as vulnerable and conflicted as she was strong. Fierce and perverse, she yearned for a larger life than was allowed a woman and for the expression of orgiastic sexuality, all the while restraining herself and subjecting her force of will to self-frustration.

16   Under these circumstances, Morgan and her lovers occasionally responded to her enigmatic potency with violence. This book traces the conflicting elements in Morgan's character where Romanticism and sadomasochism—its heartless twin—warred together to mute her intensity, stifle her achievements, and veil her legacy.

Part One

CHRISTIANA

Enormous laughter—sadness underneath.

CHRISTIANA MORGAN,
Diary

ONE

Family Trees and Their Fruit

In many lives it is the beginnings that are most significant: the first steps, though seemingly effaced, leave their imprint on everything else that follows.

LEWIS MUMFORD

On a spring day in 1906, Christiana Drummond Councilman and her father worked side by side on the hillside of their new summer home in Maine, digging into the damp, sweet-smelling earth. From where they stood, the land sloped gently down to the York River and an expanse of tidal marsh beyond. Christiana at eight years old was a slender, dark-eyed, even-featured little girl, whose freckled face predicted her later beauty. A strand of long brown hair escaped from her bow as she looked sideways up at her father, her expression somewhat shy, somewhat mischievous. She delighted in having him all to herself like this, away from his hospital, his friends and students, her mother, and her two sisters. A fresh breeze blew past them, carrying with it a briny sea-bottom smell as the ocean tide drew back from the river.

Christiana's father gardened without gloves or hat. Though he was fifty-one, he looked surprisingly youthful and bent easily to his task, his exertion and the sun turning his complexion the ruddy color of his thin red-brown hair and auburn mustache. Christiana, mindful of the reprovals of her strict Bostonian mother, chattered about dirty hands. Her father seized a handful of earth and held it up to her face. "You must never think of this as dirty," he admonished, and then he told her of his Southern boyhood and of his early love for the soil, that "wonderful and mysterious substance which nourishes all plant life." They returned to their work, and she warmed herself in the pleasure of his interest. As she shared her father's fascination with nature, his feeling for the earth, and the joy he derived from growing things, Christiana made an apt and devoted student, unlocking his secret garden world with her curiosity and allying herself with the beauty he loved. And as she embraced the slow and laborious discipline of his earthy pursuits, she became his favorite child.

In a reminiscence of her childhood, Christiana declared that her father, the volatile outsider, had created her through experiences such as these; she responded to him with intense love and an idealization of him and his values. Her feelings for her mother were more complex and echoed her father's mockery of his wife's stern Bostonianism. But at the heart of Christiana's wariness about her mother lay the realization that Isabella Councilman found her middle daughter as alien as her husband. As Christiana grew into adulthood, she adopted her father's view of his wife as a superficial woman defined by an arbitrary code of moral stricture and social grace. Christiana battled this aspect of her mother all her life; she dismissed Isabella's world as "half convention and half lie" yet could not escape feeling suffocated by that world's demands. And although Christiana was her father's favorite, he allowed her only a temporary glimpse into the masculine world he would have opened to a son.

Christiana's parents, William and Isabella (née Coolidge) Councilman, had vastly different family backgrounds. The Coolidges, bred-in-the-bone Bostonians, were part of that small society of interrelated families, sometimes called Boston Brahmins, about whom Henry James wrote so perceptively. Isabella Coolidge, though raised within this highly mannered and select circle, was unconventional in her choice of a husband. She turned away many suitors to marry, at the relatively advanced age of thirty-three, Dr. William Councilman, a new professor of pathology at Harvard Medical School. He was an outsider, a Southerner, and the first faculty member who was not himself a Harvard man. It was not lack of beauty or of social grace that led Isabella to marry late. Early pictures of her show a muted docility, a sultry intelligence. As a young matron, Isabella had olive skin, curly black hair, deep-set brown eyes, and a voluptuous though narrow-waisted figure. Later photographs show a corpulent figure and a face grown hard-lipped and plain.

Despite her mother's early sensual beauty, Christiana puzzled that two such opposite people should have married. Externally, her two parents seemed fond enough of each other, yet within the walls of their home, theirs was a tumultuous, abrasive marriage, and they used their extensive verbal flair to disparage one another's background and outlook. Isabella criticized the Southerner's uncouthness, his disdain for convention, his ribald wit, his love of strong drink, and his penchant for seeking interesting companions from outside their circle. William faulted his wife for what he called her Bostonian pretentions, for the falsity he found in Bostonian manners, for the narrow sphere of her friendships and activities, within a circle he thought of as dull. Although he refused Bostonian conventions for himself, he nevertheless expected her to behave like a conventional woman and stay within the very world he mocked. They expected no change from one another. It was the children who became the battlefield of their war. Christiana remarked that her father used fierce temper and derision, her mother nagging recriminations and icy condescension, in "waging a mortal battle over the values they transmitted to their children."

The daughters were forced to choose sides. The eldest, Isa, and the youngest, Elizabeth, adapted easily to their mother's Bostonian decorum, and they and their subsequent families remembered her affectionately as a highly intelligent, dynamic woman with woefully inadequate outlets for her energy.

Christiana preferred her father's vigorous iconoclasm. She and, later, her son viewed Isabella as convention-ridden, cold, punctilious, and judgmental. Though not denying Isabella's intelligence and vigor, they found her personality too often obscured by a grating irritability and an obsession with petty details. The father and the middle daughter allied themselves against her, making a game of never taking her seriously; instead they laughed at her and designated her the butt of family jokes. Yet in her own character, Christiana echoed some of the more interesting and complex of her mother's ancestors, who hardly hailed from exclusively Puritan stock.

Isabella Coolidge was born in Boston on March 20, 1861. She traced her family back on both parents' sides to the early colonists.

Her ancestors included John and Mary Coolidge, who came with Governor Winthrop to the Massachusetts Bay Colony from England in 1630; Isaac Allerton, who landed at Plymouth on the *Mayflower* on November 9, 1620; and William Shurtleff, who traveled to Plymouth in 1634 as a bonded servant.

22

A rather complete genealogy can be pieced together about her forebears in North America. Isabella's father, David Hill Coolidge, was the first of the family to attend Harvard College (in 1854) and Harvard Law School. He married Isabella Shurtleff, whose father was an eminent physician. The family history kept by the Coolidges, Shurtleffs, and Allertons is often a simple recitation of births, marriages, dwelling places, occupations, and deaths, but it also catches some of the adventure of these settlers' early centuries in New England, with vivid portrayals of many a character whose life differed markedly from "the stern, hard and unloving Puritan ancestors" Christiana and her father deplored. Many of the brief sketches were of hardworking, even heroic souls, who were puritanically religious. Many led uneventful lives in their roles as mothers, housewives, farmers, selectmen, militiamen, builders, and ironworkers, then, more recently, as doctors and lawyers with society wives. But there were also mystical Swedenborgians, madcap brothers, wastrels, black sheep, weird eccentrics, rumrunners, bad wives, elopements, and passionate involvements with unsuitable mates. Three characters in particular stand out: Isaac Allerton, Susanna Shurtleff, and Hannah Dustan. They are extremes—excessive distillations of general family characteristics—yet at the same time they contain elements that troubled Christiana's own character and contributed to the underlying force and passionate complexity of her heritage.

Isaac Allerton was a talented and complicated man whose place in history has been woefully neglected. By far the most colorful of the Pilgrims, he also got into the most trouble. The fifth signer of the *Mayflower* covenants, he was the confidant of William Brewster, the Pilgrim leader, and Governor Bradford's right-hand man. In 1626, Allerton's first wife having died in childbirth, he married William Brewster's daughter, and Brewster came to rely on Allerton to parlay and trade with the Indians.

Isaac Allerton's character ranged beyond the narrow confines of the Pilgrims' tenets. His religious leanings were toward the scandalously mystical Amsterdam Ancient Brethren sect, though he was nominally a Separatist and a Puritan. For a time, Allerton's trading made him the richest man in the colony; in the process he crossed the Atlantic seven times, a heroic feat in those days. Allerton took furs to England, borrowed money on behalf of the Pilgrims, and negotiated settlements for the Plymouth colonists. But he judged men poorly and traded far better and more successfully on his own behalf than for the Pilgrims. His courage, imagination, and an intuitive panache that had little grounding in practicality echo as major keys in Christiana's character, as does his more shadowy side.

On the Shurtleff side, the William Shurtleff who landed in Plymouth in 1634 had a great-granddaughter, Susanna, who lived from 1751 to 1842; she was Isabella Coolidge's great-great-grandfather's sister. Susanna lived her long and remarkable life in a farmhouse overlooking Plymouth harbor. The family biographer in his genealogical remembrances portrayed her as a charming, beautiful child with considerable social and intellectual skills, but as she grew into adulthood, she became a different person. "A change came over the young woman as silent as the midnight thief, more cruel than the grave. She became extremely excitable, restless, wakeful and eccentric. There was mental aberration, and she betrayed permanent delusions during all the rest of her life."

Susanna had what would now be called schizophrenia: she heard voices, talked to herself, had delusions and several autistically repetitive habits. Her biographer blamed her illness on her intuitive sensibilities combined with a precipitating shock. It seems that many of Susanna's friends were killed in a shipwreck off Plymouth. They were buried in the same grave at Plymouth's burial hill, with Susanna and her family in attendance. Susanna's illness began shortly afterward. The young woman spent more and more time at a little table by the fireplace, smoking a pipe she filled with her own home-grown tobacco and talking to herself. She developed her own religion, had remarkable intuitive abilities, and believed in witches and evil spirits. Still, her family and community had a great affection for her and tolerated her vagaries. She lived all her life on her family's farm, dying at age ninety-two.

The third notable personality whose character later echoed in Christiana's was Hannah Dustan, born in 1657. A direct ancestor of Christiana's on her mother's side, she was a Colonial heroine, commemorated by statues in Haverhill and on Penacook, or Dustin, Island. Hannah married a bricklayer and farmer, Thomas Dustan, in 1677 and lived with him near Haverhill, Massachusetts. Near the end of King William's War, in 1697, just days after she delivered her twelfth (and ninth living) child, a band of Indians entered her house, forced Hannah Dustan to rise from her childbed with her baby, then torched the place. (Thomas, who had seen the Indians approaching, had raced home and managed to save seven of the children.) The Indians knew they could not travel undetected with a crying baby, so they flung the little one against an apple tree, dashing out her brains, and then compelled the grieving Hannah to march half dressed through the snowy wilderness to their raiding camp, on an island in the Merrimack River.

Two weeks later, Hannah rose before daybreak one day, stole some tomahawks, and, directing a boy and another woman hostage, proceeded to scalp her Indian captors—men, women, and children—in their sleep.

Henry David Thoreau retells the story in *A Week on the Concord and Merrimack Rivers,* ending Hannah Dustan's astonishing tale by imaginatively re-creating the terror of her hazardous flight through the primeval forest. It is as if he were trying to comprehend and convey the bitter, almost unassimilable horror of her experience. "They escaped as by a miracle all roving bands of Indians, and reached their homes in safety, with their trophies, for which the General Court paid them fifty pounds. The family of Hannah Dustan all assembled alive once more, except the infant whose brains were dashed out against the apple-tree, and there have been many who in later times have lived to say they had eaten of the fruit of that apple-tree."

Dustan's descendants still preserve pieces of the tomahawk and the cloth in which she carried the Indian scalp trophies, while Christiana's niece keeps one of Hannah Dustan's wrought-iron candelabra on her living room mantel.

Hannah Dustan may have returned from the horrors of her adventure marked by more than her heroism, for she bore a daughter within the year. Occasional ancestors over the next two hundred years were unexpectedly Indian-looking, severely courageous, fiercely taciturn, so turned in upon their private world sometimes, as was Susanna Shurtleff, as to suggest mental aberration. Most, though, escaped the fruit of that apple tree, becoming consummate New England club men and like Isabella Coolidge, their social wives.

Christiana Morgan inherited excess as well as rectitude and was torn between both worlds. When she went to see Carl Jung in Zurich in the 1920s, he encouraged her almost psychic capacity for introspection and trance. Her trances simmered with an ebullient, yet oddly savage and bloody, energy in which Indians played a pivotal role. Though Jung tended to consign Morgan's Indians to a parochial American collective unconscious, Morgan's deep connection with Indians seems to have been an essential part of her individuality and creativity, rooted in her mother's link to Hannah Dustan and her Pilgrim lineage.

Isabella herself, Christiana's mother, might have been shocked by her wildly unconventional ancestors, for the Coolidges occupied their place in Boston society in an eminently sober, sane, and respectable way. Though a lawyer, Isabella's father did not have to work hard, and the family lived a comfortable life. Both parents occupied themselves with a round of clubs, duties, and social engagements that kept them closely involved with a small circle of friends and relatives.

Isabella was the only daughter and second child in a family of four. Her brothers were educated at Harvard, two becoming architects, the youngest a doctor. Isabella had very little formal education and suffered from it, but it was considered neither appropriate nor necessary to educate her much beyond the basics of reading and writing and the music, literature, and conversational languages a lady might need to take her place in cultured society. Eventually she turned waspish, focusing her unused brain, often obsessively, on the Saturday Morning Club, her Boston Garden Club, the newly founded Symphony, and a Round Table Discussion Group, where members reflected on such diverse subjects as politics, men's colleges, and theosophy. Besides occupying herself with these organizations, she fussed over her husband and daughters, the family's social life, and innumerable petty details that Christiana and her father thought absurd.

It is much more difficult to reconstruct a woman's history than a man's, especially when the daughter tends to see the mother through the father's eyes and both are veiled by the prejudices of the age. Isabella lived a very proper life and, perhaps as a consequence, was a cipher to almost all who knew her. There is a large packet of letters, however, which Isabella wrote, long before she was married, to a friend of her brother's, William Thayer. A historian, he traveled a good bit overseas, and at that distance a lively correspondence blossomed between them. Underneath the vivacious chatter, Isabella's letters reveal a flair for flouting convention and a sensibility capable of forming deep attachments.

The letters show Isabella as neither so constricted nor so in-

26

tellectually dismissible as Christiana and her father chose to regard her as being. Besides the letters, there remains an intriguing painting of Isabella Coolidge that belies the notion of her as a coldly superficial society woman. The portrait reveals, not a society matron, but a young woman with a disconcertingly emphatic Spanish or Indian type of beauty and great strength of will. She is dressed in a gypsy woman's open-necked white blouse and bolero; her laughing face glances back enigmatically over one shoulder, and an observer cannot help but be caught up by her shining brown eyes and exuberantly inviting smile. The power of her personality is fiercely apparent, revealing Isabella Coolidge in contradiction to the way she led her circumspect Bostonian married life.

Christiana Morgan may have despised her mother's puritanical streak and New England past, and insisted that her liberal Southern father was the source of all that was valuable in her. But in doing so she ignored or discounted her mother's more dramatic and equivocal lineage, full of eccentric, creative, neurotic, and intensely intuitive and powerful people. Christiana also seemed unconscious of the manifestations in her own character of her mother's unlived emotional and intellectual life, just as she was blind to the fruit of that terrible apple tree of her ancestor Hannah Dustan, herself a most barbarously heroic and Indianed Eve.

William Councilman's history is much more easily come by than Isabella Coolidge's. A far more open and approachable figure than his wife, he conducted his life largely in the public sphere, and his career was taken seriously by his peers. Councilman's contemporaries attested to his value in three detailed biographical obituaries, while he himself wrote a long autobiography for his daughters. Christiana sums up her father's personality in a panegyric that is in startling contrast to her astringent comments on her mother. He was "a ground maker for creation. A rebellion and a rebellious person . . . an abundant personality, ardent, zestful, passionate, optimistic. He was a wonderful fusion of the austere and the blythe."

William Thomas Councilman was born in Pikesville, Maryland, on January 1, 1854. His great-grandfather Christopher Councilman had come to America from Holland in the early eighteenth century and settled in Baltimore County. His mother was of Scottish and English descent; her father was a lawyer and a judge, her mother the daughter of a British soldier, Thomas Crane.

In pointed contrast to his wife's interest in genealogy, William Councilman wrote in his reminiscences that the Councilman family "is representative of thousands of families in the land; our ancestors were good simple people leading uneventful lives, good citizens doing their small part in the world with no capacity for acquiring and little desire for wealth and distinction."

27

Perhaps the most notable aspect of the Councilman family was its pervasive connection to the land. William's father, John Thomas Councilman, was the son of a successful farmer. Born in 1816, he went to Yale in 1835, taught school for a while, and then attended the University of Maryland's medical school, graduating in 1843. While a medical student, he married the seventeen-year-old Christiana Drummond Mitchell, then settled with her in Calvert County, Maryland, having been offered a partnership with an old doctor there. He returned to Pikesville in 1852, two years before William was born, buying sixty acres of farmland adjoining his father's and brother's larger farms; here he set himself up as both a farmer and a doctor.

William Councilman remembers his mother as having great natural taste and an eye for beauty. A beauty herself, she was the sturdy, energetic, and firm backbone of the household. William named his second daughter after his mother, noting that the unusual name derived from that of Christian's wife in *Pilgrim's Progress,* a favorite book of his mother's and then of his, both in childhood and later.

William Councilman's nearly two-hundred-page reminiscences are vivid in their depiction of the sights, sounds, smells, and feel of his early farm life: the changing seasons, the variety of work and pleasure offered to a young boy there, the 2:00 A.M. trips to the market with an uncle who sold his excess produce at the family stall, held for almost a hundred years by three generations of Councilmans. He portrays a vigorous, hardworking, delightful "barefoot boyhood" way of life—perhaps best appreciated by a man looking back at a time and a culture now long past.

William's immediate family were sympathetic to the South during the Civil War. Pikesville was a transition county, lying between the Democratic counties to the south, with their great plantations based on large holdings of slaves, and the Republican northern counties, with their many smaller farms and their industries. In the Councilmans' neighborhood there were a few slave-worked estates of over a thousand acres; most farms, however, had

28 two to six hundred acres. John Councilman had three slaves for sixty acres—George, Bill (a boy two years older than William and his most venturesome playmate), and Lucy—and an indentured servant, Margaret, who was the children's nurse. William's uncle, a pro-Northern man, farmed over six hundred acres with four slaves and three hired hands, all of whom were on wages and remained with him after emancipation.

While the Civil War raged just to the south, neighbors and relatives fought, as well as argued, on different sides. Maryland, as a border state, had strongly divided allegiances.

Two years after the war, William, now thirteen, went away to St. John's College, a prep school in Annapolis. At sixteen, he left to join his brother's sugar and coffee importing business. After four years during which he "led an independent existence, raised side whiskers, considered himself a very ripe individual and did pretty much as he chose," he decided to put himself through medical school with the money he had earned from his brother's business. His father urged him to go to Yale first, but a college education was not a prerequisite for medical school admission at that time.

Councilman completed the two-year medical course at the University of Maryland (his father's school) and received his degree in 1878, at the age of twenty-two. He went to work in the biology laboratory of the new Johns Hopkins University, where he was offered an assistantship in physiology. Councilman accepted, meanwhile serving as medical officer and doing autopsies for the Marine Hospital and the Bayview Asylum. He soon found that his interest in histological pathology surpassed the instruction available to him in the United States.

With the money he had saved from his salaries, Councilman found he again could afford to seek the training he needed, this time abroad. From 1880 to 1883, during the heyday of German medicine, he worked in hospitals and laboratories in Strasbourg, Vienna, Leipzig, and Prague; he studied with leaders in the rapidly developing field of cellular pathology, learning as much as he could about pathogenic bacteria and the latest methods of tissue culture.

Upon his return to Maryland, Councilman taught at two medical schools, served as city coroner, resumed doing autopsies for Bayview, and, with John Shaw Billings, started writing the *National Medical Dictionary*. He went abroad in 1888 for further study, returning to see his pathology laboratory at Johns Hopkins become the nucleus of its new hospital. He and a group of hardworking friends who lived at the hospital formed the core faculty for the university's new medical school.

When the Johns Hopkins Medical School opened, William 29 Councilman was named associate professor of pathology and resident pathologist. He is remembered as a lively colleague, a dynamic teacher, and the author of a pioneering textbook on pathology.

In 1892, Councilman left Johns Hopkins to become the Shattuck Professor of Pathological Anatomy at Harvard Medical School. (He held this professorship until 1923, a record tenure.) He met Isabella Coolidge soon after his appointment, and they were married two years later. The Boston marriage register for December 19, 1894, records the marriage of William T. Councilman and Isabella Coolidge as her first and his second. Except that her name was Anne, nothing is known of his first wife, though his daughter Elizabeth refers to him in her reminiscences as having been a widower.

Councilman, a remarkable man, brought new life to Harvard medical school, attracting some of the century's best-trained men to the faculty. He inspired enthusiastic students, who consistently named him among the few popular teachers, citing his vivacity, warmth, and open charm, the Southern drawl marked by a slight stammer, his irreverent wit, and, perhaps most important, his respect for his students.

During these years he maintained a heavy load of teaching, hospital, and administrative duties, yet managed to keep open house in his department so that interested medical students, faculty, and visiting doctors could utilize his laboratory and test for themselves the benefit of his methods. He had been appointed visiting pathologist for Boston City Hospital, and in 1913 he took over the pathology department at the new Peter Bent Brigham Hospital, where his thorough and careful departmental protocols became models of their kind and where further examples of his wit and high spirits abounded.

Between 1880 and 1924, Councilman published 115 articles and eight monographs or books, many jointly authored with students and colleagues, whose careers he encouraged. His published papers were primarily about discoveries concerning the infectious diseases of the day: tuberculosis, malaria, syphilis, amoebic dysentery, meningitis, variola, and smallpox. His last published article, though, was on the symbiosis of plant roots and fungi. Councilman's love of plants manifested itself in extensive gardening, espeically during his summers in York, Maine. It also led to some humorous encounters on the grounds of the newly built Brigham Hospital, where, in the odd free hour, he could be found selecting, planting, and tending many varieties of rambler roses. He delighted in being mistaken for a gardener rather than addressed as the important figure he had become.

This same interest in plant life led him to join the 1916 Rice Expedition up the Amazon, to a year's service, two years after his retirement, on the faculty of the Pekin Union Medical College in China (1924), and to another year's world tour.

The Rice Expedition, according to the private journal he kept of the trip, lacked purpose, definition, and planning. Partly as a consequence of the deleterious and dangerous conditions, he contracted illnesses that undermined his robust good health. After his return, he developed a painful heart condition, became less active, and grew portly. He died suddenly on May 26, 1933, at his summer home in York after a full, vigorous, hardworking, and playful life.

Councilman's warm, almost maternal Southern manner, his love of nature, his sense of wonder and curiosity, his environmental conscience, merged with a Romantic nostalgia: a secret knowledge of and longing for lost Edens. These passions and sensibilities were his legacy to his middle daughter, Christiana; they are inheritances that, accompanied by her deep love for this unconventional, larger-than-life-size man, run as leitmotifs throughout Christiana's life.

The more problematical current came from her mother's stifled talents, from the overdetermined collective world of Isabella's Boston, and from her unrecognized yet potently shadowed ancestry. There was an introspective side to Christiana Morgan that was reticent, withdrawn, inaccessible. Under an appearance of mournful beauty and preternatural calm, there lay brooding depths and ferocious dark places. Her large-souled and maternal father offered her an open and sunny masculine world that could be easily named. Her patriarchally correct mother offered her a coldly lunar world dominated by paternalistic custom and culture. And yet it was the hidden part of her mother's heritage, flowing unknown and unnamed through Christiana, that would compel her to descend into her obscure depths in order to translate its wordless darkness.

TWO

A Turn-of-the-Century Girl

. . . As when a little Girl
They put me in the Closet —
Because they liked me "still" —
Still! Could they have peeped —
And seen my Brain — go round — . . .

EMILY DICKINSON

A little before eight in the morning on October 6, 1897, Isabella Coolidge Councilman gave birth to her second daughter, a large, pretty baby with a great deal of dark hair, whom she named Christiana Drummond after her husband's mother. The birth took place at the Councilmans' home at 475 Marlborough Street in Boston. The attendant weighed the baby on the kitchen scale at an optimistic eleven pounds. Whatever her weight, Christiana needed every ounce of it, for from the start, things did not go well between mother and daughter. Isabella's journal on Christiana's birth chronicled tension and disharmony. Christiana frustrated her first by not being the son she had hoped for, then by her fretfulness and colic. Mother and baby never settled into a nursing rhythm, and Isabella weaned the child at three months. Christiana's colic only increased, and the baby continued to fret and storm, until an exhausted Isabella hired a trained nurse and sent infant and caretaker off to her mother's house. Only then did the baby settle down. When she returned to her family for her   31 belated christening at Arlington Street Church, young Christiana was cooing and laughing.

Unlike Isabella's placid elder daughter, Isa, the new baby seemed a stranger; Christiana's wayward moods and fierce will challenged the mother. In contrast, her husband professed to admire the baby's spirit and early noted that her mirth as well as the reddish tint in her hair echoed his own. Christiana's infancy continued on a stormy path, but she started to laugh, sing, and speak far earlier than her sister had. Her mother recorded that by age two Christiana was singing "Rally 'Round the Flag, Boys" perfectly.

The mother worried about Christiana's excessive crying, her naughtiness, and her lying in order to escape punishment. Though Isabella and the nurse spanked Christiana on rare occasions, their more likely punishment was to lock the baby in a dark closet. The mother noted that Christiana's "habits are slowly improving and her screaming is bettered by a judicious application of 'closet.' " Though her screaming stopped, the little girl grew suddenly quiet and clingy as a result of this draconian remedy, and she started to spend hours punishing her various dolls by putting them in the closet one after another. In this way she attempted to master her terror. Christiana was a highly imaginative child, and her experiences in the closet spurred and augmented her nightmares and dark fantasies.

When Christiana was two, her sister Elizabeth was born. Christiana adopted a superior attitude to the baby, saying, "Poor baby can't talk at all. I can. I love to talk. I talk all the time." Her jealousy showed through in her violent caresses and in her continual teasing of the younger girl. When she was five, Christiana's main delights were dressing up, playacting, singing, and telling herself stories. She had an excellent memory, was reading a bit and struggling to print and write, as well as learning to sew and knit. She continued to have tantrums, but since the inevitable result was the dreaded closet, these outbreaks became rarer.

Within that closet Christiana filled the dark with elaborate fantasies of great heroes and heroines who would join her there, either to save her or to menace her further. These were punishments she made up herself, and so, as in her projections onto her dolls, she learned to subject the closet experience to her will and control.

Though the mother chronicled Christiana's busy life, full of visits, friends, cousins, dancing classes, parties, and holiday celebrations, her tone was austere, distant, far different from the warmth of feeling that flowed when she wrote about her two other daughters. Bostonian manners and cool propriety displaced the simple familiarity her alien middle child needed. Neither the older nor the younger daughter was as sensitive as Christiana or had her strong will. Christiana battled her mother. In contrast, and possibly causing a further rift with her mother, Christiana easily charmed her father. She learned to attract his attention and please him. Even as a toddler she would run into him at breakfast and demand, "Heed me, Papa," as she climbed into his lap to talk.

Soon Christiana was earning her mother's attention in a different way. She discovered that illness gained Isabella's personal care in a way that was otherwise unavailable to her. Her childhood illnesses ranged from colds, coughs, diarrhea, croup, grippe, bronchitis, whooping cough, measles, and chicken pox, to convulsions, pneumonia, rheumatism, and scarlet fever. Before the age of antibiotics and most vaccinations, these illnesses were both more common and more protracted than they are now; yet the total quantity of time Christiana was ill in the first ten years of her life is extraordinary.

The family remained on Marlborough Street for only two years after Christiana's birth. In the fall of 1899, they moved to a larger house, at 78 Bay State Road, which was within walking distance of Harvard Medical School and William Councilman's laboratory in one direction and the center of town in the other. An undistinguished red-brick row house, 78 Bay State Road lay about midblock between Deerfield and Sherborn streets. The building was serviceable enough and suited Councilman's relatively modest salary, but it lacked the outward elegance of his wife's friends' residences. The houses on the opposite side of the street were more imposing, especially since they were freestanding and had gardens around them. The Councilman children could look from their windows through the gardens opposite and out onto the Charles River with its changing tides. Low tide brought ugly and smelly mud flats; high tide, the tugs that the girls loved to watch as the boats pushed upriver with empty barges to be loaded at the Cambridge brickyard and then down again to Boston harbor.

The children had plenty to see on the street as well: the daily comings and goings of neighbors and their children, the horses and carriages, and later the noisy new cars. It thrilled them to catch sight of a fire engine "drawn by three galloping horses abreast and spewing out smoke and flames from the back of the truck." At that time, households like the Councilmans' didn't go to market; instead

everything came to them. Besides the milk and ice deliveries, an S. S. Pierce man came around in a buggy several times a week to collect and then deliver grocery orders, while the Rhodes man did the same for meats.

The people in the largest house opposite them intrigued Christiana. The young husband and wife kept horses and rode out together in the afternoon, the wife often wearing a bunch of violets tucked into her riding habit. The girls admired her and thought of the couple as the epitome of romance; Christiana especially admired the way the husband would gallantly lift his wife from her horse and into his arms on their arrival home. It was a type of married romance that contrasted with the bickering and disharmony she saw at home. Christiana persuaded her sisters to play at being the neighbors: she would be the husband, Isa the wife, and poor Elizabeth the horse (Christiana would hitch up her youngest sister, holding the reins and using her switch in a manner far less gentle than that of their handsome neighbors). A photograph shows the sisters playing such a game, the neighbors' house visible behind them.

The girls had a large brick-tiled play yard behind their house, with a grassy plot at the end. Beside it stood a carriage house, which, because the Councilmans had neither horse nor carriage nor automobile, was used to store trunks, baby carriages, tools, and the barrels of apples they brought back in the fall from their summer home in Maine. Beyond the yard, a huge empty lot fronted on Commonwealth Avenue, as yet undeveloped at that end. From the upstairs windows in the back, the girls had an uninterrupted view all the way up what was then known as Parker Hill and could watch the trains coming and going at Back Bay Station. On weekday mornings, at breakfast, the children would see carriages driven by swift pairs of horses carrying businessmen into town from Brookline. In the late afternoon, while at their supper, the girls often caught sight of a four-in-hand coach headed for the fashionable Wayside Inn, its passage signaled by a red-coated coachman with a long brass horn.

The front door of 78 Bay State Road opened into a good-size hall, furnished with a carved oak chest, a small table that bore the requisite silver tray for calling cards, and a larger hall table, on which perched a plaster cast of the Winged Victory. To one side was an armchair, in which the children were forbidden to sit. The dining room was visible from the hall, a large Victorian table and heavy chairs dominating its somber and rather chilly dimensions; an oversize Tiffany lamp with a green shade swung above. The walls were covered with a dark wallpaper festooned with formal garlands of fruit. Imposing portraits of the children's maternal grandparents hung above the two sideboards, and Isabella's gold-trimmed glassware peered out from the shelves of a display cabinet.

The parlor, on the opposite side of the hall, was a cheerier room, with white walls, white lace curtains in its bay windows, and furniture upholstered in pale green. A piano filled one end of the room, and above it there hung a print of a vengeful God descending in a chariot and glowering down at Ezekiel. The girls practiced their scales under his terrible eye. Christiana, especially, feared him and added him to her closet pantheon of punishing heroes.

Christiana preferred the library, on the second floor, which the family used as their sitting room. The walls were wood-paneled and contained bookcases displaying Greek casts in bas-relief; a long, hard leather sofa and easy chairs made a comfortable seating area close to the wide brick-fronted fireplace, and there were two substantial desks, one for each parent.

The family gathered here in the evening, William Councilman often reading aloud to his wife and children such books as Scott's *The Heart of Midlothian, Hamlet,* and Emerson's *Essays* while they sewed, the books carefully chosen with a mind to the girls' age, if not their interest.

The room behind the library, at the back of the house, was the parents' bedroom. Partly because it was so spacious and sunny, and partly because the girls were seldom allowed there, it became their favorite. Christiana spent her days in that room when she was ill, wrapped cozily in shawls, lying on the large and comfortable sofa under a copy of Botticelli's Madonna and Child. A small third room sometimes served as the father's bed and dressing room, but much to the other sisters' envy, it was turned over to Christiana for several years while she recovered from the effects of scarlet fever on her heart.

The third floor held three rooms: a large back nursery, with bars on the windows, a front room, and a small central room. At first Christiana and Isa shared the nursery, while baby Elizabeth and her nurse shared the two front rooms. But shifts were often made to suit the changing needs of the growing girls. The children took most of their meals in the nursery; there was no dumbwaiter, so the food had to be carried up three flights of stairs from the kitchen. After Elizabeth was a bit older, the front room served as playroom and sewing room. It contained the sewing machine as well as Christiana's magnificent dollhouse, which was the central focus of the room and Christiana's favorite toy. Every spring, the girls yielded the playroom to two dressmakers, who made all the children's clothes: great quantities of summer dresses, heavy winter clothes, wool capes, dancing-school dresses, and petticoats.

The inside of the house varied greatly in warmth, the topmost floor never receiving much heat. It contained a large and a small guest room in front, one of which Isa appropriated when Christiana moved back to the third-floor room they used to share. On winter mornings, a thin layer of ice sometimes appeared in the water pitcher by Isa's bed. Nonetheless, the girls held a special love for this room, for it contained a large highboy full of their mother's treasures— her wedding shoes and stockings, old dresses, and costume jewelry—which the girls dressed up in for their games.

Besides the guest rooms and lavatory, the top floor included a large maid's room, shared by the laundress and the second maid, and a small maid's room, which was the cook's. The family, though they had no savings and lived off Councilman's salary as a professor, were well able to keep these servants, plus the nurse and a daily choreman. The maids, who were mostly Irish and often new immigrants, came and went fairly frequently. The girls remembered a favorite nurse—a Frenchwoman who spoke almost no English— who stayed long enough to teach them quite a bit of conversational French. A German woman was remembered less fondly. The girls wouldn't or couldn't learn from her. She made their lives miserable with her large and petty tyrannies and was finally dismissed after going too far with Mrs. Councilman's dread punishment. The nurse locked Isa in a closet and forgot about her, the poor child being found only at the day's end, fast asleep on the floor.

Four long flights below the maids' rooms lay the kitchen, which opened into the sunny backyard. The kitchen—a very busy place, where the cook prepared three substantial meals a day—took up most of that semibasement floor, with a laundry, furnace room, and coalbin behind it, reaching to the front of the house. Coal, which was unloaded through a chute in the window, was delivered up and down the street at about eight in the morning—a trying time for the girls, especially in their coming-out years, when the "hideous racket" interfered with the sleep they needed after dancing all night.

The Councilman girls longed to have a car, like many of their friends and relatives. Instead they had to walk or take the Beacon Street trolley, with only an occasional cab allowed. Because the Councilmans were less well-off than most of their peers, Isabella's relatives often helped them in subtle ways, such as giving the girls party dresses. Her cousin, Mrs. Peabody, would offer her box at the opera for Saturday matinees. When Mrs. Peabody came to tea, her fine carriage, with its two large coachmen, each clad in a great bearskin cape, would pull up in front of the house, then promenade up and down the block. The children would take to the back stairs immediately, not because they had anything against Mrs. Peabody, but because Mrs. Councilman required the girls to perform for all her guests. The girls would have to sing songs from a French song-book they ordinarily loved, the *Boutet de Monville*. Rebellious, and with some of her father's disdain for this sort of social visit and its pretenses, Christiana hated these performances and, even with her good voice, did badly.

Christiana's godmother, Mrs. William Endicott, "Aunt Nelly," was an Edwardian lady who traveled to Paris every year for a new wardrobe. She wore her elaborate French ball gowns once or twice and then passed them on to the Councilman girls. Christiana delighted in dressing up in them and engaging in imaginary play, but she refused to wear them to dancing school, no matter how carefully they were made over for her. Isa, more docile, obliged but felt self-conscious in the overly sophisticated finery. Aunt Nelly gave Christiana many fine presents and greatly influenced her god-daughter's sense of style and elegance.

Though Christiana liked dressing up in Boston, she far preferred her life at the Councilmans' new summer home in York, Maine. One of Isabella's friends from the Saturday Morning Club was a Mrs. Tilden, who had built a summer home on a large expanse of pine bluff overlooking the York River. In 1905, thanks to William Councilman's new hospital position and the help of his wife's parents, the family were in a position to afford a permanent summer home. They acquired the land adjoining the Tildens' and built a substantial house there, which was completed in 1906.

In the spring of 1907, just after having completed her entrance exams for Miss Winsor's school for girls in Boston, Christiana developed rheumatic fever. Her doctor discovered she had joint pain, an irregular heartbeat, and a heart murmur—all aftereffects of scarlet fever. Christiana was promptly put to bed for the next three months of the school year and thereafter in the Maine house, where "she was carried up and down stairs and up and down the hill all summer."

38

In Maine, William Councilman spent much of his time outdoors, gardening. Christiana was the only one of the girls who shared this interest. Although frail, she loved to keep him company as he continually planned and planted, adding further gardens around the house. In later years, Christiana wrote that only in these times with him did she feel completely safe and at peace as a child. She poignantly contrasted his man's world in Maine to the stultification she experienced with her mother and sisters:

> All the women of the household, mother, sisters, grandmother, aunts and cousins, are gathered on the back porch working on their embroidery. . . . It is hot and the bees drone in the flower beds. The talk is sleepy and desultory, circling pointlessly around this or that name. . . . Frightening glimpses of frustrate tragic lives begin to move in my mind like some horrible dream. . . . Then I hear wonderful sounds from the woods or lower gardens—the sound of pickaxe on rock, or thud of heavy stones going into place, or men calling sharply to each other. This day Pa, Jerry, Kimball and Alden are pulling stumps in the woods. Now, *here* talk has gristle and is spare. . . . A brief consultation, a new combination of ropes and crowbars, curses, grunts, staccato commands, bent backs, a unity of effort and suddenly it is done, the men disperse. I wander back to the house. There sit the women just as I left them, still stitching and the bees still circling and droning in the flower beds.

Though Christiana lived a tomboy's life as much as she could at her father's side during her summers in Maine, she also adapted herself gradually to her life at Miss Winsor's school, which she began in autumn 1908. The friends that she made formed a tight group, who later offered her a more active, even rambunctious type of femininity than her staid mother and sisters represented. By 1910, when the school moved to a roomy and elegant building on Pilgrim Road, it was near enough to the Harvard Medical School for Christiana to walk there after classes, visiting her father in his laboratory and then accompanying him home.

Christiana flourished at Miss Winsor's. The librarian encouraged her love of myths and fairy tales and kept her well supplied with them. Christiana's favorite place became the two huge raftered rooms in which the children built sets, designed and sewed costumes, and rehearsed their spring plays—the high point of the school year. In art class, she spent long hours learning to paint in watercolors and oils, work in clay, and sculpt in wood and stone.

Among Christiana's childhood papers is a seven-page series of drawings from her earliest school days. Titled "The Working Part of the Presidents Castle and the Presidents Slave Grounds," the drawings contain a fantastic abundance of detail; on one page, 118 slaves are enumerated, on another, 70, and so on for each page. The stick figures engage in a Williamsburg-like plethora of plantation activity, with whip- and gun-toting overseers belaboring the hardworking slaves in a way that would do credit to a Harriet Beecher Stowe. One full page depicts a macabre scene aptly named "A Torture Theatre." Here an audience watches hundreds of slaves strung up on ropes and tortured in various elaborate ways that reveal the child's fascination with guilt and retribution—an echo of the strange punishments Christiana conjured in the dreaded closet.

Her fertile imagination also led her to create her own religious ceremonies in contrast to her mother's Spartan Unitarianism. Finding an unused closet at home, she hung a picture of Christ on the cross inside, and fashioned a little altar beneath it, with candles and other sacred objects. In times of trouble or failure, Christiana would steal away to her sacred place, "away from the curiosity of her parents and the mockery of her two sisters," and light candles, kneel, and confess her sins. She would later remember these rituals in writing: "To suffer was to come nearer to him, to be more like him. The more she could exaggerate her suffering and guilt, on her knees before his image, the more virtuous and strengthened she felt."

But Christiana spent far more time on a normal girl's interests and thoughts. To her school's credit, Miss Winsor and many of the teachers appreciated Christiana's intelligence and originality as that of "the generous-minded" young woman they sought to cultivate. Under their guidance, Christiana did well as a child, made close friends, and was generally an eager, lively, and appealing little schoolgirl who found much to do to keep her from her darker fantasies.

THREE

"God Help Me, Is All I Can Say"

Real Life was singing in my ears, humming in my blood, flushing my cheeks and waving my hair—sending me messages and signals from every beautiful face and musical voice, and running over me in vague tremors when I rode my pony, or swam through the short bright ripples of the bay, or raced and danced and tumbled with "the boys."

EDITH WHARTON

C hristiana's adolescence came late and erupted stormily. From January 1913 through December 1917, she kept a diary, which chronicled a coming of age remarkably modern in its self-examination, romantic experimentation, and tempestuous extremes. She battled with the customs of polite society even as she was drawn to participate in them. It was as if one side of her wanted to join her mother's adult sphere while the other challenged its staleness and yearned to set it aflame with a Romantic blaze.

Starting in her fifteenth year, Christiana plunged into a frenetic round of dances and parties. Bostonian mothers believed that a girl's most important duty was to find a suitable husband, marry young, and assume a rightful place in society. It was a mother's duty to see that she accomplished this task well. Women planned the social season so that their daughters met the right sort of boys in a formal and chaperoned way. Initially, the excitement dazzled Christiana; she enjoyed the glamour, the parties, the clothes, and the attention, immersing herself in the life that was expected of her, sometimes to the point of almost frantic overcompensation. After a few years, however, she found the social carousel profoundly unsatisfying. She rebelled. Having tried to follow her mother into her mother's world, she learned that to do so was, as Edith Wharton once noted, to become a parenthesis to the world that mattered. Christiana realized that she had been trying to convince herself that social position and success, parties and clothes, were what counted to a girl, rather than being the "big bribe she's paid for keeping out of some man's way." She blamed herself for being unable to swallow the bribe and settle for the role expected of her, and she wondered if she wasn't hurting herself in the process, if the bribe might be, in fact, the only reward available to her.

At first, thrilled by this new world, Christiana enthusiastically filled her diary with adventures she shared with her school friends: visits, shopping, theater trips, dances, drawing lessons, house parties, summer holidays, Sunday school affairs, musical forays, and volunteer activities. Christiana not only documented her daily life; she explored her inner turmoil. Her youthful introspection revealed early signs of the warring forces that would motivate, and confuse, her relationships in later life.

Christiana began this record by listing the names of her best friends at the Winsor School. She called her pack "the boobs," and in its ranks were Sarah (Sal) Sherburne, Agnes Means, Ellen Tufts, and Hannah Fiske—friends who remained close throughout her school years and early adulthood. Christiana's group emerged as the most popular, most frivolous group at the Winsor School, soon earning the largely undeserved reputation of being "fast" rather than the roistering pack of innocents they were. Christiana, who was quickly growing into her beauty, started to gain the same kind of attention from boys that she enjoyed from her father. He had taught her charm while her aunt Nelly had shown her glamour; Christiana practiced both for the effect they produced on boys. At dances, she longed to be a "belle" but was at first unsure of herself. Before long, she noted the rush of boys to her side, but she listed these signs of boys' attention as if she didn't quite believe her own power. Even as she took pleasure in her success, her diary reveals her laboring to find the words to capture what she was truly feeling. She was at once struggling to fit into her mother's circle, to adopt its collective values, and revolting against it, trying passionately to explore the new. As a well-brought-up girl of that era, she wanted to rebel nicely, but the stage she was given for that battle was excruciatingly small, and slowly her defiance would spill indecorously out of control.

42   Like other mothers in her set, Mrs. Councilman considered Christiana's social calendar the most important part of her daughter's life and encouraged her to attend the seemingly endless round of dances and parties that filled each winter season. At the back of Christiana's 1913 diary alone, the fifteen-year-old catalogued a hectic list of twenty-nine dances and dozens of partners and callers.

From the many boys she encountered, one in particular stood out. Christiana first met Billy Stearns at a school dance in February 1913. After the next dance, a week later, she commented that he had danced with her three times in one night, and added, "I think he is awfully classy." The next day, she was thrilled when he came over to her at a horse show, and she wrote, "Gosh, but I *do* hope he will come to call, I am all simple over him now."

Gradually, as they continued to meet, Christiana turned her diary into a history of their relationship. With almost scientific scrupulosity, she examined the extravagant extremes of longing, embarrassment, ecstasy, and despair of a young girl's infatuation. Self-doubt, though, became the companion to her pleasure as she alternately protested that she adored the boy and then wondered whether she really felt anything for him. Billy and she fought and made up; when they grew closer, she spurned him; when he grew distant, she liked him better than ever. Confused and aroused, she wondered at her own behavior, declaring, "Oh I wish I knew what I wanted & how I felt. As soon as I know he adores me, I don't feel half so keen about him." And so she would turn away, and so they would fight again. The intensity of the fights clearly held an exciting sexual resonance for Christiana. Her experience of first love seesawed in this increasingly tumultuous way over the next three years.

Christiana's initial relationship with Billy Stearns, adolescent as it was, reverberated through her later loves. It is as if she were laying down the template for her adult attachments. Billy Stearns was a type of person to whom she would always feel attracted, a type she could imagine as a young Anthony Adverse hero: stalwart, upright, idealistic, and most of all devoted; evidently he worshiped Christiana. Among the many detailed entries on their romance, Christiana recorded surprisingly little about Billy Stearns himself, although she assiduously wrote down everything he told her about herself. When the two met, he was in his last year at Noble and

Greenough preparatory school in Boston; he went on to Harvard, where, until he became ill with spinal meningitis, he went out for crew and took his studies somewhat more seriously than did many of his peers. He drove his own car and was a regular at the pre-coming-out parties and dances of the Boston and Cambridge Brahmins. A photograph of him at age eighteen or nineteen shows him to be a handsome boy with a somewhat brooding expression. He had dark, curly hair and gentle eyes to contrast with a determined-looking cleft chin. Like the man Christiana later married, Billy Stearns was highly idealistic and a bit young for his age; also like him, Billy had charm and conviction, which she mistook for force-fulness. Absorbing the platitudes then current about men and women, Christiana viewed herself as feminine and therefore in-constant; while she considered Billy constant and straightforward, and therefore manly.

Christiana believed the dictum that it was somehow wrong or unladylike to let a boy know she liked him. Reasoning that love was a game she might lose if the other player learned her true feelings, she busily flirted with numerous boys and pretended to be cool and uninterested. None could be sure where he stood with her, possibly because Christiana wasn't entirely sure herself. When her attention did shine on a boy, his rewards were large, for she charmed and dazzled and made him feel the very center of the world. But she was well aware that flirting with other boys quite merci-lessly heightened her beau's attention and passion. When this hap-pened, Christiana became addicted to the charge she received from Billy's overheated response. On March 8, 1913, she recorded this:

> When the dance began after supper I felt like a tack so I said I would sit out with Lloyd & turned two people down. Then Bill came along & just by way of conversation I said Lloyd and I were getting the measles. Then Bill asked me to dance & I refused. Well later, he danced with me & we sat out. He told me almost in tears, saying he knew it was foolish, that he was so jealous of Lloyd Nichols he was almost dead. So to cheer him up, I told him I liked him better than Lloyd. Then Lloyd Nichols cuts in, & insists on sitting out, & presents me with a pin. Then Billy comes up in tears again almost, & says Lloyd said I gave him a flower. Then I had to explain all that.

It is no wonder that Christiana acquired the reputation of being a heartless flirt. When she acted naturally, though, and didn't behave as she thought young women should, things went more smoothly. At a spring house party marking the final dance of the season, she described just such a moment with Billy: "The last dance we had together was paradise. The only word he said was to ask to walk home with me tomorrow, then we neither of us said a word; & he held me so tight! Every now & then he would almost crush me, he held me so close, & it was all I could do to help pressing his arm."

That fall, the sixteen-year-old Christiana wrote valiantly about her hopes for the school year: she was going to make friends, study well, and have a good time. Soon, though, she was noting her fatigue and her growing habit of staying home from school. She started to get in trouble for not knowing her lessons and was obliged to stay after school for extra tutoring. Perhaps because Isabella was unable to value Christiana's intelligence, or because her own had been sacrificed, or because it was, in Edith Wharton's memorable phrase, "the custom of the country" to devalue women's minds and keep serious business or intellectual pursuits for the men, the mother failed to encourage her daughter's quick mind. Instead, during these critical years, a subtle foot-binding of Christiana's talents occurred. While her male companions underwent a rigorous course of studies at such schools as Noble and Greenough, Milton, Volkmann, Andover, Exeter, Groton, or St. Paul's, and were expected to go on to Harvard, Christiana's schoolwork was increasingly neglected. College was considered out of the question. Isabella allowed her daughter to stay at home from school pretty much whenever she found an excuse. Even the family doctor cooperated, as Christiana noted: Dr. Brigham "said that I could go to dancing school and the theater tomorrow but not to school."

These absences were compounded by another custom: menstruating girls would take to their beds. Christiana, like her peers, had started puberty a few years later than girls do today. Her period came for the first time when she was fifteen and a half. Thereafter, she would make a monthly note in the diary that she "was laid up today," and then she would spend the days in bed or on the sofa in her mother's room. Christiana increasingly used minor indispositions to gain much-needed solitude and to catch up with her studies, faithfully noting the subterfuges in her diary: "Honestly, I must pretend to have indigestion tomorrow as I need to study for my French exam." But even though her mother emphasized the importance of Christiana's social life over her schooling, she faulted her daughter for her flightiness and castigated her as lazy, selfish, and frivolous. Christiana started to view herself in the same, confused way.

Miss Winsor, in turn, seemed not to expect her older students to be too studious. She was canny enough to know that while a few of them would go on to college, the majority had been brought up to come out, take their place in the social whirl, and marry young. Undoubedly familiar with the pace of her students' social engagements, Miss Winsor noted Christiana's fatigue and asked her to drop literature, insisting that she was working too hard.

Christiana's father was of little use to his daughter in helping her channel her energy constructively or taking her intelligence seriously, for in the main he held expectations similar to his wife's. The condescension that accompanied Councilman's treatment of his wife and women in general now began to be directed at all three daughters. It was especially wounding to Christiana after her years of successfully obtaining his approval. Councilman, like most of his peers, took it for granted that his womenfolk would, in Edith Wharton's words, neither "share in the real business of life" nor ever be called upon for "help in the conduct of serious affairs." Instead he sent out markedly confusing signals: he worked hard to support his wife, while mocking her priorities. And then there were times when he would turn and undermine his wife entirely, offering Christiana two dollars for every dance she skipped.

Though her parents were not troubled by Christiana's absences from school, they grew increasingly worried about her turbulent behavior and her group's reputation. What concerned them especially was the cumulative effect of the five high-spirited "boobs" on one another, as well as Christiana's madcap intensity, her fiery relationships with boys, and her pleasure in flouting conformity. Every so often, Christiana felt impelled to tear loose from the stultifying niceness demanded of young girls. She and her friends would go off on long trolley rides, then sit by the roadside and smoke cigarettes, wandering aimlessly from place to place.

In May 1914, after a house party in Barnstable, Christiana drove back to Boston unchaperoned, the only girl in a carload of boys, and on the spur of the moment went with them to racy Revere Beach—out of bounds to a well-brought-up young girl. Christiana's family was outraged when they learned of her escapade, and Christiana herself anguished over the way she could become so giddily caught up in the exhilaration of the moment. Overcome with shame, she saw her behavior through her mother's eyes: "when I went to bed I was so repulsed with myself for what I had done. I loathe myself so and I hate myself for lowering myself to do such a thing, and although they won't admit it, I know I have lowered myself in the eyes of those boys. I am so repulsed at it all I could kill myself. God help me, is all I can say."

46

In response, Mrs. Councilman urged Christiana to go to boarding school for the year before she came out, to keep her from harm. Isabella feared her daughter's impulsiveness and wanted to prevent her tentative sexual experimentation from going further than it already had. It was here, perhaps, that the daughter's rebelliousness and the mother's conservatism conflicted most explosively. In her diary, Christiana had guilelessly documented her sexual attraction for Billy, and it would not have been surprising had her mother secretly read it.

Though notably restricted by the conventions of the day, Christiana's vital eroticism bloomed that year as she and Billy walked together on spring evenings along the esplanade or sat close on the sofa. By the time Billy came to Maine, for a summer house party, he was resting his hand in her lap and finding excuses to hold her hand, while Christiana, in turn, leaned her head so close to him as to be "almost" touching his shoulder. Christiana recorded her body's awakening without any conscious idea that she was writing about sexuality and passion. Even in her diary, now, she was concealing from herself the extent of her involvement with Billy by her "almost"s and "not deliberately at least"s. These words exemplified the breach between Christiana the upright Bostonian mother's girl and Christiana the sexually awakening renegade. The two coincided at this time, because, in her innocence, Christiana could still keep one part of her from knowing the physical reality of what the other part was doing.

> I lay almost absolutely flat on the hammock right on my side [she wrote], and two or three times his head was right on top of mine but I couldn't get up a worry. Then our faces were so near that it was really almost repulsive but I just *couldn't* think it as repulsive because it seemed so divine with him. My imagination worked so that I could have sworn I felt his lips on my forehead but I absolutely know that it wasn't. I couldn't talk at all and he didn't say much except that he was absolutely earnest about this afternoon. The feeling I had on that hammock was ab-

solutely too terrible. If that isn't hitch I should like to know what is! I suppose it was gloom of me to lie that way but I absolutely could not help myself.

In searching for herself, Christiana continued to look outward. As a child, she had examined her father in order to find her own reflection; now she looked to boys to discover her opinion of her teenage sexuality. She overheard Billy talking obliquely to Charles Ames about what she and Billy had been doing on the hammock, and immediately she plummeted into worry over her behavior. The diary again took on the shocked tones of Isabella, surprised and aghast at a hoyden's exploits. In an era and a place where young ladies were still supposed to be spiritual and beyond reproach, Billy and she were holding hands, touching, embracing, and talking of love. "I know that I have no right to encourage him that way when I really don't know my own mind but I get perfectly drunk when I am with him." Isabella Councilman's observations led her to insist that her daughter finish her schooling away from Boston and away from Billy Stearns. Christiana intuitively dreaded the notion and had recurrent nightmares about it; she feared that her first love would not survive her mother's clipping of her unladylike wings.

The school to which Christiana was sent, Farmington, was at that time primarily a finishing school, which many girls attended for a year before they came out and got married. Christiana's sister Isa had been there the year before and loved it. In contrast, the weight of the place crushed Christiana's soul. Without the support of her band of high-spirited friends and the admiration of her beaux, Christiana found her usual swings between extroversion and illness now casting her down into a significant depression.

Christiana was so wrenchingly homesick at first that she couldn't eat. She found the school oppressively narrow; she mocked the little rituals the school took so seriously, had problems with her lessons, hated her room and her roommate, and went from being one of the most popular girls at home to being the least liked at Farmington. Christiana lived for the letters she wrote to and received from her friends in Boston; she also found some respite in illness and the infirmary.

Though the school kept her out of trouble, it offered little outlet for Christiana's high spirits. Its values were based on even more conventional attitudes toward women than Miss Winsor's, its goal being a single-minded inculcation of ladylike behavior. Farmington's program was stultifyingly restrictive compared to the imaginative one at Miss Winsor's, and there was little to do after class. Instead of rollicking around Boston with her friends, Christiana now spent her free time crocheting, sewing, or taking formal walks with other girls, which had to be organized far in advance as "dates."

Christiana longed for the outside world, bemoaning how little news of it seeped into the claustral confines of the school. War was fast approaching, and she was seized with interest about it; she chafed at the paucity of details available to her, only hearing of the sinking of the *Lusitania* by chance. The school kept the real world out as much as possible, though students were allowed to sew bandages for the Red Cross.

The girls, by and large, seemed content to fill their empty hours talking, playing cards, dancing with each other, or just hanging about. Sundays were especially bleak and endless. Christiana grasped at what life she could—an occasional outbreak of giggles, an outing, a game of baseball. Finding her studies dull, she ignored homework and began to read and reread the Cantica III, "Purgatory," from Dante's *Divine Comedy* at night under the bedclothes, conjuring a world of fantasy as Farmington crowded in on her with the ominousness of her childhood closet.

Besides Dante and her fantasies, Christiana found solace in religion; this time it wasn't the closet rituals of her preteen years but inspiration from the young minister who came to teach the school's Bible class. She studied the Old Testament, fascinated by the stern power of the patriarchs. In late February, after a stay in the infirmary that she accurately called a "semi-collapse," accompanied by unremitting headaches, she was taken out of school by her family. Already slender, the unhappy girl had no appetite and continued to lose weight; she could only respond to her father with tears, not knowing, herself, why she was so unhappy. After a short consultation at home, her father and the family doctor hospitalized her at Peter Bent Brigham. Christiana wrote dolefully: "I have an awfully nice little private room but I never felt more dead discouraged, and I was such Niagara." The doctors tested her heart and X-rayed her, but everything proved negative; they then brought in Dr. George Waterman, who specialized in nervous illnesses. Dr. Waterman diagnosed her as suffering from depression—the first of the depressive episodes that were to recur throughout her life. After a week in the hospital, she was sent home to recuperate, with doctor's orders that she remain at home for the rest of the school term.

Dr. Waterman followed James Jackson Putnam, George Beard, and Weir Mitchell in considering this sort of neurasthenia or melancholia a woman's particular problem that derived, not from restriction in too narrow a sphere, but from her improperly exciting her mind in a world too large for her. These doctors decreed a cloistered stillness and an exaggeration of the very passivity that afflicted her. The patient was to be closeted away from the world, to avoid stimulation, give up reading, and, above all, not use her mind. Creative but troubled, the afflicted women, it seemed, injured their psyches through cultivating or exercising potency.

Throughout the rest of her adolescent years, Christiana's exuberant gaiety returned occasionally at a dance or with a boyfriend, but generally it was curbed. A consistently sober note of self-questioning appeared in the diary now. Farmington and Dr. Waterman's course of treatment had done their jobs well: Christiana subdued her vigor and energy at the cost of recurrent bouts of depression, which were an acceptable part of the custom of the country. What woman, reading this even today, does not recognize some echo in herself of the change brought about in Christiana, and some memory, however slight, of a death in herself as she was socialized into the mores of late-adolescent femininity. All too often, some sad breakage of the spirit occurs, where the wild, free passions of girlhood are given up, sometimes through external pressure, sometimes voluntarily in exchange for popularity, conformity, and collective values, or else that same energy turns inward in fantasy in its very effort to keep itself alive, or becomes weighed down by the exertion of revolt. Tractable girls, like Christiana's older and younger sisters, could enter adolescence seamlessly, as if their girlish vigor were but a passing phase that yielded smoothly to the values of their mothers and society. Christiana found that the custom of the country threatened her very essence, yet lacking outside support, she faulted herself and soon conspired in her own defeat.

On her return home, Christiana felt out of tune with her old friends, though they visited her, and Agnes Means, especially, skipped school to keep her company. Christiana now dreaded the dances, and the boys had begun to bore her; everyone felt too young. When not blaming herself, she longed for something beyond herself and yearned to be taken seriously. "I am crazy to meet some older person and be able to talk sensibly to them." She started to turn against women too, disparaging them for their undeveloped minds, finding them petty and frivolous, noting how uninteresting their lives were in comparison to men's.

Over the winter and early spring of 1915, Christiana's first depression slowly lifted. With her spirit now somewhat broken, she returned to a happier, even placid spring term at Farmington. "Hat said she thought I had changed more than any girl this year. I think I have too, and in spite of all the terrific gloom I went through, I feel that what I have gained is worth it all." She joined in her schoolmates' interests and in their rituals with untypical meekness. Her diary entries became briefer and equivocal. The radiance of spring itself helped the girl and nourished her aesthetic sensibility; she found solace in the beauty of the gardens, in walks in the woods and among the blossoming trees, in the odor of the lilacs and the pleasures of hearing mandolin music under a full moon. That these were the last months she had to remain at Farmington also helped, and she found a subdued pleasure where she could.

Christiana regretted that she had not made better use of her time at school, yet much of it had seemed to offer her so little. She reread her diary and turned against her younger self and her rapscallion vigor: "Tonight I was reading over my diary and honestly some of the things I said last year repulsed me so. It perfectly revolts me when I think last year I really thought I loved. I think I've really grown lots older this year since I've been here [at Farmington]. Billy has absolutely gone out of my life now & I never give him a thought. It seems so funny after all last year." One of her last entries of the school year indicates the finality with which she faced her difficult coming of age: "It just came over me how I was leaving school to go out into the world and have all the worries and cares and big experiences. It seems too dreadful to think that I am grown up."

Like a Stain
of Blood

White & cool & fresh I thought her
As she came to me—
All white.
But the whiteness of her scorched my eyes
It turned to red, red & deep purple,
Shot through with flames of blue
That quivered, died down
And leaped up hungrily again;
Making her fiery robe more scarlet
And the crimson of her lips more aching.
Blinded I was;
Torn and panting.
And my soul felt seared with crimson
Like a stain of blood upon the whiteness of
    her purity.

CHRISTIANA COUNCILMAN,
March 30, 1917

I t was only a temporary capitulation, but for the time being at least, Christiana had neither the energy nor the will to pursue her risky course of exploration. For the next few years, her diary took on a heavier, darker tone and became a record without originality and verve. By her coming-out year, she was blasé and fatigued; lacking the high spirits that had formerly attracted a rush of new partners, she was now seldom the center of attention. More troublingly, she turned against the most creative part of herself. It was as if her youthful spirit had peaked and passed but nothing of substance had taken its place.

    She kept pretty much to the same small group, feeling herself less successful than she had been in the past but carrying on with a full schedule of lunches, teas, and dances. The newspapers made much of her, calling her "one of this season's most popular debutantes" and mentioning her membership in the Sewing Circle or the Vincent Club, exclusive groups of Boston society girls. She poured at club teas, ushered or played small roles in their plays,

52 and joined her friends in their bandage sewing and other charitable ventures, trying to make the most of what they offered. A photograph taken the year of her coming-out ball captures her radiance; in it, she looks straight at the camera, without disguise. It is a strong and beautifully proportioned face, with high cheekbones, large dark eyes, and full lips. But the image cannot hide a darker current of melancholy that shadows her face.

For a moment, however, Christiana could recapture the old thrill and find everything "too marvelous for words," especially when the ball was fancy, when she looked beautiful, and when the attention she received approached what she had experienced in the past. The temporary vivacity, though, usually came off with her ball gown, revealing an underlying sadness. Christiana's heart seemed no longer in the social whirl—it was just something to do for a season or so until a girl married. The social "bribe" for a woman's insignificance seemed increasingly hollow to Christiana as the sadly merry young group convinced one another of the marvelous time they were having, busying themselves with yet another ball, doing the same thing, dancing the same dances, saying the same things to the same people, night after night after night.

Christiana wondered why her spirits were so low in a year that was supposed to be so wonderful and why she was finding so little meaning in her life. William and Henry James's sister had experienced a similar coming of age in Boston; Alice James blamed herself but also attributed her misery to the terribly restrictive social stage offered a young lady in Boston, the "stupidity and want of imagination of the Bostonians, whose highest idea of doing a pleasant thing for you is to ask you to meet someone you see every day." In her adult diaries, James recorded a turmoil and a psychic castration that resembled Christiana's a generation and a half later: "I had to peg away pretty hard between 12 and 24, 'killing myself,' as some one calls it—absorbing into the bone that the better part is to clothe oneself in neutral tints, walk by still waters, and possess one's soul in silence."

One event that temporarily reconciled Christiana to her narrow world was the engagement and marriage in February 1916 of her elder sister, Isa, to Frank Wigglesworth, a fellow Brahmin, who had just graduated from Harvard. Christiana liked and respected Frank and enthusiastically adopted him as a new sort of man in her life—an elder brother who could help and advise her. Meanwhile, the wedding itself represented the highest point of a young woman's life for girls like herself. Christiana's mother planned the affair with even more attention than was paid to the girls' coming out. Christiana captured her happiness for Isa in a letter she wrote to her aunt Alice in Maryland. "Well, even if she is my own sister I don't mind saying she was the loveliest bride that I ever dreamed of. . . . She had beautiful coloring and the expression on her face was enough to make you cry when you looked at her. I can't describe her at all or make any attempt to—she just looked sublimely beautiful for words, and perfectly calm."

The clipping Christiana inserted in her diary contained a full description of the formal and social aspects of the wedding, including the names of the ushers, one of whom was Henry Alexander Murray, a man to whom Christiana paid little attention but who was to assume a pivotal importance in her later life.

Following the exuberance of the wedding, Christiana again plummeted into the self-doubting depression that, since Farmington, increasingly marked her winters. Toward the end of her coming-out season, she wrote: "Went to the last Saturday evening and had a punk time because I was so awfully tired & I just felt that I didn't care if I never saw one of the people who were there again. I was just so tired of them. They all seem so young & so trivial. . . . I just long to find my place in the world and get out of this. Of all the people I've seen this winter Bill & Floyd are the only ones I'd ever care about seeing again."

Bill Meeker had caught her attention early in the season, but though he sought her out and danced with her, he shied away from a romantic involvement, preferring to be her confidant. Floyd Blair was a different sort of boy; against her better wisdom and her friends' advice, he soon became her steady boyfriend and, for a time, lifted her out of herself and into a temporary but powerful infatuation.

Although he was a Harvard graduate and a student at Harvard Law School, Floyd Blair came from outside Christiana's class. He was not popular among Christiana's group, being older and considered a bit too ambitious, too serious. Unlike her friends, Floyd was expected to earn his own money during school holidays. He had a robust coarseness and power that both attracted and repelled Christiana. She carried on with Floyd in much the same way she had with Billy Stearns; she became bored when he was under her spell and fascinated when he seemed least interested. Floyd was primarily drawn to Christiana's beauty; he remained profoundly uninterested in her ideas. But their relationship was far more darkly layered, enigmatic, confused, and complex than that of Christiana and Billy. Part of the reason for this was Christiana's new awareness of her sexuality.

Isa, after her engagement and marriage, started to share her sexual knowledge with her sister, while Christiana's mother enlightened her about the facts of life. Consequently, when Christiana and Floyd picked up where she and Billy Stearns had left off a year or so before, she understood what was going on.

> March 28, 1916
> I am so sick of thinking about F. that I am nearly crazy. I can't get him out of my head and I feel as though I had grown years older during these last two weeks. I look at everything with such a different point of view. One minute I feel as though I was keen about him & the next as though I could never think of such a thing. It is all turmoil and I wish I would hurry up & decide altho of course it is much better to wait. It makes me furious now to think of having told anyone or having let anyone suspect— which I certainly have—but it won't happen again. I think I made a mistake in not seeing him oftener and I am going to suggest the idea to him. Honestly the whole thing is hell. I worry & think about it so much that it is too awful. Frank [Isa's fiancé] said he would find out what Dick Wig [Wigglesworth] thinks of him & I am dead to know. You can tell so much by what other men think.

The men's reports were not what she expected. They did not approve. Besides that, after Floyd had visited the house a few times, Christiana's father added his warning on the young man's unsuitability. Yet Christiana remained deeply attracted to Floyd's ardor and single-minded pursuit; that he was an outsider and forbidden only excited her. She enjoyed playing with fire. At the next dance, Christiana told Floyd of her family's views on the impropriety of their relationship. Whereas Billy Stearns would have retreated at once, Floyd advanced more forcefully. Christiana wrote in her diary: "He agreed about its not being fair & said it made him feel so bitter to think he had nothing to offer me—no money, no social position. He danced with me every second after that & once I have an idea that he kissed my cheek altho I'm not sure. I have an idea that somehow I have given him some encouragement & I am rather worried about him."

In spite of her parents' admonitions, Christiana, so unsure of her own mind that she alternately spurred Floyd on and decided to break it off, kept seeing him. Her values remained elusive, her judgment provisional, as she first followed his lead, then retreated to her mother's world. The relationship seesawed for over a year. Floyd insisted he would make her marry him; his force of will and passion aroused her, and they got more and more deeply involved sexually.

> I knew I was playing with fire but I revelled in it, so I guess it was mostly my fault when his self control broke down absolutely and he kissed me madly & passionately on the lips over and over again with all the strength that was in him, half suffocating me but the more I resisted the worse it was so I just had to give in and wait until his passion exhausted itself. For almost half an hour his lips never once left mine and I felt as though I were being crushed to death, but he didn't seem to hear anything I said. After he had gone I felt so weak and sick that I could hardly walk. I felt as though the bloom of my girlhood had been desecrated & torn from me. Hot hands had been laid upon me, & I felt my face sort of seared with those passionate kisses. From now on I will know the meaning of passion all right—as I never could know it otherwise and with a sort of horror to think how anyone could lose their self control that way, & the power of it—not to be able to stop it because it sweeps you off your feet with the terror of its intensity. I feel as tho I had grown so much older and wiser as tho there wasn't a thing that was awful that I didn't know, as though I wasn't fresh anymore, and every time anyone kisses me on the lips I feel sort of sick. The memory of it haunts me. When kisses are full of reverence, they seem wonderful even with passion, but there was no reverence in these—as though any woman would do, and that's what makes them so awful & what makes me feel as though I wasn't any longer fresh. How horrible it would be to endure that when you didn't want it. I realize as I never could have before what some women have to endure, and also how easy it must be for some women to go wrong.

Christiana's diary began fully to explore her inner war. One side of her listened to her family and convention and decided her entanglement with Floyd had to stop. Searching for reasons, she faulted Floyd for being narrow and materialistic; she saw herself as

his opposite—cultured where he was uncouth, idealistic where he
was Machiavellian, and with a large heart and wide view of the
56   world, while he "absolutely lacks poetry in his nature." She compared him unfavorably to her family and criticized him as incapable
of offering her the intellectual stimulus and aesthetic sense she drew
from her mother's and father's worlds. But when she looked again,
she found he did answer her desire for the outrageous and excessive—for the intensity that her own world denied. When he didn't
listen to her and forgot himself in his passion, Christiana wrote that
his "mastery always gives me a wild thrill." Her indecision took
on a frantic tone as she and Floyd progressed beyond kissing and
he refused to accept her increasingly frequent brush-offs.

> I am so upset & depressed. For the last two weeks I have
> been meaning to send Floyd away but somehow when I
> come to the point my courage seems to desert me & I just
> can't do it, & when he leaves I loathe myself for a weakling
> & a coward. When I am all alone with him he sort of
> compels me—he is so quiet & forceful & insistent, & I
> care enough for him to be an awful coward about facing
> that wounded, hurt look that his eyes would have should
> I tell him. I can't bear to see him suffer. Then, too, I realize
> perfectly that I get more or less carried away by his passion
> when I am with him. . . . I know I am a lie & living a lie
> and that each time I put the inevitable end off I weaken
> myself who am only too weak already,—& make it in the
> end harder for him. I may not mind telling a lie but I loathe
> living one. I wonder what the matter with me is.

Nothing could sound less like a Farmington debutante.
Through her tentative affair with Floyd and its ultimate resolution,
Christiana regained some of the passionate intensity that her
finishing-school year had almost muted. Their final breakup allowed
her to regain a sense of her own individuality and to perceive how
much more complex and layered her feelings were than what she
saw around her.

> I don't think that I ever suffered so much in my life as I
> did tonight. Floyd came in & when I saw him I felt all
> my courage go, & I broke down completely. He was so
> much more intense and passionate than he had ever been
> before that it seemed too unbearable. When I finally told
> him that I couldn't go on—that I didn't love him enough,
> I felt the suffering in the silence that followed as I have

never felt suffering before. Somehow then it seemed as
tho all my superficiality had slipped away, & my heart
which before had seemed so cold & hard, was finally
pierced to the quick & bleeding.

Part of her revolt now turned inward into self-blame, as the
frustrations and inhibitions of her narrow Bostonian world continued to drain the blood from her life spirit. Where her male contemporaries were encouraged, channeled, and disciplined to make
something of their talents, Christiana's intelligence was not taken
seriously, nor could she find a useful outlet for it. Instead of making
a mark in the world, she was expected—and herself expected—to
marry someone who could do so while she occupied herself with
a social and cultural life: a little reading, some sewing, visits, perhaps
some charity work, and, above all, being useful to her husband.
As her closeted world pressed in on her, the outside one was fast
drawing the United States into war; she felt infuriatingly peripheral.
"In my diary this year," Christiana wrote, "I have resolved to write
mostly just my thoughts as what I do each day amounts to so little."

As she wished for someone who could take her out of herself,
Christiana started to explore and formulate her own longings and
desires. "I want to feel everything for myself—great sorrow or
great joy— Oh God, I want to feel to really find myself in feeling."
She bemoaned her lack of grounding in this: "I have no creed to
live up to no religion to fall back on, no framework to hang anything
on and my feet are drifting and I am drifting and while I go on this
way I never can do anything."

A new friend burst into Christiana's life in May 1916 and gave
a powerful impetus to her search for self-definition. The two
women had met the previous summer, when Christiana visited
mutual acquaintances in Cape Cod. Lucia Howard was an unmarried
woman of thirty-six, a rather tall and imposing New Yorker with
a long, sallow, and somewhat horsey, intelligent face. Unlike Christiana's socialite friends, Lucia had not only gone to college but
traveled widely; she had even met the small group of intellectual
women who were to center themselves in Bloomsbury. She read
Lawrence and Freud and German philosophy. At first her frank and
sometimes outrageous opinions simply made Christiana laugh, but
before long the younger girl became Lucia's disciple. Lucia recognized Christiana's intelligence and responded to her questing
spirit; Christiana's enthrallment with Lucia echoed the infatuation

she first felt for Billy and Floyd. In the spring of 1916, her diary was as full of Lucia as it once had been of the two men.

58 Christiana's new friend was intense, excessive, oppressive, high-strung, opinionated, and given to aesthetic rhapsodies about feeling and beauty. Like Hermione in D. H. Lawrence's *Women in Love,* Lucia somehow made Christiana feel *"unbounded* and *uplifted,"* as if everything about Lucia came with emphasis attached.

The older woman brought a strong gust of new ideas and new life into Christiana's deadened world, appearing almost providentially as a simultaneous antidote to Isabella Councilman and to Floyd. Lucia was very much a "new woman," eagerly involved in politics, women's issues, and self-discovery. She and Christiana read and talked endlessly about "serious things"—religion, politics, sex, the war, aesthetic beauty—that Christiana thought only men could discuss. It was as if this strange woman allowed Christiana to examine her own doubts through new eyes.

> These days in Barnstable have been perfect heaven for me. Lucia is such a wonder. It seemed all the time as though all conventionality was stripped from my eyes and she was showing me the world as it is without the artificiality that there is to our lives. *Why, why* do we have to cramp our feelings & our natural desires. It seems so awful to think of people not being able to expand or think naturally or feel different experiences, but to be crushed and choked with it. It is too awful and I will fight against it. I won't be one of the ones who are. Ma is & so is almost everyone I know. Of course I realize that a certain amount of convention is necessary but why do we have to make our feelings so. Lucia says that the only two real forces in human nature are religion and sex.

Lucia embraced Christiana as a fellow free mind and aesthete. Christiana in turn opened herself to Lucia's enthusiasms for religion, for music, and for all "the great things in life." Through Lucia, Christiana discovered a mirror for her own fervency. "Lucia has such a wonderful appreciation of beauty that my soul was just flooded and filled with it."

As the summer of 1916 progressed, Christiana expanded when she was with Lucia and then contracted into confusion and doubt when surrounded by her old friends and family. Few of them cared much for Lucia, though she welcomed Christiana's friends and, in spite of her age, seems to have become part of the same young group at Barnstable. Nevertheless, Lucia's influence on Christiana worried her parents.

With Lucia as her guide, Christiana started to realize how little 59 she had used her mind. "Thank God, I am beginning to think & pray that I may never slip back again into that peaceful narrow groove of no thought." Under her friend's tutelage, she dove into new territory, noting the titles of thirty-five books read in 1916, among them Tolstoy's *War and Peace, Resurrection,* and *Anna Karenina.* Christiana also read contemporary history, Walpole and Galsworthy, and books by Arnold Bennett, Omar Khayyám, Edith Wharton, Henry James, Jane Addams, H. G. Wells, and the poetry of Browning.

Lucia appears to have been one of those large-souled new women who seized her own power through the life of the mind but had little use for men. Christiana pondered Lucia's aversion as opposed to her tendency to idealize men. "I can't believe that all men are bad, as Lucia seems to think." Lucia also shook Christiana's acceptance of the imbalance between the sexes and the opposition to suffrage for women that she had learned from her father, an opposition that was based on women's inability to enter men's worlds. After her exposure to Lucia's thought, however, the inequality of social relations between the sexes began to worry Christiana:

> Lately I have been getting this horrid idea into my head of rebellion against the position of women, sometimes it seems to me that their whole life is merely for men's pleasure, & they have to endure all the suffering & all the drudgery & it seems so unequal. I know it can't be helped but I hate the idea, I don't know what has come over me & I hope & I pray I get this out of my head bec. I loathe a woman who is always talking about rights etc. It would be good for me now to fall madly in love & get these horrid ideas out of my head. I seem to hate the idea of marriage & being used. Oh, I don't know why I have got this horrible sordid turn of mind—taking all beauty out of life.

Though the hugs, hand-holding, and touching that Lucia demanded were not unusual among women of that era, to a more sophisticated reader in a more sophisticated time, her interest in Christiana clearly held a lesbian element, whether conscious or unconscious, acted upon or not. Christiana, however, seems not to have responded: "Lucia rather irritated me the way she kept wanting to hold my hand. I loathe demonstrations in public & anything like that is so foreign to my nature that it is always an effort." She was further repelled by Lucia's loverlike jealousy and proprietary claims and by something too intense, "too tragic, too serious for my youth . . . such a sort of exaggeration of emotions. And then I was beginning to weary of her excessive devotion—all the time kissing me & expecting it in return which is always an effort on my part, because it is so foreign to my nature to act that way with women." Yet for two years this relationship provided Christiana with permission to explore parts of herself that her family, her teachers, and her Brahmin companions had preferred to ignore. In spite of, or maybe because of, all Lucia's excesses, she gave Christiana back a part of her soul that had been temporarily lost and from which she would never again entirely turn away.

Christiana summed up her debt to Lucia:

> "Be true to the highest within your own soul, and then allow yourself to be governed by no customs or conventionalities or arbitrary man-made rules that are not formed upon principle."
>
> Lucia sent that to me today and it seems to fit me exactly—the words that I have always felt. She is a blessing to me and I adore her—she understands so much that no one else does. She wants me to go to Honolulu with her this winter. What I wouldn't give to go! But of course it is impossible only I long to travel so and get away and see things. The sameness of Boston & the same people—of course you adore your friends but the others you don't [care] a bit about, and I haven't gotten a bit further about making up my mind as to what I want to do next winter, & I drift & drift & can't seem to get hold of anything definite. I'm afraid I make Ma unhappy.

Her troubles intensified that autumn when she returned to the emptiness of her Bostonian social life: "Back to the whirling rush and hardly a minute to breathe. It's really so foolish because I never do anything, but spend my whole time dashing around accomplishing nothing, but it seems to sap your whole soul in a way—because I never have time to think or to read." Her father had left for an extended exploration of the Amazon, which would keep him away all winter. Christiana worried about him, and with good reason, for the trip was badly planned and hazardous. Without Lucia there to discuss things with and to mirror her discontent, Christiana woodenly went through the motions of her usual life.

By January of 1917, the depression that seemed now to afflict 61 her each winter, again intensified. Her father was stuck in Brazil for longer than he had planned; without his breezy presence to lift her spirits, she suffered even more acutely from the unbalanced narrowness of her mother's and her friends' provincial emphasis on homely duty, feminine subservience, and the social whirl. Christiana responded with an exacerbated self-hate. She found herself smug, conceited, shallow, wanton, selfish, and trapped.

Torn with self-blame and confusion, she logged one of the more introspective passages to be found in her diaries:

> I still feel too wretchedly to go around and yet I am so sort of bored, staying at home here doing nothing. . . . There is a feeling in me that I want to live *really*. I want things to be vital to me and pierce my heart. I want to feel joy and sorrow to the utmost—I want to drink every draught to the utmost. . . . I suppose that is why I crave now for books that are strong—that have splendid new thoughts and ideas and that really hit one. . . . I am always groping frantically for some new thought—or old one that is new to me. I think that is more or less the tendency of this age anyway. We are living in such tremendous times.

Part of Christiana's unrest and the desire to live did come from "the tendency of this age." It was 1917, and the United States, along with much of the rest of the world, was locked in a great war. And it was Christiana's dance partners, cousins, and friends who were to fight for its causes and die in its battlefields.

The Clouds of War

The little things of which we lately chattered—
  The dearth of taxis or the dawn of spring;
Themes we discussed as though they really
    mattered,
  Like rationed meat or raiders on the wing;—

How thin it seems today, this vacant prattle,
  Drowned by thunder rolling in the West,
Voice of the great arbitrament of battle
  That puts our temper to the final test.

SIR OWEN SEAMAN,
Punch, April 3, 1918

B y the spring of 1917, the Great War absorbed more and more of Christiana's attention. She was fascinated by the conflict's mix of horror with lofty ideals and longed to play some part in its drama. The war's reality came home to her in unexpected ways. One day, she encountered a group of wounded French soldiers in Harvard yard, and she wrote in her diary: "When I think of what they have seen and how much they must feel about the war, it makes me feel perfectly ashamed at not being in it heart and soul."

At a dance that same evening, she met a boy named William Morgan and sat out with him so that they could talk. She had been to so many dances and sat out with so many young men that one more encounter must not have been worth recording. Two weeks passed before Christiana first mentioned him in her diary. By then her feelings about the war and her feelings for him rushed together in an urgent epiphany of wartime romance.

I have been seeing a lot of W. O. P. Morgan lately. . . . He has never been around with girls at all and so doesn't seem very polished, but he isn't at all awkward. He is very much of a man's man and has perfectly splendid ideals and is really thoroughly fine through and through. He is a marvelous person to talk to because being so very genuine he isn't at all bashful about talking of his aims & ideals in life, and we have some very deep talks, and some very interesting ones. He appreciates books a lot & gets a lot out of them, altho he isn't at all brilliant. He has a delightful sense of humor and can be awfully funny. He is funny-looking and you can't help being awfully fond of him, although physically he doesn't appeal to me very thrillingly, the way Floyd did. . . . Well, anyway after all this preface about him, we were walking out at the country club this afternoon and he told me he should have to go to Fort Sheridan tonight. He asked me if I ever thought I could care for him because he had found in me his ideal. Somehow I had the feeling it was coming, although we had always been rather impersonal. He was too sweet talking to me and seemed so shy, as though he were afraid to walk on such sacred ground. Somehow I don't think of him as a masterful man, but a perfectly dear boy. We sat there under the pine trees and saw the sun come out and it really was so pathetic because over it all hung the cloud of war, & I felt as tho' he were going out on that great unknown & all the suffering of it, so little knowing what was coming. We walked home arm in arm, somehow I couldn't believe it, I had known him for such a short time.

During the following weeks, Christiana's diary brimmed with news of the war and of friends who, like Bill Meeker, had left Harvard to enlist. Bill Morgan's long letters from training camp at Fort Sheridan soon brought her news of army life. Christiana responded to his idealism and his humor, but what captivated her was the aura of fated romance that encircled them: the idea of him going off to war, with her as the object of his affection. In perhaps her last clearheaded diary entry about their relationship, Christiana wrote of her misgivings:

"Bill" Morgan . . . seems sort of young. We are wonderfully congenial but he isn't ahead of me intellectually. I have a feeling that I shall never fall in love until I meet

64

someone who is way ahead of me intellectually—some one with whom I will have to make a great effort to keep up with, and who has big broad stimulating ideas—who had seen enough and read enough to have these ideas carry great weight. He must have a very keen sense of humor, too. Somehow I don't think I shall ever get up a thrill on anyone whose brain isn't way ahead of mine. I just long for that stimulus and inspiration, and so far I have always felt myself a little beyond the man in that direction. It seems a cocky thing to say, but it is perfectly true.

Bill's appeal lay in his easy friendliness and his acceptance of Christiana as a peer; he resembled her first boyfriend, Billy Stearns, far more than the more exciting and forbidden Floyd. Photographs of Morgan during this time show a boy's face with an open, friendly innocence. His small, even features and remarkably sweet expression suggest his sensitivity, humor, and charm. He fit the role of the perennial best friend more than the romantic hero Christiana fantasized, but it was wartime, and sending a boyfriend off to war generated its own romance.

Christiana and William Morgan embarked on a lengthy correspondence that recalled her mother's lively exchanges with William Thayer a generation before. War heightened the intensity and lowered the barriers between the young couple and propelled their friendship toward a rapid declaration of love. One hundred eighty of Christiana's letters survive from these years, many stained orange with trench mud, acrid, and crumpled by the confines of a soldier's pocket. While only forty of Bill's handwritten letters remain, Christiana excerpted and typed over a hundred that he wrote while overseas, deleting whatever personal and loving messages they contained. She kept these more formal copies in two large black notebooks for posterity, making the letters available—some for the family, some for use by local newspapers, others in hope of later publication.

Like her mother before her, Christiana used her letters to hone the self-scrutiny she had begun in her diaries. In the letters, she relinquished much of her social and flirtatious Boston debutante's persona, allowing her deeper self to emerge, as well as her love of ideas. Her correspondent responded with equal enthusiasm and, cut off from his college confidants, gave Christiana what she had longed for since her early days with her father: access to a man's inner life, ideas, and emotions. The letters grew ever more intimate and self-revealing.

The young man who had entered Christiana's life so suddenly and with such impact was not a Boston Brahmin, nor had he been one of the boys Christiana encountered at dances and coming-out balls. Like Christiana's own father, he was an outsider to Bostonian society. A native of Chicago, William Otho Potwin Morgan was born on May 14, 1895. His grandfather was Otho H. Morgan, a Civil War veteran who had served under General Sherman and cofounded the Chicago Varnish Company. By the time of his retirement, Otho Morgan had made a small fortune.

Bill's father, William Otho Morgan, was a scientist who had studied chemistry in Vienna; he returned to Chicago to become chief chemist and director of his father's company. Bill's mother was Clara Marks, whose immediate relatives were clothing merchants and real estate tradesmen. She fell ill soon after Bill's birth, and shortly thereafter Bill's father caught pneumonia, had to stop work, and moved away from the family on doctors' advice. He died within the year. Bill was a little over a year old when he was christened at the close of his father's funeral service.

Clara Morgan's father had died before he reached thirty, her husband at thirty-one. As a result, she became obsessively concerned with her son's well-being and her own, becoming hostage to a variety of megrims and prostrations. Bill grew up an overprotected only child under the thrall of a hypochondriacal and fearful mother. In ninth grade, however, he was sent off to St. Paul's, a boarding school in New Hampshire, which proved a lucky antidote to his claustrophobic and fatherless home. Many prominent Chicago families of that era sent their sons to St. Paul's as an introduction to the Eastern establishment and in preparation for Harvard. Released from the queasy concerns of his mother's house, Bill flourished, throwing himself into an energetic boys' world of friendships, athletics, and school activities. He was well liked, played baseball, excelled at ice hockey, becoming captain of the hockey team in his final year, and was secretary of the school's athletic association. Elected president of his sixth form, he also served as associate head editor of their news and literary magazine and was active in many other school organizations.

He went on to Harvard and was in his junior year when he met Christiana. Not particularly studious, he did well enough while concentrating on club life and varsity athletics, again excelling at ice hockey. He joined the AD Club; it and the Porcellian were the most prestigious clubs at Harvard. Bill's varsity training schedule kept him away from dances and girls, but in fact he preferred the easy company of his male friends, perhaps distancing himself from a boyhood spent too much in women's company.

66   Bill left college in the spring of 1917, becoming one of the first of the forty-two members of the Harvard class of 1918 to join various U.S., French, or English armed services. He was assigned to an officers' training camp in Illinois, Fort Sheridan, near his Highland Park home. The ten-to-twelve-page letters he wrote to Christiana showed his need to succeed as a good soldier. He told her that he'd "spent all [his] life with fellows," laying a wistful, if not entirely accurate, emphasis on himself as a man's man, more used to masculine endeavors than to feminine company. Nevertheless, he didn't deny taking pleasure in getting home nearly every weekend or his problems dealing with his mother's apprehensions. Bill delighted in basic training—sounding, at times, as if he were in training for an athletic team rather than for war. Part of his eagerness came from his feeling that, unlike his delicate father, he could "endure anything and everything."

By late May, at only his fourth letter, Bill was writing about love. "I have wondered when something bigger than [my former life] would happen—when I would become awake—and things would become more vivid and clear. . . . I have always believed it would be love, when some girl, whom I had imagined to myself, would come into my life."

Bill willingly poured out his impressions, feelings, and thoughts to Christiana, while she, in turn, delighted in being a man's special confidante. She confided to her diary that "they are the kind of letters I have always dreamed of having a person write me—but I never thought that any man would feel things the way I do, & love the same things that I do." She must have shown how much this new role pleased her, for Bill remarked, "I remember your saying that it would be wonderful to feel you were giving to the war some man who meant everything to you—and it is wonderful for a man to feel he can sacrifice himself for a girl." By June, Christiana and he were planning a meeting in York during his first leave. In late June, their letters crossed in the mail, each having written about watching the full moon on the same night and thinking of the other; they were amazed, as lovers always are, by this extraordinary coincidence. More and more, Bill's letters became an ebullient paean to the life of hard training, to patriotism, to their growing closeness, as the clouds of war heightened the intensity of their emotions.

In August, Bill received his commission as first lieutenant and was one of five men chosen from his company for early active duty in France. Sounding a bit as if he had once more made a varsity team, his words almost jump off the page in the excitement of an untried soldier.

> Imagine Chris, what it means . . . to train the troops as they get ready for fighting. I can't express myself—Chris—to think that this should come to me after all my dreams of going over there—I feel like smashing things (windows, furniture or something) and then at the same time I have that peculiar tightening in my throat which you get when you are so wildly happy that you can't say a word. . . .
>
> It seems as if a great door had suddenly opened—revealing beyond another world—the one I have thought of so often—the one in which men come to their own and at last really are valued as men should be valued, for what is at the bottom of them; a world where men have seen things with new visions and feel things in a way which only future generations will realize.

A few days later, he arrived at the Councilmans' summer home in Maine. In uniform, about to go off to war, and taking leave of his girl, Bill professed his love. Christiana reflected that he brought out the best in her, but she wondered whether he would be masterful enough. Floyd had appealed to the passionate side of her nature, not at all to her intellect or ideals. "It is just the other way with Bill," she wrote. "We are so utterly congenial, and so perfectly easy with each other."

They walked under the moon and sat under the pine trees by the river. Looking up into the stars, Christiana decided she loved Bill, and, there, she promised herself to him. "There was no mad thrill," she wrote, "it was much deeper than that. . . . I know that with him I shall give a far finer and more beautiful life to the world than I ever should alone. It filled me with such a deep infinite peace, a peace and joy so deep and searching that it could only find expression in tears—it came so near to tears."

Less than a week after Bill arrived in Maine, he asked Christiana to marry him, and having known him for less than five months, she accepted. They walked together once more by the ocean, aware that his orders to embark were imminent and that they would have to say goodbye. Feeling the bittersweetness of these moments, Christiana wrote:

> Now I know what love really is—and already I can feel myself changed—softened perhaps. It is so dignified and so beautiful, and calm. It seems to be just a part of my soul, interwoven in all that is finest and best in my nature. I love everything about him, even his faults, and I want to be with him all the rest of my life. God alone knows what the future may hold, but if need be I pray that I can make my sacrifice as nobly as others have made theirs, and if he comes back, I pray that we can make a life together worth living.

After telling her parents of the engagement, Christiana noted: "It came as quite a shock to the family and they are all rather upset." Isabella objected at first not only because the Morgan family was unknown to her but because of Bill's extreme youthfulness, the pair's naïveté, the suddenness of the engagement, and the sense of pressure caused by the war. However, the very circumstance of war and Bill's commitment to it caused her to relent. William Councilman, usually Christiana's ally against her mother's social qualms, turned on his daughter with biting mockery; raising a glass to Christiana and her betrothed, he toasted "the Babes in the Woods."

A photograph of Christiana and Bill at the time of their engagement may have been taken by Councilman to emphasize this epithet. The couple are seated in a woodland corner of the York gardens; Christiana's beauty seems muted, pensive, as she shrinks into herself and away from Bill, who, handsome and eager in his officer's uniform, leans toward both her and the camera. He looks more like a younger brother than a future husband.

Bill's ship sailed for Europe on September 12, 1917. Two days later, Christiana learned that Bill Meeker, who had enlisted in the Lafayette Escadrille, the crack French flying corps, was killed when he crashed his plane on a training mission a scant three months after his arrival in France. Christiana was overwhelmed by this first loss and mourned deeply.

Before the war ended, fifty-one members of the 1917 and 1918 Harvard classes would die. One by one, Christiana and Bill Morgan mourned twenty-five close friends from within their small social set, among them Christiana's first boyfriend, Billy Stearns. By the end of the war, three out of Bill Morgan's five Harvard and St.

Paul's roommates were dead; the remaining two were crippled for life.

There are no epic tales about the women's side of the war. Women's war stories most often remained invisible, their roles ignored, belittled, or sentimentalized as, at best, supportive. Women of Christiana's background were expected to stay home, cheer, wait, and mourn. Like some patient Penelope, Christiana could have woven and unraveled the familiar and protected pattern of her life day after day after day. But she was profoundly unwilling to take the passive role expected of her. Her family gave her little if any help. Isabella couldn't understand her daughter's wish for anything beyond what was normal in Boston society, while Christiana's father, usually her ally, turned away from her aspirations with old-fashioned Southern vehemence. The more Christiana grew restless, the more he mocked and disparaged women's ambitions in the world, fulminating that a woman's place was at home, where she should occupy herself solely with domestic pursuits. Because there was no clear route, no adequate female model, and no support, Christiana expended a great deal of energy in formulating her quest and worrying whether she was doing the right thing. It took courage and ingenuity, for none of it came naturally.

Bill's war experiences were horrifying but straightforward; he took part in some of the most notable and terrible battles of the war. Christiana's attempt to break out of the life expected of her made for a heroic trail that was difficult to follow and to chart. She made many false starts.

She tried writing, but impeded by her lack of education, she failed. She rarely wrote of everyday details; carried away by vast ideals, she soared into lofty and often meaningless abstractions. Her most interesting writing occurred in her daily letters to Bill, in which she revealed her daily life, her joys and sorrows, her personal responses to events, and her fight to discover a role for herself in the war.

Christiana's engagement yet separation from Bill proved invaluable in this period of her life. Being betrothed removed her from the ranks of the husband-seeking contestants of the drawing room and relieved her from having to attend the endless dances, parties, and teas, waiting for the right suitor to come along. The social whirl could be left to spin without her.

Being separated from Bill meant that her new vitality was not

70

entirely wrapped up in him. She did not have to lead her life conventionally in his shadow or remain completely enmeshed in their relationship. There were hours and days now when she was rested and free; she no longer danced past dawn, nor was she attending to her husband-to-be in the frantic throes of marriage preparations. Instead she had the time and space in which to pursue a larger self, which felt more compatible with the changing times.

Christiana spent several months absorbing this new situation and trying out the customary activities of a young woman of her class. At first, she busied herself with her clubs and volunteer work at The French Wounded, where she and a few friends made bandages. Her afternoons were spent either at the Red Cross or with an infant class at a charity run by Lincoln House, where members of her club volunteered to care for needy children. Otherwise she was with friends, going to shows and teas, leading a quiet and manless approximation of her prewar life. But this life could not satisfy her. On the final day of 1917, Christiana took leave of her diary, the last one she would so scrupulously keep. The final entry dwells on Bill's life, now, as the important one and sums up the way she occupied her day, struggling unconvincingly to conform herself to its petty script and its unnaturally docile role.

> I find that I haven't written in this diary for months—the reason being that I have little time—I write Bill every night, and tell him all that I used to write in this. I no longer need this diary, for I can tell all these longings and ideas and daily doings to Bill.
>
> He is now in the 28th Infantry of the Regular Army, and I think things are a good deal harsher for him now than they were at first. That wild enthusiasm has all gone leaving in its place grim determination. He is beginning to realize and appreciate the horror and the sordidness of it all, and it is only by great strength of will that he is able to pull himself above it. He had a chance to come back here and train but he chose to stay over there. I think it was splendid of him, and really everything he does tends to make our love so big that I admire him more and more. . . .
>
> I am awfully busy all the time now. I go to the French Wounded and work every morning, and I generally do something in the morning [sic]—so the days seem to fly past. I wish I had more time to read, but I realize the only way to keep happy is to work. And now in the face of

these great events, and in the face of the sufferings ahead
for the country, I feel that service is the only thing for us
here at home.

The passive, long-enduring *dolorosa* role could not contain
Christiana's energy and spirit, however, and she fell into another
depression. Her letters to Bill veered from paeans celebrating war's
glories to moody critiques of trivial days spent wrapping bandages,
gossiping, dancing, and going to the theater. Hungrily, she sought
an alternative on which she could focus herself and make a contribution as vital as Bill's.

She found the solution in the Red Cross. She and her best
friend, Sal Sherburne, hatched a plan to get away from restrictive
Boston and enroll in a rigorous three-month nursing course in New
York City. Christiana's letters again looked outward. She wrote of
the shortage of coal and the dimming of the streetlights, the offices
and schools closing early and the clubs closing altogether, the food
shortages, with meatless and wheatless days, the effects of these
deprivations on her family, and their far graver effect on the poor.
She also wrote of the tension, the constant anxiety, the restless
apprehension that she and others "on the home front" suffered as
they heard of the terrible battles.

Her family opposed her nursing plans, seeing them as nothing
but whim and another sign of Christiana's "difficult character."
Her father, who had taken her side as a child, responded to Christiana now with outbursts against her gender, ridiculing women who
didn't know their place and duty. As William Councilman grew
older, and particularly when he was drinking, he had a marked
tendency to rant, and Christiana found his tirades difficult to combat; they sapped her energy, but she could not bring herself to stand
up to him. "I wish you could have seen me tonight," she wrote
Bill. "Pa was in one of his rampages, and said that he thought
women were the cause of all war. I knew it was just silly and he
loves to make these ridiculous statements—but, like a fool, I started
to argue about it. Finally I got so mad that I burst out crying. Did
you ever know anything so childish? I was so mad at myself."

Christiana persisted in her nursing plan, at the cost of increasing
rows with her parents. Her difficulty and perseverance in the face
of their obstruction brought home to her the argument for woman
suffrage. She now defended feminist causes, arguing with her family
as if she were pleading for her own emancipation. She wrote to

Bill about the new women's movement and her study of it, concluding: "It is fundamentally *right* that we should have the same freedom and the same privileges. . . . I see that it is right and now I am a woman I feel that I have the right to ask for it."

Christiana came to these conclusions the hard way. She still idealized her father, so it pained her to oppose him. Because she had heeded his needs and wishes for so many years, because she loved him and yearned for his approval, and because he was so unconventional in other ways, his misogynist harangues weighed heavily on her. Her mother was easier to challenge, as she used propriety and conventionality to hobble Christiana—weapons William Councilman had long ago taught his daughter to disregard.

Because of her family's opposition, Christiana kept the full scope of her plans from her parents, simply telling them about the first part: a three-month nurse's aid course in New York. Her ultimate goal was to serve in a field hospital at the front. To this end, she planned to stay in New York for an extra three-week Red Cross course, gain practical experience in a hospital during the summer, and then either specialize in physical therapy for the Red Cross or enlist as an army nurse. Because she knew no one from her social class who had done any of this she had no one to help her execute her plan.

The first step of her escape succeeded. Christiana, Sal Sherburne, and their friend Frances Clarke moved into a rooming house at 52 East 53rd Street in New York and enrolled in the YWCA for the nursing course. She described her first days there to Bill:

> What a day we did have yesterday. We went to class in our uniforms and I just wish you could see them. How you would laugh! Sal looks like a district nurse and I look like nothing human. The teacher is perfectly wonderful. She is very intelligent, and gives a large enough outlook on every subject to make it awfully interesting. . . . Our rooms look too divinely now—nice and bright and sunny and really very pretty. We are too thrilled for words.

The nursing course turned out to be as intensive and demanding as Christiana had hoped. She was assigned to Flower Hospital, at Sixty-eighth Street and the East River, and worked there three mornings a week from nine until twelve. Before long, she volunteered for an extra morning's work. The afternoon lectures included such things as medical terminology, basic patient care, pharmacology, and first aid; she found them detailed and informative, full of practical knowledge as well as psychological aspects of the work.

Christiana's hospital duties rotated her among the wards, where 73 she enjoyed the hard physical work, washing, feeding, and caring for patients. She found that she preferred men to women patients; the men's gratitude made her feel more needed and womanly. The men also reminded her of her goal—to nurse soldiers like, and in place of, Bill; nursing them was, in some ways, an extension of her love for him. Christiana's spirits soared now that she had something constructive to do. After the initial shock of dealing with wounds and the most basic of bodily needs, she discovered she had a real talent for nursing.

Besides a thorough grounding in general patient care, Christiana learned to assist in the operating room; her duties also involved sitting at the bedsides of those past hope so that they wouldn't die alone. After she had overcome her initial queasiness, her biggest problem involved sticking to hospital protocol rather than blithely doing things her own way. Doctors' arrogant treatment of nurses posed a difficulty too: her growing feminism and her pride warred with the demeanor required of her. She wrote Bill: "This being a doctor's handmaiden gets on my nerves more than anything else."

Christiana's success in her training gave her a newfound self-esteem, which she gloried in. The city itself gave her a further taste of independence; with her hospital training as anchor and her uniform as a shield, she felt free to explore its streets. She, Sal, and "Frank" Clarke wandered the city together, took long bus rides, dined unchaperoned in restaurants, and, in their precious free time, did pretty much what they wanted. Christiana walked where she pleased and mingled with different strata of New York social life, which she observed with Whartonian appreciation of its gradations. A Dr. Lambert, who had trained under her father, accompanied her to concerts, the theater, and about town, and introduced her to a vastly different medical world that that of her rather shabby hospital. She felt most at home, though, in the circle inhabited by Bill Meeker's family, which she found similar to her Boston world. The Meekers welcomed and cared for Christiana like a daughter of the house and drew some comfort from her memories of their dead son.

Christiana conveyed the atmosphere of wartime New York in her constant flow of letters to Bill Morgan:

I came out of the opera yesterday and walked thru to the Avenue. Everything was in a blaze of sunlight, and all the flags were out, while on every corner & in every window were great posters announcing the beginning of the Third Liberty Loan drive. Overhead two aviators were flying quite low over the city, one in a dirigible balloon, and one in an Italian Caproni plane. In front of the library a great band was playing to advertise the War Saving Stamps, and people were shouting hoarsely to the crowd gathered and shrill women's voices cut through the crowd urging people to buy stamps. The sidewalks were so crowded that you had to almost elbow your way along. Such confusion I have never seen or heard in all my life . . . but this afternoon it struck me as being so aimless and futile, and sort of mad, with no meaning and no sense. I felt as though the madness of the whole city was concentrated right on that corner. I walked down to the Plaza where I was to meet Lucia and Miss Cobb for tea.

Christiana's friendship with Lucia Howard had not survived her engagement to Bill Morgan. Lucia took the engagement as almost a personal affront, as if Christiana had rejected the finer, truer world tendered by Lucia herself and the companionship of women. For her part, Christiana had not been able to return the signs of affection Lucia demanded. Their meetings grew fewer, with Christiana complaining of Lucia's coarseness and Lucia berating Christiana's lack of feminine solidarity. They met infrequently now and somewhat guardedly. The meeting at the Plaza Hotel was made easier because of Christiana's exciting job but more because Lucia's affection now focused on her great new friend, a Miss Cobb, whom Christiana had also known in Boston. After this, Lucia faded from Christiana's life, having served as one exemplar of the independent, sophisticated, and intellectual woman Christiana hoped to be.

Christiana completed her course with unabated enthusiasm. The three friends were now not only working constantly but studying for a demanding set of exams. Sal fell ill with typhoid fever and was unable to finish. Christiana and Frank passed, both receiving a 99 percent grade on their five exams and their clinical work. Christiana wrote: "We get our diplomas the day after tomorrow. . . . Really & truly Bill, I feel such years older than before I left. I don't know why I should but I do. I suppose it's because I have much more self respect for myself knowing that I can do something if I set out to it, and it gives you so much more initiative too, I think."

To her great dismay, the next step in Christiana's grand plan had to be delayed. William Councilman had been in poor health ever since he returned from the Amazon; at the end of May he suffered several mild heart attacks. Isabella Councilman ordered her daughter home immediately after her graduation, to care for him at York. This was far from the nursing work Christiana had hoped for, and the digression troubled her; it was a clear reminder that she and women like her were first and foremost hostages to their families' needs. The first duty of an unmarried woman of her class, it seemed, required the sacrifice of personal ambition and resolve for the well-being of a family member. Christiana agreed to return home but knew herself well enough to fear the danger to her future goal. She also feared that, unexercised and unsupported, her newly acquired skills, confidence, and ambition would wane. They were too new, too vulnerable, and too untried.

On her return to York, Christiana sank into the quiet beauty of the place, but, her world contracting, she again became depressed. She tried to turn the emptiness into passion for Bill and wrote of her longing for him. Her parents, meanwhile, responded to her restlessness by trying to limit her even more as if the problem were her moods rather than her restricted environment and the torment of inaction.

To Christiana's great relief, her father made a quick recovery. Christiana resumed her nursing studies and volunteered for a three-day-a-week job in the small hospital in nearby Portsmouth, New Hampshire—part of her plan to gain practical experience. Frances Clarke wrote with news about the army nursing course at Fort Ayer in Devon, Massachusetts, and the two planned to apply together in the fall. As soon as Christiana had meaningful work at Portsmouth, her depression disappeared. Though her father had been a beneficiary of her nursing care, he ribbed her unmercifully, making no attempt to hide his old-fashioned contempt for nurses. She ruefully confided to Bill that "Pa is so amused by this whole proceeding. He looked ready to laugh his head off when I told him what I had arranged."

It was no laughing matter. The hospital at Portsmouth was desperately short of nurses. Its doctors were superior to those at Flower Hospital, and they treated Christiana with far more respect than her father did, perhaps because her father was a noted Harvard physician. Christiana assisted at patients' bedsides, in the operating room, and once, inexperienced as she was, at a prolonged, hazardous, and difficult birth. Though the daily routine at the hospital was no more strenuous than her experience in New York, Christiana found it more wearing. Rather than returning from a difficult day to the mutual support she had had with colleagues and friends, she now came home to her parents' indifference and disdain.

A medical exam was required for the Fort Ayer nurses' program. Christiana consulted the doctor who had taken care of her after her collapse at Farmington. Dr. Brigham, a good friend of her father's, who doubtless shared his values, voiced his views about the impropriety of Christiana's plans for a girl of her class and refused to recommend her. Instead he delivered a long lecture about her health, warning her that the scarlet fever she'd had as a child might have weakened the muscles of her heart. He found nothing wrong except slightly elevated blood pressure, but said she would be a fool to risk any vigorous activity.

Christiana returned to York with her plans crushed, her little world closing in on her once more. She struggled again with depression, feeling restless and unable to sleep. "It's the old awful feeling that I am wasting my life these days. I am letting great things slip by me and I stay on the outside of events and take only a little part. I think I shall go mad unless I can have the peace of mind that I had in New York again."

In an extraordinary step, Christiana went against her doctor's orders, her father's wishes, and her mother's fears; she continued her schedule at the Portsmouth hospital and resumed plans for further training. But her energy was sapped by Brigham's alarms, by her parents' lack of support, and by the easy comfort of idle days at her summer home. Part of her wanted to yield to the inertia and fragile lassitude that was acceptably feminine, while another part bounded forward to join the vast army that toiled together in the war. On August 13, 1918, she applied to Fort Ayer, confiding to Bill that she could always give up the training if it proved too hard. By September, she was writing joyfully to him of her plans to be in uniform by the new year and in Europe by spring.

Christiana's tenacity slowly earned her father's grudging respect, as did the fact that she was taken so seriously by her colleagues. An influenza epidemic had spread from Europe to the American troops and from a ship in Boston harbor into the city itself. The Red Cross desperately needed good nurses and drafted Frances Clarke and Christiana for emergency duty in Boston.

The Spanish flu, as it was called, spread across the globe in   three increasingly virulent waves that year, infecting about one fifth of the world's population. The most deadly strain landed in Sierra Leone, Africa, in Brest, France, and in Boston almost simultaneously in late August 1918. Within a few weeks, thousands were falling ill and hundreds were dying. It didn't peak in Boston until mid-October but expanded south and west almost immediately after it arrived. Within a year, it claimed half a million lives in the United States alone, thirty-five hundred of them in Boston. The influenza killed rapidly, its highest death toll not among infants and the elderly but among young adults aged twenty to forty.

Christiana was assigned to a temporary hospital for soldiers who had been in training camps or on ships near Boston. The Massachusetts Home Guards set up a series of tents on Corey Hill. Christiana started her job there on the same day she learned that she was underage by two years for the Pershing Reconstruction Aide course that could get her to Europe. She wrote Bill of her disappointment, then went on to describe her difficult and interesting work. The temporary hospital was efficient but overloaded from the very beginning. In her first days, there were three hundred men, of whom twenty had pneumonia and four died; two days later, the pneumonia cases had almost tripled, and ambulances were bringing more and more men from the troop ships. The nurses' only protection against the disease was a gauze mask dipped in antiseptic. She gave Bill a lively picture of her responsibilities:

> Just at present I am writing this in bed—and if it doesn't feel like heaven to be in bed I don't know what does. I must have at least ten blisters on each foot—and my back and arms ache so that I can hardly sit up. . . . I just wish you could have seen me at the hospital today. I was on duty from one until 8 tonight—and such a day. I have never imagined that it could rain so hard. It simply *poured* and there were perfect rivers of water around all the tents. I had on a great pair of rubber boots—and some private's overcoat and no hat. The rain simply poured off my hair— and every time I tried to do anything for the men, I would get them soaking wet, of course. And you can imagine what a mess it was trying to carry up the supper—as we had to walk miles from the kitchen in the pouring rain.

Then of course, just as it was getting dark—a whole lot of ambulances had to arrive—and the men . . . had to be gotten into bed, and their temperature and pulse taken. Then I had to go from tent to tent with a lantern and make out their charts—and they were an awfully sick bunch too. Then the doctor came along and I had to carry the lantern for him and take down the orders for medicine. Then I had to go around to 24 tents and tuck them all in for the night and fix them up and give them their medicines—and altogether it was really hectic. . . . But all the same it is just like the breath of life for me and I *love* it.

By September 28, the flu cases in Massachusetts had climbed to fifty thousand; the state could not keep up with the emergency and requested a thousand nurses from the West, where the epidemic had not yet broken out. On her way to and from work, Christiana passed carts stacked with wooden coffins, weaving through Boston to collect the dead. Her friends Frances Clarke and Hannah Fiske eventually came down with the flu, as did an increasing number of nurses. But Christiana worked on sturdily and in robust health in spite of her aching arms and back and her blistered feet.

The Red Cross had drafted all nurses' aides, in order to assign them where they were most critically needed. They shifted Christiana around, and she found herself learning her profession under the pressure of crisis and increased responsibilities. Perhaps the high point of Christiana's nursing career was in Methuen, a small mill town near Lawrence, Massachusetts. She was sent there to assist the only health care provider in town. Miss Robertson was an intelligent, dedicated elderly woman, who immediately embraced Christiana as an angel sent to help her. She had Christiana accompany her on rounds and then sent her out alone to minister to dying patients. Christiana threw herself into the work, profoundly affected by family tragedies but carrying on with fortitude.

In Miss Robertson, Christiana found a motherly and competent woman who, in contrast to her own mother, had spent her life working; in turn, Miss Robertson recognized and welcomed Christiana as a bright, hardworking daughter after her own heart. The two made an impressive couple as they worked together in crisis, tending to the nightmare around them; they shared their few moments of free time and their lodgings in an easy exchange based on

mutual respect and affection. It was for Christiana a rare opportunity to serve with an older woman and build bonds of feminine
solidarity. Just as they had both settled into the rhythm of their
mutual work, however, Christiana received a telegram that commanded her to report to Colonel Brooks, the head of the medical
department of the Massachusetts State Guard. She was to help set
up a mobile hospital similar to the tent hospital on Corey Hill. Her
unit consisted of Frances Clarke, two trained nurses, Colonel
Brooks, and Christiana.

The hospital they established turned out to be a successful
prototype for a series of emergency hospitals. The team worked
well together; during the first hectic days, the four nurses were each
on duty eighteen hours out of the twenty-four, but after two days
the shifts were decreased by six hours. In a few weeks, they treated
over five hundred influenza patients, losing only four of them—a
record for the time. Christiana was put in full charge of the pneumonia ward.

While William Councilman grudgingly appreciated the value
of his daughter's wartime nursing, he refused to take Christiana's
dedication to her career seriously and continued his dismissive teasing. Christiana arrived home exhausted for a weekend break and
reported ironically to Bill that "Pa didn't know whether to laugh
or whether to be serious about it when I told him all that I had
been up to. He was so delighted when he heard about the 12 hours
work a day—and when he saw my awful looking hands all poisoned
by corrosive disinfectant. They all said I looked very healthy so I
guess that work must agree with me."

Colonel Brooks planned to move his group around the country, setting up mobile tent hospitals wherever they were needed,
intending to adapt them for military use once the epidemic
abated. They called themselves the Brooks Unit now, and they
set off for Springfield, Massachusetts, with a formal title and uniforms.

"Our uniforms," she wrote Bill, "are dark blue capes with red
lining—and a blue cloth cap. . . . We are living in the house of [an]
estate. . . . There aren't rooms enough for everyone—so ten of us
are sleeping in a room—on canvas army cots with no mattress &
no sheets. By the time I get through this, Bill, you won't be able
to tell me a thing about the army."

Christiana now oversaw all the aides, assigned ward coverage,
and was herself in charge of the men's influenza ward. And so the

pattern of her work settled down to what she believed would be its course for the next year. She cherished the hard physical labor, the endless days and nights on duty, the endurance of cold and damp and fatigue, the ability to survive on strength of will alone, as a counterpart to and sharing of Bill's war at the front—at least it was the closest she could approximate.

SIX

Maybe Forever

Desires and Adorations,
Wingèd Persuasions and veiled Destinies,
Splendours, and Glooms, and glimmering
Incarnations
Of hopes and fears, and twilight Phantasies;
And Sorrow with her family of Sighs,
And Pleasure, blind with tears . . .

SHELLEY,
"Adonais"

Like so many of their idealistic contemporaries, Christiana and Bill Morgan welcomed the glamour and nobility of a war they thought would bring an end to all wars. In October 1917, soon after Bill landed in France and sometime during his five weeks in the British Army's infantry school at Toutencourt, he wrote to Christiana with unconvincing swagger: "Killed—but what matter? . . . We are all crazy to get to the trenches & to go 'over the top,' and if death comes to us it is only you who will suffer."

Shortly thereafter, during a furlough, Bill rode his horse up to the front, as if to some football game, eager to see it and to meet friends there. "I must tell you of my wonderful Sunday at the front," he wrote. "I am sending you a pansy. I picked it beside the grave of an Englishman. It seemed so beautiful to see it growing there. The grave was fresh and in a bottle was a note, 'Here lies an unknown English soldier, Sept. 1917.' " In November, he reported to the First Division of the American Expeditionary Force. His recommendation from infantry school read: "A good keen officer

81

who should make a fine leader. He is of cheerful disposition with energy and determination. He is quick to learn and with more experience should be able to instruct in military subjects but would also be a good officer on the line. [Signed] H. Bacon, Major, Commanding No 1 platoon." The commandant added in his own handwriting: "Keen and cheerful; will make a leader."

Assigned to the Twenty-eighth Infantry, Bill began to experience the grim realities of trench warfare. He wrote to Christiana of the superhuman endurance this kind of combat required and of his men's courage in the face of intolerable conditions. While participation in warfare tempered his idealistic fantasies, it also sharpened his affection, even love, for his troops. As the months passed, Bill shared the rigors of their day-to-day existence and witnessed the carnage in the battlefields around him. "It is hard to keep new life in your heart during these endless days of hardship; when your limbs feel like lead and your spirit is almost done in, when the mental strain is coupled with physical exhaustion, and you see nothing ahead but the endless days and nights in the trenches."

Bill served at the front, first in the infantry and then as leader of a machine gun corps with his own platoon, from November 1917 until he was wounded at Soissons in mid-July 1918. He survived the battles of Cambrai, the Ansauville sector, Cantigny, the Montdidier defensive, the Marne-Aisne offensive, the Somme, and Soissons. The Germans referred to his division as the Black Snake Division, because its soldiers attacked with deadly effect and then slipped away, snakelike, out of German hands.

The First Division was composed of four regiments—the Sixteenth, Eighteenth, Twenty-sixth, and Twenty-eighth—whose histories can be traced back to the American Revolution. Before April 1917, they were a relatively small body of men stationed along the Mexican border. When the United States entered the war in Europe, each regiment was split into smaller units and the ranks filled with new officers, recruits, and draftees, until by 1918 the division had grown to about thirty thousand men. It was the first U.S. division to land in Europe, and it fired the first American shot of the war. Because it was considered well trained and reasonably fresh, the division initially was used battalion by battalion to relieve the exhausted French and British troops in the trenches. The new troops quickly proved they could fight as independently and as valiantly as their allies. Bill's regiment, the Twenty-eighth, held the trenches in front of Cantigny in some of the fiercest fighting of the war and then went over the top to break through enemy lines, capturing the village of Cantigny on May 28, 1918, to give the United States its first victory.

Marshal Foch, in charge of overall planning, ordered the First Division back from its victory in order to take part in what *The New York Times* called "the most decisive battle in history." The battle of Soissons was fought to dislodge Germans who held a salient that threatened Paris itself. Bill's division was given "the place of honor," the most difficult and important position southwest of Soissons, near Missy-aux-Bois, with orders to capture and secure the heights above the town. The battle involved the division in even more savage fighting than at Cantigny, but its success turned the tide of battle. The area was captured, along with 3,375 men, 125 officers, 150 field guns, and 300 machine guns. The First Division swept on that fall to play decisive roles at St.-Mihiel, the Argonne, and Abaucourt.

These last battles were waged without Bill Morgan and his platoon, all of whom had been killed or wounded during the battle of Soissons. It is hard for someone who has not lived through it to comprehend the experience of an infantryman or a machine gunner on the front lines. As a lieutenant with his own platoon and battery, Bill endured heavy and prolonged combat exposure including life in the trenches for months at a time, and led his men in the insane ordeal of going "over the top." He encountered poison gas, suffered constant bombardment, saw men dying around him, and was, in short, at the very center of the particular hell that constitutes front-line fighting, whatever the war. As a machine gunner in charge of other machine gunners, he experienced the naked barbarism of war, unprotected by a command post, by rear-echelon work, or by any of the many training, planning, and support jobs that occupy most officers. Bill described one deployment against a German offensive:

> We will set our gun up at night in a shell-hole and try to hide it in the day-time, as well as to hide ourselves. We shall have no trenches, no dugouts and only one meal every twenty-four hours cooked way back and carried up at night. I don't think it will be too comfortable lying around in the mud, especially as we do not get relieved like the infantry every four or five days. It is simply a question of sitting at the gun all night, just waiting for them to come. . . . A French Sergt. . . . said that the Boche came over last month absolutely shoulder to shoulder, wave on

> wave as far as you could see. . . . Our captain is sitting
> opposite me making out his will.

84

On one side, Bill felt the exhilaration and sharpening of the senses that comes with confronting such a danger and finding one-self equal to it. On the other, the long-term effects of warfare on this sensitive and imaginative man began to be apparent. Bill's letters slowly reveal the cumulative damage. He tried to give Christiana some sense of the squalor of the dank and filthy trenches, of life under siege with perpetually wet feet and wet clothes, the smell of the poison gas lurking in pockets of ground, the roar of exploding shells, the sudden attacks and the slaughter. He wrote about his fragmented sleep and the need to be on constant alert. Like any lieutenant, he fought alongside his men, and he described how they would be hit beside him or fall on top of him, how personally he took their injuries and deaths, as well as the pain of watching them fall prey to shell shock, trench fever, and tuberculosis. Bill's grad-ually eroding resilience and the way his idealism degenerated into the bitterest cynicism chart the virulence of his combat fatigue.

Because of huge losses and ridiculously inefficient planning, Bill's platoon did not get the rest and relief of other battalions. The men remained constantly at the front, under unremitting waves of bombardment and enemy fire. Bill received a citation for bravery for keeping his men together and repelling a seventy-two-hour barrage, but extended active duty without time to recover his nerves led to inevitable shell shock. Letters Bill wrote during this period veered between descriptions of superhuman endurance and passages of precarious, almost manic, elation, as if his sanity rested on glimpses of nature's beauty amid the slaughter. In one lull, he wrote Christiana that

> this is such a beautiful little green wood, all checkered
> with dancing sun-light. I wonder why I should have felt
> this way this afternoon. I think it's the contrast, to hear
> the birds singing and to see the spring all around, and then
> to know that for hundreds [of] miles on either side of you
> men are killing each other, throwing gas, sneaking up on
> each other with little trench knives. At times I wish I were
> in the infantry. They claim that it is better to fight man
> to man and hack and slash than to sit cold-bloodily by a
> gun and wipe out a battalion by pumping 250 shots a
> minute into men with the pressure of one finger. We kill

them more cleanly, our bullets are such nice smooth clean-cut affairs.

The violet he picked and enclosed served as mute testimony to the heart-searing contrasts that unbalanced him. Bill tried to conceal his shaky nerves, but the veneer of bravado was wearing painfully thin. In response to Christiana's continuing flights of idealism, he revealed a grim shift in his mood and outlook.

> You've got to have a bit of will-power to keep things from tearing loose in your head. Some men just haven't got that will-power. It's not their fault—you've got to kill your imagination and on top of that swing into a certain savoir faire "To hell with it" mood, coupled with the idea that the Boche hasn't a piece of lead in all Germany which can hit you. . . . It is all these little things, the little strains, which stretch your nerves to the breaking point, that makes a fight out of this war—the little things you never read about, the things you can't see. It is all covered by that vague malady called shell-shock. Sometimes it results in insanity for a while, but from insanity down it covers a great many things.

The battles continued with unremitting intensity, the deaths of his comrades unhinging him bit by bit. But the death of George Haydock, his best friend and companion since the day they landed together, affected him most. Bill mourned Haydock, telling Christiana that the war had always struck the two men as repulsive, unnatural, mad. For a time Bill stopped sleeping and was unable to concentrate or even read. In letters that Christiana separated from the ones she kept in the two notebooks, he confided that he feared he was falling apart, then a day or so later, he apologized for his nerves and his bitterness.

By the time Bill's platoon was ordered to start for Soissons, the men lacked sleep and sufficient food. The battle started during the night, in an oozing quagmire of mud. Bill's unit was used as shock troops, being sent first to one advanced position and then to another. As they tried to advance, the Germans fiercely bombarded them from the heights above, and five more of Bill's men died. Bill fought the mud as well as the enemy, struggling to get his platoon's four-horse combat wagon through the muck, around holes and trenches, and into each new position, leaning his own weight against the wagon to help its advance. The heavy vehicle slewed in the deep mud, and in a most inglorious accident, its metal-rimmed rear tire skidded over Bill's foot, partially crushing it. He continued with his men for as long as he could keep up. Later, Bill recounted his subsequent ordeal:

86

Toulouse, July 23rd

. . . Never shall I forget that walk. It isn't in me to see what I saw. . . . They were gassing us, and a man came up and said he had been gassed. (The mustard doesn't affect you seriously right away.) I told him to walk back with me. We got into a shell hole for a while to see if the artillery would let up, but it didn't so we decided to shuffle on. We had gotten a few steps when all I remember is a blinding flash and crash, and then a few seconds later a horrible cry behind me. The man had landed just at my heels, with his leg torn off just below the knee. I can't seem to forget his expression. I bandaged him as best I could, and put on a tourniquet, and cut away his clothes. Finally I quieted him and told him he would be all right, and that the First Aid would come with a litter, and so I left him. No one was in sight coming back who could carry him, so I had to go on to get a litter from the rear. It took me over an hour to get back. . . .

That field. I never shall forget it. From a selfish point of view it would be so much easier to die than to see all that suffering. Somehow it hits me hard. . . .

For two days and nights they transferred us to four different hospitals, sending the slightly wounded in trucks. The third day I was a stretcher case. Then thirty-six hours on a train, and here I am way down here, at last in the land where there are lights at night, and no guns.

I thought this rest in the hospital would be great but I can't seem to get over the strain. It gets so on my mind that it drives me almost mad at times.

I expect to be here about a week, and then to Paris and get some equipment. What a sight I am. Uniform torn, and only one shoe, no equipment, and blood all over my hat, and not one cent to my name. Perhaps after that a leave to Nice, and then on with the war. Sometimes I wonder how much longer I really have in this game.

Bill's convalescence took far longer than he expected. He was transferred to another hospital, in Vichy, to recover from what, after Vietnam, would be known as post-traumatic stress syndrome, with its accompanying nerves, sleeplessness, nightmares, sudden flashbacks, and the anguished guilt that came from surviving when so many of his men had been killed.

On August 15, Bill went before the hospital disability board; he was advised to request a return to the United States, but haunted by his platoon's deaths and in an attempt to master his broken nerves, Bill asked to be returned to the front. He was classified B2, for a back-area job, and given a leave. He continued to make light of his condition in letters, but he had lost weight and grown pale, and his shell shock continued unabated, his nerves feeling like live wires.

Arriving in Paris on leave, Bill found that he was believed to have been killed at Soissons. He also heard further appalling news about the destruction of his platoon, the terrible losses suffered by his division, and the deaths of more of his close friends. His bitterness gnawed at him as he heard less experienced soldiers boast about their valor and idealize the war. In disgust, he tore the battle-service chevrons from his jacket, and drank, and mourned his lost friends. Before long, his back-area assignment came through; he was to be an instructor at the gunners school at Goudrecourt, the First Division's main training center.

There was no way now that Bill could enter into the routine of a job like this. Confronted with men who were as innocent as he had been the year before, he saw clearly that what he was supposed to teach would be bitterly ineffective in the bloody chaos of combat. The difference between his experiences and the life around him clashed poisonously, yet he dreaded returning to the front. Bill's tense irritation targeted everyone and everything and permeated his letters. Perhaps worst of all, Bill found himself racked with guilt that he had survived when his whole platoon had perished. Though he functioned well enough at his job and assuaged the grief with alcohol, nothing repaired his stripped nerves. Finally, he tried to return to the United States, as he had been advised.

Christiana did not understand. She continued her own patriotic rhapsody to glory and their letters grew jarringly discordant. The lag in mail delivery exacerbated the misunderstandings, so each was responding to events and emotions at least a month old. Christiana fell into Bill's category of people who hadn't been to the front; she persisted in meeting his "nerves" and shock with a steely insistence on his valiant heroism. Yet in encouraging Bill to write about his experiences, she facilitated some release of the horror that gagged him; hitting intuitively on this "debriefing" process—now considered one of the best treatments for post-traumatic stress syndrome—she played a crucial if ambivalent role in Bill's recuperation. Christiana also drew Bill away from his obsessive ruminations with avid questions about books, propaganda, education, politics, Marxism, the peace proposals, and other neutral subjects. Perhaps if she had responded more tenderheartedly, her own pain would have silenced Bill; instead Christiana's almost clinical interest in his feelings and experiences permitted him to share his agony with her. With bracing normalcy, she openly admired him for his candid accounts. "Bill my own dearest, . . . I knew you couldn't go on much longer the way you were going—it was just impossible. There were times when I thought you were losing your hold on things—& I admired you so for the way you kept on dear."

Christiana's descriptions of slogging through the mud at Corey Hill, her aching back and arms after twelve-hour days, her efforts to set up new hospitals, all met Bill on his own ground. What else could one write to a man in such condition except an account of the baby one watched die and the way its death stuck in one's mind and wouldn't leave? Christiana came as close as she could to Bill and his experience. Her letters to him during the flu epidemic were from one battlefront soldier to another. Christiana demonstrated her love through a comradely valor that was to become an essential part of her life. She would pit herself against whatever ordeals her lover faced and strive with him as an equal on the battlefield. She counted the days until she would be able to join him at the front.

But before she could join Bill in Europe as a nurse, the guns of war were stilled.

On Armistice Day, November 11, 1918, Bill happened to be on leave in Paris. He greeted the news with outward celebration but inner ferment. "I certainly am in the queerest state," he wrote that day to Christiana. "I don't know whether to lie down and go into hysterics, or stride forth breaking things into small bits. I can laugh with the best of them, but underneath there lies a Hell which can't be forgotten even though it is past."

In the final blow of the war, Bill's long list of fallen comrades had ended with one last death: his dearest school friend, Alf Gardner, had been killed along with a handful of men attacking an unassailable little hill of no military relevance whatsoever. "All I can say is Alf knew the outcome before he even started. . . . Sometimes I sit and just stare into space . . . there have been so many tears over here and the strain has been so great."

Christiana was working in the new mobile unit in Springfield when the news of the war's end arrived. In her letter to Bill that day, she continued to soar above him in idealistic elation, even as he sank ever deeper into grief.

Nov. 7

My darling,
We have just heard the news of Germany's surrender and Oh Bill it *can't* be true. I don't dare to believe it. Frank and I have fled the camp—it was in an uproar, & people were *clapping*. It seemed like a sacrilege—a horror to see them. . . . But I can think of nothing but the price that has been paid for this day—and then people *clap*—and talk about how fine it is. . . .

I keep wondering about you. How you are taking it. Can the day really have come at last. I can't write all I feel—you know dearest—some things just make you speechless. I didn't know one *could* feel as much. Bill darling—don't you pray that the dead can know. They must. And we will never forget them as long as we live, my husband, we will never forget them. And our lives will be worthy of this day—I know. I know

Chris

Christiana's nursing career ended with the war. Though she considered going abroad to help with the wounded, she didn't want to commit herself to anything that would prolong her separation from Bill. Not needing to earn her own living, and no longer part of the war effort, she found herself back where she had started. Her letters now took on a fragmented quality; new possibilities bobbed to the surface, only to disappear. Slowly the exchanged letters that were once filled with battle tales and stories of each other's wars shifted to dreams for their future. Christiana's most consistent themes were her strange unrest and her inability to find a replacement for the nursing. And beneath it all was the fact that her romantic hero had not died a tragic death on the battlefield but was coming home in the flesh to marry her.

Christiana's struggle for meaningful work went unnoticed—at best it was a personal idiosyncrasy. The war ended and the influenza epidemic abated. Christiana wavered, lost clarity of purpose, and closed the book on that chapter of her life. Never, in her journals, letters, or diaries, did she mention her nursing career again. She returned home and resumed her appointed place on the periphery of life.

In late November, she finally came down with the flu. Her letters vacillated between enthusiasm about Bill's return and their approaching wedding and dismay as she found herself in the old rut but incalculably changed. Her depressions returned as she pondered what she could do to regain her sense of purpose. While Bill drank heavily with his friends in Paris, Christiana recommenced her pointless social round; she even encountered Floyd, dancing with him and again feeling his power over her and hating herself for it and for her irrelevant existence.

Christiana occupied the months until Bill's return with studying and reading; she shopped for her trousseau and planned her wedding gown. She wrote Bill, telling him flirtatiously of the lace she had bought for a chemise. What she didn't tell him was that her grandmother Coolidge had given each granddaughter five hundred dollars (about four thousand dollars today) for her trousseau. While Isa had used the money to supply her new house with all its linen, Christiana splurged the entire amount on lingerie.

She discussed where they would live and proposed New York, because Boston felt more claustrophobic than ever. New York seemed new and fresh and was, of course, the place where she had first broken away from her family. "I hate this place," she wrote Bill. "I think everyone you meet tries to kill all ambition and intelligence that you have." She suggested that Bill apply to law school in New York.

Christiana started a self-imposed schedule of study in the mornings, her interests now literature and current events. She began reading *The Dial* and *The New Republic* regularly and was drawn to lectures on timely subjects. Her politics became decidedly liberal and, for a time, even radical. She read Rousseau, Veblen, Machiavelli, Trotsky, Marx's *Das Kapital,* and many books about Russia and Bolshevism. Bill followed her lead and responded to her ideas, voicing a similar though less vehement radicalism. Christiana enjoyed the convergence of their ideas and wrote to Bill at the new year from Portland, Maine, of her view of him as the ideal companion with whom she could share a lifetime of good talk. Her craving for learning increased, but she lacked guidance and a college education, and her readings (as well as her opinions) were sometimes haphazard and indiscriminate.

During these postwar months, Christiana longed to join a suffrage or women's socialist organization and, in order to learn more about the labor situation, briefly considered taking a factory job.

But in a letter brimming with talk of labor, union politics, and the need for radical reform, she confessed to Bill that she was repelled by ugliness and adored luxury too much to adopt socialism.

Though William Councilman accompanied Christiana to lectures, shared her interest in Russia, and discussed politics with her, the weight of his views on women added even more limitations to Christiana's Boston Brahmin upbringing. She loved and admired her father, yet could not agree with him.

> We had a wonder of a row at lunch today [Christiana wrote Bill]. Pa started on his favorite line of talk about woman's place is in the home—and she should learn to sweep and dust and cook etc. It always makes me mad and I thought of a wonderful comeback. I said I supposed if a woman's place is in the home a man's was in the office and did a man ever think it was a beautiful and inspiring task to sweep and clean and tidy up his office. I rather think I had him there because for once he couldn't think of an appropriate reply.

Her father was suffering from a bad heart, high blood pressure, and the cumulative toll of years of heavy drinking. He increasingly counted on his favorite daughter's company, disparaging her initiative all the while. Though he couldn't envision a creative or independent life for his daughter, he had grown to approve of Bill Morgan, and had followed his war experiences with the greatest interest and sympathy. Because it pleased her father, because she was brought up that way, and because she was in love, more and more of Christiana's energy centered on Bill. Her wishes for herself and her ideas of useful work were slowly transmuted into dreams about his career. She looked at his options from the point of view of her own background and ruthlessly, if unconsciously, disparaged the business orientation of Bill's Chicago family. She wrote that business was "disgusting and a waste of human intelligence." She suggested politics instead.

When Bill replied that he was considering diplomacy but, as a courier for the peace conference, having a firsthand experience of the type of people attracted to it and the internecine fights, on the whole preferred politics, Christiana jumped to answer: "I'm so thankful Bill you want to go into politics," and the following day wrote that diplomacy was "no man's job." And a few weeks later: "I'm so glad dearest you want to go into public work of some sort. . . . I had always dreamed that my husband would have some ambition beyond just plain business."

92   Christiana's now partially imaginery Bill, heroic because of his war experiences, turned into someone as intrepid as Floyd, some of Floyd's characteristics intermingling with her picture of Bill. Christiana wrote to him of this change: "remember the first time when we were sitting on the porch of Gran's little house—and I told you that I didn't think you were reckless enough to suit me . . . well I think you are now." She harked back to their early letters and the bond of idealism that had once united them, exhorting her pseudo Bill as if he were a visionary firebrand: "Ideals, Bill, we'll always work for them, they'll be the great point in our life. And these ideals will never fail us, Bill, because they're real, constructive and they're the only sure path toward progress for human beings."

The trouble was that Bill, after enduring six campaigns of the war and spending four and a half months of recuperation as a courier for the Peace Commission, came back to the United States with his faculties less than intact and with a bitter contempt for high ideals. Bill returned inwardly scarred, with his body harboring the trenches' seed: the tuberculosis that would overcome him fifteen years later. In April of 1919, however, he was a soldier back from the war and passionately in love with his fiancée. Reunited, they decided to marry in early May, and then Bill departed for a hurried trip to Chicago to see his mother.

Christiana had insisted that they get married as soon as possible and then slip away alone together, perhaps to York, where they would have no distractions. She wanted a beautiful wedding, but one that could be planned within the month. This ran counter to her mother's wishes for a delay and for a large wedding with its usual fuss, and led to another wearying series of fights. Christiana had her way, and the date was set for May 9, 1919.

Christiana chose the Arlington Street Church, where her sister had been married, and the same clergyman, Reverend Paul Revere Frothingham, her mother's friend. In Christiana's case, only close friends and relatives were invited. Christiana decorated the church with a single garland of white roses and greenery. She had no attendants, nor did she wear white. Instead she had designed an elegant wedding dress of cloth-of-silver, with a court train of the same material, lined with grass-green chiffon.

Bill had rounded up several friends to serve as ushers along with Christiana's relatives. After the ceremony, there was a small reception and wedding breakfast at the Councilmans' house on Bay State Road. Christiana and Bill left before it was over. They spent their honeymoon in York, Maine, occupying Christiana's grandmother's cottage and walking again on the bluff and in the pinewoods by the tidal river where Bill had courted her.

And so these two babes in the woods, who knew each other chiefly through letters written during the two years of adventure, upheaval, and loss that divided their meeting and their marriage, embarked on a complicated life as husband and wife. World War I had overturned their past and all its safe certainties. Nothing could ever be the same. Yet like others in that dislocated generation, Christiana and Bill sealed off those turbulent years and faced the future without speaking of them. They had experienced the savage and ugly side of life and witnessed its power. She was no longer the young postdebutante Boston girl he had left behind, nor was he the innocent and plucky Harvard lad whom she had sent off to war.

Through their daily correspondence they knew parts of each other to a depth that would not have been possible in normal life. Christiana served unknowingly as Bill's therapist, allowing him to wrestle with his demons in his letters. She had wanted to hear it all, yet the knowledge was perhaps more than she could live with as his wife, especially since she was drawn to harder, fiercer men than Bill. She ignored his more subtle masculinity, convincing herself that her returning soldier came back as tough as Floyd.

Both Christiana and Bill had matured through their ordeals. Christiana had been brought up to be ornamental and had instead proved to be intelligent, quick, and vital—a woman of purpose. She now knew that she could do something and do it well. She also saw her faults: she lacked an educational grounding, she lacked tenacity and self-discipline; she was best at throwing herself into a crisis and working magnificently to meet it, but then too easily she lost interest.

Both she and Bill were acutely sensitive and thus fragile and easily scarred by events. While she would soar and crash and soar again, Bill slid into soggy black holes of despair. This tendency, though not as marked as Christiana's mood swings, was aggravated by his harrowing experience of the raw hell of war. He had lost forever the high ideals with which he had catapulted himself into the battlefield. Bill returned with much of his strength, health, and vigor gone; these lay trampled and wounded in fields where his friends had fallen, and he emerged far less whole than Christiana.

94   As a newly married couple, they were oddly out of balance, being both too old for each other and too young and inexperienced. The most difficult complication for their marriage, perhaps, was that Christiana felt her strength, while Bill, in spite of his courage and perseverance, was a shattered man. Though neither of them realized it, she was the stronger of the two, yet she continued to accept society's inherited notions about a woman's place. Christiana, along with so many women of her generation, believed she could and should live through her man: "I want to put all my energy and interest into the work you are doing." At the same time, she needed a hero, and she expected Bill to take on the world and carve out a glorious place for them both.

Maybe there would be no more wars, and maybe they would live happily forever after, as they planned. On May 9, 1919, as they walked down the church steps together as husband and wife, they believed it all was possible.

The Origin
of the Hero

*The finest of all symbols of the libido is the
human figure, conceived as a demon or hero.
Here the symbolism leaves the . . . realm of
. . . images and takes on human form, changing
into a figure who passes from joy to sorrow, from
sorrow to joy, and, like the sun, now stands high
at the zenith and now is plunged into darkest
night, only to rise again in new splendour.*

JUNG,
Symbols of Transformation

Christiana and Bill returned from their honeymoon to an apartment at 985 Memorial Drive in Cambridge. Overlooking the Charles River, it was across and upriver from her parents' house and a few doors away from her sister Isa's. In a large, red-brick apartment building, it had mullioned bow windows, high ceilings, and large, somewhat dark rooms. During the war, Christiana had daydreamed about living by the Charles. "In the spring evenings we can have tea, and then walk along the river together and see the sunset every evening. . . . How wonderful it will be in the spring with the gold light on the water and on the buildings across the river—and we two together."

Though they often had tea and walked together in this romantic way, they had difficulty adjusting to their new life. Christiana attempted to limit her high-flying aspirations to the task of becoming the model wife of a successful man. Bill was worn with exhaustion and disoriented by his oddly leftover life. He chose Cambridge over New York for its familiarity during this time of transition.

96 Harvard had granted him and its other soldiers their bachelor degrees in honor of their heroism, but Bill had had only three years of college and didn't feel ready to start a career. He tried Harvard Law School for a desultory year, only to discover that he detested it and the type of people there. Bill preferred his friends at the AD Club, but drinking at the club did not help assuage his discontent. When he turned to his marriage for relief, he found he could not meet Christiana's expectations for his future. Together they represented two poles of the mood in America just after the war: Bill's the bitterness of the sad young men who had watched much of themselves die with their comrades in the trenches; Christiana's the elation in a new world made possible by a war that had swept away the old.

Christiana welcomed this new spirit of freedom as a vital antidote to Bostonian conventionality, yet as a newly wed woman, she found herself expected to play the role of a socially correct housewife. Bill's Chicago upbringing, reinforced by the firm religious grounding of stalwart St. Paul's School, made him more traditional than his bride, in spite of his war experience and the political skepticism it inspired, and in spite of his intense longing to be different. It was as if Christiana had picked a husband who brought her down to earth in the same way that her mother limited her expansive father. Christiana had noted Bill's suspicion of her iconoclasm early on:

> I guess you don't know Bill, what an unconventional wife you have. I am just like Pa in that way. It fascinates me to do out of the way things. It's so interesting. You'll probably have a fit dear, won't you? because you're really very conventional. . . . I decided that you were ever since that afternoon at the Brookline Country Club, when you wouldn't let me stay out and have supper with you. Do you remember?

Christiana instinctively found herself at the forefront of her taboo-shattering generation. She felt and responded fiercely; this intensity, though encouraged by the spirit of the time, was intrinsically her own. It spurred her desire to explore and express herself, while contemporary values helped release her from convention and prudery. Eagerly, she combined her own sense of adventure with the liberating message of the new literature she was devouring while Bill was reading the law; D. H. Lawrence, James Joyce, Nietzsche, Freud, Jung, Proust, and Marx mirrored, as well as formed, facets of her moods and beliefs. With these as guides, Christiana felt the need and the right to channel her intensity into sexual explorations that were usually reserved for men.

Marriage gave Christiana license to discover the extent, depth, and power of the passion that had been awakened in her dalliance with Floyd. If her lustiness derived from Christiana's Pilgrim and puritanical blood and brought into her bedroom the vigor with which Hannah Dustan had once faced the Indians, no wonder her ancestors guarded so violently against it. But even with the new currents of thought stimulating Christiana's urge to experiment and explore, she was reined in by custom, which upheld traditional gender roles and a different standard for women. It was a thorny paradox for a highly sexed woman in a culture that often retained Victorian ideas of womanhood. Most male freethinkers lagged in their attitudes toward women and seemed blindly indifferent to women's needs. Bill echoed this in their marriage, being not only sexually naive but no different from the majority of his peers in making love according to his own abrupt tempo, unaware of his wife's need for satisfaction. Nothing Christiana read gave her the words to express what she felt or required; as a woman, she was denied any but a passive part in her newly awakened erotic life. And so, though their lovemaking was frequent and passionate, it conformed to Bill's untutored precipitousness and left Christiana constantly aroused but seldom if ever fulfilled.

Christiana was caught in the age-old dilemma: how to be a free spirit in a woman's body—a body that was soon taken over by its most ancient and traditional task, childbearing. Christiana found herself pregnant near the end of her first year of marriage. She had not wanted a child. She rejected the process as alien and profoundly unaesthetic. The condition of pregnancy repelled her as her body grew swollen, clumsy, and misshapen, host to a foreign being who sapped her vigor and forced her physical appearance to stand in mockery of her lithe spirit.

Before her wedding, Christiana had written Bill of her desire not to have children. Her aversion had been intensified by what she had seen of hospital births, especially the agonizingly prolonged and difficult one at the Portsmouth hospital in 1918. Christiana later visited Isa after the birth of her sister's twin boys, and her dislike of childbirth now extended to the infants themselves. She wrote Bill: "I stopped at the hospital to see my young nephews. They were too awful looking. I hate little babies."

Christiana's antipathy remained profound and was aggravated

rather than ameliorated by her own experience of pregnancy and childbirth. On September 6, 1920, sixteen months after her marriage, she bore a son, Peter Councilman Morgan. At that time, home births had been superseded by hospital births, which provided neither the privacy, the comfort, nor the support of a birth at home. The attitude of doctors and nurses tended to be crude and brusquely impersonal, with little, if any, appreciation of the psychological needs of women in labor. The callous new style of safer, "more scientific" childbirth was especially hard on Christiana, who was isolated in her hospital room to endure the long hours of labor alone. She received no information about what her body was experiencing and whether it was "normal" or not, and she had nothing but her own fears and the screams of women in adjoining rooms to warn her of what was still to come. In truth, she was bearing her child at peril of her own life: the high blood pressure first noted in 1918 now escalated dangerously. In the final stages of labor, Christiana lost control, yelling and grunting, but ether rendered her insensible to the last violent contractions and the pain. She was returned unconscious to her room, and the baby was whisked away to another part of the hospital.

Critics of childbirth customs have deplored the way the impersonality and brutal isolation of such births can turn a natural process into a cycle of pain, tension, and fear that can interfere with a woman's feelings for her baby. But in those days, cold efficiency was considered scientific and modern, as was the initial separation of mother and child. Peter was brought to Christiana on a rigid four-hour schedule during the day, but was otherwise cared for in the nursery, away from his mother. Christiana spent the customary twenty-one days in the Phillips House, a private wing of Massachusetts General Hospital, removed from her usual surroundings, her family, and her baby.

The lonely and frightening ordeal, followed as it was by extended psychological isolation, precipitated a full-blown postpartum depression. Once home, in a repetition of her own infancy, Peter failed to flourish on Christiana's care, so she turned the baby over to her mother and sister Isa, with whom he did much better; but Christiana did not recover as rapidly as her mother had, and Peter stayed with relatives far longer. She consulted Dr. Waterman again. Believing that the postpartum period was a time of physical bankruptcy in the same way that her depression was a sort of nervous bankruptcy brought on by mental overactivity, the doctor prescribed bed rest, further isolation, and seclusion.

Bill, meanwhile, confronted his own ambivalence to his son. The early perils of his infancy—a sick mother and a dying father—reverberated in Bill, unconsciously making Peter a threat to his very survival. Further, owing to Christiana's depression and Bill's unease, their lovemaking ceased and Bill held his wife accountable.

Nine months after Peter's birth, Christiana took up her old baby book and started to write about her son in its back pages. She noted her son's birth, weight gain, and other details as if they were a laundry list, filling a scant two pages in telegraphic style, then leaving the rest blank.

> William Peter Councilman Morgan Son of Wm. Otho Potwin Morgan & Christiana Councilman. Born at Phillips House, Mass. Gen. Hospital, September Sixth, 1920. Labor Day. Dr. Huntington officiated. Weight at birth—7 lbs. 8 oz. 21 days old: Left hospital—8 lbs. Oct. 6—10 lbs. 2 oz.; Nov. 6—11 9; Dec. 6—12 9; April 6, 1921—10 7 [sic].
>
> Short clothes April 5th
> Lived with Grandma until March 1st
> Went to NY—58 West 58th for a month with Father and Mother . . . returned to his Grandma Councilman on April 12th. Immediately became an angel.
> First tooth April 16th. Lower right incisor.
> Scolds & grunts whenever he sees his bonnet.
> May 2nd—8 months: Weight 20 pounds. Teeth—2 lower, 2 upper, April 29.

Christiana's connection to her child remained tenuous at best. The easy warmth and bonding, the delight in symbiotic attachment to an infant, the pleasure of its smell and looks and responses, were denied her not only by her experience but by the medical thinking of the day. For this was the time that John Watson and his teaching about child care were becoming popular. Watson distrusted maternal instinct. Mothers, he believed, tended to be hysterical and unhygienic, and they benefited from rigorous schedules and restraints. In the thinking then current in England and the United States, a nurse could take care of Peter as well as if not better than his mother and would be less swayed by maternal weaknesses. Watsonianism's chilling astringency further alienated Christiana from her child and further sanctioned and encouraged her severe asperity.

"I think you get so little satisfaction with children," Christiana wrote. "We had a long discussion on the mother of the family who always puts her children first and her husband second. I hate that spirit and I think it ought to be the other way around."

100   A photograph of mother and child shows Christiana carrying her little boy unnaturally and regarding him with a tentative, oddly hopeless glance, as if they hold each other hostage. She looks pale and fragile; her depression is evident, shadowing both her beauty and her child.

Soon after Peter was born, the family moved from Cambridge to New York. Bill's uncle controlled his mother's money and meted out a paltry sum to Bill. When Bill gave up law school, his uncle urged him to go into business and arranged for him to start training as a banker in New York. In spite of Christiana's attitude toward business, Bill needed to support them; she also had been feeling suffocated in her domestic role in Cambridge and looked forward to the open and creative life available in New York. They found a small apartment a few blocks from the rooming house where she had lived as a nursing student, but the sober tone of a letter Christiana wrote on their arrival contrasted markedly with the joyous one heralding her first entrance into New York during the heady days of 1918.

58 West 58th Street
October 20th

Dearest Ma,
The entire family arrived safely at the Grand Central, assisted by two porters laiden [sic] down with bottles, blankets, etc. and poor Peter in a state of utter confusion and exhaustion. However he settled down quickly and has since been very good indeed. The new maid is very nice and a whole hearted sort of person—but I can't say that she has great finesse in waiting on table as yet. But I hope to improve her in the course of time. But it is a *great* relief to have a happy and contented household.

Your picture arrived from York without a blemish— and it looks wonderfully in the room. I never saw anything fit in better.

I haven't been doing much since I arrived but unpacking trunks, silver, etc.—and getting things generally in order. Bill is working hard at the Guaranty but says that he will be perfectly thankful to get out of it. We are going off to the country somewhere to spend this weekend in the car. . . . When Bill leaves the Guaranty we are going to take a week off and make a trip up the Hudson to

Pittsfield. We think we are very lucky because we have found a garage only about 2 blocks away where the storage is only 20$ a month—It is 40$ in practically all of them. We use your urn for tea every afternoon and find it very satisfactory. I am crazy to have you see the apt. . . .

Aff.
Chris

Though Bill worked at the Guaranty Bank, both he and Christiana preferred to think of him as a potential political journalist. As part of Bill's job as a courier for the Peace Commission in early 1919, he had traveled around Europe witnessing the commission's propaganda and the suffering that it denied. Bill returned to the United States with notes and a full diary to add to the letters he had written to Christiana. The Morgans worked on these papers a bit during the first year of their marriage, then took them up again as raw material for his journalistic career. Christiana's depression lifted when they worked on the papers; her hopes for her husband rekindled. Bill would sketch the outline for an article in pencil in a notebook, then the two would engage in long discussions and he would pen a revision, which she would amend and type. Of course, the essay was to appear under his name. Christiana simply served— as wives often have done for their writer husbands—as motivator, editor, typist, muse, appreciative audience, and organizer. Through conversation, she helped Bill form and pin down his ideas, then rearranged and edited a bit to help shape them. At their best, the small group of articles they produced would not have been out of place in an equivalent of today's *New York Review of Books*. What worked in the articles was their careful documentation, an eye for the telling though sometimes arcane detail, sympathy for the common people and the underdog, and their generally leftist tone. Effective writing, however, came much harder to both Christiana and Bill than conversation.

Perhaps the most interesting and successful article appeared in *The New Republic*. In it, Bill adopted the journalistic voice of a frontline soldier looking at the world for which he had fought and the peace that had been forged as a result. He wrote of the ordeals and deprivations he had witnessed in blockaded Austria and Central Europe, exposing the Peace Commission's tactics and warning that they were about to surrender their mandate. He went on to describe the shattering of President Wilson's Fourteen Points for peaceful recovery and the decimation of the League of Nations, concluding

102 that "the politicians of the world have sold their peoples. This is the last war I will ever enter. The diplomats of the allies have had the opportunity to bring about a new era. Any policies that may follow which bring us into another war will not be the fault of the peoples who will be called upon to fight that war." In contrast, Bill called for thoughtful men to join together with labor; only in this way, he felt, could they dismantle the bankers' peace treaty and implement the Fourteen Points.

It was an awkward if creditable first article. Where Bill wrote simply and stuck to the facts, it was a soldierly job, but the piece lacked organization and was inbued with an unpleasant tone—part Christiana's gung-ho utopianism and part Bill's schoolboyish truculence—that puts off rather than convinces the reader. The article riled even the liberal audience who read *The New Republic*. Bill was accused of Bolshevism, the great new bogey that had replaced Germany as public monster; he responded with a hotheaded and disastrously impolitic defense, which resounded with Christiana's rhetoric and her Brahmin contempt for Main Street's shibboleths.

In these postwar years, much was changing in the United States. The conservative voice of Henry Cabot Lodge soon replaced President Wilson's vision for the world, pragmatism replaced idealism, and strongly self-interested, isolationist business interests replaced plans for world healing. Bill soon abandoned journalism and, drawing on his family's business connections, spent his time trying to turn himself into a pragmatic young banker, learning business, and supporting his family. Christiana still yearned for a hero and openly despised the occupations that now employed her husband; her ideals clashed with their economic need and troubled their marriage.

In a letter to Christiana's parents a few months after their move, Bill tried to put a positive light on his work and on the couple's adjustment.

> Chris has been much better these last two days. She went to Cedarhurst for luncheon yesterday and was gone from 9:30 to 4 PM and did not look tired when she returned. She is out for luncheon today—and I am glad she is going out and seeing her friends now, because the city is depressing when you are more or less alone—you recoil so from the people you see and their luxury. I am glad that she can get these hours of thinking about nothing because she would otherwise find it hard to break a more serious

frame of mind—and it makes the change to this type of city less of a sudden contrast.

She is trying very hard to find a balance in this environment and she is understanding more and more of the reality and the effort which is required to attain what we both want.

From 1921 until the fall of 1923, Bill worked as a banker and then as a trader for R. D. Skinner & Company, but as with his journalistic efforts, neither brought him happiness nor success. Bill's mother, meanwhile, was dying of breast cancer, and he started spending several months at a time in Chicago with her. At first, both the bank and Skinner were generous in granting him leave, but as his absences prevented him from advancing in his work, they added to the precariousness of his marriage. Christiana accompanied him to Chicago once, bringing Peter for his grandmother to see, but it was not a successful visit. Christiana felt paralyzed and oppressed by the Midwest, especially by Bill's stultifying house and by his narrow-minded and bourgeois relatives. The couple fought, Christiana accusing Bill of weakness and lack of vigor; the baby mirrored their disharmony and fretted and cried. Christiana returned to New York, the baby to Boston, and Bill made his two- and three-month trips to Chicago alone. In choosing between career, marriage, and his dying mother, Bill clearly favored his mother and tenderly cared for her during her slow decline.

Christiana started to spend her mornings taking classes at the Art Students League, enrolling for the full academic year in 1921 and 1922 and for parts of 1923 and 1924. The classes provided her with happy memories of her days in the art room of the Winsor School and were both outlet and succor for her narrow and now often lonely domestic life. The Art Students League was a convivial, free-spirited place, then occupying the three top floors of the lovely old building it now owns on West Fifty-Seventh Street. It was just emerging from its traditional past into a vigorously experimental era, though the classes were still modeled on the Parisian École d'Art and used French terminology. The school encouraged innovation and attracted dynamic teachers. Christiana entered into a life-drawing class attended by thirty or so other female students; blending in, she concentrated on her art and was able to come and go as she pleased.

She studied most often with Frank DuMond, who was at the start of his fifty-year career at the League. Though he had been brought into the school as an innovator, DuMond still held rather old-fashioned stylistic ideas. He was a very popular teacher, with a strong sense of composition and plastic form. Christiana also studied with the more modern and daring Guy Pène du Bois, whose jumpy line caught the frenetic energy of her generation. She modeled with clay under Leo Lentelli and also learned wood carving and sculpting in stone. Though her attendance was less than regular, her mornings at the school became for a time the center of her days and gave her the basis for a lifelong avocation, which flowered in the paintings of her later "visions" and in the wood and stone carvings that became emblematic of her philosophy.

The other great interest Christiana had was depth psychology. She read Sigmund Freud's *Interpretation of Dreams* with fascination because of her own vivid and haunting dreams, but she found herself unable to accept his limiting assessment of dreams. She much preferred C. G. Jung's *Psychology of the Unconscious* (later retitled *Symbols of Transformation*), which traced a conglomeration of symbolic parallels in art, literature, mythology, religious thoughts, ethnology, folklore, superstition, and psychology. Jung's understanding of the libido resonated with her own experience. Jung described the libido as a form of psychic energy and life force that vitalized not only sexuality but innumerable creative activities as well. She read and reread the book, marking the pages, especially those that seemed to name her own feelings; most heavily marked was Jung's chapter about the origin of the hero, in which he equates love for the hero with love for the unconscious realm. In 1923, Christiana would be among the first to buy Jung's *Psychological Types* in its American edition, but it never appealed to her as strongly as his former, more imaginative and literary work.

Apart from her art and reading, Christiana initially led the same sort of vapid social life that she had been accustomed to in Boston; it brought her the same alternations between hectic activity and depression and was accompanied by the same feeling that she was frittering her life away. Her friends were drawn from the circle she had met while studying as a nurse, especially the Meeker family, and from Boston and Harvard expatriates—acquaintances from her coming-out years and class- and clubmates of Bill's. With her husband often away and the problems between them growing, with her child primarily cared for by his nurse at her mother's or sister's house in Massachusetts, with her days unpinned to anything but her art, her reading, and her social life, it is little wonder that

Christiana's curiosity eventually combined with her generation's belief in experimentation and she began to take lovers.

One of the first, Cecil Dunmore Murray, was a young man of her own age; a Harvard and AD Club man, he was a native New Yorker from a well-off family connected, through his mother, to many of old New York's elite Four Hundred. Having returned from his heroic exploits as a naval bomber assigned to the RAF (for which he earned the Naval Cross), Murray had completed medical school at Columbia and married a fellow student. Friendly and gregarious, "Mike" Murray was known for his humor, gentle good spirits, and empathy, though his more brilliant older brother, Henry, frequently overshadowed him. (This was the same Henry A. Murray who had been an usher at Christiana's sister's wedding.) Christiana eventually met Mike at the houses of mutual friends in their small Whartonian circle of New York society, but the two had been drawn together before, in a chance encounter one day as Christiana was wheeling her baby's perambulator up Fifth Avenue toward Central Park. This led to other, private meetings, and before long they became lovers. He was a type she had known and charmed as a debutante—more like the high-spirited, witty, gentle, and worshipful knight of a Billy Stearns and Bill Meeker than the commanding and dangerous Floyd Blair. Mike Murray had a young child too, but he was realizing that he did not love his comradely student wife. Christiana seemed another species of woman altogether, at once glamorously mysterious and an enchanting conversationalist. He adored her and came to see her whenever she would permit it.

A far more powerful older man soon entered Christiana's life, the fiery Zionist Chaim Weizmann, later the first president of Israel. From their first meeting, in April 1921, he captivated Christiana. Christiana and her younger sister, Elizabeth, had been introduced to Weizmann at a fund-raising dinner in which he spoke brilliantly and glowingly of his dream of an ideal promised land and of his work for his people. He had come to the United States to organize the Jews in support of his World Zionist Organization and had just received a hero's welcome in New York, including a ticker-tape parade and accolades from the press and all sectors of society. Christiana was drawn to his dynamism and his charismatic strength, while he was entranced by her beauty, her enthusiasm, her interest in his cause, and her response to him.

The heroic Weizmann was more exotic and compelling than

105

106 any of Christiana's previous beaux, and dimmed them into obscurity. She was in awe of this strangely vibrant man and amazed at his interest in her. They both loved serious and deep discussions that bubbled with wit; she admired the way he could temper the most profound topic with humorous anecdotes. When they met, he was in his mid-forties, a wiry, energetic man just under six feet tall, with an expressive, appealing face. His large head was dominated by a high, balding forehead, a black mustache, and a pointed goatee. He had a firm Semitic nose, a sensitive mouth, and large, liquid, deep-brown eyes which his first wife, Vera, described as humorous, seductive, and containing all the sorrows of the Jewish world. They were remarkably like Christiana's eyes.

Weizmann's scientific way of thinking, his broad outlook, and his wit reminded Christiana of her father. More than twenty years her senior, Weizmann also possessed her father's forcefulness, vitality, and his authority. Weizmann advocated and was an example of qualities she most admired: diligence, hard work, self-discipline, brilliance, and flair. Fired by his cause, Christiana readily yielded to his magnetism and was swept into a passionate affair.

Weizmann had a propensity for being bowled over by sudden and intensely ardent infatuations. Christiana was, like former loves of his, a Gentile *princesse lointaine,* attractive to him not only because of her beauty and intelligence but also because she was a Bostonian aristocrat. His biographer Norman Rose describes Weizmann's liaisons with such women, although he does not mention Christiana by name. Weizmann's charm and power often drew women to him, and he would respond with fatherly yet passionate affection. Psychologically, he resembled Christiana Morgan in many ways, flying easily between elation and despair, craving admiration, able to arouse the imagination and inspire a profound response. He was one of those men who are high in both masculine and feminine attributes; he could be at once tender, demanding, loving, dominating, and charmingly submissive. Having found that women understood him best, he flourished under the attentions of particularly intelligent and beautiful young confidantes, whose love and adulation became the solace and revitalizing erotic force behind his continued frenetic political activity. Women found his need for them irresistible; in a memoir Christiana wrote almost forty years after their affair, she disguised him with the name Mr. Frankel:

In her early twenties . . . in the middle of her protracted season of tumultuous discontent and anarchy—she had been taken by friends to hear the charismatic Mr. Frankel speak on Zionism. Never had she been so instantly enthralled. Here surely was a man whose strong passions and towering intellect were wholly and unequivocally involved in a single, historic enterprise. . . . What zeal, what eloquence! The wholeheartedness of his commitment, his certainty of purpose, the fervor of his language were as an invigorating, powerful West wind blowing through the stagnant atmosphere of a long-closed house. The ambiguities, skepticisms, dilemmas, and confusions that made up the life she was leading were all momentarily dissolved, submerged, or swept aside as trivial, by the overwhelming tide of Mr. Frankel's words. Here, without a doubt, was an inspired man, made in the image of an Old Testament prophet with a hot coal on his tongue, a man worthy of her trust and her discipleship. . . . [Their meetings served to] excite Eros. . . . Though shaken by her discovery, she was not deterred, perceiving, as she did, the hunger of this man for the adulation of a young Gentile woman who was so particularly and sincerely yearning to participate in the advancement of his cause. Abetted by these and other conspiring dispositions Eros drew them irresistibly together.

Though no record of the daily particulars of their affair remains, the two met both as lovers and as intellectual companions at Christiana's apartment throughout that spring and early summer. Their affair had such an effect on both of them that Christiana planned for a time to convert to Judaism and they both, though married, considered eloping together to Israel. Christiana went so far as to reserve passage on the SS *Celtic* with him, planning to accompany him to England, but then a greater awareness and some common sense overtook them. Weizmann sailed without her in July, returning to his wife in England and to what was most essential to him—his political work on behalf of a Palestinian state. Though they met again in New York in 1923, and probably also in England when both were there during the following year, and then again in Switzerland, the affair never regained the intensity of those ardent months in 1921.

The effect of Chaim Weizmann on Christiana Morgan was far more powerful and more lasting than that of her on him. She was younger, less formed, and he was not only a famous man but an incorrigible flirt who needed affairs such as this to stimulate and renew him. Weizmann's passionate force and depth of character left an indelible and lifelong impression on Christiana; he became the ideal against whom she measured less dynamic men. Given the intensity of her four-month affair, her life with her undeveloped and introverted husband now seemed utterly banal. Compared to the heroic Weizmann, Bill, Mike Murray, and the other New York youths of her class seemed inadequate to stir Christiana's imagination.

Unaware of Christiana's experiment with Mike and her later passion for Chaim Weizmann, her husband solemnly told Christiana in the letters and poetry he wrote her from Chicago that her passion derived from and belonged to him. Bill had awakened Christiana's sexual passion, but with a youth's understandable egoism and ignorance, he took her ardor as his own creation and possession. He expected to be the romantic center of her world—and that she be his mirror and his property. The letters the couple exchanged during Bill's increasingly long stays in Illinois provide an important insight into the pivotal first years of their marriage and its ultimate outcome.

Christiana and Bill got on better by mail in those days than face-to-face. Their correspondence recalled them to their courtship and the almost daily letters they wrote while he was in the army. For a time, Bill's absence and their letters seemed to bring them into a better harmony. Christiana's affair with Weizmann also helped, because she stopped harping on Bill's attaining heroic achievements. Many of his letters reveal a man torn by his mother's illness and childhood memories, by his lack of a career and his inability to do the writing he had planned. In one letter, he broached the painful subject of her past mockery of him and his relatives:

> Three times you have said there was "Marks" [his mother's family] in me when you knew it was the cruelest thing you could say. . . . You have said it more than three times—but these three I remember because I knew they were true—and for a very long time the "Marks" characteristics have been a ghastly spectre to me—as if following night and day. It is . . . because I have struggled so hard—because I have destroyed behind so much . . . that I am stirred beyond all knowing when I detect a fragment still alive. And can you know what it is to have blood which in you is incompatible with the rest of you—and be given by nature instincts and a mind which rebel.

He protected himself from Christiana's disparagement with paeans to his vigorous manhood, which are, to a modern reader, rather disconcerting, for he presented himself not as the conquering hero for a cause, like Weizmann, but as the subjugator of his wife.

In a crucial misunderstanding and devaluation of Christiana's 109 sexuality, Bill assumed that his arousal alone determined their love-making and that she was simply the object of his desire. Unable to understand why she failed to respond, he sought to prove his man-liness to her and to himself through admiration of his returning physical strength and, perhaps above all else, in claiming that Chris-tiana's sexuality was proof of his power over her. The odd thing is that the virile chest-beating excited Christiana, and although Bill was not hero enough for her, she took these violent expressions of power as a proof of his manliness. She wrote to him demanding that he tell her how he loved her, that he thrill her and make her afraid. Bill had grasped an element of sexuality they shared—the excitement of pushing passion into measured violence. Lovemaking began to occupy much of their letters, each competing with the other in verbal excess:

> My wonderful Christiana woman—you do know how to make me love you. There is beneath this last letter and the one before this a strong current of love which is plainer than any words you have thus far spoken—and you have reached to the very soul of me—you have wrung the depth of me until all else is so paltry that I can take notice of nothing else, only of you and of my love. Something stirringly poignant was in your letter and your love seems more real than at any time these long weeks.
>
> You have given to me more than in all your letters combined— I am therefor more happy—yet I am infinitely more depressed, more maddened by all this than ever be-fore— I used to get grim over it in a mean way—but now the grimness tears at my soul, at my life and I am drawn toward you irresistibly with a power of tides— And I lean far out toward you—straining and reaching until I am incensed with love for you which blinds me to all else in life, and I care nothing for person, thing or sky—
>
> . . . My woman, you speak of the whiteness of your body and the hair falling over it, and your warm legs and how you will move for me, slowly, strongly, sinuously— Would you say those things to bring wild madness to my mind which I cannot control—and make me love so that I recognize no force, nor no life but that of love.
>
> It seems that there comes to me from you insanity now and feelings which blacken my mind and obsess me

to distraction—and you dash them before my eyes with *cruelty* (it seems to me when the blood surges over me) and I say with cruelty because you must well know what you drive me to—and you must know the desperation of my extremes now, and the terrible moments when I would have physical pain to quell me and take away from me what would cause wild abandon of wanting and craving.

It is so that I am composed—and I suppose you will tear me always to madness, though you have never known me as I am now, and you would not dare to go so far— You did it with my jealousy and now you do it with the beauty of your body and soul— You write to me naked and you must know what it does to me—

I want you so that I would take you into unconsciousness of passion and pain, for nothing but that could satisfy my craving and here lies the blackness of my love. I dare you to be so when you see my face again, and when you see my body, and my arms—when you see the intense liveness of my body and mind and the way of its strong, instinctive, determined impulsiveness. Your lover will exceed all dreams of the commanding, ruling, urging, strong, man of your dreams—the man who cannot be denied nor moved—but has his way. And it seems to me that could I but see your body, could you but see my eyes and expression you would be stirred as you never thought you could be or would be.

I would love you a thousand ways.

I can see you standing before me naked, and I would throw myself to kiss your feet and stand off to worship the exquisite beauty of you—and upon the instant I would crush you to the ground at my feet, beaten, wrenched down before me—then would I throw you back for me— I would insanely press my lips to the moisture of you and you would be swept away and know nothing from that time on—

I love you—I love your letters—my woman—Christiana—

Goodnight dearest—I want you—and it shall be forever different soon—very soon—

Your lover

Alternating with these letters were others about Bill's mother's health and his unhappiness in Chicago, and criticisms of their marriage. Christiana's coldness also preoccupied him; he railed at her for withdrawing from him in the months after Peter was born and for not appreciating the magnanimity of his abstinence. There is no conscious understanding in either of them of the reasons for Christiana's need for privacy during that time—even galvanic lovemaking could not have solved their doubts and misgivings, nor could it have helped Christiana recover from the trauma of childbirth. She and he both seemed, at least in the letters, to prefer a Dionysian frenzy of excess than the simpler but also deeply binding pleasure of two people giving each other comfort and gentle affection. They had to be always, in Christiana's words, "at the crest," posing for each other as superman and superwoman.

Both by then had read Nietzsche's *The Antichrist* and *Thus Spake Zarathustra;* Christiana, especially, was seized by Nietzsche's ideas of power, his celebration of primitive strength and the heroic ego. Bill's letters of that time were strongly erotic but in a Nietzschean way. Feeling weak and unmanned, the gently masculine Bill assumed a tone of brutal domination that might have excited them both but was alien to the real state of affairs between them. For the truth was that Christiana was more the hero and the leader.

In the midst of Christiana's affair with Chaim Weizmann, an experienced, tender, gentle, yet passionate lover, Bill wrote to Christiana:

My passion woman . . .
Now we are to go away again, you with me this time as it should be. You have been long without me and your body has become small again. Your skin has grown cold these months and you are to be kissed again—every part of your body with a relentless man love— You are to be made large again for me— Nothing can come thru you but only as you give to me and you are therefor to serve me. There is to be no question of that and you are to know what I must have. The first night that you are away with me, I shall take you as it is meant to be with man. First I shall make you hate me, I shall make you feel your utter lack of power over me that you will fight bitterly at first, then desperately—with every ounce of your strength you will fight and I shall make you serve me there on the floor—I shall render you helpless—and withal you shall love as never before you loved. . . .
I want to see you in bed in my room—I want to see you lying there where I am to go and lie the full length of you—close to me that I may kiss the hair of you & feel

it—and the warm breathing of you and your hands upon me—and your full arms about me and your breasts pressing soft and your thrilling, living legs crushed between mine and the heat of you—the soft hair of you falling about your face and the perfume of it clouding my mind. So would I kiss & kiss, as you have dreamed your lover would—every bit of you, plunging my lips into you and the lying long upon you my lips on yours drawing all from your mouth and knowing nothing else of life nor of living.

But know you this my woman: you serve me— You are mine. No one can touch you—I must have you my way and as I conceive of woman, instinctively,—if it should be possible to lose you by cruelty, hardness, by force then better to lose you because I can never be happy in any other kind of love. But know that if such is the case you do not go free from me until I have broken you— until you are unable to have other men, until your body is wrent and made too large, too brutally taken to be satisfied by other men and even until I have made you bear more children for me.

You have felt vaguely that I did not dare many things; that I was afraid and was too impressed with restrained life, to ever throw it utterly to the winds. But I know full well what life is—and I do not intend to miss one atom of the freedom that each individual life is given—nor do I intend, for instinctively I cannot do otherwise than risk even life itself, that I have utter happiness & utter love & that I have & use in every way my woman (for I love too much); or nothing. Better that, than to have half attained, though it mean torture to you and abject, arbitrary subserviency.

Goodnight my superb passion woman. Oh you shall be close to me and as personal as my kiss

Your great lover

Perhaps it was at Christiana's behest that he was reading Nietzsche, but assuming his tone could not make Bill sound like a hero. Christiana and Chaim Weizmann also shared an enthusiasm for Nietzsche, especially for his philosophy of a will to power, which, during this period, Weizmann was quoting extensively in his own letters. Weizmann personified many aspects of the heroic superman; Bill Morgan used the concept only rhetorically.

But Christiana was as confused as Bill. She had read what

woman's sexuality was supposed to be and had tried to remain what her husband believed her to be. Yet by taking lovers, she sought to admit herself into the company of those who chose for themselves and pleased themselves. As such, she became the center and source of the flame of her own sexuality, claiming her right to it. When Bill was able to tap into Christiana's desire, he gloried in the results, hovering around her flame, all the while announcing that *he* was at its center. Preoccupied with Christiana's response to him, Bill tried to legislate both their doubts away, limiting her fervor to his own boundaries and holding her to traditional notions of marriage. Their problems with each other and with their marriage, however, demanded reality rather than the heroic Nietzschean bombast that disguised them from themselves and from each other.

After his mother's death, Bill finally returned to New York. He continued his work for R. D. Skinner until his mother's will was settled and then, in the fall of 1923, left to attend courses at Columbia. Christiana busied herself with her art classes and continued to see Mike Murray occasionally. She became intrigued by the courses she and Bill had started at the New School for Social Research and by their fellow students in class. It was then that she came to know Mike's brother, Henry A. Murray.

Christiana loved opera and attended performances at the Metropolitan as often as she could. One evening, Bill, Christiana, and her brother-in-law Frank Wigglesworth shared a box at a Wagner opera, and Christiana sat out intermission in the box's romantic, mirror-hung recess, with its deep-pink damask silk walls. Bill had run into Mike's elder brother in the lobby and brought him back to be introduced. Christiana recognized Henry from her sister's wedding and greeted him briefly in the rosy dimness of the box, but she was too busy talking to Frank to pay him much attention; nonetheless, the combination of her slender beauty, the rich blue of her evening dress, the headiness of Wagner, and the exquisite romance of the setting made a lasting impression on Henry Murray. A month later, all four Murrays came to dinner at the Morgans'. Harry sat on Christiana's left; while others talked business, she leaned toward him and asked him whom he preferred: Freud or Jung. Henry Murray could not answer, but he hastened to buy Jung's *Psychology of the Unconscious,* and their subsequent conversations explored this subject. Harry (as Henry was more familiarly known) was drawn to Jung for the same reasons as Christiana. Jung once had told a friend that his book was an account of adolescent psychology, with its clarion call toward heroic heights and depths. In spite of Christiana's and Harry's sophistication, this was just the realm that fascinated them both.

114

Harry was a young doctor doing biochemical research at the Rockefeller Institute. He and his younger brother, Mike, had been members of the AD Club at Harvard along with Bill Morgan and Frank Wigglesworth. In spite of poor eyesight and an incipient stutter, Harry grew to be a popular and successful oarsman at Groton and Harvard. Harry was made captain of the Harvard varsity crew, but in his final year he became somewhat too aggressive and too blatantly zealous for his classmates' taste. At the critical race of the year, he refused to cede his place in the first boat to the coaches' choice (a popular younger AD man). If Harvard had won, Harry would have been a hero and his strategy a brilliant coup, but the boat lost, and a small scandal ensued; the crew and fellow club members questioned Harry's sportsmanship, which was the same thing as questioning his honor. Graduating from Harvard in 1915, Harry took the unheroic path of staying in medical school during the war, serving only in the reserves, in spite of having asked Teddy Roosevelt's advice and being told to enlist or always regret it.

Now, in New York, Harry's ambitions and energies were chafing against too small an arena. Having just finished his surgical internship at Columbia-Presbyterian Hospital, he was studying chicken embryos at Rockefeller. His wife, Josephine, née Rantoul, a beautiful girl from a very well-to-do and prominent Boston family, had been the pick of her debutante year. Christiana had admired Jo Rantoul since 1916 and had recorded in her diaries Jo's adventures as the first girl in her set to own and drive a car. Jo impressed, even dazzled, Christiana with her verve and sophistication and her genuine goodwill toward the younger girl. Now Christiana met her as an equal and a friend, but it was Jo's husband who shared Christiana's interests.

Harry's interest was more than intellectual. He found himself haunted by Christiana's face. Something of the sort had happened to him a few years earlier, while he attended a dying patient at Columbia-Presbyterian—a young woman with a lurid and violent past, who was dying of syphilis compounded by influenza. Harry did an extensive case study of her and took her photograph. In spite of her disease, her wasted face, and her rotten teeth, her tragic brown eyes glowed with the inner light of a Sienese Madonna. Christiana's face held the same fascination for Harry.

When Christiana fell into another depression that winter, what lifted her was her involvement in a series of lectures at the New School, which she and Bill attended with Harry, Mike, and their group of friends. They studied nineteenth-century Romanticism and German philosophy, enthusiastically discussing these writers as well as the mysterious and unfathomable world of the new depth psychology. Christiana took an active part in the discussion group, listening and contributing as much as any of the men.

By this time, 1923, Jung's *Psychological Types* had been published in the United States and was required reading for the so-called Extravert-Introvert Club, named in honor of Jung's major categories. The book was perhaps Jung's best-known contribution to personality theory and the basis for Christiana's and Harry's lifelong interest in this subject. The personality types, as Jung formulated them, fall into two opposite categories, introversion and extraversion, each with four functions or ways of adaptation: thinking, feeling, sensation, and intuition. All energy for the introvert flows within, reality being his or her reaction to an outside event, thing, or person rather than the thing in itself. The extravert does the opposite reaching out to external reality and defining the world through contact and connection to external objects. Each of the four functions can be experienced in an extraverted or an introverted way:

> For complete orientation all four functions should contribute equally: thinking should facilitate cognition and judgment, feeling should tell us how and to what extent a thing is important or unimportant for us, sensation should convey concrete reality to us through seeing, hearing, tasting, sensing etc., and intuition should enable us to divine the hidden possibilities in the background, since these too belong to the complete picture of a given situation.

Jung went on to explain that most people used one primary function extensively and a secondary one somewhat less, while the weakest function—such as feeling for the thinker, or sensation for the intuitive—remained shadowy and undeveloped. Harry and Christiana played at devising a type test for the club, based on further intricacies of Jung's typology; though too psychologically naive to measure anything reliably, the test presaged their professional work together in the 1930s.

Together, Christiana and the group shared beliefs and values with the most innovative and forward-looking members of that generation. These young iconoclasts yearned to be left alone to do and think what they pleased. They abhorred censorship and social restrictions, and they eagerly advocated freedom of action and progressive politics. They rejected old forms of religion and religious observance; they scorned mediocrity and the bourgeoisie and delighted in toppling bourgeois idols, disdaining the business world and its increasing love for mass production. Perhaps what defined them above all else was their discovery of their own libidos whether in sexuality or through depth psychology. All these concepts motivated Christiana and her fellow freethinkers to explore a wide range of possibilities in themselves, free from puritanical oppression, convention, and standardization.

The more they studied and read, the more dissatisfied some of them felt with the way they were living their lives. Bill, Harry, Mike and Christiana were all growing heartsick at the failure of their buoyant postwar aspirations; they saw America as an increasingly money-grubbing and conservative society, but they'd failed to find a more satisfactory alternative life for themselves. Seeking refuge from their dismay, they decided, as did many of their generation, to flee temporarily to Europe and imbibe loftier air. The group decided on the University of Cambridge, where the men could pursue graduate degrees in biochemistry and related fields. Harry and Jo had a small daughter; Mike and his wife, Veronica, had a son about the same age as the Morgans' boy. The wives, they decided, could keep each other company and the children would have each other as American playmates. In 1924, each family gathered itself together, and one by one they set sail, to meet again in England, where they would return to the broad, safe sheltering arms of academe.

EIGHT

Brother and Sister

Midway along the journey of life
I woke to find myself in a dark wood,
For I had wandered off from the straight path.

DANTE,
Inferno, Canto 1

O nce at the University of Cambridge, the men took up the life of expatriate American students, but with different aims and results. Harry and Mike pursued doctorates in biochemistry, Harry working in the laboratory of the eminent F. Gowland Hopkins, along with fellow students J. B. S. Haldane and Joseph Needham. Mike wanted his doctorate in order to qualify for a teaching job at Harvard, while Harry wished not only to advance his career at the Rockefeller Institute but, more important, to instigate a radical change in direction. While in Europe, he intended to consult with C. G. Jung in Switzerland about becoming a psychoanalyst. The Murray brothers needed only a year in England to earn their degrees, but Bill Morgan would have to stay in Cambridge a few years longer, for he had switched fields, joining the Murrays to study physiology under L. J. Henderson, a visiting scholar from Harvard and one of the most renowned figures in science of that time. Though Morgan collaborated on a paper with Henderson, he again became disillusioned, this time with the 117

style and content of the instruction, and, in his final year at Trinity College, turned toward anthropology, a much more congenial field
118 for his talents. Christiana, Veronica, and Josephine resumed their roles as wives and mothers, but in the even more restricted atmosphere of this medieval learning center. The women were thrown into close proximity, as at first they knew few other people.

The Morgans rented Lawden Cottage at 1 Newnham Terrace in Cambridge, a rambling, ivy-covered stone house with charming but small and low-ceilinged rooms. Perhaps its best feature was that the back garden ran down to the Cam River, enabling the couple and their friends to punt to the house in beguilingly romantic, Venetian style. Christiana occupied herself hunting for old English furniture and adding an elegantly exotic flair of her own that contributed a bohemian, Art Nouveau touch to the house. Peter had a governess and attended nursery school at the innovative and experimental Malting House School, so Christiana had very little to do. During the first year, she slowly made friends, entertained visiting Americans, frequented lectures (such as John Middleton Murry's on the Romantic poets and the art historian J. S. Lucas's on Pre-Raphaelite art), read, shopped, and accompanied Jo Murray on many of her sightseeing expeditions. Christiana still occasionally welcomed Mike as a lover, but the affair was tempered by their proximity, by her friendship with his wife, and, even more, by her growing attraction for his brother. She saw Chaim Weizmann a few times, but he was a far different man in England, involved as he was with his wife and his domestic circle, as well as his seemingly endless work for a Jewish homeland; she decided his obsessive labor was a run for martyrdom and took his flattery now as empty words. Christiana and he were no longer the same golden American and glorious hero they had encountered in each other in New York; she held no authentic place in his life, while his more mundane existence cooled her ardor. None of this life—not her flirtations, not her dalliances—gave Christiana a sense of meaning or purpose. Looking back many years later, Harry Murray wrote that he saw Christiana during this time as

> a profoundly depressed woman. She appeared to [have] everything a woman could desire, and yet, despite it all, she was basically, tragically, and incommunicably unfulfilled and un-self-realized. She was resistant to all that Western culture had to offer her, to the type of life which tradition prescribed, dissatisfied with Christianity, dissat-

isfied with the accepted role of woman as wife and mother. She felt there must be something better than all this. Her one deep attachment was to her imaginative father, and in his criticisms of society she found confirmation of her own revulsions, and intimations of other possibilities.

The University of Cambridge in those days provided a welcoming cornucopia for men, but women, even women students, received at best a cold reception and were reminded of their inferior position at every turn. Virginia Woolf, writing of Cambridge during this period, described her own exclusion; even the college "beadle" lorded it over her, the officious little man racing over the lawn to keep her, a mere woman, off the men's sacred grass.

Christiana wandered the parts of town she was allowed in, marveling at the beauty and the gardens and entertaining the possibilities of the place, but she felt herself alienated from the cultural life around her and more than ever an outsider. She played her role and made what she could of the circle of expatriate young people, losing herself in her books, seeking comfort in the evanescent conversations she created around tea tables and at dinners, and finding imaginative ways to decorate herself and her house without the money available to wealthier friends. Christiana had put on a little weight since the worst of her depression in 1921, but she was still slender, though even with her hair cropped, there was nothing boyish about her. The sensuous depth of Christiana's beauty added a disquieting opulence to her American good looks, even a touch of the seraglio, and she casually displayed it with full consciousness of the effect she produced.

Christiana discovered little to nourish her, and her long days often lay barren. The fierce loneliness and sterile emptiness of her "accepted role" echoed her youth in Boston: if she engaged in the social activities customary to a woman in her position, she felt she was squandering herself, but she did not know how to find her objective or what it would be. With time, Christiana's and Harry's fascination with Herman Melville and Jung started to fill that void. Their discussions opened them to an exciting world beneath custom and good form—a world they approached as if they stood hand in hand like brother and sister at the entrance to a dark wood.

Bill Morgan still experienced the hyperarousal and fragmentation of chronic post-traumatic stress. He began making more demands of his wife, but the more he pushed, the more Christiana withdrew. He was too jittery to settle down to his studies and found them as barren as journalism, the bank, and business, but encouraged by supportive letters from his father-in-law, Bill decided to stick it out.

While the Morgans struggled with both careers and marriage, Harry and Jo Murray seemed to thrive. In contrast to Christiana, who felt her wings had been clipped by marriage and motherhood, Jo Murray flourished. Less complicated, less intellectual, and less questing than Christiana, Jo excelled in the role of wife and mother; she found it easy to enter into the spirit of whatever was going on. The Murrays had leased Leckhampton, a large Georgian house with great lawns, a tennis court, a quasi-natural stone-lined swimming pool, and fields and woodland besides. For that year, it became the center for the more interesting expatriates, as well as for members of the Trinity College rowing crew and new English friends the couple soon attracted. Useful connections for Harry poured in, while Jo managed the house, her child, and the visitors with seemingly effortless care and attention. In her diary, she mentioned the stream of visitors Harry and she entertained—among them the Cass Canfields, who were in London that year, the noted professors L. J. Henderson and J. B. Priestley, and the poet I. A. Richards, in addition to a group of intellectuals and society people centered in Cambridge.

Jo relished her presentation at court but took pleasure as well in attending lectures and church services; in going on outings with her husband, her father, her friends, and her child; and simply in dining in the nursery or enjoying a good talk with the governess. She organized her daughter's life as effectively as she did her husband's, and was a loving mother in the days when many women of her class saw little of their children. Jo structured visits, entertainments, and outings for other children (primarily for little Josie's pleasure) and was there to care for them when their parents were busy. She wrote with beguiling enthusiasm and love about her five-year-old daughter's accomplishments: her dancing classes, her behavior in church, her adventures with her playmates (Peter Councilman Morgan, now called Councie, being one of the closest), and the little girl's penchant for being their leader and organizer. Jo joined a woman's field hockey club, adding that sport and tennis to her already busy life. Harry received her full attention, and she entered his triumphs into her diary as if they were her own; she took particular pleasure in his friendships with noted people, his speech before the British Physiological Society, and his climb up the ranks of rowers to be in Cambridge's first boat in time for the Henley Regatta.

The Rantoul money made things much easier for Jo than they were for the far less affluent Morgans. More significantly, Jo took enormous pleasure in her wealth and the life it afforded. The practical details of daily living were more important to her than they were to the more creative and original Christiana. Whereas Christiana's world turned inward upon her moods, ideas, and feelings, Jo focused on external, physical satisfactions. She made Leckhampton a place where Harry could have all the benefits of being a good host without doing any of the work; instead he socialized, worked at the lab, and read Melville and depth psychology. A photograph of the couple reveals Jo to have a clearer, more straightforward beauty than Christiana's; Harry, meanwhile, stands assertively and slightly ironically, dominating the camera with his tall, broadshouldered, lithe, yet muscled body. The thirty-one-year-old's face is at once cocky and eager to please; his high scholarly forehead is already balding at the temples, and his strongly thrust jaw and narrow lips give him a suggestion of hardness, in marked contrast to his tender and humorous hazel-brown eyes. Altogether a fascinating face in its incongruities and one that would take Christiana a long time to fathom.

Jo's face, in contrast, reflects unambiguous ease, satisfaction, and goodheartedness—a spirit echoed by the diary she kept that year. At first, the only somber note was her failure to have a second child. Several times that year she thought she might be pregnant; she described Harry's joy and her elation and then the regretted arrival of a belated period. It had been difficult for her to get pregnant the first time. A year or so after their marriage, Harry had consulted a doctor in Boston about their failure to conceive and his problem with potency. The doctor examined him, then sent him off to instruct his wife to travel south alone, see other men, and write to him about her imagined adventures. This was done, Murray and she were reunited, and, soon after, they conceived a child. By now, however, they had ceased playing such games, and Jo quickly overcame her sorrow, immersing herself with renewed zeal in her daughter, her friends, and her life.

Before the year ended, however, a shadow crept into Jo's diary and over her life. She began to note Harry's turmoil, which was made up of one part Carl Jung, one part Herman Melville, and one part Christiana Morgan, each inextricably intertwined with the

other and threatening to separate him from Jo. In early March, Harry
had left Cambridge for the long spring holiday and traveled to
Zurich to consult with Jung. To Murray, Jung represented psychoanalytic theory as Melville represented literature. Harry saw
parallels between the two, immersed as they both were in myths,
Romantic philosophy, and the labyrinthine depths of the unconscious. Melville's, Jung's, and Christiana's influence over Harry
rose, and Jo felt her husband moving away from her; her wifely
pleasures dimmed, and the alien refrain "I feel strangely depressed"
increasingly marked the pages of her diary. Subsequent photographs
of her never portrayed the earlier clarity and verve.

Not unjustifiably, Josephine Murray blamed Carl Jung for
much that was to follow, although her problems had started long
before—on the evening when Harry Murray had been reintroduced
to Christiana Morgan at the opera. The seed of Harry's attraction
to Christiana had been planted there, to be watered by common
interests in Jung and Melville and by their long discussions of
nineteenth-century thought; and now, with their sojourn in England, attraction grew into passionate fascination. Christiana realized from the first that what drew her to Harry was far more forcible
than the malaise and self-exploration that had heretofore tossed her
into passing affairs. In spite of the bohemianism accepted by their
contemporaries and the unhampered sexuality prevalent among
both men and women in intellectual Bloomsbury and Cambridge,
and almost obligatory among the British upper class, Christiana
made no move to take Harry as her lover, though she flirted with
him and kept their friendship and discussions intense. While at the
New School, she had met several radical Greenwich Village women
and pondered their ideas, ideas that were also current in Bloomsbury
and Cambridge. These women grappled with what it meant to be
a radical and a woman—how to be autonomous, assertive, and free
from traditional female restraints. Some, like Christiana, looked
for freedom and self-definition through heterodoxy—the right for
women to choose different and multiple sexual partners, without
any bonds or obligation, and dependent on neither husband nor
lover. Harry's forceful personality, though, threatened to overwhelm Christiana's own precarious struggle to find herself.

Harry, on his side, at first also shrank from an affair with
Christiana. Jo was Christiana's friend—her closest woman companion in England—Mike, his brother, was still her sometime lover
and continued to hold strong feelings for her. Added to this was

122

the group's, especially Harry's and Christiana's, emphasis on honesty and openness about their personal life. They, in tune with their peers, believed they had the right to explore and discuss their sexuality as freely as any other aspect of their lives. Yet this freedom forced Christiana and Harry to consider the consequences of their desire. Harry felt that an open move toward Christiana would take too great a toll on his comfortable life; he would sacrifice not only the earthly and social comforts Jo provided but also Jo's talent in backing his career. Besides this, the profound effect Christiana exerted on him filled him with fear; he yearned for her and resisted her at the same time. Though Murray in later years publicly proclaimed that he went to see Jung out of professional interest, his fascination with Christiana and their possibly explosive juncture had filled him with confusion, and propelled him to consult with Jung about their situation.

At this stage, when Harry and Christiana were merely talking about the *idea* of erotic love, they expressed their unclear feelings by comparing them to what they were reading. This added a complicated literary overtone to their infatuation, in which Jung's ideas and Melville's literary parallels merged to become the instruments by which they opened up their world and their psyches. Besides mythology and Jung's broad understanding of the libido, the specific aspects of Jungian theory that appealed to them were his understanding of the collective unconscious and its archetypes, especially the anima, the hero, and the shadow.

Jung described the collective unconscious as a heritage that underlies and is common to all humanity; it manifests itself through archetypes—eternally inherited psychic forms—expressed in images, myth, symbols, and dreams that recur across culture and time. According to Jung, the archetype is never fully knowable, remaining an eternal, unchanging, primordial, and collective deposit of "certain ever recurring psychic experiences" common throughout the history of the world. Its outward representation, the archetypal image, can be positive and negative, good and evil, clothing itself in accordance with the values, culture, and experiences of a particular time or place and the attitude of a particular individual. In the article he was working on in 1924, "Marriage as a Psychological Relationship," Jung defined the archetypes of the anima and its masculine counterpart, the animus. Not only do they combine all of the experiences of particular women and men in a person's history but also:

124

Every man carries within him the eternal image of woman, not the image of this or that particular woman, but a definite feminine image. This image is fundamentally unconscious, an hereditary factor of primordial origin engraved in the living organic system of man, an imprint or "archetype" of all the ancestral experiences of the female, a deposit, as it were, of all the impressions ever made by woman—in short, an inherited system of psychic adaptation. . . . The same is true of the woman: she too has her inborn image of man. Actually, we know from experience that it would be more accurate to describe it as the image of *men,* whereas in the case of the man it is rather the image of *woman.* Since this image is unconscious, it is always unconsciously projected upon the person of the beloved, and is one of the chief reasons for passionate attraction or aversion. I have called this image the "anima." . . . [It] has an erotic, emotional character, the animus a rationalizing one.

Both Christiana and Harry resonated to this description. Certainly it explained their sudden and powerful attractions to people such as Chaim Weizmann and Harry's syphilitic patient. Christiana also pondered how it was that she seemed so often to be the object of men's anima projections. The two were also both drawn to Jung's concept of the hero and the heroic ideal. Jung had dealt with the hero archetype in *The Psychology of the Unconscious,* where the hero's quest was emblematic of a young man's striving toward wholeness—a striving that both Harry and Christiana perceived in themselves. Jung also thought of the hero as a positive aspect of a woman's animus, later writing that in the animus's truest form, "he is a hero, there is something divine about him." The animus and anima are not only unconscious internal images that an individual projects onto other women and men, but more important, they connect the personal unconscious with the collective unconscious. As such, Jung found the animus and anima heroic guides to an enormously rich inner world common to all humanity.

The shadow archetype is often the enemy of the hero and his other face, but Jung's theories held a far more comprehensive idea of the shadow. Since Jung believed that the goal of development was wholeness—what he called individuation—the development and understanding of all parts of oneself demanded understanding and acceptance of the shadow within the self, that aspect of the archetype heretofore ignored or rejected by the ego. Both Morgan and Murray instinctively understood the importance of these ideas. Jung's concept of the integration of the shadow in individuation provided an alternative to the nice, and Christianly correct, denial of evil and pursuit of perfection, which they found hollow and unsatisfactory. The shadow provided them with another, much more equivocal and suspect, guide into the underworld.

Jung's ideas about the different personality patterns in the book *Psychological Types,* which had so interested the two in New York, cast light on the ways the Morgans and the Murrays interacted and on some of their problems with each other as well. Christiana was an intuitive thinking type who loved to gather external facts together into theories often based upon her dreams. Harry also loved to create theories and the two bounced their ideas off each other with an almost drunken abandon. Bill, an introverted sensation-feeling type, mistrusted this kind of mind-play, relying on his inner sense of the world and his like or dislike of what he found. Jo, meanwhile, was extraverted and sensation-feeling, and so valued concrete reality and all its pleasures. Each marriage partner was thus, for the most part, the other's typological opposite, a combination where attraction, loathing, and misunderstanding combined, yet each proffered what the other lacked. Christiana's and Harry's match was far more tantalizing, because it was much closer. They talked the same typological language; Harry's thinking was the more highly trained and honed, while Christiana's intuition blossomed. Part of the joy of their discussion lay in the fact that they responded as if they were one person, Harry having the formed thoughts that Christiana could admire and Christiana making the leaps of imagination that transported Harry. Typologically brother and sister, they each gazed at the other's face in the pool, failing to perceive that they were attracted to their own reflection.

Since their arrival in England, the group had been reading Herman Melville together, and this added a literary torsion that intensified the current between Harry and Christiana. The two read Melville with the same eyes and, through him, found themselves immersed in a powerful, if unconscious, erotic experience. They were not alone in this rapture. Many of the initial discoverers of the dynamic unconscious grappled with the same Romantic interest. In *Moby Dick,* Melville pictures the collective unconscious as a vast ocean within which the archetype of the terrible mother, the whale, enthralls and lures Ahab, a hero of the shadows, in a desperate chase to his death. In his novel *Pierre,* Melville traces the collective unconscious through Pierre and his half-sister, Isabel; mysteriously

126   attracted to Isabel, Pierre is intent on fathoming her soul as if it contains the key to his own. Melville's books exemplified Jung's ideas, not in dry theory but in a splendid extravaganza of desire, where good fights evil, light challenges dark, and the ego dramatically pits itself against all the forces of the unconscious.

Beneath Harry Murray's extraverted and scientific demeanor lay a yearning for the mythopoeic aspects of the unconscious represented by Melville, Morgan, and Jung. An anima figure in its dark, suffering, yet mysteriously generative form had attracted all three of the men—each man wanting to rescue her in her many disguises. Murray, as well as Melville and Jung, failed to understand that this anima enrapturement inflated its adorer with a sense of heroic identity, the image inspiring each to feel virile and at the same time throb in sympathy with her, thus experiencing emotions he had long denied himself.

D. H. Lawrence wrestled his way through a similar fascination, perhaps proving himself the better psychoanalyst. He freed himself by studying his own response to an invented anima figure's torment; through imagining the woman suffering "from the depths of her soft vulnerable victimized female self," he could make himself feel extraordinarily potent. He also discovered that a real woman rarely matched this romantic anima image, her type occurring most clearly on the stage or in books written by men. He understood the self-referential narcissism implicit in the whole concept, for in projecting such an anima image, a man could safely feel himself both the hero and his shadow: "What a villain I am what a black browed passionate ruthless masculine villain I am to the leading lady on the stage and on the other hand, dear heart, what a hero, what a font of chivalrous generosity and faith. I am anything but a dull and law abiding citizen. I am Galahad full of purity and spirituality. I am the Lancelot of valor and lust. . . . I am myself only I'm not a respectable citizen . . . how I admire myself!"

Neither Murray, Melville, nor Jung was as clearheaded as Lawrence was here, nor did they perceive how self-serving their anima enrapturements could be. Like Ahab, they found themselves inextricably bound to the mysterious depths of the figures they were compelled to pursue. Christiana Morgan, in her depression, passionate disquiet, and lacerating reveries, embodied for Harry an unknown yet injured aspect of himself. He yearned for her, yet he also loved his wife and his vision of a successful exterior life that seemed to be his for the taking. While Jo stood for all that was light in his life, Christiana came to personify the plangent, the obscure, and the inspiring. He desired both equally and simultaneously.

Perhaps the problem should be placed earlier than the scene at the opera. Christiana was not the only woman to affect Harry so turbulently, to catch and form the components of his anima image. Harry's older sister, Virginia, had once played the imperious and heroic Amazon to the then delicate and thin-skinned little boy, overwhelming him and, often with great cruelty, making him her wounded (and feminized) slave. Harry's earliest, polymorphous, boyhood sexuality derived from the excitement of challenging and then being dominated and overcome by this darkly powerful and often extraordinarily mean little girl. Under her bullying, Harry made a great effort to hide his tender and intuitive side, until he almost totally repressed it. In early adulthood, during his medical training, he had seen an aspect of this sensitive and badly wounded feminine self resurrected in his syphilitic patient. Harry very nearly wallowed in his pity for her and, in true Lawrencian fashion, decided he would rescue her through his healing love. Christiana now seemed to proffer a similar echo of his lost self and exerted a similar fascination. But her effect was far more profound, because she was of his class, a friend with a comparable mind and comparable interests, who was searching, herself, for ways to translate her own unfathomed suffering.

The couple's attraction approached a crisis as the group started reading Melville's *Pierre*—a book whose parallels in Murray's life crashed in on them all. The hero of *Pierre* is the son of a dynamic but ambivalent woman—Harry's imaginary self as the center of his mother's life and without the encumbrance of his overpowering sister. Pierre had grown up in privileged ease at home, as Harry had at Groton, Harvard, Columbia Medical School, and the prestigious Rockefeller Institute. Their careers and futures seemed secure, at least by conventional standards. Both men loved their sensible, good, competent, and very appealing wives-to-be, Jo Rantoul and Lucy Tartan, and, through their marriages, would come into a substantial fortune. Melville's Pierre throws all this over for the darkly introverted Isabel, whose face has long haunted him. He senses in her not only profound melancholy but an accompanying knowledge of vast mysteries that teem within his own mind. Discovering that Isabel is his own long-lost half-sister and soul mate,

Pierre sacrifices everything in his exterior life for her. He moves with Isabel to a hovel in New York, and with her as his muse, attempts to write the book she has inspired in him. *Pierre* ends tragically, but not before Melville brings together two aspects of the feminine, personified by Isabel and Lucy, united in service to the hero's genius.

On a psychological level, Melville's Pierre and Harry Murray both contended between and tried to unite aspects of themselves represented by Isabel/Lucy and Christiana/Jo. Harry, in notes made many years later, supposedly about Pierre, pondered what the two types of women represented for him. Harry made two columns, putting Isabel on the left as "grief, night, dark, unconscious, pride, sea, rejected, isolate, deep, non-maternal, spiritual, supernatural, primitive, introvert, mirror, unstructured, unconventional," and Lucy on the right as her opposite: "pleasantness & gaiety, day, light, conscious, benevolent, land—solid of veritable reality, accepted, social, shallow, maternal-marriage, natural-heavenly, cultivated, extravert, structured, conventional." He went on, not only equating Isabel with Christiana and Lucy with Jo, but conflating himself with Pierre—Harry was the physician here, not Pierre, who needed to confront his shadow and ponder his own situation:

> Why does Lucy not hold him at this point? 1. She does not greatly *need* everything he has to give. He is a physician. She is conscious—well-accepted. Isabel is sick—rejected—unconscious. [Lucy/Jo] is conscious light & goodness—cannot understand, meet, call forth, sympathize with his lies. No place for his lies—grief, hate, sex, pride in her. This would have to be all repressed with her. . . . It is his creative strength that takes him out of the constricted little sphere—narrow reverence—haughty ritual—too small for him—space—cooped in suffocating stuffy conventions—cannot breathe. Isabel is like the ocean.

During the months in England, Christiana and Harry read and talked and came ever closer together, Christiana calling him the way Isabel called Pierre and the whale called Ahab. *Pierre,* with its flagrant parallels and tragic outcome, shocked the quaternity of Bill, Christiana, Jo, and Harry Murray. Jo noted in her diary that she had "read Pierre all afternoon and it made the deepest impression on me that almost anything else has—talked to Harry all evening about his plans and his ideas with reference to 'Pierre.' Had a bad

128

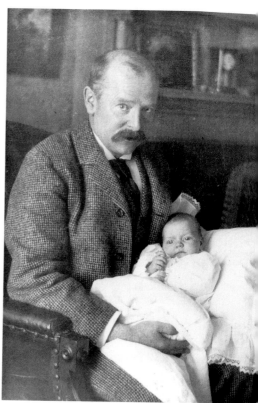

Isabella Coolidge Councilman, Christiana Morgan's mother, posing as a gypsy in the early 1890s.

Dr. William Councilman, holding Christiana shortly after her birth in 1897.

Christiana adored her father, photographed here in the garden he designed at the family's summer home in York, Maine.

THREE PHOTOS: HOLDEN FAMILY SCRAPBOOK

Above left, Christiana (center) with her sisters, Elizabeth and Isa (left and right, respectively), playing house in front of 78 Bay State Road, the family home in Boston.

Above right, at age seven, Christiana's ebullience often brought her the punishments of "closet."

Below left, at fourteen as a student in Miss Winsor's school, Christiana was very active in spite of periods of illness.

Christiana was sent to finishing school at Farmington, where, after initial rebellion and a severe depression, she learned to channel her energy into the social whirl of debutante life.

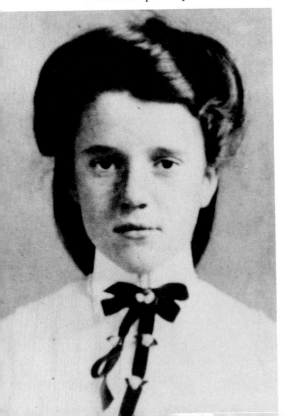

In 1916, when her sister Isa married, Christiana was one of the bridesmaids. She is in the center in the back row, wearing her hat with a difference.

Lucia Howard, who opened Christiana's eyes to a more intellectual and emancipated view of her womanhood.

Left, at the hearth of the Bay State Road House at the time of Christiana's involvement with her first love, Floyd Blair.

Right, "Miss Christiana D. Councilman," reported the Boston papers, is "one of this season's most popular debutantes. She is a prominent member of the Sewing Circle and a leader in the social activities of the younger set."

Below, in 1917, alternating between a hectic social calendar and bouts of depression, Christiana met William Morgan, a junior at Harvard who had just volunteered to serve in World War I.

After her engagement, Christiana was happy to drop out of the Boston social scene. Here she is with Bill just before he shipped out to war. That same year, she went off to New York to start a career in nursing and contribute to the war effort.

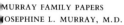

Christiana's beauty was an arresting blend of the magnetic and the melancholy. She is pictured here in 1926 at the time of her analysis with C. G. Jung.

Cecil (Mike) Murray at aviation camp in 1918. Mike and Christiana became lovers in the early years of her marriage.

Left, Henry (Harry) Murray, who would be Christiana's lifelong lover, with his sister in 1908. Virginia, a domineering girl, enjoyed tyrannizing her brother.

Below, Harry Murray in 1915, at about the time of his graduation from Harvard.

Below left, Harry became engaged to Josephine Rantoul, a well-to-do and popular debutante in Boston.

TWO PHOTOS: MURRAY FAMILY PAPERS
COURTESY JOSEPHINE L. MURRAY, M.D.

HARVARD ARCHIVES, HARVARD UNIVERSITY

WEIZMANN ARCHIVES, REHOVOT, ISRAEL

TWO PHOTOS: MORGAN FAMILY PAPERS

Above, Christiana married William Morgan after he returned, ravaged by the horrors of war. Councilman (Councie) Morgan was born the next year, and they moved to New York, where Bill worked as a banker and the two studied at the New School for Social Research.

Above right, during the New York sojourn, Christiana met and had a brief affair with Chaim Weizmann, one of the founding fathers of Israel.

Right, in 1925, Bill and Christiana traveled with the Murrays to Cambridge, England, in order to pursue studies in biochemistry and psychology. Their relationship showed great strain as Christiana and Harry's attraction for each other grew.

Fascinated by Carl Jung's work
in depth psychology and particularly by his book *The Psychology
of the Unconscious,* the Morgans
and Harry Murray traveled to
Zurich to meet him.

Jung urged Christiana Morgan to
be for Murray what Toni Wolff,
shown here in the late 1920s, had
been for him—a lover and *femme
inspiratrice.*

TWO PHOTOS: KRISTINE MANN LIBRARY

Did you have one of those too? — was it black? Did it move ???

Robert Edmond Jones, "Jonah," the theatrical set designer who was an ardent advocate of Jung and was Bill and Christiana's best friend in Zurich.

Christiana holding one of her vision drawings, the remarkable artwork that moved Jung and inspired his theories.

Female abraxis.

Christiana Morgan's active imagination led her to produce dozens of these vision drawings, which Jung later mined in his "Visions Seminars." The visions suggested a new and revolutionary concept of feminine psychology, but they would never realize their potential.

Uniting with the god of earthly passion.

The giant.

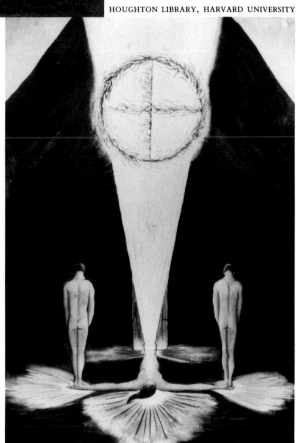

Three men, one woman.

The Harvard Psychological Clinic during the 1930s. It was here that Christiana Morgan worked with Henry
Murray to establish a more humanistic
approach to psychology.

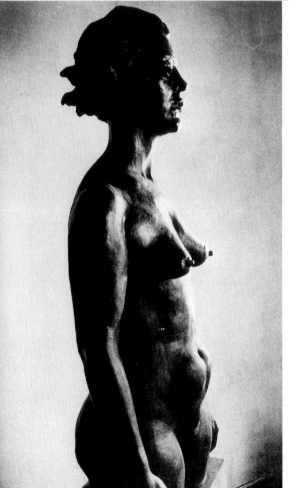

Gaston Lachaise created this sculpture
of Christiana Morgan in 1935. Upon
seeing it, British philosopher Alfred
North Whitehead—one of Christiana's
later friends and lovers—described it as
"Woman becoming."

Christiana in the clinic's library.

Portrait of Christiana by Mary Aiken, 1956.

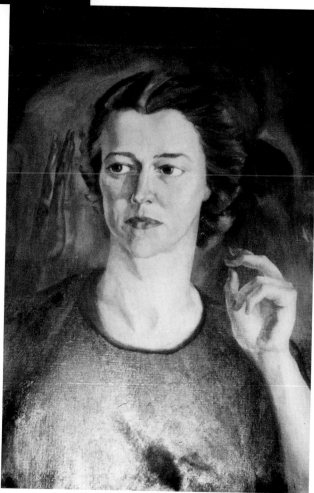

THE TOWER
ON THE MARSH

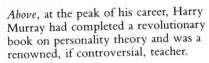

Above, at the peak of his career, Harry Murray had completed a revolutionary book on personality theory and was a renowned, if controversial, teacher.

Above left, the three-story structure in which Harry and Christiana did their most creative work was modeled after the retreat Jung had built to write in and be alone with his mistress, Toni Wolff.

Left, Christiana at thirty-eight, standing at the doorway of the Tower house, the place she and Harry built to memorialize their love. It was here they carried out their erotic rituals.

Above, in the garden.

Above right, working at her desk.

Right, Christiana in her sixties, standing in the doorway to her ritual and trance room.

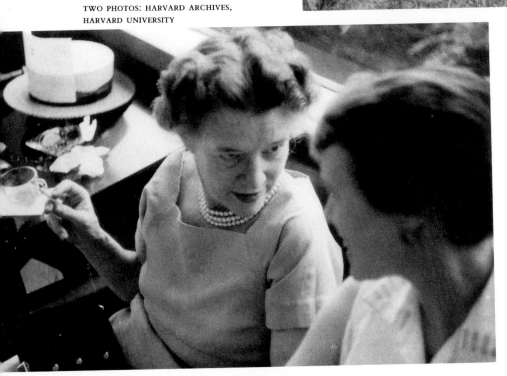

With her son, Councilman, in the 1940s, just after her radical sympathectomy. The operation, obsolete today and remembered for its ravaging effects, severs the sympathetic nervous system along the spine.

At a clinic party, showing the effects of her alcoholism. Christiana would fatally drown at the start of a subsequent bout, nine years later.

TWO PHOTOS: HARVARD ARCHIVES, HARVARD UNIVERSITY

headache—the 2nd in a week." In *Pierre,* Harry Murray confronted a tragic version of his conflict. Aroused and troubled, he hastened on to Zurich to consult with Dr. Jung.

When Harry Murray first met him, Carl Gustav Jung was a vigorous fifty-year-old man, tall, robust, charismatic, a brilliant talker and intuitive thinker. Widely read and educated, Jung had been trained as a physician and then as a psychiatrist, living among and studying his patients for nine years at the Burghölzli mental hospital in Zurich, one of the foremost centers for research into mental illness, before setting up a private psychoanalytic practice at his house in Küsnacht, a suburb of Zurich, on the shore of its lake. Jung gained international notice through originating the idea and term "complex" for the emotionally charged ideas or images at the center of neurotic behavior and, in 1904, devising a test to elicit them. Through this work, Jung had attracted the attention of Sigmund Freud, a man Jung admired as his leader in their investigations of the unconscious. In 1906, the two men joined forces, and Freud soon acknowledged Jung as his favorite son and heir. However, their own complexes intervened: Freud as an edgy and somewhat paranoid patriarch defending his kingdom, and Jung as the hero and son compelled to overthrow the father. They soon found themselves embroiled in a personal rivalry and a battle of Oedipal intensity. In 1912, the younger man broke with Freud, ostensibly because Jung could not accept Freud's dogma of sexuality and because to Freud, Jung's idea of the collective unconscious was heresy. After a severe mental crisis brought about by this rupture, Jung emerged with his own theories in the form of *The Psychology of the Unconscious,* in which he postulated a collective as well as a personal unconscious, a potentially optimistic view of the psyche rather than a pessimistic one, and an amplificatory as well as a reductive mode of treatment that aimed at individuation rather than a narrow adjustment to reality. When he resigned his position as first president of Freud's International Psychoanalytic Association and as managing editor of the *Jahrbuch,* the first Freudian journal, his break with Freud was complete.

By 1925, when Harry Murray came to consult him, Jung's creative new theories were attracting artists, intellectuals, and the rich, as well as some of the more forward-looking doctors in Europe and the United States. A small and devoted band of these patients and followers had gathered around Jung, a number of them training to be analysts themselves. The thirty-two-year-old Murray found in Jung both a father figure and the model for his future career.

130   In a most fated and fateful coincidence, however, Murray sought the counsel of a man who was himself entangled in an anima complex. Jung's interest in the depths of the labyrinthine unconscious had focused itself on and become personified in an anima figure similar to the one who so enthralled Murray. Jung, too, had been abused as a child; as a physician he had taken an exceptional interest in his predominantly female patients' inner worlds, fulfilling his own need to fathom the wounded feminine. In the process, Jung, like Murray, became fascinated by particular patients, and he fell into at least one probable liaison with a patient. In his memoirs, Jung traced this anima image in his own life back to its first personification, a maid who took care of him while his mother was hospitalized. Jung wrote:

> I still remember her picking me up and laying my head against her shoulder. She had black hair and an olive complexion, and was quite different from my mother. I can see her, even now, her hairline, her throat, with its darkly pigmented skin, and her ear. All this seemed to me very strange and yet strangely familiar. It was as though she belonged not to my family but only to me, as though she were connected in some way with other mysterious things I could not understand. This type of girl later became a component of my anima. The feeling of strangeness which she conveyed, and yet of having known her always, was a characteristic of that figure which later came to symbolize for me the whole essence of womanhood.

Jung's choice of psychology as a profession may very well have been influenced by his need to understand his fascination with this type of woman and what she represented. While still at the university, Jung, accompanied by his mother and his sister, had attended a series of family séances where Helene Preiswerk, his fifteen-year-old cousin, acted as the medium. In physical appearance she resembled the servant who held and caressed him as a child. This cousin inspired and was the subject of Jung's doctoral dissertation. Laurens van der Post wrote of the young girl's importance to Jung: "One cannot stress enough here how significant it was that in taking even this first step toward his destiny, his guide was already what one is compelled to call, for want of a better word, the abnormal and unrecognized in the feminine spirit of his day."

However, the mysteriously creative and mournful figure who tantalized both Murray and Jung was not the type of woman each chose as his wife. Jung had married someone remarkably like Jo Murray. His wife, Emma (née Rauschenbach), was the daughter of a well-off and socially correct industrialist. Jung credited her common sense as well as her practical housewifely and motherly skills for creating the ideal background for his work. Her substantial income enabled him to build their large and comfortable house at Küsnacht; it also gave Jung the financial security to embark on his highly unconventional career. Emma Jung's practical steadiness served as ballast for her husband's more volatile nature, while she had the intelligence to share his interests and support his theories.

Jung first psychoanalyzed his wife and then involved her in analytic work. Yet he had the common prejudices of the time and regarded her as his satellite: above all else, she was his wife and the mother of his five children. Jung also held a nineteenth-century view of masculine sexual prerogative. He found that his marriage did not, and did not need to, contain him. In a letter he had written to Freud, Jung proclaimed: "the prerequisite for a good marriage, it seems to me, is the license to be unfaithful."

In the psychological theory that he evolved and that so impressed Harry Murray, Jung, with nineteenth-century hubris, divided women according to the roles they held for men. In Jung's private life, his wife cared for his family and for his material needs, while he looked to the anima-type figure to inspire him. Applying this to women's psychology in general, Jung concluded: "One could characterize these two types of women as the 'married mothers' and the 'friends and concubines.' . . . When you are wife and mother you can hardly be the hetaira too." Emma Jung fit well into the former role but was then defined by and limited to it. Jung allocated the role of the romantic, hetairic muse to a series of other women. Of these, Antonia (Toni) Wolff was by far the most important. In many ways, she and Christiana Morgan resembled each other. Both were highly intuitive as well as troubled women, both had a similar elegance and intensity; they had pale-olive complexions infused with light, and large, inward-looking dark eyes that gave them a haunting air of mystery.

Toni Wolff, an educated and patrician woman from Bern, who was thirteen years younger than Jung, had been his patient, then his lover, and subsequently helped him in his work. During the time of his traumatic break with Freud, Jung had descended into his own Melvillean depths and carried on a three-year "self-analysis," during which Wolff listened to his dreams and fantasies. She steadied and guided him in this underworld, serving as "analyst" and anchor. By the time Murray came to see Jung, Wolff was not only Jung's acknowledged mistress but a colleague and analyst in her own right, trained by accompanying Jung as his sister/lover/guide—what Jung called his *soror mystica,* his alchemical sister—through his inner journey.

Both Emma Jung and Toni Wolff seemed to accept, or yielded to, this division of roles and tried to make the best of it. In fact, the two women analyzed each other's dreams, the wife included the mistress in family dinners, and each acknowledged the importance of her separate role in Jung's life. Friends of theirs noted, however, that the arrangement wounded both women profoundly, that both suffered loneliness as well as injured self-esteem, and that both struggled heroically to keep themselves to the single sphere to which Jung and his culture restricted them. Both Emma Jung and Toni Wolff had far larger personalities than Jung's view of women allowed. Though his support and encouragement afforded each woman a chance to develop and function as an analyst, Jung went on to confine them to separate areas of his own public and private worlds. He then created a theory that reflected and rationalized his own propensity to split the feminine image in two and project each half separately.

And so Harry Murray came to consult with Jung about the dilemma of wanting to hold on to his wife while being enchanted and inspired by Christiana. Within the first long session, the older and more experienced man had told Murray not only about his theory of the uncontained partner in a marriage needing to roam, and about the different types of women, the mother and hetaira, but—the need for psychoanalytic reticence not yet recognized—also about his personal life. Jung spoke of Emma Jung as filling the role of wife and mother for him, while Toni Wolff filled that of lover, mystical sister, and muse. Jung suggested that such an arrangement was difficult but possible and, for some men, psychologically advantageous. It had risks, Murray reported him to have said, but if handled honestly and clearly, and if Harry was up to it, it would only add to his creativity.

Murray met almost daily with Jung in the ensuing weeks and took up other theoretical issues, as well as the subject of Murray's career, but the question of the anima and the two types of women, wife and hetaira, were the crucial personal ones to which they returned. As Murray was preparing to leave, Jung agreed to see Christiana Morgan later that year. Harry left Zurich on a high tide of enthusiasm for Jung's psychological theories and eager to impart his discoveries and probable lifework as a psychoanalyst to his wife and to the Morgans.

133

The Murrays were reunited in early April in San Remo; Harry immediately shared his new insights with his wife. It seems from her report that he did this with his usual extraordinary vivacity but also with amazingly obtuse tactlessness. Jo wrote of her reaction in her diary: "Met H. at 2 o'clock train & took him home for a hot bath. Then drove up on top of lovely village on mountain top & felt strangely depressed. He was absolutely hypnotized by Jung and impenetrable. We had a talk before dinner—then a nightmare meal & an awful outburst of long pent up feelings. I was absolutely wild & unable to contain it." The next day, Jo added: "To Rapallo for night. Took a nice walk along shore that evening and then sat out under stars and moon listening to music till I was reduced to tears again. Can't seem to re-adjust & vowed that never again would I let him go off alone—that was certain."

A few days later, the Murrays joined up with the Morgans, who had been in Rome with Christiana's parents and younger sister. Harry hastened to tell Christiana about Jung's relationship with Emma Jung as his wife and the mother of his children and Toni Wolff as his anima ideal; he went on to propose the same thing for them. Neither Jo nor Christiana accepted the idea. If Christiana was to take Harry for a lover, she wanted a more stable commitment, which recognized her for herself and not just as his inspirer; nevertheless, she felt attracted by the extra energy his idealization gave her. In her notebooks, she pondered their relationship and the power element involved.

> I wish that with Harry I didn't have this feeling of a snake in the grass somewhere. It always seems to be interfering with my sensing of his personality. Its head always crops up immediately after I think it is not there. This snake is the desire for power, always present. It is this which gives that quality of coldness in the personal relations. After he has gone it comes over me. There is no genial basking in the friendly presence on his part. There must be ideas given and taken, new ideas always, more and more of them. Delightful, stimulating, attractive, life-giving through so

much energy, but somewhere from the deep regions of my mind I am reminded of Frederick and the orange. [Harry as Frederick and Christiana as the valued but ultimately devourable or rejected orange.]

However I love him at this period. This tension between the two selves is so beautiful and so youthful, with all the touching appeal of youth. For me he is more beautiful now than I think he ever will be in the future. I feel unsure of him in the future, and dread the thought that long after this conflict has been satisfactorily solved it will be remembered and transferred to the purely intellectual field, and we will hear words once beautiful and full of passion and meaning used to gain a point in an intellectual argument. . . .

He asks me, "Do you remember the dark-haired woman in *Pierre?* Do you remember that Pierre says to her—'you fertilize me'?"

A strange relationship, and one which for the first time in my life I fear. I am taken beyond my powers. I am made strong. I am given my own life, which by myself I am hardly conscious of. I see and understand my own spirit. It is as if my spirit were embodied, and for the first time at Tristan and Isolde I translate it into the figure of another person and it becomes more comprehensible. It is strange the effect of looking into a mirror and find that the image comes back intensified, clear cut, resplendent. I had thought this only possible as a response to art. I am greatly and terribly moved to find it in a human relationship. Its dangers are manifest. Narcissus gazing into the pool.

Both Christiana and Jo refused to copy Jung's example because they had much more to lose in this sort of triangle than did Harry Murray. Both also had a bit more sense of themselves and slightly more independent values than European women, who had long endured the convention of mistresses. But Harry remained convinced. The rest of their Continental tour became an ordeal for the two women and extremely awkward for Bill Morgan, the often overlooked fourth in the quartet. The couples attempted to be straightforward, friendly, and civilized with each other and to discuss Jung's theories both abstractly and in reference to themselves. With Harry's verbal wooing of Christiana now out in the open, he took off for hours in order to persuade her; Jo couldn't hide her anger and upset. Both Morgans combated the strain by drinking too much at the foursome's evening meals. Each couple tried to avoid the other. Then, to complicate things further, Mike and Veronica Murray joined them; Mike felt betrayed by his elder brother, now his rival for Christiana's attentions. Thus, in a maelstrom of talk, desire, and injured feelings, the group made their way together through Italy and France and back for the summer term, the Murrays' last in Cambridge.

The most painful thing for Bill Morgan and Jo Murray was to watch Harry's and Christiana's growing intoxication with Melville and Jung now focus on each other. Harry used Jung, Jung's theory, and Jung's private life as exemplars and justifications for his plan; and he persisted in discussing these things with Jo, who reacted with rage and tears to what she called his "Zurich rantings." She felt even more left out as Harry and Christiana started to plan a future together as analysts. Jo responded by defending their family and accusing Harry of not valuing her. He reassured her, insisting he "would not go an inch without her," and spent about as much time wooing her as he did trying to convince the two women he could love them both. No wonder Jo hated Carl Jung and blamed him for this new and disastrous train of events.

They returned to England in this state for the final Cambridge term. The group continued to see a lot of each other, reading Melville and discussing Jung. Christiana fell ill with a lingering flu. She and Jo spent many painful hours together, discussing their situation. Jo made a renewed effort to get pregnant and increasingly wrote in her diary of being in tears, angry, or "strangely depressed." Bill felt bitterly hurt and fell into a morose withdrawal interrupted by sudden rages. He attempted to win back his wife through a manic sexuality that his weakened body could not sustain, and the strain exacerbated his problem with premature ejaculation. This further enraged him, while Christiana was left aroused, resistant, and unsatisfied. The Morgans' son not surprisingly started to have problems in school. The five-year-old found himself involved in the heartbreaking business of being open to and affected by all the currents of his parents' lives but powerless to mediate any part of them. A comment in the Malting House record stated "who could possibly think that this clowning, intelligent, delightful looking child was the most disturbed student in the class?" Peter Councilman Morgan would later write: "There must have been awful things going on around me, but if I knew them they have vanished. Plenty of reason soon to be disturbed, but why so early?"

Christiana fled back to Lawden Cottage from an arranged two weeks with the Murrays at Henley and dreaded their regathering. She was feeling jolted by the force of Harry's attention and frightened by her growing response to him, even though, at this date, it was all still talk. She wrote about Harry in her journal: "I knew that he would wake something in me again and I scarcely wanted it. He seemed to be pounding & battering at me. All that I had thought I had learned for my own peace—the life well lived—he seemed to be shattering."

Everything was out in the open, but nothing had been agreed on, and they all persisted in being civilized and attempting to do the right thing. Wanting to be the modern radical intellectuals they believed themselves to be, they decided to work through the problems together, however excruciating the process might be. They did not consider canceling their projected final month of travel before the Murrays returned to the United States. Just as Christiana had avoided Henley, Jo avoided part of the trip, remaining behind to close Leckhampton and sell their car. She went on to Paris alone with little Josie and the governess and consoled herself by ordering an elaborate wardrobe from Vionnet and party dresses for herself and her daughter from Lanvin. Jo planned to rejoin the group in mid-August and meanwhile looked for suitable seaside housing for the children and their governesses for the month the adults would be traveling together. The tone of her diary became bleak. Though she didn't delve into her feelings, Jo had resolved to make the best of the situation and to enjoy whatever was left between Harry and herself. Perhaps worn down by his enthusiasm and persuasiveness, she agreed to remain in the marriage and to abide by Christiana's decision as to the rest. Harry rejoined her briefly in Paris, and then she saw him off on the train to Carcassonne to meet the Morgans and Mike and Veronica Murray.

Though Christiana and Harry hadn't actually become lovers, they were very much in love and tried to spend more and more time alone together. One evening as they sat in a restaurant discussing themselves and Melville, someone asked them if they were married. Harry looked across at Christiana and, thinking of Pierre and Isabel, replied, "No; she is my sister." When Bill joined them that evening in the square at Carcassonne, Harry and Christiana openly questioned what would become of them. While Harry and Mike had fought over Christiana like two randy dogs, Bill replied in agonized simplicity: "You must do what you think is right."

Bill sank deeper into himself during these days, and when he wasn't drinking, he became increasingly formal; Christiana couldn't bear to hurt him, and yet she struck out against him in frustration and increasingly forgot him in her absorption with Harry. Her wish for heterodox autonomy swept aside, her journal was filled with Murray:

137

> We spoke to each other through Melville. We understood it as one. We both realized an intense relationship. There seemed to be only the slightest definitely focussed sexual feeling —only a great live awareness when we were together.
> For three days I had this great & intense feeling of being impelled to write him & did it against my will & after much conflict—in which I said "The veil has lifted. Together we are on the open sea & I have met you where I expected to meet no man."

At Saint-Jean-Pied-de-Port, in the Pyrenees, Bill wandered into town while Christiana slept. Harry climbed up some heavy vines outside her porticoed window and entered her room and bed, enfolding her in his arms. There are contradictory reports of what happened next, but a close reading of Christiana's journal and her notes of her analysis reveal that Harry probably still kept some distance between them, not making love to her completely. Nevertheless, Christiana felt the tension between them resolved:

> Then the thing broke & from the moment our arms were around each other there seemed to be a great alive peace. I felt very quiet but intensified in all my personality— sure—confident & powerful. My whole past life seemed only to have been for this & suddenly I became aware of what they had all been for to keep this thing alive in me which was answered by Harry. I never felt so quiet. I never felt so surely a woman. . . . I know that with him this Ahab that I have that can either destroy or create would forever be creative with him & never destroy. That I could put it in his hands & be a woman as I have never been one.

Several times more on the journey they lay together in the same way: naked body to naked body, like a twinned Narcissus frozen by the power of their feelings and desires.

Jo had joined them on August 11 at Toulouse, and the group went on to Tarascon, Tardets, and Périgueux, ending up with the children at Honfleur. Jo tried to fight off her desolation but increasingly resented the incessant talk about Melville, Jung, animas, and wives. She took to leaving the group and going to bed early, confiding to the privacy of her diary her heartache over Harry's Jungian stance and his all-night discussions with Christiana: "Melville bouts," she called them. For the next twenty days, Jo's diary reveals her to be vacillating between isolation and painful efforts to tag along with the two lovers or listen in on them. Perhaps the most poignant entry came at Périgueux: "Chris and I ordered $50 worth of underwear on arrival here from Mme. Rudeau & afterwards I wondered why I had as 'what's the use?' " Jo's diary broke off abruptly on August 30 at Honfleur, with a final entry about a lovely day at the beach, which concluded: "On our return I got all dressed up in Paris clothes for dinner—then changed & went to the beach club where Hiawatha & Madelon served us wine till 1. H. went swimming till 4 A.M."

At the same time, Christiana had been confiding to her journal her worry about Harry's unembodied lust as well as his almost abstract treatment of her. Harry seemed to approach her like an imaginary idea, a sisterly anima from whom he could tear meaning rather than a woman he could physically embrace.

> I felt that—I was a divine goddess to him and he kissed my feet. I fertilized his mind, he felt creative as he had never felt before—but he fled from my lips. That same night out on the beach—he came to me quite naked and I touched him all over with my hands—but even then there was a sort of white and sublime purity. If he can understand through me really to love to be earthy then perhaps something fine could be made of it. But if he keeps this waste spot of desolation in him then I feel that he will be a raging force of destruction that will destroy me and everyone he comes in contact with.

The vacation ended with the Morgans seeing the Murrays off at Le Havre. Harry stood on the ship's deck, tears pouring from his cheeks as he looked at Christiana standing below. When the boat slowly pulled away, Jo was at his side; she held his hand and put her arms around him to comfort him. Young Josie spent the voyage with her new Scottish nurse, feeling abysmally alone. Her parents had little energy left for her: her father distracted by his romantic embroilment, her mother by seasickness and the agonizing pain of comforting a husband who loved another woman. Josie would wonder in coming years why her mother now cried so often behind closed doors.

Harry Murray returned to the Rockefeller Institute in the fall   139 and received his doctorate there for the work he had done at Cambridge University. Jo gratefully settled into her New York life again, resuming friendships and managing the couple's busy social calendar. Murray used the winter to switch from biochemistry to psychology. Like Jung, he considered training in psychiatry at a mental hospital, Boston Psychopathic, but through Professor Henderson's help and much negotiation, he was offered an appointment as Research Fellow in Abnormal and Dynamic Psychology at Harvard instead. Morton Prince, a psychiatrist renowned for his work in abnormal psychology, planned to start a psychological research clinic at Harvard and chose Murray as his second in command. Harry included plans for Christiana to become his research assistant when the Morgans returned to the United States.

Meanwhile, in September, Christiana traveled to Zurich to see Jung, who agreed to take her on as a patient the following June and also to consult with Bill. In preparation, she looked back at her life and wrote down what she thought was salient for Jung. She included a brief life history, which exaggerated her deficits and her childhood invalidism. It was a cold, hard, and sadly clinical look at herself— perhaps conveying what she thought would most make her an interesting subject. Jung promptly ignored it, focusing on a deeper level. Christiana wrote to Harry from Zurich immediately after she met Jung to tell him how inspired she felt. Intuitively, she grasped Jung's method and theory and experienced the profound healing effect of his presence even at that single meeting. She also envisioned Harry and herself together carrying Jung's theories forward at the Harvard Clinic.

> And now I want to write you about Jung, although to tell you what I think of him seems peculiarly difficult. As you said, he has indeed the true fire. I never dreamed that anyone could talk so directly and so instantly to the spirit or the core. There is a fine comprehension and a large sweep about it all, rather a splendid fearlessness. I had the curious feeling of having ages of New England ancestry quietly and noiselessly taking flight after two hours of conversation with him. Not all of them took flight—not the pioneers and the whalers or the hewers of wood and the drawers of water—only the tight-lipped cold-eyed

dogmatic variety. These withdrew themselves so noise-
lessly that I didn't even waste my breath to hurl an epithet
after them.

It is really wonderful to see in the man this quiet
rejection of the Christian attitude. (Rejection isn't quite
the right word—rather his passing beyond it.) He is the
only person I have seen who somewhere didn't have it
however much they protested. . . .

He seems definitely to have achieved a new attitude.
He is honestly attempting a new way. There is no question
that he is the prophet. And the new way means the reconciliation of the thought of the present day with the spirit.
He has achieved the attitude in himself. The full philosophy remains to be worked out. Let's do it, Harry! To go
on with what Jung has begun would be the biggest thing
that could be done at the present time. Is there a bigger
whale or a whiter whale than the chains of the outworn
attitude which fetter and hinder the spirit? . . .

Don't think, dear, that I have lost my critical sense
entirely. But Jung is a big person and I see the significance
of him and his work. It goes infinitely far beyond the
therapeutic aspect. The germs of what we seek are in
it. . . . Goodbye, dear one. It is late and this letter grows
long. Hold me close to you. There are big things in the
air. I need you.

P.S. I can't feel quite right about writing to you to
the Rockefeller unless Jo knows that I am doing it.

Christiana's letters to Harry and her notebooks thereafter
abounded with discussions of both Jung and Melville and contained
ever-increasing efforts to work out her own position in relation to
them as well as to express her love for Harry. At this time in her
life she surpassed Melville, Murray, and Jung in one important
respect, for she refused to split women into illusory pairs of opposites, writing that it was only "when they are one being, combining both, then a great synthesis is achieved, perhaps the
greatest." Morgan went far beyond Murray, too, in both the scope
of her ideas about love and the concreteness of her physical passion
for him.

During that long winter, the Morgans and Murrays wrote to
each other quite often. Christiana's letters were mostly full of the
books she read and the endless ideas and theories they sparked in
her. She spent the winter in England pondering her relationship

with Harry and preparing for her analysis through study and introspection. Without the effervescent Murrays, the Morgans withdrew into themselves and saw comparatively few people. They 141 endured a damp and surprisingly cold winter and a delayed spring, which caught and reflected Bill's mood. Christiana sculpted in clay, carved in wood, and read psychology. She did extensive work as a research assistant to a Professor Bartlett on comparative theories of the unconscious, both in anticipation of her analysis and in preparation for her job with Harry. Bill studied hard but joylessly to try to complete his work in physiology, slogging along at a subject that could not hold his attention.

At winter break, the Morgans traveled to northern Africa; they took a trip through Provence in the spring. During that long year of separation from Harry, Christiana seemed to be formulating her own philosophy for the first time. The hiatus kept the intensity of Harry and Christiana's still unconsummated passion alive; the memory of his bodily retreat before the object of his love seemed to stoke their mutual desire. Harry and Christiana wrote letters in which they engaged in long discussions and arguments about their ideas and made increasingly warm avowals to each other in much the same way Christiana and Bill Morgan had built up their love for each other during the war. The two lovers planned to meet in Munich in August, when Jung would be away on his summer holiday and when, almost too transparently, Bill needed to be in Chicago to see his sick uncle. All this was discussed in an odd series of letters that revealed everything while saying nothing; perhaps enough had already been said. Harry meanwhile reported that he had started a biography of Melville. Christiana responded, revealing her heat for her brotherly lover as well as her interest in his book on Melville:

> Oh, Harry, please, please bring the ms. to Munich. I have been immersed in Cambridge for so long that nothing else will bring me to life. (I might add that it needs both you and the ms.!) I got all hot with excitement when you wrote that you were going to look at Arrowhead [Melville's house]. What has happened to it?

Harry heard Christiana call over the immense distances of sky and air just as surely as Pierre had heard his sister, Isabel. Bound by an intense and indescribable longing for each other and for their glorious ideal, they awaited their reunion in ambiguity.

Part Two

WONA AND MANSOL

I too exclusively esteemed that love,
And sought that beauty, which as Milton sings,
Hath terror in it.

WILLIAM WORDSWORTH,
The Prelude, Book XIV

NINE

The Whale

Not drowned entirely, though. Rather carried down alive to wondrous depths, where strange shapes of the unwarped primal world glided to and fro before his passive eyes; and the miser-merman, Wisdom, revealed his hoarded heaps.

HERMAN MELVILLE,
Moby Dick

Christiana arrived in Zurich in early June 1926; Bill (now preferring to be called Will) followed two weeks later, after the end of his college term. She settled into the Hotel Sonne, an attractive old inn on the Seestrasse, overlooking Lake Zurich and about fifteen minutes from Jung's house; Harry had stayed there the year before, and Robert Edmond Jones, a friend from the Extravert-Introvert Club days, was already in residence and being psychoanalyzed. Christiana found herself immediately at home in the intense atmosphere peculiar to analysis. She delighted in Jung's attention and the turbulence fermented by the analytic relationship. Though some people stayed in Zurich for many years and created an almost religious life centered around their analysis, most foreigners came to Jung as they did to a spa—for whatever time they could afford, perhaps returning in following years for brief but intense visits. Jung thought this especially useful for young people like Christiana, who at twenty-eight had not yet formed a coherent life for herself.

Four years later, when Jung lectured on the fantasies and art-work Christiana Morgan produced during that period, he disguised their author but sketched an outline of her at the time as a thinking intuitive type,

146

> very intelligent . . . and exceedingly rational. She has a great deal of intuition, which really ought to function, but is repressed because it yields irrational results and that is very disagreeable to the rational mind. . . . People with such an extraordinarily one-sided development of their thinking function have, on the other side, an inferior feeling-function, because feeling is the opposite of think-ing. The feeling is archaic and has all the advantages and disadvantages of an archaic function. The inferior function is generally characterized by traits of primitive psychol-ogy, above all by *participation mystique;* that is, it is pe-culiarly identical, or makes one identical, with other people or with other situations. She had the feelings cir-cumstances gave her. She could not feel hypothetically, but she could think hypothetically. As a matter of fact, her intelligence was so highly developed that she thought things people in her environment did not think.

Christiana Morgan brought the following problems to Jung: her sexual and love complication with Will and Harry; her depres-sions; the "red-hot conflict" so often caused by her undifferentiated and primitive feeling function—a feeling Jung later described as "something fearfully strong but primitive, barbarous, animal-like, and you cannot control it—it controls you." She also had a father complex, which kept her looking to strong and wise men to solve her spiritual conflict in the same way she had looked to her father in childhood as the resolver of her problems. Even more basic to her disease, Christiana suffered from being a powerfully gifted and creative woman in a culture and milieu that made no room for her, not even to give her an adequate education or the words with which to name what was wrong. From the notes she made of her analytic sessions, it appears that Jung focused primarily on her love problem. Christiana Morgan made rapid headway, at first seeing Jung several times a week for two-hour sessions, with an occasional visit to Toni Wolff.

From the beginning, Christiana discussed her relationship problems with Will and her quandary about Harry. Jung dealt with these issues objectively but also investigated some of their under-lying dynamics. He demanded that Christiana take responsibility for her own analysis. He encouraged her to focus her mind and to take her dreams seriously for what they had to teach her about her condition. He also urged her to take more responsibility for her life through active awareness and consciousness of her sexuality, yet at the same time he appears far more directive than an analyst would be today, especially about her connection with Will and Harry. Jung had little patience with her intellectualizing and sought to go beneath it. Within days of the start of the analysis, Christiana stopped writing her usual long theoretical and literary letters to Harry and changed to a more lyrical tone. At the next visit, she showed the result to Jung, who faulted the letter's airy poetics, instructing her to come to grips with reality if she wanted to begin a liaison with Harry. She recorded that Jung told her to discuss with Harry the practical possibilities of their plans and deal with them concretely.

In response, Christiana wrote a pivotal letter:

> Hotel Sonne, Küsnacht–Zurich
> June 17, 1926
>
> Dear Harry, You have spoken to me and I have spoken to you from the innermost places where storms and profoundest quiet lie together in dark embrace. From that terrible and beautiful world can we now come and speak to others? If you don't want to do this, dear Harry, then let this letter go. Always there will be something in us which we share together. If it cannot come to fulfillment then it cannot. I love you—and you cannot hurt me by telling me that what I write is impossible. God knows it is hard enough.
>
> I think the only way that we can ever know whether our love is great enough to be fulfilled is to test it against the love we have for Will and Jo. And we will have to take their pain and somehow or other carry it with them. It seems to me at times that I would almost rather die than have to hurt Will so by even talking of this with him. But he is strong and beautiful in spirit and perhaps will be able to fully understand two human souls. I don't know. Perhaps I ask from him a greater understanding than is possible for any man to give. I cannot possibly conceive breaking my relationship with Will, because him, too, I love. And it must be the same way with you and Jo. Can we give ourselves to each other within our relationship to them?
>
> If we can be enough to each other to walk this terribly

difficult and lonely path and to carry two other people with us as we go, I will come with you. Only we must walk in the light of fullest possible understanding between us four.

Perhaps we are neither of us strong enough to do it. Perhaps to try it would kill what we now have together. Perhaps the pain of the others will be too much for us. How shall we know?

You must not feel that you carry me, nor I you. I am trying to look at this with a steady gaze. At such moments one is quite alone.

Will arrives today and I will talk of this with him. In some respects my relationship with Will has not been all that it might be. But he will now be seeing Jung and I hope that certain things with him will be cleared up. This may make some difference. In any case he must have every chance.

Dear Harry—if you wish let all that I have said in this letter go by. After all we are human, and we may undertake something that will be too great for either of us to manage. We might live thereby, or we might destroy ourselves and others, for we would have to walk where there are few footsteps to show us any way.

Chris

If you want, show this letter to Jo.

As a result of her analysis, Christiana began to allow herself to speak without disguise; she also started to learn a middle way in her old habit of forcing everything, even the deepest emotion, into pressured theoretical terms, on one side, or into airy poeticism and flirtatiousness, on the other. With the help of her gifted therapist, Christiana started to make sense of herself and to understand her depressions and the meaning of her actions and fantasies. Her dreams set out the core problems that Jung and she worked on together. Jung taught her to focus inward, allowing space for her feeling sense to develop. She learned to avoid the strained over-rationalization that had masked her psyche, and she started to trust herself.

Christiana Morgan made an ideal patient for Jung; she worked hard, was intelligent, witty, honest, and talked in the language he could best hear: that of intellect and intuition, dreams and imagination. She also appealed to Jung as a woman, for in her dark reverberative beauty and her deep connection with the unconscious,

she resembled his own anima image. The two got along famously—too well, in fact, for Jung never adequately dealt with her ideali-zation of her father or himself. Though her admiration and Jung's   149
propensity for projecting his anima ideal onto women of Chris-tiana's type energized them both, it ultimately detracted from her therapeutic progress. Initially, however, the collusion helped by making Morgan extremely receptive to all that Jung said, while his attraction for her made him willing to give her extra time and energy.

During these months in Zurich, Christiana experienced an al-most mystical return to nature, especially when, before or after her session, she took solitary rambles in the beautiful woods that were above Küsnacht; she also started, for perhaps the first time, to take her art seriously. Christiana felt she lacked a language to translate the sense she had of her own possibilities and that this, perhaps, was the root cause of her depressions and discontent. She had en-tered analysis yearning to find herself but with no idea of what that self was or how to withstand outside influences. At the same time, she felt that others, particularly men, sensed something subterra-nean in her and drew on it without her knowledge. Metaphorically, it was as if she occupied the two familiar top floors of her house but was only dimly aware of another self living on the ground floor. She understood little of this self's peregrinations and nothing of the exotic traffic flowing through the vast cellars and waterways below. Jung sensed this subterranean quality in her sexuality and called his patient's attention to it. He explained the way it carried her down to wondrous depths, where, in *participation mystique,* she merged with the unconscious of other people and situations. Mor-gan recorded that Jung told her:

> Well now first comes the point of your sexuality between you and your husband. It must be fully gone into and that situation straightened out first of all. You see if you are not fully satisfied in that way you begin to sexualize every-thing. Even now while you are in here your face is white & your neck red & you have all the signs of vague fear. The atmosphere is heavy and charged with this sexuali-zation that is going on in you. It is like the turkey spreading out its feathers saying to the male—you see how frightened I am and how cold my hands are. Everything is intense and heavy. This is the same thing that I was telling you about the other day of the *participation mystique.* You have

this with many people. That is . . . because your sexuality is not satisfied and so you put it into everything. Now you must wait and see how you feel when this thing is right between you. You see you may be sexualizing him with this energy that you have left over.

From his relationship with Toni Wolff, Jung understood that Christiana Morgan lacked comprehension not only of her own passionate earthiness but also of the spiritual side of her sexuality. Wolff had awakened Jung to these two sides of women's sexuality, and through it they experienced a doubly potent conjugation; Jung recognized that Christiana and Harry might be capable of a similar union. Jung also realized that she was confronting one of the major dilemmas of the age: how to be responsibly alive to all aspects of herself without restriction. The religious aspect in her erotic conflict and behind her love for Harry might lead her beyond Christianity's denial and repression to a far more perilous and complex integration of the body and of evil.

Yet at the same time, the very fact that Christiana Morgan was a woman blinded Jung to many of her possibilities. Neither his understanding of women's psychology, nor his conflicted attitude toward his own mother, nor the era itself could allow for a truly autonomous woman. Jung knew that he and his patient were struggling with a similar problem but, rather than viewing her as his counterpart, he instructed Morgan to live her life very much in the same way Toni Wolff lived hers—as adjunct to and in the service of her lover. In the analysis, Jung soon started to shift his focus away from Morgan and onto Murray as the center of the relationship; Jung began telling his patient not what she needed to do for herself but what she needed to do for Harry. In moments like these, and there were many, Jung forgot Christiana Morgan while he glorified her role as an anima figure and *inspiratrice* for a man. Jung's antitherapeutic, nineteenth-century masculine lens could only see women fulfilling themselves through fulfilling men's needs. In the middle of helping Morgan regain her voice, Jung's attitude served to silence her. She recorded that Jung told her:

> We all have to do something collective—create something for the world. If a woman creates a child then she is doing something collective for the next generation. If you create Murray now—make him a complete man then you are doing something for this generation and what is the difference? But this is a very difficult question. One can never

know one's powers until one has tried. Perhaps it will fail. Perhaps it isn't meant to be. When you do this you play with dynamite. It may destroy you—or you may find the new way. . . . You are a pioneer woman. Your function is to create a man. Some women create children but it is greater to create a man. If you create Murray you will have done something very fine for the world. Such women are never recognized—but they should be. They should have the Legion D'Honneur pinned to their breast. It is a great thing to be able to do that. . . . This relationship will be terribly expensive—expensive of your libido. And you must keep as much of it as you can—to bring to this problem now. . . . This is what as a woman you should have. So you become a really wise woman a *femme inspiratrice*—and so you give to man what he has not. So he turns to you and you create in him.

Jung had discussed these same ideas with Harry Murray the year before. Christiana now spoke of Harry's elation and noted her analyst's response:

Yes—I gave him a hell of a good time. I let him look through my telescope. I showed him Heaven. I knew after that that he would fall back into all sorts of infantile things—but at last he has seen. Now what you will have to do is to make him work—so that he can attain. I mean he must come up every step of the way living it all through. If he can't do this then he can never be an analyst. Heaven knows what he might be. Perhaps a writer. To live through the steps is what you can help him to do. You have your ideal of him. You must make him live up to it—because you have seen the vision of what he might be.

Jung's analysis of Christiana Morgan constitutes almost a primer of what a good and a bad analysis involves. Though Jung could not have been more helpful to her in his interpretations and support concerning many of her problems, and although his warmth, deep interest, and liking for her were healing, the analysis faltered when Jung's own complexes and the cultural norms of the time interfered and became arbiters of psychological health. Christiana tried to take in what her analyst kept telling her about herself and woman's psychology, but though it flattered her ego, she found herself exhausted and further depressed by his mandate to create Harry rather than herself. She outwardly agreed with Jung that this indeed could be her mission in life, yet she revolted against having to sacrifice herself for men. In her journal, Christiana flung down her objections to men's demands:

152

> Came home raging over what he had said about my being too lyrical. Then it flashed on me that he is throwing me back right into my problem—face to face. It dawned on me that the whole trouble has been a conflict about Will & Harry which I have repressed—hence deadness & lack of sexuality. . . . To me the world is Harry—he entirely surrounds me and I feel that although I am more alive when I am with him than I ever could be alone—so alive that I feel greater than myself still, I have peace. . . . However there is this about him. I feel him to be clutching and tearing at me for something—as though he would tear the secret of his own love out of me—and at times with him I feel absolutely exhausted and drained dry. Although he gives me much of his mind & spirit he gives me nothing of warmth and of earthiness. . . . A strange oppression has been on me for the last two days. It seems to be overwhelming and sad and awe inspiring. It is different from a pure depression. It is as though it were the breaking of the last shell of consciousness. It is like gazing at something full in the face—the fact that to my child to my husband and to H. I must be a mother and that nothing will ever stand between me and the forces which are around me—that I will be eternally alone—looking at these naked things always unprotected, and then measuring them to the capacity of these several individuals— veiling them and transforming these things that I see to meet the needs of each one—while I see them in the raw. I have the feeling that this may be the real awakening consciousness of woman. It makes me feel appallingly alone.

The "naked things" to which Christiana alluded were her visions or trances. Under Jung's guidance, she had descended into the waterways of the collective unconscious, bringing back up with her "the strange shapes of the unwarped primal world." Jung had just begun to teach trancing as a way of introducing archetypal elements into clinical use, but it was only after Christiana Morgan's arrival that it started to catch on as a potent adjunct to therapy. At the time of his break with Freud, Jung had used the same process to explore his own inner turmoil. He voluntarily dropped into the unconscious in the way his young cousin, Helene Preiswerk, entered her mediumistic trances. However, Jung always kept part of his ego 153 present to monitor and then record what emerged. It was very much like taking part in a waking dream and then recording the images, myths, and stories that unfolded; Jung took his visions as archetypal amplifications of unconscious elements in his own personality and as images he could draw on for support and for information about his psychic processes. Through this method and with Toni Wolff as aide and witness, Jung analyzed himself.

Jung described the process to his patient as turning inward, clearing the mind, and concentrating intensely, in order to incubate and activate inner images; the trancer then entered into the scene, letting himself become part of the picture or action. Jung guided and encouraged her, telling her that the single images appearing before her inner eye were

> only the beginning. You only use the retina of the eye at first in order to objectify. Then instead of keeping on trying to force the image out you just want to look in. Now when you see these images you want to hold them and see where they take you—how they change. And you want to try to get into the picture itself—to become one of the actors. When I first began to do this I saw landscapes. Then I learned how to pull myself into the landscapes, and the figures would talk to me and I would answer them.

The difficulty lay in allowing the unconscious images to reveal themselves with the least conscious intervention. The trancer needed to pay relaxed attention, then, after the images ceased, to write, draw, or paint the story. During his own analysis, Jung had filled two large and elaborate books, his Red Book and Black Book, with the products of his "active imagination" or visions. Though Jung did not show Christiana Morgan these books until her final visit with him, he had shown them to her friend, Robert Edmond Jones. Jones, a sophisticated and extremely talented artist, whose stage sets are forever connected with Eugene O'Neill's plays, was thrilled by the theatricality of Jung's books of imaginings, whereupon Jung suggested that he try the same process. Jones took to trancing immediately, finding that it deepened and speeded up his analysis. Jung then asked him to coach others in Zurich.

During the summer of 1926, about thirty or so analysts and patients had gathered at the Hotel Sonne in Küsnacht or in other

154 pensions and houses nearby; they put more demands on Jung's personal attention than he could manage. Besides the resident group of analysts that centered on Carl Jung and, to a lesser extent, on Toni Wolff and Emma Jung, most were patients or disciples, some of whom were themselves training to be analysts by going through analysis until Jung thought them ready. Among the English-speaking group were the analyst Tina Keller and the doctors Beatrice Hinkle, Kristine Mann, Esther Harding, and Emily Bertine, who often spent their summers in Zurich and were thinking of starting a New York program (the future C. G. Jung Institute). Others included an assortment of mostly English- or German-speaking poets, literary figures, novelists, artists, and doctors. Several well-to-do Americans were also starting to consult with Jung, such as Paul and Mary Mellon, the Fowler McCormicks, and his brother Harold F. McCormick, who had brought his wife, the former Edith Rockefeller, to be analyzed by Jung. Hermann Hesse and Richard Strauss dropped in on the occasional lecture and stayed to talk, while James Joyce, who was then living in Zurich, consulted Jung about himself and his schizophrenic daughter.

In 1926, there was no formal program, no center, and only occasional lectures or seminars. The patients gathered around Jung were adrift together in Switzerland, away from their old lives and families, often with nothing to moor them but an analysis that flung them abruptly down into the most private and startling depths of their psyches. It was as if each person there were participating in the same mysterious and sacred ritual; the patients and analysts were further drawn together in their knowledge that they were in on the beginnings of an exciting new psychology and affecting it, no matter in how small a way, by their presence and participation.

Jung felt increasingly pressured by the demands of his success; he could no longer write, teach, and give to these ever-growing numbers of people the same amount of time that he had allotted to patients in the early days of his career. He solved part of the problem by holding seminars and overseeing study groups; he also conducted what today would be called highly abbreviated analyses and let certain patients whom he had analyzed briefly become analysts under his supervision. Jung, like Freud and Adler and the other psychoanalytic pioneers, evolved his own ground rules for what had been called the "talking cure." He adapted his ideas as he went along, learning from his successes and his mistakes. Jung worked very differently from analysts today. Not only were his sessions sometimes many hours long, but Jung moved faster, making strong interpretations but leaving little time for the slow psychic digestion analysts now believe mandatory, nor for a thorough working through of complexes or early-childhood material. It often seemed enough then to grasp and name the internal image of what in fact might take the rest of a lifetime to incorporate. Perhaps dissatisfied with the demands of time, Jung cast around for something that could intensify, vivify, and maintain the analysis and engage the analysand actively in his or her own cure without taking up more of Jung's already overbooked schedule. He decided to investigate the possibility of active imagination—trancing or visioning—as a clinical and therapeutic tool that an analysand could employ privately. It was then that he engaged Robert Edmond Jones to help introduce the method.

Jonah, as the Morgans called him, was their closest friend in Zurich. Coached by him and encouraged by Jung and by Toni Wolff, who was now seeing Will, the Morgans discovered that active imagination made a highly productive addition to their analysis. They were Jones's star pupils and then his equals. Showing a lively fervor and a marked talent for trancing, each would go off separately to enter a meditative, self-hypnotic state and then afterward write and illustrate his or her vision. The Morgans and Jones discussed their creations intensely among themselves, often on picnics in the wooded hills above the lake, or on the lawn or porch of the inn, where the other analysands, the *Jungfrauen* and *Jungherren,* could not help but overhear. The friends openly shared the pictures and stories that emerged from the trance state, greeting each other in the streets of Zurich with "How's your Indian?" "Are you still in the cavern?" or "What's your magician up to today?"—innocent, perhaps, of what even a single response to an inner picture revealed about their psychology. Jonah, elaborating on Jung's wish for the trancing to plumb the depths of the emotions and the psyche, took to directing the stage setting for them: "Ah, but is it dark enough? Is it deep enough? Is it black? It must be dark, darker!" and Christiana might add from her own analysis, "It must have more blood!" Behind their enjoyment, however, all three were deeply committed to their analysis and to the visionary dramas unfolding within them.

Active imagination, especially in the vibrant form of Robert Edmond Jones's and Christiana Morgan's visions, seemed a promising solution to Jung's dilemma. He reveled in the Morgans' and Jones's graceful, light humor and their effect on the more somber members of the Zurich group. Their presence and the very extravagance of their trancing (and, possibly, of active imagination itself) caused quite a stir among the solemn "handmaidens" who were then in Zurich and who tried to learn active imagination with the same sanctimonious spirit they tended to bring to their analysis. By the following summer, active imagination had caught on in earnest, and the next few years must have made Jung's circle seem even more bizarre, with trancing analysands wandering about Zurich. In later years, active imagination, though used far less often than in its heyday in the 1930s, became an important part of Jungian analysis for those patients with sufficiently strong egos and was a useful aid when patients could not remember their dreams or needed to elaborate an obscure part of a dream.

For Christiana, active imagination slowly began to oppose her propensity to translate everything into theory, because her images evoked her feeling response. Between early July 1926 and May 1927, she generated an extraordinary series of fantasies. Perhaps intuitively, and very much as a father's daughter, Christiana came up with an unprecedented production of artistic and imaginative archetypal material just when this was the very stuff that would most interest her doctor. The technique Jung was developing caused images to well up in her; she experienced and then recorded them, later transferring them, as Jung suggested, to three folio-size books. She illustrated her text with a potent image from almost every vision, her art training enabling her to catch the feeling and much of the extraordinary magic realism of her visionary realm. The near-Coleridgean intensity with which the visions claimed her led Christiana down into the most primitive and archaic parts of herself, yet she was able to maintain a rational and directed outer life without being swept away.

On July 2, about a month after she had started her analysis, Christiana Morgan returned to the Hotel Sonne after a session with Jung; she felt sleepy and lay down in a self-hypnotic state, whereupon a clear image of a peacock appeared behind her closed eyes. The peacock rode on a man's shoulders, its beak threatening the man's neck. Then came an image of her own shoe, with a hole in it, no longer usable. A few days later, when she again risked letting her consciousness drop, a face capped by a three-cornered velvet hat materialized, only to vanish in a puff of Faustian smoke. Christiana related all this to her analyst and complained about the lassitude that accompanied her semi-hypnotic state.

Jung, recognizing the lethargy as a typical temporary aftereffect of an altered state of consciousness, reassured and encouraged his patient. Once she started to vision, it was as if Morgan possessed   157 something Jung had met before only in himself: the equivalent of perfect pitch, a gift enabling her to plummet into the collective unconscious with accurate immediacy and then resurface to translate the images coherently. Jung did not go into theory with Morgan, nor did he show her his visions (until their final session together); he merely indicated the general waters and their briny possibilities. She relied on Jung as an inexperienced navigator would rely on a seasoned skipper who had charted the area before her. Jung told her that the visions were the channel to her inferior function:

> Now this is the way that your inferior function, feeling, speaks to you. It speaks to you like an oracle and you must listen to it as though an oracle spoke . . . and these visions show now that your feeling can meet it and will help you. . . . I feel your greater calmness you are very different. Of course you feel that way because by doing this you are feeding the soul. You are giving some libido to it— Then you can be no longer destroyed. Before you had a self destroying tendency and so people could destroy you. Now you are creating yourself instead of destroying yourself.

More images appeared before the next session: an arrow shooting at a moon; a head with a halo-like spoked wheel behind it; a double-ended goblet holding wine that a shadowy figure drank; an Indian's tepee. Further isolated images started to pour in on Morgan; Jung helped her to put them in a cultural and psychological perspective, telling her:

> These are the origin of magic in the primitive. Now you are beginning to get at the real self. Yes, you turn your eye in. You use the inner eye as you have always used the outer eye—and so you know the completeness of life— the life that is behind life. The picture of the double goblet is symbolic of just this. You can drink from either. The men against the wheel means the beginning of individuation. The 8 spokes here are the eight functions. The wheel is a very ancient symbol of the soul. . . . The moon & arrow is spirituality through sexuality. The wigwam is the abode of the primitive hence symbolizes the unconscious.

158 Christiana worried about the risks involved in trancing, the agony she sometimes felt when she was pulled down into the depths, and her exhaustion when she emerged. She told Jung about her concerns and wondered if she should continue to vision either under his guidance or without him after she left Zurich. Jung encouraged her as much by his interest and support as by his advice.

> Yes, you can always do this. In this way you get to your own sources. . . . So you grow and come to know yourself. This you see with your own eye—so they are real. I would suggest that you paint them as beautifully as you know how. In this way they become very objective and mean more to you. This will be true even though you don't know the meaning of them.

He went on to warn her of the enormous power of the unconscious and its many dangers. It was as if Jung remembered the rush of images that swept him up after his break with Freud, his own tenuous state, and his courageous decision to bring the images to consciousness. Jung warmed to Morgan at this point, treating her with unusual delicacy and care. He welcomed her as a rare companion who explored the depths he, too, had sounded. Jung talked to her about his own experiences and the risks he had endured and accepted. Warning her that she needed a strong "ego stance" from which to face her visions, he encouraged her to steady herself by giving form to the visions in her art as he had done, but also to remain centered in her responsibilities to her husband, her child, and her possible relationship to Harry. He debated whether or not Christiana had the strength to continue, because the visions were coming with such intensity. As if in answer to Jung's concern, she envisioned a solitary image of fire inside her mouth; Jung took this as a sign that she had to proceed, her vision recalling the unwilling prophet in the Bible on whose tongue Jehovah had placed burning coals as a sign he must give voice to what was within him.

Her analyst paid a great deal of attention to Christiana, changing his schedule so that he could see her almost daily. He not only monitored her condition as her physician but also enjoyed her as a creative partner, an alchemical *soror mystica*. When the future analysts Sabina Spielrein and Toni Wolff had been Jung's patients at the Burghölzli hospital, they too had led him into unfathomed reaches, but they were psychotic at the time and their voyages chartless and hallucinatory. Christiana was no psychotic; she formed her material with lucidity and maintained the ability to stand outside and observe it along with her analyst. They explored her surreal world together, then pondered where they had been and what had befallen them. Jung charted the process as her visions became more detailed and more powerful. He urged her to refine her illustrations of them:

> I should advise you to put it all down as beautifully & as carefully as you can—in some beautifully bound book. It will seem as if you were making the visions banal—but then you need to do that—then you are freed from the power of them. If you do that with those eyes for instance they will cease to draw you. You should never try to make that vision come again. Think of it in your imagination and try to paint it. Then when these things are in some precious book you can go to the book & turn over the pages & for you it will be your church—your cathedral— the silent places of your spirit where you will find renewal. If anyone tells you that this is morbid or neurotic and you listen to them—then you will lose your soul—for in that book is your soul.

Christiana Morgan responded not only to Jung's affectionate interest in her but to his mastery. Encouraged by him, she dove even deeper in her fantastic journey. The visions began to take on an epic quality, becoming more elaborate and appearing almost daily. Jung translated the phantasmagorical flow into conscious and recognizable archetypal elements. His interpretations, though brief, served as guideposts and equilibrium for his patient. Jung cautioned her not to force the visions but to rest, take care of herself, and be content with dreams when the fantasies no longer came.

A depressed American Indian stood on the shores of a lake, his dead horse beside him; the Indian dived into the black pool and emerged on the other side, transformed into a Chinese. Christiana reencountered the Indian, much renewed by his plunge and temporary shape-shifting, and followed him along a plain and backward in time. They traveled past a Christian woman, past a Mithraic bull, and down into an exotic world of chthonic initiation, where Christiana united first with a black god and then with a dread matriarchal realm. As Morgan descended into the unconscious, she engaged in powerful shamanic acts: swallowing, then being swallowed by, a snake; passing painfully through fire; bleeding, then immersing herself in a river of blood; experiencing violent, sometimes terrifyingly orgiastic, rituals of union. She encountered many fierce and transformative animals on her journey, including a ram, a black stallion, bulls, goats, and snakes. A number of guides, male and female, came to her aid, while dwarfs, giants, and mechanical men acted as barriers to her progress.

In her visions, Christiana confronted the unconscious in its starkest, most primitive form. She plunged down to the most basic instinctual and vegetative sea bottom in order to unite with the natural world, from which she had been cut off. Then she resurfaced, bringing this knowledge back up with her into conscious life.

A vision that frightened her early on with its power was an animal face in which she "beheld what no man is meant to see, eyes full of beauty and woe and light." She rendered this face in a drawing and asked Jung about its uncanny power over her. Jung cautioned that she needed to respect her fear and not call the image up again; he praised her drawing because she had not only caught the eeriness of the image but also, through her effort to portray it, gained mastery over it. Thus reassured, she went on to envision a blood ritual in which she married a Dionysian black god and physically united "in the blood" with him. Reading the vision, entering into it with her, one feels the force of this dark figure's potent sexuality, conveyed though it is with late 1920s style and restraint.

> I beheld a great Negro lying beneath a tree. In his hands were fruit. He was singing. I asked him "What do you sing, oh Negro" and he answered me "Little white child, I sing to Darkness, to flaming fields, to the children within your womb." I said "I must know you." He answered "Whether you know me or not I am here." While he sang blood poured from his heart in slow rhythmic beats. It flowed down in a stream covering my feet. I followed the stream of blood which led down and down. At last I found myself in a rocky cavern beneath the earth. It was very dark. I saw a glowing fire and above the fire—a phoenix bird which continually flew up and beat its head against the top of the cavern. I saw the fire create little snakes which disappeared—small dwarves and men and women. I asked the bird, "Where do they go?" The bird answered "Away, away." Then the bird said, "Stand in the fire woman." I said "I cannot. I will be burned." Again the bird commanded me to stand in the fire. I did so and the flames leapt about me burning my robe. At last I stood

naked. The fire died down and the bird disappeared. I walked about the cavern searching for a way of escape but could fine none. Then I was afraid & walked about like one demented. At length I heard the Negro descending. He sang in a full throaty voice, "I sing to you of darkness and of flaming fields." He opened the door of the cavern. He laughed when he saw me and said "Now you are wedded to me." We ascended the steps into the daylight and he said again, "You are wedded to me."

Christiana's sexual union with this passionate, elemental figure having been consummated, she sunk to an even more basic level, a vegetative one in which her body started to penetrate the ground. She felt her feet oozing forth roots that pulled her down into the subterranean blood, while her arms stretched far above her toward a sky that pulsed with the same stream of blood. Extended both upward and down, she felt herself drawn between heaven and earth on a chthonic crucifix of desire. This paralleled her journey down through the ancient matriarchal religions and up again in time through Greco-Roman, Mithraic, and Christian mysteries. It was as if her psyche required her to integrate each layer of experience serially as she experienced the full power of uniting pagan mysteries with Christian mysticism.

After Christiana's intercourse with the black messiah figure, he shape-shifted into a snake, entered a church, and mounted on the cross, thereby uniting the pagan and the chthonic with the Christian Mass. For Jung, this marked the climax of his patient's visions. He told her that they were a sacrament holding "material for the next two or three hundred years. It is a great *document humaine*. It is the rushing forth of all that has hitherto been unconscious."

As Jung supported and encouraged her visions, his countertransference to his patient grew. He had known that she was going through a process similar to his own, but now he realized that she was doing it in a passionate feminine way. It was as if he were seeing an alternative world full of dynamic images that simultaneously excited and repelled him; they caught him between erotic attraction for their discoverer and a need to dismiss her power.

During the summer, while Jung took his yearly vacation and Will Morgan visited his sick uncle, Christiana brought her visions with her to Munich, for her reunion with Harry. Through her immensely creative experiences and through Jung's fascination with

162 her case, she had become far more self-confident than she had been the previous summer. Christiana showed Harry her vision book and allowed him to dive with her into its world; he thus confronted her reintegration of dynamic feminine power unconstrained by the limits of analysis. Harry responded with an explosive passion of his own—a passion that had churned and grown within him for the year they were apart. Christiana's trances, with their erotic power and chthonic sensuality, accompanied the lovers through Germany and became part of their lovemaking.

Each day, Christiana recorded the visions that were pouring out of her, painting scenes from them and entering them into a leather-covered parchment book. She surfaced in white heat daily, meeting Harry fresh from her inner world of dark gods, in which she had congress with bulls, green-eyed satyrs, libidinous stallions, golden youths, grape-leaved priests, and writhing snakes, to each of whom she opened herself, drinking the wine and the lifeblood they offered her. Christiana's sexuality and eroticism rose up, drawing a potent response from Harry, calling forth his own long-repressed Melvillean side, and his yearning and capacity for intensity and depth.

The pair spent their days in the beer gardens and small inns and towns around Munich, all the while gliding deep into Christiana's inner universe and their own passion. Together they navigated her barbarous world and then made love according to the spirit and character of each fantasy that swirled around them. The trances fertilized their lovemaking, which in turn reanimated the trances. Harry exulted in and was humbled by Christiana's potent feminine figures and by the power of the sexuality unleashed between them. In a rare stationary vision at the end of their stay together, Christiana crystallized the spirit behind their passionate encounters. She envisioned herself and Harry as two naked lovers united within a circle formed out of the splendid body of an enormous crowned black snake. The snake enclosed the entwined lovers, protecting them while infusing them with power.

Harry had the imaginative capacity and the erotic resourcefulness to meet Christiana in both her worlds while helping her to keep one foot strongly in reality. What had called out to him long before from his ambivalently provocative experiences with his sister, from his crazed patient, and then from Melville and from Jung, came to rest in Christiana Morgan. All that was injured and feminine within him resonated to the healing vision of Christiana's heroically dynamic feminine figures, while all that was masculine coalesced to embrace her vast deposit of raw, erotic fire.

At the end of the month, they rejoined Jo and Will, together with the Extravert-Introvert Club member Alfred Cohn and his wife. Though jolted back to earth a bit, the lovers made little effort to hide their delirium. Will acceded to its power; Jo soon departed again for Paris and the solace of new wardrobes for herself and Josie.

In October, Christiana returned to Zurich with Harry Murray. She showed Jung the vision book and told him that she had never felt so alive or been so fulfilled sexually. Everything seemed to have come into focus for her; she felt in touch not only with wisdom and strength of feeling but with the meaning of her life. Jung was thrilled with her vision book but, alas, responded as a man rather than an analyst. Despite his having encouraged her union with Harry, Jung now started to sound jealous, as if the force unleashed in the visions belonged to him. Jung reacted to Christiana Morgan's potent sexuality with signs of passionate countertransference. Harry Murray had returned by then to his wife and his job at Harvard, and Christiana resumed her analysis, writing guardedly to him about the change in her analyst:

> Küsnacht–Zurich, Hotel Sonne
> October 12, 1926
>
> My Beloved, I am moved by a great impulse to write you tonight. I wonder whether I am merged in the dark depths of you so that in some sense I am strange to you again, or whether I am beside you in the strong living power of you.
>
> The Old Man is in his best and most vigorous form— charged with thunder and lightning. The forge is good and hot and we are getting close to things. The spirit grows, tried by strange fires.
>
> And you, my dearest one. What can I say? I love you. You are beside me always. The darkest and the lightest power of me is given into your hands.

The tragedy of what happened next, as much a product of the culture as of Jung's personality, was a circumstance that has been too often repeated in the analysis of women. Jung did not know how to deal with the power he had helped unleash; he began to view his patient primarily as a woman, and his traditional gender prejudices overpowered all psychological observations. It may have been doubly problematic for him when a woman, especially a beautiful woman, harbored her feelings in her unconscious and outside her conscious control. Christiana's vast, unconscious, primitive, and often barbarically erotic feminine realm entered the consulting room with her. This potent and fiery side connected her back to the dynamic feminine, opening the way to something that had been lost to more traditional women. It is just here that Jung must have been faced with a profound enigma. Neither Jung the man nor nineteenth-century theory expected this sort of unconsciousness in a woman. Men faced with this feminine power tend to flee, or to combat it by seizing it for themselves, trying to surmount it through lovemaking or rape. The great whale, so long sought and with such yearning, suddenly becomes a threatening monster that must be conquered or harpooned. Jung's dual reaction was to cloak himself in his authority regarding what a woman is—a "feeling" type— and what was going on: something "no longer law abiding"; yet at the same time he fell into a powerfully erotic pull, wanting to possess the whale. What Morgan needed at this point in her development was someone to help her embrace her connection with the chthonic feminine and understand that it is the source of a potent feminine self. Jung, instead, started to attack the very power that attracted him. He began to restrain the flow of Morgan's images and reemphasized her mind, suggesting that she buy an etymological dictionary and take up the study of the mythic parallels of her visions. He also told her:

> Yes, the summer was very fascinating. You were living the life which had hitherto been unconscious and this seems as though it could go on forever. It is a great renewal of life and energy. It is a wonderful flowing. But at the same time . . . to grow you must also use your mind. If you only flow then you only reach a deep level where there is no tension—all levels become the same.

Morgan's visions grew abruptly telegraphic and detached. Jung noted the change and criticized his patient for it, but he never questioned what this communicated about the analysis or his relationship to his patient. He now began to disparage Harry Murray, finding his rival notably immature and flighty. Jung felt himself to be much the better man and continued to insist not on Christiana Morgan's creation of her own self but on her role as an anima woman and *femme inspiratrice* whose "positive attitude [may] free [Harry] and give him something to go ahead with."

In response, Christiana's psyche seems to have created recurrent and ever more powerful images of the strong feminine. Embarking on a series of flame and snake visions that were paralleled by a series wherein she regained her own weapon—a flaming spear—Christiana brought the series to a climax with a vision of a naked goddess on fire: The goddess stands, arms outstretched, before a flaming wheel; great snakes writhe from her head, while a spear alight with blue flames supports the woman and forms a central spoke of the wheel. It is a key image and could have formed the central focus of her analysis, but Jung brushed it aside in a few words, muting her with a barrage of amplifications from Plato and Greek mythology. Morgan insisted on returning to her vision, asking her analyst why she sweated so when she saw it. Jung's response was to compare her snakes and her sweat with bigger and bloodier ones of his own: "Of course you sweat to get up to it. It is the greatest effort that you can make. This is the picture of individuation and the snakes are the evil principle without which the spear cannot exist. I too had such a picture— My snake was so great that it coiled about my body and I sweat blood. When I accepted the snake then my anima which had been blind gained her sight."

Two days later, the analysis disintegrated further; Jung sounded not only jealous of Harry Murray but envious of his patient's newfound feminine strength. He started to attack Christiana's virile sense of womanhood by disparaging it. "The female thing in you doesn't really come up into strong being. It is not crystallized— not powerful enough. You must become more of a woman," and he spent the next few sessions assailing her for what he had formerly encouraged. Where he had once praised the relationship with Harry as a way of Christiana's finding herself, Jung now harshly belittled it and the passion the pair had experienced in Munich: "but that whole relationship is on the unconscious side. It was your animus which gave you life and though you felt like a woman it was his anima that made you feel it and that ran you. . . . You weren't really a woman."

Christiana's visions were making her a woman, but one too large and complex to fit into the confines of tradition's female shell. Jung mistook his patient's intellectual side for masculinity and forgot that it was her newly discovered feeling that needed support. At the same time, Jung started to use the analysis to take potshots at Christiana Morgan and her relationship with Harry Murray; Jung's tone is not only hostile but coarsely brutal, as if everything of value were male and could be obtained through the masculine. Jung proceeded to reduce his patient's inner feminine figures and her blossoming sense of herself to nothing but neuroticism. He told her he expected a reversal in the former positive course of the analysis, but the reversal was Jung's own reaction to the whale. Her derivative response was: "I felt very defiant . . . and thought to myself Whatever they say I believe [in my visions]."

The following session appeared to be equally embattled, with Jung whipping his patient with her animus and calling an image of heaven in her vision "ludicrous." He suggested that she drop all the inner work she was doing and settle down and have another child. Christiana does not write about the psychological devastation of having her visions tossed aside this way and her new feminine strength left not only unmirrored but unaccepted. She simply noted her response to being reduced to one biological function. "My conscious attitude is absolutely against it. It would be death to me and I could give the child nothing," she told him.

This recalled Jung to himself for a bit, and he softened, suggesting that the internal child/star of a new vision and her inner and outer attitudes might in time come together. But at the same time, his reaction to the daemonic feminine was no longer to flee it or destroy it but to seize its energy for himself. Jung introduced his own image of the hero Siegfried, which had already played an ominous history in his life. His identification with this hero had gotten him in trouble at least once before, in his calamitous relationship with Sabina Spielrein at the Burghölzli hospital. Now Jung interjected his image of Siegfried between Murray and Morgan, all the while denying the reality of their passion. He told Christiana that Siegfried was the fitting agent to bring about her feminine development and faulted her newly discovered strength: "I only say watch—to pay attention. You see now you are the strong virgin. You are like Brunnhilde. You have never been broken in. There ought to come to you a Siegfried who would break through your ring of fire—who would make you into a woman." With this loaded image, Jung consciously or unconsciously intimated that he, not Harry Murray, would make the only suitable lover for Christiana Morgan.

She temporarily deflected Jung from his personal interpretations by crediting him with inspiring her visions. Jung fell for the

flattery, accepted the credit, but further distanced her by spending
the rest of the session spinning out a long fable about a Chinese
rainmaker. Though Christiana struggled to bring her analyst back   167
to herself and her visions, he escaped into further abstractions.

The tension between the two increased as Jung was torn between breaking through his patient's wheel of fire and discounting
her. At the next session, she abruptly stopped the journal of her
analysis. The final sessions were not chronicled. For the record,
there are the blank pages; Christiana's reports of her analyst's change
in behavior; the signs of his fear of the strong feminine; his inclination to belittle Harry Murray in comparison to himself; Jung's
mentions of Siegfried; the deterioration of the analysis; and a marked
increase in number of sessions (Jung was now insisting Morgan
come for both morning and afternoon appointments). But the record is in fact more substantial: there is a packet of correspondence
between patient and analyst. After Christiana Morgan's death,
Harry Murray sent the correspondence to the British analyst Gerhard Adler, who was editing a collection of Jung's letters. Adler
decided that all but one of the Morgan-Jung letters were inappro-
priate, but instead of returning them to Murray, he sent the whole
packet off to Jung's executor, his son Franz Jung. Until the Jung
family releases the documents they own, there can only be sup-
positions about Jung's problems with his anima and with countertransference, and about the gossip that Jung, in his identification
with Siegfried, broke through a number of his patients' rings of
fire by sexually exploiting them.

Harry Murray commented on the single letter Adler published:
"In passing let us note (without exclamations) that measured in my
scale of libidinous affection, the letter yields as high a rating as any
letter written to any one of the more than 450 correspondents included in Jung's two-volume *Letters*."

In December 1927, a little over a year after Morgan left Zurich,
Jung began to consider writing a book about her visions, and she
sent him her completed books. Jung thanked her, writing:

> In early December your face haunted me for a while. I
> should have written then but there was a question of time.
> Thank you for everything. "*Don't blame me!*" You are
> always a living reality to me whereas other former patients
> fade away into oblivion, becoming unreal shadows in
> Hades. You are keeping on living. There seems to be some
> sort of living connection (but I should have said that

long ago I suppose). You probably need a confirmation from my side of the ocean just as well. . . . But my dear, dear (!!) Christiana Morgan, you are just a bit of a marvel to me. Now don't laugh, there is nothing to laugh about. You were quite right in scolding me.

Whatever happened or did not happen—and the lacuna of the missing journal pages is augmented by the silence of the Jung family—Jung, by the end of October 1926, was urging his patient to leave analysis and take up her real life. She was still immersed in her visions and still hadn't resolved many of her analytic issues but agreed with his suggestion; her analysis came to an end in early November. Morgan left Jung in order to try to keep hold of what she was recovering—a feminine self situated not in any masculine agency but in the womb of the dynamic feminine. She attempted to regain through her visions something that her own mother had not been able to give her: a sense of her own power.

Christiana's final visions, which continued on the boat back to New York and, with decreasing frequency, for the following six months, left male figures behind. At first, she plunged into the realm of the mothers, a world "that is alien to man and shuts him out." After integrating the loathsome feminine of these depths, Christiana embarked on a primarily upward pilgrim's progress of her own drama. In these visions, she underwent trials and engaged in heroic action, full of blood and violence. Her ensuing descents were now accompanied by recurrent but transformative flame and snake motifs.

One trance started with a male figure, whom she left to follow her star. She passed through a gate into a cavern, where, guided by a more powerful feminine double—the Woman in Blue, who was both old and young—she confronted the harpies, ghosts, and dragons in "the dark regions" of her own soul. Unlike a traditional masculine hero, her female guide served the terrible feminine instead of killing her. This revolutionary figure let the chthonic feminine attack and merge with her, thereby gaining its energies and absorbing them into consciousness. Neither Christiana nor her double slew the chthonic feminine. Instead, healed by contact with this aspect of feminine power, the two emerged, bringing the power they integrated up to the plain and into consciousness.

Powerful feminine images continued to burst up from Christiana's unconscious at this time, including witches, ancient mothers, dragons, volcano goddesses, sky mothers and earth mothers, harpies, maenads, wise women, loathsome women, women heroes, and women guides; slowly they replaced the male images on which Jung had concentrated. While in her outer world Morgan struggled to readapt to her life away from Zurich and to form both a personal and a working relationship with Harry Murray, in her inner world her vision quest continued. At this juncture, as this uprush of female figures attests, she was much occupied with her own sense of herself as a woman; the visions seemed to instruct her that she had to separate herself from men's (including Jung's and psychology's) view of women and from women's traditional passivity. In a most telling picture of this, she visioned an encounter with the "Black Serpent":

169

> I came to a great river. The water of the river was green and it moved with a slow and sluggish current. In the water I saw floating the white bodies of women. Slowly they floated past. Beside me grew great reeds of gold. I saw no way to cross the water. I waded in. Instantly I felt myself being sucked down. In horror I seized a gold reed to pull myself out. The reed broke in my hand and drops of red blood spurted out. Then I seized the branch of a tree and pulled myself out onto a sandy beach. Again I gazed at the women floating by. One came near to me. I pulled her out and laid her on the sand. She opened her eyes. I said why do you float. Where does the river go. She answered When I was young I was cold. The water was warm. I plunged in. Since then I have been floating. The river flows nowhere. Always on and on. It has no source and no ending. I said Why don't you walk. See I have saved you. She answered Behold what the river has done to my feet. I looked and saw that she had no feet only long pieces of seaweed where her feet had been. She said Put me back in the water I cannot be saved. I put her back into the water. She floated away. Then a great wind arose and the green water whipped into waves. The women rose with the waves. With hungry faces and screaming voices they called on me to enter the water. I said I know you. You have no feet. I must walk. Then laughing with derision the women screamed Oh you who talk of feet where are your feet. I looked down and saw that my feet had sunk into the sand. I pulled them out and ran and stood upon a rock. Then I called to them Behold my feet. My strong feet. As I spoke a black snake arose

from the water and coiled itself tightly about my feet. I reached down and put my right hand deep into the mouth of the snake. Then I drew the snake up from my feet. Its tail coiled around my neck. I could not free my hand from its mouth. I looked into its eyes. I walked to the edge of the water and put the snake in the water. The water receded and left a dry place around the snake. I thought Perhaps this is the way I can cross the river. I was afraid lest in the middle the snake would drop away and the water would carry me off. I called for help to free my hand from the snake. No one answered. At last I knew that I must try to cross the river. Holding the snake before so that the water receded I crossed the river in safety. On the other bank I began again to ascend the rocky path. My hand was still in the mouth of the snake. Try as I would I could not shake it off. As I walked the snake became heavy. I dragged it along the ground. I could scarcely pull it.

For months, Christiana continued to struggle through a series of encounters of this sort, and then she began an ascent, bringing the depths up with her. The fantasies of this period portrayed her torment as she labored unassisted to bring to birth a radically new feminine image. The trances' masochism increased, as if her rebellion against Jung was reconstellating her rebellious childhood and her attempts, through fantasies of suffering, to master the closet.

The Gate of the Dark Will

The road on which I traveled cracked open beneath my feet. I saw deep in the dark earth figures hammering many forges. Suddenly they thrust up before me a great gate of red hot metal. The ground closed. I beheld on top of the gate a woman lying pierced through by five red hot spikes. Smoke rose from her burning flesh and mounted up into the sky. In the smoke appeared a great goblet. Many stars hovered over the goblet and water poured from them into the cup. The cup brimmed over and water fell upon the red hot gate. Soon the water cooled the gate and the gate crumbled. I ran to take the woman off the spikes. I laid her on the ground and bent over her weeping. I said I must heal your wounds. She said wait. Then I saw five great stars above her. They sent down five rays. Each entered a wound in her body. She lay back and said lift me up. She was lifted up and I saw a dark rider on a black horse take her. She disappeared in the sweeping folds of his great black cloak. Then horse and rider descended to the earth. He set the woman upon the ground then rode with black fury up into the sky and vanished. Then the heavens became light. I looked at the woman. She was shining with a white light and her body was healed. I said to her Oh tell me what all this is. Where have you been? She made answer, I have been to the place where there is darkness in heaven, the place where man and animal are one. The gate is the Gate of the Dark Will. There is great suffering. I knelt at her feet. I saw that in the flesh of her feet were delicate veins of gold. I said Show me the way. She took my face in her hands saying Now you will suffer. Then she took my hands and whirling me around flung me onto the gate which had arisen anew. Like the woman I was pierced by five spikes. The smoke from my burning flesh rose and formed a black cloud above me. The light from the star on my breast pierced the cloud of smoke. I looked up and saw a red flaming spiral. I looked through the spiral far up into the sky and saw the Woman in Blue. She was in a red womb. She raised her hands above her head and her hands made a tiny opening in the womb thru which light entered. I wept in agony. My tears fell upon the red hot gate and the gate crumbled to the ground. I rose weary and faint. I saw that I was surrounded by a dark red womb. I lifted my hands to the woman in the sky and stood as she had stood. The womb which surrounded me opened in a tiny crack. I looked up and saw the sun in the sky. Then I saw my star around the very sun. A ray of light touched me. I was healed. The womb fell away. Slowly I walked along the never ending road.

A few weeks later, Christiana again redeemed rather than killed a terrible mother dragon, on a still more conscious plane. The classical male hero would have destroyed the dragon once and for all. Here, though, after they fought, the dragon explained that they each had been searching for the other "day after day," believing that they had to conquer and destroy each other. The dragon bestowed gifts on her and said that each of them made up half of the other. However, "now we are met . . . you have conquered." The dragon then transformed herself into a luxurious red plant with an alembic-like stem. Christiana again used the inner star of the previous visions to unite and interact with the dragon in this more assimilable form.

Christiana's vision showed her that a woman hero's task was not to kill the dragon but to keep it alive, even as she separated herself from unconscious fusion with it and its power. Through

172

entering into conscious relation with her dark dragon, Christiana integrated its power inside herself. She redeemed her raging, fire-spitting dragon along with the treasure and brought both up to the surface. Crucially, she did not make the dragon nice, or socially acceptable, nor did she kiss it in the hope she would become a beautiful princess and live prettily and happily ever after with and for some man. She realized that a woman hero needed her dragon to stay a dragon. Christiana was doing difficult work because she dealt with images of the feminine that had not been put into words before and contradicted everything she had been taught about women.

Christiana went on in her trances to find and release an anima-like captive; she united with a dark double and discovered her own anima, at a time when the anima concept referred only to a man's psychology. Christiana did not defeat the depths but instead, and originally, *united* the depths with the heights. Toward the end of her visions book, in February 1927, she discovered what the masculine era had tried to hide: that not only the primitive and spiritual feminine needed uniting, but also the masculine figures of Satan and Christ. Christiana visioned a Satanic Christ lurking behind the one-sided Christian mask of God. She raised this Satanic Christ up out of her own unconscious, and as it surfaced, the Judeo-Christian world crumbled beneath her. The men in the vision fled, though Christiana's recovery of the dark light proved to be the very thing capable of freeing and healing them. The masculine Satanic Christ firmly in consciousness, she embarked again on another powerful series of ascents and descents. This stunning vision prefigured and may well have inspired Jung's important theoretical work on the same subject in "Answer to Job," while the visions as a whole anticipate Jung's final work, *Mysterium Coniunctionis: An Inquiry into the Separation and Synthesis of Psychic Opposites in Alchemy.*

In May 1927, Christiana had the last vision of the series. Though she would occasionally trance later, never again would her visions have the immediacy or the narrative power of those that began in Zurich the year before. Christiana's last vision summed up the goal of her journey: in her final task, she eventually freed herself from the masculine and, by inference, from Harry Murray:

> I ascended the mountain. Rain fell upon me, & grass and flowers grew at my feet. I looked up toward the radiant white light on top of the mountain which shone down

upon me. Suddenly the light was obscured by a figure of a great black man standing in front of me. He stood silent and still like a statue, his arms crossed. I approached him. When I came near to him he tore the skin of his breast open, & stood with his arms outstretched holding the skin of his own body so that all the bone & muscles & tendons of his body were exposed. Upon his chest was a mirror. I looked in the mirror & saw my own reflection. Above my head was the tiny winged child of gold with out-stretched arms. Around it was a golden light. The man alternately hid & exposed the mirror. At last I said "Cease this. I will crack your mirror." I smashed the mirror & placed my right hand on the breast of the man where the mirror had been. The man closed his skin over my hand. I could not free it. I struck at him with my other hand but I could not free myself. Then I said, "Well, I will wait." I looked at the man again. Suddenly I saw that he was transparent, that the light from the mountain pierced through him. I cried out, "Why, you no longer stand between me and the light. You are transparent." The man said "You have freed yourself." He disappeared. I as-cended the mountain.

Christiana recorded this vision in her notebook, never placing it with her other visions, as their conclusion; nor did she allow Harry Murray or Carl Jung to see it. Instead she ended the book with the penultimate vision—one more fitting for a woman of her time. In it, she is on the ground, impaled on an earthy cross at the foot of the mountain. She supports Will Morgan with her right hand, Harry Murray with her left, while a wise old man stands on her feet. Christiana is pinned to the cross by these male figures. However, a divine child in a flaming circle of blue fire rises above her and approaches the mountaintop in a promise of her final vision.

Christiana Morgan's visions in their entirety depicted an ar-chetypal representation of women's psychological development for which neither she nor Jung was ready, one that is coming into consciousness only today. Her visions instructed Morgan that she had to free herself from traditional ideas about women and discover her own, vastly different idea. Part of this feminine self, she found, contained a powerful chthonic element that appeared as the dragon, or as snakes or serpents, or as forms of loathsome women, whose daemonic power was essential in bringing the new form to life. If this potent image of the feminine could have been understood by

Morgan and Jung, it would have meant a confirmation of herself to Morgan and a leap ahead for Jung's antiquated theories of a wounded, pallid, and mourning feminine.

Morgan's visions depicted a way of development that was far ahead of the traditionally feminine one of her era; it was a woman's heroic quest, a type of quest that Morgan may have been the first to envision. Seen this way, the visions in their entirety become a vital and energizing mystery. They have much to offer women exploring and recovering the darkly potent side of women's psychology and have much in common with aspects of Inanna, Lilith, Hecate, and Kali—aspects of the powerfully active, dark, and sometimes loathsome feminine archetype. The visions portray an assertive and active feminine along with the more conventionally passive one. Morgan's visions stand complete in themselves, the way sagas and myths have stood. Entered lovingly and with a feminine eye for the whole form, the visions reveal their intensity, their beauty, their author's fierce courage, and, above all, the visionary power of her bold and joyous quest.

Christiana Morgan inspired Jung and Harry Murray, but she got overlooked in the process. Morgan allowed them to use her connection to the chthonic feminine without their knowing *what* they were using in her, or through her. It wasn't, as Jungian psychology would have it, that Morgan was a *femme inspiratrice,* a woman whose energy was meant to nurture a gifted man. Morgan's visions struggled to capture a purely feminine force, and Jung couldn't help her with this. Jung, Murray, and Morgan herself may have been blinded to her true relevance, not only because Morgan's psychology didn't fit into Jung's and his time's view of the feminine, but also because being a *femme inspiratrice* was what fathers expected of their daughters.

The daughter's eros in a patriarchy had to be placed at the service of the father. Morgan needed a mother who had realized her feminine potency. Without such mirroring, this type of daughter's undeveloped, though passionate, capacity for feeling lies darkly in the unconscious, invisible; it then gets defined by men as an empty receptacle, uncannily sucking in men's projections. It is the woman's own energy and libido that inspire, but the men take this unseen mercury to back the mirror of their own reflection. Morgan's visions offered her a vital alternative. They created a battle within her: on the one side was Jung's demand that she inspirit, reflect, and create Harry Murray while herself remaining veiled in a male point of view; on the other, her visions demanded that she free herself and regain her own power. This battle was to frame the rest of Morgan's life.

175

During the months the Morgans were in Zurich, Will had seen Jung for a few sessions, but things were not going well with him. Jung seems to have undervalued Will Morgan, dismissing him as a mother-bound man and sending him off to Toni Wolff. Wolff, who at least according to Will's notes, often conducted his analysis by teaching him about the theory of analytical psychology as it applied to him rather than listening to him. Will's dream of Toni Wolff after their first session depicted her talking down to him and giving him toys to play with. She interpreted his dreams and visions as those of a typical male—a thinking type. Though Wolff emphasized the need for Will consciously to assert himself and settle on a career, she insisted he be manly in a logical, thinking way. She regarded his strong feeling function as inferior and weak, as if it were an anima possession and a deficit, rather than his strength. Will was able, however, to discuss deeply personal issues with her, such as his problem with premature ejaculation and his habit of frequent urination. Wolff interpreted these as typical of the young naive hero who is still overly connected to a widowed mother. There is no evidence that she considered possible underlying medical problems.

The type of analysis that was being developed in Zurich gave neither time nor depth enough for the analysis of early wounds and did not meet Will Morgan's need to deal with his childhood or, even more essentially, with his war traumas. Will had recurrent nightmares, not only war dreams indicative of a chronic post-traumatic stress disorder but other dreams and visions that alluded to gassing, lung disease, and death. In one recurring dream, he was being asphyxiated by his own breath, a breath that frightened him because it smelled of onion gas. He had another of "two eyes—clear pupils—the whites a horrible scum: in each lower lid a drop of clear amber liquid. The skin is brown, the warning of coming DEATH in heavy large letters." It was as if the dreams were calling specific attention to his illness. A Jungian analyst today would focus on these areas immediately and suggest a complete medical evaluation. In hindsight, what Wolff and Jung took to be Will Morgan's infantile pull back into the mother could as well be taken as a far more critical pull forward toward his death.

The rather flagrant devaluation of him exacerbated Will Morgan's own feelings of low self-worth. Jung and Wolff seemed to consider Harry and Christiana as the main stars in a drama that strikingly resembled their own, with Will and Jo serving as peripheral characters. Jung and Wolff succeeded in persuading Will to support his wife in her double relationship. Wolff did help Will, however, by demanding that he take his future seriously; she helped him shift some energy from worrying about Christiana to focusing on a career. He left Zurich sadder and little wiser than he had been and with an oddly distorted archetypal grasp of his situation. Positively, through friends he had made in Zurich, Will found a new direction for his career and, while he finished his degree requirements in physiology, joined the small Jungian contingent studying anthropology in Cambridge.

In a journal entry he made just before returning to England, Will pondered the interplay of Harry, Christiana, and himself; his newly acquired psychological terminology was mocked by the raw power of his feelings:

> His [Harry's] mother her mother driven by fiends, his sister; my wife more conscious than any of them but urged too—Harry & she urged to a greater thing. Can he give up all that he has, can he die, for otherwise he will not make it beautiful. Will he rush into this situation with my wife as he has done heretofore, before he is conscious. But all this does not cause my excitement. My libido has gone in, and as I sink nearer to the Unconscious I will find undifferentiated feeling. I do not want it. I tried to keep feeling down since Friday so that my thinking & intuition could be clear: I feel stronger, I had no remorse from pouring muddy feeling. Now it is difficult to imagine that I go back in a few days to England. What is happening to me?

The Morgans' close friend Robert Edmond Jones perceived qualities in both Christiana and Will that Wolff and Jung, perhaps blinded by their theory and the blaze of their own personal drama, could not see. As the Morgans departed, Jonah wrote almost a summation of their experience:

> Dear Will—
> I am sorry to scrabble off a note to you. I told both [Wolff] and [Jung] about my vision of you because I wanted to know whether I had gone mad—as of course I have—or

whether I had really seen something. [Jung] said that he had not seen it in you but that he had *felt* it in the last morning very strongly—something formidable in you— then he said that I had seen the [archetype of] The Old Man. He said that you had developed a remarkable quality and could do great things. . . . It is awfully lonely here without you two. But I feel, mystically, that we three are together, really together, as people are not often in this world. I *must* know how it goes with you in America. I love you too Will. We found our common love thru initiation.

Always,
Jonah

I am going to write to Christiana.

Dear Christiana,
I am terribly disturbed and sad at really saying goodbye to you and Will. I have got it into my head at last that I am going to be here all alone. It is not so pleasant. But I feel, and I know you feel too, that we are bound together very closely in one of the strangest and most sacred experiences that three people have ever had together. Who knows how it all has come about or what occult influences each of us has had on the others to bring us nearer to ourselves? A strange threefold flowering— Will has been most extraordinary these last days, and yesterday morning he came back from an hour [with Jung] in a state of exaltation so intense that it rushed out of him like a light and all his movements became ample and large and his face was that of a seer. I—practical!—made him go and lie down. It was thrilling to see. I bless you both and send you my love. It will be something! when we sit around a table once more with our various drawings.

Always,
Jonah

Will Morgan did not return to the United States but stayed in England to complete the work for his degree. His son and the boy's nurse remained with him. Councie attended Malting House for another term, while Christiana embarked alone with her visions on a ship in wintertime to meet Harry across the great expanse of sea.

178 *From Mansol's Book*

(WRITTEN BY HENRY MURRAY)

August, 1927

How did you know how to create me,—to create us both in some new unity? Your instinct was sure and certain— For years I have known only one thing and that was that consecration was life. I have sought in concrete and abstract realms the principle that was to bind me; and now I know that I have found it. I am linked to your destiny by unbreakable affinities. I am yours everlastingly.

I conceive of our life,—and I have no other life but ours, as first an experience together to be lived, felt, formed and expressed. I believe that it depends for its structure and continuous evolution upon your trances. I think that if we do not know what we are doing, if we are not self-conscious about what is evolving within we shall cease to evolve, and it will be forever a chaos, mere sensations. As I see it the central problem is to fashion our feelings and sensations into meaningfulness, and your trances do that for us. It is my complete conviction that these trances of yours must be worked over and lived and merged into our life, so that they are reality and the essence of our tangible existence. They must be enriched by our blood and our thought. You have given me the topmost crest of my imagination at one instant.

September, 1927

You cannot possibly deny that you have created me and carried me across the stream and given me light and led me out of darkness. Remember I am talking facts. You could never have gone on this way without me. You are everlastingly dependent upon me. But *you* are the center, the re-creating fire and nourishing water.

Now it is true that your ordering principle—which is our life—works by way of the trances. There might have been some other ways but this happens to be the way now. And so it follows that your trances represent, express, *order,* our love. Thus they are central. We cannot go ahead without them. They are our language.

Everything I have said so far is a fact in experience. It has come about this way. It happens that you have a cosmic eye; that you look over the entire span of life from the germ to the farthest affirmative bright yea-saying star. But even if this were not so our private destinies would be linked up with your creating principle, because we have nothing else. I can do nothing else but feed you with my powers. This is the only life that can be real to me.

179

I see you as the woman that I love and also as a cosmic divine essence of light. You must know this and accept it. To do this means to take a step much greater than you have ever taken, because it means the assimilation of the formidable pretentious conviction that your visions will govern us both, forever.

Before you carry your truth over to the world you must carry it over to me. You have no affirmative life really, until you are certain of your genius for *us*. When you become absolutely egotistically assured that I must govern my life according to your vision, then you will *really* have me to nourish you. You must take this as fate determined. I have an absolutely clear perspective of it. I see you with your personal beauty and creativeness, and the universal essence of which you happen to be the modern representative. If you can say the truth, the universal truth for your epoch, as you have in the trances, then that is the highest life possible, and we are aiming for this.

You are only straight and clear to me, and yet it seems funny that I should feel this because, in another sense, you are not at all clear. You are covered with layers of protective investitures which seem to be all of a defensive nature. It is our problem to strip these coats. Let us let our natures run their proper course.

Our purpose is to create a trance epic. I know that whatever I can give that is good, will make your trances good. When I am wrong the trances will be wrong. They will be nothing but a lonely, solitary and hence meaningless song without me. But if you know that except through your trances as a core I cannot express myself, how can you have a humble attitude about them? I shall enrich them for you and they shall include all time and space and all life struggling within the confines of time and space— A sure voice has told me that I can no longer live without them and that I must enter into your vision— That peculiar force, call it what you will, that is at the center of your being, that is expressed in the trance is the New Thing, which mixing with man's thing, makes a third thing,—which is IT. We are going to try to live the new way and express IT.

180   Our focus will be this epic, an Epic of *Your Life*. It will be divided into three parts.

1, a realistic account of your waking life with all your outer contacts. 2, your trances, more or less poetically transcribed. 3, an objective cold analytical thing which will take in all that psychology, history, myths and modern psychology has to say about it. Every problem, every great problem will have its place, successively looked at from these angles. Christianity, paganism in you, the sexes in you, woman creativeness vs. the child, then the emergence into *us,* etc. I do not know of anything as big as this ever having been attempted, but I feel fully capable of doing it *with you.* The Melville book will be a training ground. I am ready to have you repudiate many of the details of this, but I will be crushed, I think, if you repudiate the core of it.

This poetic transformation, this fashioning of a world-force in you, which is really beyond one sex and yet is gloriously feminine, is the only thing which can hold my imagination, and, as it seems to me, the most natural outflow for my energies. How could anything be better than this?

Perhaps you may not see this this winter because our energies will be used in the world, but when you know yourself, then we shall start in the fire together and keep ourselves to it. "Write the Book" we shall say,—which will simply mean developing our passion more and more for each other and letting what-will flow from our love. You are the center of my world and the compass of all my hopes. Your center is spiritual, and your truths soul-truths, so you must determine the climate of our life, and be the leading principle of our life. I live gloriously when I mass upon your vision. Keep me at the center. Drive me always toward The Book. Only so can I write. Only so can I surpass myself, and overtop my highest imaginations.

I may terribly analyze and criticize your trances. We may fight horribly, but this may all be necessary. The great vice will be fear, false modesty, shallowness. Are we brave enough for this? Will you be infinitely jealous and never allow me to disperse? If so I will write your life though it may take twenty years to do it, for it will be a big canvas. This will be my only work, and will reach a mountain that none has ever climbed. The whole spiritual course of man will pivot on you.

From Wona's Book

(WRITTEN BY CHRISTIANA MORGAN)

My spiritual loneliness is stark and terrible and brings with it great fear. Sometimes I feel that I come close to the verge of insanity. I feel unutterable terror, holding all alone to this that is within me. All my trance passion you defer to some later date. When my energy for our life is so powerful that you cannot resist it you follow it for a few brief days, we create understanding and new recognitions, but then it threatens your work and your plan of life as you pull away and I am left gutted and lost. My spirit feels broken by your perpetual return after our ecstasy to the same life without any change having happened out of your great recognition. Sometimes I curse my own creativeness because it seems to me that what it has done is to create a form for the spirit which can't be lived. I feel impotent and depressed, and your recognitions seem hollow and remote to me if you cannot live them. Is the spirit to remain forever only a vision?

I was Epiphany once—in myself. I was an "empowering factor" for father, Jung, and finally for Mansol. In our religious synergy I was "empowering our transformation." The achievement of ever deeper states of being in which they could be met, became an end (Walpurgis). This was up to a point, since it created unity in each, and generated great life because each met the other in ever deepening understanding,—in ever deepening and varied states of being. But since Wona never insisted that M. should formulate their steps,—a new split in life developed. The sad aspect is that Wona never demanded a formulation out of revelation from M. Her trances and her experience showed her that the world held no life for her unless it was formulated anew in terms that held the meaning of the trances. Here she failed dismally. . . .

Thinking of myself—my beauty—as a bridge for the archetypes for Mansol. Me trying to be the vehicle through which the archetype for our time can come to birth in M. M. being an instrument. But I can't *feel* for what he is doing because my feeling is connected with the archetypes. . . . The terrible danger of an archetype. . . .

182

M. asks me why I am not happy. Until our form is right, and clear between us, there can be no happiness for me. I must find my right function,—the new form. . . . I have lived as instigator—a starter of life. The archetype (Epiphany). Jung was the right one until recently. Now the time has come when I must *create myself*. I cannot live in that archetype any longer. Now I must learn out of myself, in and through myself the long slow process.

The very *crux* of this change for me is that I don't have to be effective . . . out of myself, but in what I do, and in what I cherish.

TEN

Let's Do It, Harry!

The Harvard Psychological Clinic

The full philosophy remains to be worked out. Let's do it, Harry! To go on with what Jung has begun would be the biggest thing that could be done at the present time. Is there a bigger whale or a whiter whale?

CHRISTIANA MORGAN

When Christiana embarked from Cherbourg that November, no one saw her off. Her husband and son had gone back to England for the winter. She traveled frugally and alone on an old, almost empty Cunard ship, occupying a windowless second-class cabin but, thanks to a sympathetic steward, using the adjoining one as well. She continued to trance amid the bleak surroundings and cold November storms. When the weather quieted, she walked the decks and pondered what returning to Boston and Cambridge would mean. Because of her analysis and her passion for Harry Murray, she felt she returned as an outlaw and a stranger. At the same time, she was full of joy about traveling to meet her lover and to embark on their new and untried life together—a personally secret, publicly professional collaboration at Harvard. Chistiana wondered whether or not she could find will and wisdom enough to build the kind of life Harry and she desired. At times the difficulties that lay in her path overwhelmed her, for the life she envisioned diverged radically from its surroundings;   183 though Christiana had found a new sense of organic unity through her visioning, she questioned if it would prove solid enough to combat both her own inner puritanism and that of the world she would be rejoining in New England. The storm-tossed ocean liner approached the Ambrose light in New York harbor at dusk in a leaden gale; Christiana braced herself against the wind and worried: "Why should I be pushed to this course which no one else seems to be taking or even to have seen? And what . . . kind of world would confront [me]?"

As if in answer, she ran into old Bostonian acquaintances just as Mike and Harry Murray appeared at the Victoria Hotel to welcome her. She completed her journey by train to Boston and to the apartment building on Memorial Drive in Cambridge where she had lived two years before. She spent that first winter organizing the apartment, making plans for the clinic, continuing to vision, and contemplating her future relationship with Harry. When her family returned, Will took up the study of anthropology at Harvard and Councie attended Shady Hill, a school that was an easy and successful transition from Malting House, as it was conducted on the same principles yet had a solid academic focus that suited the sensitive and serious little boy. He loved the school and was well liked there. His mother's attention, however, was elsewhere.

Morgan started work at the Harvard Psychological Clinic that winter. The clinic bloomed like some exotic yet aberrant tropical plant in the middle of Emerson Hall, the glacial bastion of Edwin G. Boring's scientific and experimental psychology. As chairman of Harvard's psychology program, Boring strove to instill rigorous scientific methodology throughout his department. Limiting psychology to what could be stringently controlled in the laboratory, he and the majority of university psychologists of his time labored to codify the fundamental elements of consciousness and correlate them with physiological processes. William James described the positivist and empirical psychology then in ascendance:

> There is little of the grand scale about these new prism, pendulum, and chronograph-philosophers. They mean business not chivalry. What generous divination, and that superiority in virtue which was thought by Cicero to give a man the best insight into nature, have failed to do, their spying and scraping, their deadly tenacity and almost diabolic cunning, will doubtless someday bring about.

Yet Morton Prince's contrary new clinic erupted right in the middle of Harvard's mecca of scientific precision. Prince wandered the murky depths of psychopathology and hypnosis, charting man- ifestations of the subconscious, hysteria, and multiple personality through dramatic case studies that eluded the quantification and control so valued by his peers. Prince, even in his early seventies, lived on a grand scale, displaying the showmanship of a Jean-Martin Charcot at the Salpêtrière; he gathered sensational patients around him, showing them off, as Charcot had displayed his *grandes hysté-riques,* in equally florid teaching presentations, which appalled the fastidious businessmen of Emerson Hall. Murray described Prince as a dapper little man and a vivid lecturer, whom students relished for his theatricality and zest. But Murray added, perhaps with a touch of rivalry, that Prince had "little inner life, [and] no dark shadows, no all-pervading skepticisms, no tragic depths, and hence with age he did not open to a mellow wisdom."

Morton Prince was perhaps best known for his fascinating study of the multiple personality of a Miss Beauchamp. He treated the young woman under hypnosis and slowly helped integrate her various personalities in what the French historian Henri Ellenberger has called an enthralling example of group therapy on a single individual. By 1926, however, Prince was an old man, and his mind had grown less sharp; not only was he making no new discoveries but he jealously repudiated the newer explorers of the unconscious like Freud and Jung. Prince wanted to keep his own method and name paramount at Harvard; the clinic would stand as his final and highest achievement.

Prince, who lived in Boston and in the early 1870s had been an old collegemate of Harvard's president, Abbott L. Lowell, now persuaded his good friend that Harvard needed not only Boring's experimental-psychology laboratories but a place where Prince could use his own patients to demonstrate psychopathology and teach its cure. Lowell agreed, on condition that Prince raise the money and endow the clinic himself. He succeeded, "extracting from his enormously rich skinflint brother just enough stock to pay for a secretarial novice and some accompanying equipment" and, eventually, a small clapboard building on Beaver Street. There was little money at first, about three thousand dollars for the entire staff, and so Prince recruited part-time or self-supporting dollar-a-year therapists from a wide variety of backgrounds, preferring, in fact, to train them himself, in his own methodology.

186 Prince paid scant regard to their academic qualifications, approving, as did the majority of depth psychologists at that time, of lay analysts but also making the best of what he could get since funds were lacking. Prince accepted Murray—who lacked psychiatric training but had an M.D. and a Ph.D. (albeit in biochemistry)— as his second in command through the urging of Murray's friend and mentor L. J. Henderson. Prince had little in common with Murray except an interest in the unconscious and an abhorrence of the type of experimental psychology Boring revered. Perhaps Murray's greatest selling point was that he was independently wealthy and would work for no salary. Murray in turn introduced Christiana Morgan to Prince, who took an immediate liking to her. Given Murray's backing, her evident knowledge of depth psychology, her informal study of it at Cambridge University, and her analysis with Jung, Prince welcomed Morgan and offered her part-time work as an analyst in training.

Prince slowly assembled an eccentric polyglot group, full of disparate outlooks. While Prince lectured about his patients with dramatic flair, often demonstrating their recall of pathogenic events under hypnosis, Murray taught a course on abnormal psychology that downplayed hypnosis and emphasized Freudian and Jungian theory. Murray proved to be a remarkable lecturer in spite of his stutter; he spoke with vivid and enthusiastic immediacy, illustrating his points with a Melvillean interest in the complexity of individual lives. But Emerson Hall threatened to blow apart under the tensions between Boring's strict laboratory and Prince's innovative clinic, as well as from competing currents within the clinic itself. It was a great relief when the small group moved to its new home at 19 Beaver Street.

Morgan had been entrusted with furnishing and decorating the new quarters, Murray supplying most of the money and even some of his family's furniture. The couple consulted on paint, furniture, and the rich Oriental carpets as if they were decorating a house of their own. While Murray busied himself preparing lectures, Morgan turned what had been an old and faded New England two-family house into a remarkably vibrant workplace, including a lecture room, a library, six rooms for behavioral experiments, and ten studies or consultation rooms. In decorating them, Morgan combined originality of style and use of color with elegance: not a stiff Bostonian elegance but a warm, vivacious one that did not intimidate. It gave, as Henry Murray wrote, "a lived-in atmosphere . . . which puts patients at their ease and . . . is conducive to good-feeling, industry and thought." Morgan's aesthetic sense pervaded this and every house the clinic occupied for the next forty years, creating a consistently harmonious setting for the clinic's working life. In contrast to Harvard buildings' often sterile exteriors, gardens were planted around each house the clinic inhabited, which Morgan designed and cared for as her father had once tended the rosebushes around Massachusetts General Hospital. She even transplanted a cedar tree from her father's garden in York to the entrance of the Beaver Street house. It flourished and in a relatively short time obscured the front door sign; its stalwartness and sweet odor augured well for the clinic's vitality.

187

Though Morgan thoroughly enjoyed the tasks of decorating the clinic and seeing patients, she found Prince's approach alien and grew to dislike his histrionics as well as many of her colleagues' Freudian orientation. She felt that both outlooks devalued patients and treated them unsympathetically. Neither philosophy expressed her own notions of self, or her sense of respect for her patients, or the work she was doing with them; her alienation exacerbated the split she felt between her inner life and her participation at the clinic during its initial years.

So that Morgan and Murray could meet privately, Harry rented a small apartment at Fairfax Hall, 1306 Massachusetts Avenue. He paid the rent under the semblance of purchasing rare books from its owner, Maurice Firuski. Conrad Aiken had used the same apartment several years before, and Murray lent it to him a few years later when he was wooing one of the clinic's young secretaries, Clarissa Lorenz, who eventually became Aiken's second wife. The apartment was on the second floor, above a tobacconist's shop, and had the advantage of being entered through either the building's front door, across from Harvard Yard, or an upstairs room at the side of the shop. Their entry obscured by the comings and goings of customers, Morgan and Murray could meet unobserved. Or so they thought. Their trysting place was discovered by Jo Murray, but she kept the knowledge to herself. As it happened, the building's janitor knew the cook at the Rantoul country house, in Beverly Farms. Jo, on good terms with the cook, made sure she kept tabs on the professor's rendezvous with his companion, gaining thereby the grim satisfaction of catching her husband in the lies he was telling, though she said nothing to him about her knowledge. The lovers referred to these rooms as Fairfax and met there at least once a week, but with a strain of furtive subterfuge that Christiana detested.

188   In August 1927, Morgan and Murray stayed a few days at the apartment the Murrays kept in New York; here, they first named themselves Wona and Mansol and, in a pattern they would repeat throughout their life, they examined their relationship and looked for a new form that would better help them remain lovers and working partners. Harry wrote in his diary that he often felt inferior to Christiana that first year; he was torn between love and a competitive jealousy of her inner life. Murray had not yet made a name for himself; his effort to do so at Harvard and through the books he planned to write would derive not only from personal ambition but from his need to compete with his lover's power. He described Christiana and himself then as "two whirlpools" engaged in a battle of wills. While outwardly they appeared to be discussing their love and work with calm, he felt that they were engaged in a fierce power struggle for dominance and centrality. Behind Murray's support of Morgan's interest in depth psychology and behind his encouragement of her contributions to the clinic lay his battle to draw her into his world and avoid being drawn into hers. For a time, the two focused energy on creating their substitute home at the clinic. Christiana lost the first and perhaps most important battle as she adapted herself to the age-old role of mistress; nevertheless, it was her relationship with Harry that gave her an unparalleled opportunity to do creative work with patients as a team member at the clinic. She found her professional role increasingly rewarding. Though she did not have Harry to herself as a wife would, she had him at her side as a working partner.

Morton Prince died during the summer of 1929, and Harry Murray was chosen to replace him as head of the clinic. Many of his staff were Freudians and at first, Murray allied himself with them. He had surveyed the state of psychodynamic psychology in the United States and found the Freudians better trained and better organized than the American Jungians; the Freudians had practical ideas on training analysts, and were—in part because the majority of them were male while the Jungians were preponderantly female—somewhat more accepted by the medical community at large. One result of Murray's interest in the Freudian camp was his role in the formation of the Boston Psychoanalytic Society. Besides Morgan and Murray, who thought of themselves as Jungians, the other initial members of the society were an Adlerian, a Rankian, and three Freudians. Since most worked part-time at the clinic, the society's early meetings were held there. Murray then persuaded the Freudian analysts Franz Alexander and Hanns Sachs to come to Boston to analyze each of the would-be founders of the society. Sachs remained, while Alexander soon returned to Chicago, requiring those he analyzed (including Murray) to spend months at a time in Chicago until their analysis was completed. In order that Morgan could fully share in the life of the clinic and have standing in the society as a lay psychoanalyst, she embarked on a training analysis with Hanns Sachs and had him supervise her work with two of her clinic patients. She presented case studies of these patients to the clinic and before the fledgling society.

Sachs's analysis and supervision felt stiflingly reductive to Morgan. She found the Boston Psychoanalytic Society meetings equally restrictive and was especially repelled by their views on women. She sat in silence about this for meeting after meeting, until a forum on the sexuality of women proved too much for her: Morgan listened as Alexander, who had a notorious predilection for chorus girls, expounded on the natural superiority of the male sex and castigated women as passive, masochistic, and marred. He called a professional woman's wish for an active life outside the home nothing but a childish striving for a penis and spoke of creativity as beyond the province of the female sex. The other men then joined in with a relish that verged on the vindictive, while Irmirita Putnam, a Jung analysand, collaborated, speaking about girls as deficient by nature and about babies as poor substitutes for penises. Morgan contained herself for as long as she could, only to burst out with objections, especially about women's sexuality; the members' icy response to her protests caused her to flee from the room and sob out her frustration secretly in her office. Murray excused himself to follow her, but only privately concurred with her views.

Sachs's Freudian outlook, with its draconian construct of women, allowed no room for Morgan's more Jungian explorations with her patients, nor for her ideas of the creative and healing aspects of the unconscious. Sachs pronounced her visions aberrant and worth discussing only as manifestations of pseudomasculinity—a futile surrogate for the penis she lacked. He further limited Morgan through reinforcing Jung's dictum that a woman's feminine task was not to develop her own ideas and creativity for their own sake but to support a man—Murray—in his. Sachs felt that woman's creativity, if there was such a thing, lay in substituting childbearing and homemaking for her deficient anatomy. It was not until Morgan met Karen Horney in the 1930s and read her papers on the psychology of women that she and Murray found a Freudian view more reflective of their own. Karen Horney repudiated Freud's concept of penis envy and posited a masculine womb envy instead. Not only did she treat female sexuality with much more resonance than Freud or Jung, she evolved a typology of personality that Morgan could adopt as an expansion of Jung's introverted and extraverted types.

Morgan's initial experience with the Jungians in the United States was as disappointing as her confrontation with the Freudians. Shortly after her return from Switzerland, she traveled to New York to consult the Jungian analyst Beatrice Hinkle. Morgan wanted to continue the work she had begun with Jung and looked to Dr. Hinkle for reinforcement of her growing sense of herself and her vital creativity, and also, possibly, for an ally in her tangled effort to live an unconventional life. Hinkle, however, recoiled from her visions, viewing them not as a path toward individuation but as a pathological, even psychotic, phenomenon. She insisted that Morgan stop her visioning at once or risk insanity. It was clear that therapy would involve a procrustean effort to pare the patient down to narrow mediocrity. The night before her only visit to Hinkle, Morgan dreamed of her childhood confinement by Dr. Waterman; the night after the encounter, she dreamed of marveling at a clear mountain range others were too nearsighted to see. She left Hinkle's office and never returned, feeling rebellious and even more alone. In her diary, she valiantly asserted that "she would not disgrace her own experience, however perilous, to be cumbered any more by such prudence and return to the narrow and airless vaults of her past which this woman, despite her professional standing, represented by her attitude of fearful repudiation."

Within the clinic's Freudian mold, Morgan continued to forge her own sense of herself as a therapist, but she had to keep her ideas in the privacy of her journal. Her skill as an analyst is hard to measure, because what she did with her patients occurred under the rules of confidentiality. Morgan's patients, however, by their letters, and by Murray's and others' accounts, were devoted to her, and many went on to lead active and creative lives that they attributed to the results of their analysis with Morgan. A number became her lifelong friends. From her writing about therapy, it seems that

Morgan's greatest talent as an analyst, besides her empathic and sensitive mirroring, lay in her understanding of the mutuality of the process. She did not treat her patients autocratically, as Hinkle had treated her, but evolved a method not unlike feminist therapy today, in which she looked on herself and her patient as a team working together to build self-esteem while they discovered the meaning and value behind the patient's neurosis.

Morgan received recognition and support for her analytic skill and her clinical work during these years, but she had to mask herself in alien terminology. Murray was the only one, however sporadically and ambivalently, who championed what was most essential to her—her sense of herself as a woman and her development through her visions. Without female peers and with no mirror except Murray's wavering one, she began to lose the sense of herself that had started to emerge in her work with Jung. Morgan put her creativity into her patients, her clinical research, the furnishing and upkeep of the clinic and the property Murray had helped her to buy near Newburyport, and, perhaps most significantly, into advancing Murray's career. There was no voice but her own to call her back to herself and her needs, and that voice was drowned out by the external world and its demands. As for her visions, perhaps out of her own insecurities and Murray's insistence that he have all of her, Morgan began sacrificing them to the service of their relationship. A dream's or a vision's value lies in its reflection of a different view of the psyche than the conscious ego holds; it can reveal images that potentially enrich, broaden, even correct, an individual's conscious viewpoint. Instead of witnessing her visions and seeking their meaning, Morgan started to bend them into weapons in the competition between herself and Murray. The final vision of the first series, on June 14, 1927, recorded her solitary ascent of the mountain. The visions thereafter no longer rang with the pure timbre and accuracy Jung had praised; they became muted servants of Morgan's will to power.

Morgan's and Murray's erotic excitement and the fascination of their mutual projects left Will and Councie Morgan as bereft as Jo and Josie Murray; husband, wife, and children placed a poor third in time and interest to the inner and outer worlds the couple were creating together. Will Morgan had returned to the United States with the essential work for his Cambridge University doctorate completed, but he still lacked a career that interested him. Thanks to his small inheritance, he attended classes at Harvard, now pursuing a career in anthropology, but he was also fighting a losing battle for his health and for his place in Christiana's life. In a final

192 attempt to reclaim her, Will had demanded that Christiana and he have another child upon his return from Europe. Murray, probably unable to sire another child himself, tried to encourage Christiana, declaring that he would love and take care of the baby as if it were his own. Christiana managed to avoid pregnancy, knowing that another child would further burden her increasingly empty marriage. Her refusal was only one sign among many that though she remained married to Will and still professed her love for him, she had abandoned him far more completely than Harry ever had Jo. Will's passive acquiescence in this state of affairs left him inwardly marooned. As his health continued to deteriorate, he was diagnosed as having asthma and treated accordingly; on medical advice, Will Morgan made long trips to the drier climate of the Southwest. He looked forward to doing research on the Navajo Indians, whose culture he had become interested in at Zurich, examined at Harvard, and finally studied in field research backed by Yale.

His doctor's prescription of a stay in the Southwest temporarily lifted Will's spirits yet also recalled his father's similar journey the year before he died. Will fled Cambridge, Massachusetts, in 1929, eager to leave the miserable amorous triangle behind, and for a brief and productive time he enjoyed the new life he found. A natural anthropologist, he examined Indian beliefs with sensitivity and respect; he gathered a large amount of data, which he later converted into a series of monographs. He also felt at home with the Navajo and made many friends among them; they grew to respect his gentle, self-contained ways, which matched their own. Before long, a Navajo medicine man was involving him in their more private religious ceremonies, including a nine-day healing chant in which Will, as patient, was one of the participants.

It was during the summer of Will's Southwest journey that Morton Prince died. Harry succeeded him as clinic director that fall and shortly thereafter, the clinic moved to a larger house, at 64 Plympton Street. Slowly, in the years that followed, the spirit of the place changed and a surge of new life began. One by one, the Freudian psychoanalysts dropped away as Murray and Morgan shifted the emphasis of the clinic from psychopathology and hypnosis to research on personality. Though the two remained for a time a part of the Boston Psychoanalytic Society—Murray even became its second chairman, succeeding Irmirita Putnam—they withdrew from active participation, finding the society increasingly humorless, dogmatic, and swept with its own power rivalries. To the public eye, however, the clinic remained closely identified with 193 the society's now exclusively Freudian group, Murray attributing Harvard's new president Conant's first rejection of his request for academic tenure to this linkage.

Now the only patients referred to the clinic for psychoanalysis went to Murray or Morgan, and therapy became almost extraneous to the main agenda. The new program evolved into a heroic study of the full range of human potentiality. Instead of learning more and more about less and less, as the laboratory psychologists were doing, Murray and Morgan envisioned a complete survey of human personality through examining individuals in depth; Murray focused on the grand sweep of the idea, while Morgan's interest lay in fantasy, values, and creativity. The resultant theory synthesized what they had learned from Jung, Freud, and Adler with a very American interest in personality as a whole made up of many measurable states. The humanistic psychology Murray and Morgan conceived derived as much from William James, Herman Melville, and nineteenth-century American literature as from European depth psychology. The method behind their personality theory sought to measure the component parts of the whole through a battery of assessments that produced an in-depth biography of the individual. The clinic staff went on to test a group of Harvard students with the wide diversity of assessments and methodologies they had invented. These tests were grounded on Jung's ideas of psychological functions, his introversion-extraversion parameters, and his interest in active imagination; Freud's concepts of id, ego, and superego; and William James's work on manifest needs, traits, and behaviors.

Henry Murray and his often silent partner attacted an enormously gifted and energetic group of graduate students to the Harvard Psychological Clinic, many of whom went on to become distinguished psychologists in their own right; among the first were Isabelle Kendig, Ken Diven, Donald MacKinnon, Nevitt Sanford, Robert White, and Saul Rosenzweig. For ten years, and for brief resurgent periods thereafter, the clinic assumed the aura of a Camelot, with Murray as head and Morgan by his side. The atmosphere of excitement, even enchantment, and the almost erotic magnetism of the work itself was the outward manifestation of Murray's and Morgan's inner marriage. As such, the clinic took on a deep family

feeling infused with passionate intensity and daring, though its
source remained hidden except to an observant few. Two of the
194 clinic's original members—Robert White, who initially joined the
clinic because of his interest in hypnosis, and Saul Rosenzweig, a
nascent Freudian in 1927—recalled Morgan's essential contribution
most clearly and, over sixty years later, still spoke with exhilaration
about the magical quality that permeated the clinic and was felt by
each participant in those valiant early years. White perhaps best
conveyed the change from Prince's tenure to Murray's new clinic:

> I was present as a graduate student during the year before
> and the year after Prince's death, then absent for the next
> three years teaching at Rutgers. When I returned, it was
> to a wholly different world. Everyone was talking about
> needs, variables, and a mysterious process called thematic
> apperception. Strange people were wandering in and out,
> neither staff, patients, nor students, but simply person-
> alities undergoing study. The ship had radically changed
> course. . . .
>
> In hindsight it was easy to see what it was in Murray
> that fell into this new shape. There was the research phy-
> sician's respect for detailed histories, multiple assessment,
> and careful description of variables. There was the curi-
> osity, inspired alike by Prince, Freud, and Jung, about the
> realms of unconscious motivation and fantasy. There were
> the influences of history, literature, and the arts. There
> was Murray's own special fascination by the profound
> experiences in people's lives. But it was the necessity to
> arrive at systematic description that gave these diverse in-
> terests their new creative shape: the vision that the time
> had come when it might be possible to develop a full-
> length, full-depth, dynamic, scientific account of human
> personality. A comprehensive system was the ultimate
> goal, and it was the time to put up the scaffolding.

The inspiration flowed in large part from Morgan's trances and
from Murray's and Morgan's desire to comprehend what such fantasy production revealed about an individual's personality. Morgan
thus extended her search for the meaning of her visions through
the clinic's research on fantasy production in others. White noted
the profound effect of her presence at the clinic:

> Working at the Harvard Psychological Clinic was the great
> experience of my life, and when I try now to imagine what

it would be like if Christiana had not been there with us, I can see that an indispensable dimension would have been left out. She was the natural, spontaneous depth dimension that completed the whole enterprise. I can remember a lot of things I thought and might have said but didn't, because Christiana was there and I knew they were not true.

Cleome Wadsworth, a research associate and later a friend, recalled how on her first day at the clinic she became aware of Morgan's importance to the clinic and to Murray. In a taped interview, she reminisced about Christiana Morgan:

Well, they had a little house, a very cozy little house off the Yard. It was like going into a home. The room where they ate was also where they had seminars. The table would be laid, and they would have sandwiches and coffee. . . . And she was always there, sort of like a mother in the background, the Great Earth Mother. The way I discovered her, you might say . . . at a seminar one evening, Harry came in and sat down at his desk (we were all sitting around), and I saw him look around the room and then I saw him look down and he looked up again; he looked around, then he bent over like this and looked in one direction, then he straightened up and started on his lecture. Well, now, being an intuitive type, I got all that gesture and I said, "Ah, there is something over there in the corner." I looked around and saw this handsome lady who always wore fantastic Indian jewelry and usually a red dress, and she wasn't quite as old as I was, but she was more or less my age. I said, "Ah, that's it, that's the other part of this little house; that's what makes things run."

Then she came to talk to me once or twice, and Harry seemed to like me. One day I was quite overcome with joy; she invited me to go to her place in the country for a weekend and I said, "Well, of course, I know that you're the other part of Harry Murray." She said, "But how do you know this?" I said I just felt it, and so this endeared us to each other, because she became very intimate with me and told me the other parts of her life.

During the early 1930s, Christiana Morgan was not only handsome but at the height of her beauty. Her face had filled out a bit, while her expression both softened and strengthened. Her nervous edginess was giving way to a calm assurance that combined authority with a lush, even voluptuous, acceptance of her sensuality and power. She was a striking presence at the clinic. A succession of clinic members and students regarded her as their mentor and as the de facto hostess who organized and supervised the clinic's day program, as well as its famous lunches around an Arthurian oval table. She presided at staff meetings, pouring afternoon tea as people gathered to discuss their subjects and make presentations. At first, she and her housekeeper made sandwiches, but Murray soon brought in a cook to prepare and serve more elaborate lunches. Besides her clinic and analytic work, Morgan, as lady of the house, supervised the cook, planned the meals, and saw to all the many details, such as flowers for the table, that maintained the homelike yet quietly luxurious environment that awed and delighted the graduate students and visitors.

At the lunches, which were often accompanied by wine, Murray and his guests and colleagues strove to outdo one another in Camelot-like jousts for their associates' and their "Lady Morgana's" favor. The conversations and ideas sparkled with a brilliance that was never quite matched in their execution. Tuesday and Thursday lunches were kept for in-depth discussions of various puzzling and interesting cases, while Murray reserved one day a week for an often renowned guest, who discussed his own work and added to the excitement of their own. Among the more noted of the visitors were Harry's friends Conrad Aiken, Alfred North Whitehead, Archibald MacLeish, Lewis Mumford, and C. G. Jung, as well as such diverse people as Katharine Cornell, Felix Frankfurter, Jean Piaget, Paul Robeson, and Aldous Huxley. Harvard's best minds, regardless of their discipline, came to cross-fertilize, as Murray declared, "with cuttings from [their] field." It seemed that anyone of note who interested Murray and came through Cambridge was invited; a calendar for a February in the early years, for instance, listed among the guests: George Miller, I. A. Richards, Paul Tillich, Wallace Stevens, and Karl Binger. Christiana Morgan was not always present, but when she was, her ability to draw people out caused Murray and others to shine brightly and choose their words with particular care.

Those who knew Morgan well and may have suspected her relationship with Murray spoke of her laugh and Murray's sensitivity to its occasionally ironic and mocking tone. This would cut into Murray as nothing else could, and served, as Robert White noted, to keep the group and Murray honest amid their flights of fancy. One member of the clinic, the Finn Risto Fried, who became a distinguished psychologist, teacher at the University of Jyvaskyla, and authority on terrorist personality types, later reminisced about his years at the clinic. He had heard a rumor that Morgan and Murray were lovers and used a room at the top of the clinic for trysts. The young graduate student was so full of admiration for the two that when he found himself in need of a place to woo a responsive Radcliffe woman, he brought her to the same room after hours, finding the encounter superbly erotic. In a more serious vein, Fried was impressed by the amount of work he and others accomplished at the clinic and went on to recall Murray, the lunches, and one of the clinic visitors:

> Certainly [it] was the most exciting place I have ever worked at. Murray radiated an enthusiasm that was infectious. He was excited about his own ideas, he was excited about other people's ideas, he made people feel that they themselves were exciting. I especially remember the lunches. The cook was a black woman of great culinary skill, who invariably served fresh-baked rolls along with the main course. And we drank Chilean white wine—Murray had discovered a brand that was of a quality unusual for its relatively low price and had stocked the cellar with a generous supply. Around the table would be various members of the staff, assistants, and, not infrequently, a distinguished visitor from out of state or abroad. Sometimes we planned research, sometimes we talked politics ("Did you know that a native American male has a much better chance, statistically, of becoming President of the U.S. than president of Harvard?"). I think that Murray came up with more original research ideas during any one luncheon session than most psychologists do in a lifetime. . . .
>
> The visitor who most impressed me was Jean Piaget. Accustomed as he was to visits from well-known scientists, Murray himself admired Piaget so much that he was uncharacteristically nervous in anticipation of the visit. A few minutes short of [the lunch] hour, he happened to look out the window and noticed that the front lawn was littered. He asked me to help him clean it up. We both were bent over, picking up trash, when a courteous voice inquired whether this was the Harvard Clinic Annex—and there was Piaget, right in front of us, extending his

hand for a handshake—and there were Murray and I, both hands full of Popsicle sticks and chewing gum wrappers. Piaget had a very warm, informal manner and was easy to get close to; after he had held a first-rate lecture, he had an animated discussion with us, and I had an opportunity to ask him many questions.

The clinic welcomed and accepted women far more than was normal then or for many years afterward at Harvard. Besides Christiana Morgan, and because of her example, the clinic admitted a succession of strong and talented female research assistants, graduate students, and administrative assistants. The number of women who were trained at the clinic and then went on to productive work elsewhere was high. This was due partly to the relative openness to women in depth psychology in the 1920s and '30s, and partly Murray's perception that his subjects behaved differently with different interviewers and testers, so that he valued diverse ages and genders on his staff. More important, though, was Murray's own admiration for quick wit and intelligence and his receptiveness to talent. Thanks to Morgan's success, Murray became a proponent of women as working colleagues and considered himself a feminist in this respect even before there was such a word. Though he was a humanist, welcoming and encouraging excellence wherever he found it, he considered his female staff, colleagues, and students women first and scholars second and, because he was a man of his time, did not expect them to progress in the same way or require the same advancement he gave to male scholars. Still, Murray wrote of the high caliber of these women and their contribution to the clinic in a way that echoed his appreciation of Morgan, though—like Jung—he perceived women's talents as useful, first of all, to men:

> the skill of women in therapy and psychological research [is] on a par with that of men—but today they can fulfill a special function: to correct what men have said and to say what they have not said about female psychology. Moreover, there are a few women—gnostic women—who have the gift to quicken minds to their fertilities, a power which some creative men in their indebtedness have had sufficient stature to acknowledge.

Perhaps the most notable, besides Christiana Morgan, were Isabelle Kendig, a member of the original team; Marjorie Ingalls, Murray's longtime secretary and administrative assistant; and Harriet Robey, a novelist and trained analyst, who joined the second research team. Robey was a motherly, middle-aged woman who struck up conversations with the subjects and later recorded acute clinical observations, which were usually verified by subsequent test results. She and Morgan were remembered as two of the clinic's best interviewers and test administrators. In the early years, they were joined by Maria Rickers-Ovsiankina, the future expert on Rorschach interpretations; and research assistants Elizabeth Cobb, Ruth Peterson, and Esther Whitman. The influential Norwegian psychologist Ase Skard studied at Radcliffe in 1931–32, making the clinic her headquarters. In her brief autobiography, she stated that at the clinic, "the purely human values were as important as scholarship. I have never been part of a milieu and a working team where research at the highest level was combined with so much of warmth, mutual good will and assistance, without a shadow of suspicion or envy."

Christiana Morgan would never have considered herself the pioneer that she was. She was well aware of her limitations in academic circles and, although she played a full and creative part in the clinic as a psychologist and research assistant, she neither discussed with her women colleagues, nor had the consciousness even to formulate, the differences in how she and her male colleagues approached their jobs and the ways their contributions were received. She would not have been working at the clinic but for her relationship with Henry Murray, nor would she have had the clinic's support were it not for his backing; thus it seemed obvious to her to focus on Murray's advancement rather than her own.

For the first ten years of the Harvard Psychological Clinic, Morgan and Murray delighted in discussing their plans for it as well as for their more private life. Together, they enjoyed the clinic's growing reputation and nurtured it as if it were a favorite child. Morgan, especially, focused on the spirit of the place. She insisted on the value of fostering a good working atmosphere and helped create a program that balanced hard work with restorative lunches, lectures, formal and informal gatherings, and play. She spoke on behalf of the staff, ensuring that they were allowed to create their own working rhythms, with much leeway in their hours. Though Morgan and Murray kept up professional appearances, the intensity of their connection imbued the clinic with special vitality. Morgan enjoyed reinforcing the undercurrent of sexuality in their day-to-day work together. To this end, she invented signals that communicated erotic messages to Murray in public:

The Signs: Red Bracelet = I want your body. Sapphire Pendant = I have something to tell you. Navaho Necklace = I want to help with therapeutic problems. Red beads = I love you very much but do not need you—Play, talk etc. White = I am tired, quiet, depressed. I want your arms. Gold necklace = I am exultant but do not need you. Navajo metal beads = I am working Clinic, everything is fine. I do not need you. Nothing = domestic troubles.

It both amused and excited them to play with the provocative nature of their double relationship as colleagues and lovers. Calling herself "Wona" and Harry "Mansol" for their identity as lovers— names they used for each other in private and in their notes, letters, and diaries—Christiana noted some of this in her diary.

Winter 1934. Wona's extreme erotic consciousness— awareness of her bodily physical sexual sensations— Accompaniment to lunches & meetings at Clinic.
1934. *The Wisdom of the Body*
Winter 1933–34. The winter at Fairfax—lunching together—and making love afterwards almost every day. Then going to Clinic meetings aflame with Mansol's body.

In contrast to periods of such intensity, there were times when Christiana was overlooked in the press of Harry's many other interests; these were the times when she fought her winter cycle of depressions and stayed away from the clinic, seeing her patients at home. Maintaining the relationship became her responsibility, as Harry began to consider the clinic the major focus of his attention. Once, disturbed by their failure to reach equilibrium in their work together, she wrote to Murray about her fears, attacking him as less than her perfect knight.

I am filled with pain about it.
The Old Man [Jung] said that this wouldn't go because you were too young and so your work wasn't at the point of being routine. It would demand too much creative energy on your part to make your place in the world and deal at the same time with your unconscious. So far we have managed. But this is a dangerous place. You have your lectures to write which is a great effort. Your energy must be withdrawn from your unconscious. This forces you apart from me. Your ideas are not yet formulated or

organized. You don't want what I have to give you in your work. It would only serve to disturb you. We are not ready to be together in work yet. Nor do you want now the intensity of our life together. So then what have we ahead of us? If I become unreal to you and fade out during this period which may last several years, all that we have made is lost. You will repress things in yourself for a certain time and then this process which we have been through will have to begin all over again for you with some other woman. This is why I have such a terrible sense of wanting to make myself real to you with a ruthless intensity. We have nothing else to go on now but to cling to the stern reality of each other and to have faith that moves mountains. We must be so real to each other that such a situation as at the Clinic today will never be possible again. We were vague, amorphous, polite. You were entirely withdrawn from me. We had no contact other than surface politeness. Under the circumstances ahead of us we will often be withdrawn in our souls from each other, and if we have no actual sense of each other's reality, then this whole thing falls down. Oh, my Love, this is so dangerous. I am utterly terrified. Only by a mighty faith shall we live now.

Only a few of their colleagues observed the depth of the struggle Morgan was undergoing. Saul Rosenzweig was the first. He occupied the office opposite hers and came to know her as well as anyone at the clinic. From the beginning, he had been deeply affected by her depth and her beauty, though his infatuation soon turned into respect and love. Rosenzweig, a brilliant young scholar, was still an undergraduate during his first year at the clinic, and nobody took him seriously until Morgan became his supporter and mentor. He credited her with seeing his talent, wholeheartedly accepting him, and giving him a start in his exceptionally productive career. They liked each other at once, Morgan coquettishly telling him how much she was attracted to Jewish men and how much he reminded her of Chaim Weizmann, but also taking him under her wing like a son or brother. After their work was finished for the day, she and Saul would have long discussions in the privacy of their offices over sherry and the cookies he kept for her. She impressed him with her knowledge of psychoanalytic theory, especially the contributions of Nietzsche, Freud, Adler, and Jung. She listened and reflected back to him what he most needed to see—

the importance of his own ideas. Rosenzweig and his career flowered. He remembered far preferring Morgan's deep and steady support to Murray's initial intoxicating exuberance, which, in Rosenzweig's case at least, turned into neglect as Murray's enthusiasm leapt away to embrace ever new persons and projects.

Neither Morgan nor Rosenzweig had felt comfortable with the original emphasis of the clinic in Prince's time; after his death, they became the chief supporters of Murray's effort to shift its focus, Rosenzweig becoming the spearhead for psychodynamic experimental rigor. Rosenzweig attributed this new orientation, especially its emphasis on the production of fantasies as a method to study personality, in large part to Morgan's visions. For a while, Rosenzweig worked with Morgan on a team that was devising ways to measure personality through the subjects' production of fantasy material; his task was to create measurements that would validate existing psychoanalytic concepts, such as Freud's repression theory. They were among the few early measurements that stood up empirically. Sixty years later, Rosenzweig wrote that Morgan deserved recognition for her groundbreaking contributions to personality theory; he believed she was perhaps most overlooked for her work on values. Fairly competitive himself, he recognized her lovers' contest with Murray but was amazed at her lack of interest in receiving acknowledgment for her work. Rosenzweig criticized Murray's sometimes overwhelming charisma and narcissism, as well as the era's pervasive blindness to a woman's—especially a beautiful woman's—scientific accomplishments. But Rosenzweig also noted Morgan's diffidence and her lack of skill or practice in standing up for herself in an academic situation. Often after a meeting during which one or another of the men, including Murray, presented her ideas as if they were his own, or took credit for concrete work she had done, Rosenzweig would ask her why she had not fought for recognition. She would smile ironically, implying that she was too proud to enter the fray; though she pretended not to care, saying she had more important things to do than concern herself with boyish competition, he noted her subsequent anger and low spirits. He felt she obtained silent satisfaction, nevertheless, from knowing how much she had created, whether credited or uncredited, and to what degree her visions and work had become key components of the clinic's program.

For the first fifteen years of the Harvard Psychological Clinic, Morgan not only saw patients but contributed fully to the clinic's comprehensive series of studies. Though Murray recognized her special skill in interviewing subjects and administering and interpreting projective tests, as he grew older he downplayed, or grew increasingly forgetful of, the extent of Morgan's work at the clinic, subsuming it under his own and speaking of her lack of involvement. However, Rosenzweig, Robert White, and many other colleagues attest to her contribution as a vital, active, and original team member who was central to all aspects of their work.

Perhaps Morgan's most original contribution was the Thematic Apperception Test. Rosenzweig sat in on the meeting at which the idea for it first came up. After he left for postdoctoral work in Worcester, he recognized Morgan as the chief author of the completed work and requested that she present it at his hospital's grand rounds. He recalled that the idea of the Thematic Apperception Test (TAT), which was to become one of the most popular projective tests in clinical psychology, germinated from a question raised by a student in one of Murray's classes. The class had been discussing fantasies and Jung's idea of active imagination. Cecilia Roberts reported that her son, when ill, one day greeted his mother when she came home from work with stories he had made up about the pictures in the magazines she had left for him. She wondered if pictures couldn't similarly release fantasy material in a clinical setting. Murray discussed this enthusiastically with Morgan, then presented the idea at a lunch meeting. Morgan and Murray subsequently developed a set of pictures whose objective was to elicit responses that revealed the drives, sentiments, emotions, and complexes a subject either harbored in his unconscious or wanted to conceal. Through analyzing the fantasy material, a trained observer would be led to the underlying variables in his patient's personality. The test shortened and clarified therapy in the same way that active imagination had helped Morgan in her work with Jung.

For a time, everyone in the clinic and his or her family scoured magazines for pictures, experimenting with ways to elicit fantasies. One method Murray especially liked was to have his daughter, Josie, and her friends play a game called Murder, which took place in the dark and during which a secretly designated "murderer" would stalk and "kill" his prey while the detective would try to discover him. Afterward Murray would show the children photos of faces; he compared stories they made up when scared or excited with those they produced at a more halcyon time. Both Harry's daughter and Christiana's son remembered these games, as well as days spent responding to a variety of images. Morgan played a main role in choosing the final pictures and assessing different ways to administer them; she was the first to utilize the test, giving an early version to an anorexic patient (one of the first diagnosed cases of anorexia in Boston). Her patient's responses indicated that the test, even in its rough form, could facilitate therapy by uncovering an individual's core complexes.

After Morgan's case presentation, many a clinic meeting was spent discussing the TAT, while the analysts' closets began to overflow with pictures. At first, they were simple black-and-white photographs of people's faces. However, recollecting her own active imagination and the power of the drawings that she, Robert Edmond Jones, and Will Morgan had produced, Christiana started collecting and then drawing ambiguous scenes, many of them in the style of her old instructors at the Art Students League. In the final form of the test, eighteen cards (nine pictures specifically for males, nine for females) depicting humans in equivocal situations, plus one blank card, were presented to the subject over two sessions. The trained administrator of the test elicited a story for each that could be subjected to a somewhat standardized interpretation.

Morgan stressed the importance of the setting for the TAT and the personality of the examiner. Well versed in the delicacy of working with fantasies, she emphasized the need for a friendly, congenial, and encouraging approach. From her notes, it is evident that Morgan spent much time both at the clinic and at home during the following years writing up parts of their findings. When their article was finally published, in 1935, Morgan's name preceded Murray's as chief author. The test was immediately successful and soon became a best-seller at Harvard University Press; for many years it was second only to Harvard's music series. Morgan's voice and style pervade the text, intermingled with Murray's more scientific interpolations; she drew six of the nineteen pictures in current use— "the old standbys," as the third revision of the test describes them. Though Morgan's name was inexplicably and inexcusably dropped from later editions of the test, her contemporaries vouched for her authorship. Murray, in later life, would argue that he had just put Morgan's name there to encourage her, or that Morgan preferred not to be listed. Robert White, who eventually took over the clinic, especially stressed her right to be cited as first author, without slighting Murray's equally vital contribution.

Morgan went on to write two further articles on the TAT with Murray. One was a Jungian and psychoanalytic explanation for a 1935 journal article in *Archives of Neurology and Psychiatry,* the other a chapter for the clinic's first book, *Explorations in Personality,* published in 1938, where she is given pride of place with six first coauthors after Henry Murray (twenty-one other clinic workers appear in ranks below the first six names). In both articles, Murray and Morgan drew on her visions, stressing how fantasies give the trained reader (or analyst) an excellent view into his or her subject's unconscious.

Further work by Morgan often remains in note form or as part of team research and appears throughout the clinic records, on almost every project. Especially significant are Morgan's interview and testing techniques; a tentative "Philosophy of Aesthetic Criticism"; research on what she called "Attributes and Vectors," which included interesting work on superiority, attention, bondage and rape fantasies, masochism, freedom, and nurture, again mining examples from her own visions, as she had done for her work on fantasy in art, religion, and science. A further contribution to the TAT itself was a fourteen-page document Morgan wrote on the theme of the claustrum, or enclosed space. What was especially idiosyncratic to Morgan, and prefigured the stance of later feminist psychologists, was her emphasis on herself as part of the experiment or therapy, herein recalling her early childhood experience and trauma. Through careful analysis and copious use of case material, she proposed a rethinking of the Freudian (and Jungian) concept of the desire to return to the womb. The article would still be welcome in analytic journals today. Morgan first analyzed the concept and its use, defining claustral fantasy as that of a safe and secluded space to which one could retreat from the "dangerous turmoil" of the world and within which creativity could bloom. She traced the fantasy back to a longing to be safely contained within a nurturing mother's arms. She found this type of fantasy indicative of introversion, the subject typically having "one or more secluded and safe havens," where he or she could daydream, ruminate, and escape from extraverted demands. The presence of claustral images indicated the introverted subject's need to avoid harm, and showed that he or she was substituting a geographical and physical spot for an absent loved, supporting figure. Morgan posited that a person who produced many claustral images would also typically remember certain places and activities of childhood with special nostalgia and yearning, and be drawn toward death. "Due to the resemblances between birth and death or more precisely between death & the prenatal condition of unconscious, & due to the nearness of passivity & death the S. [subject] may become preoccupied with the thought of his own death. He may even contemplate a passive type of death such as taking a drug or drowning."

It would not be going too far to assume that the subject she named "Chris" in this article was herself. The subject shared Morgan's early lack of maternal care, her mother's rigid aloofness, Morgan's own labile emotions, introversion, artistic interest, and manual dexterity, in addition to her predilection for certain safe places and scenes (in Christiana's case, her beloved childhood summer home at York and gardening there with her father); Chris occupied Christiana's own family position as the middle of three children. In a few pages, Morgan caught the essence of an artistic and wounded introvert and set out her thesis with sensitivity and precision. Morgan was clearly capable of extensive original work of this sort but spent far more time at the clinic with patients and doing basic research for Murray, especially on needs and values, as well as on Melville, Romanticism, and the Byronic hero.

During these years of productive work, Christiana fought to maintain a viable personal life with Murray and with other friends and lovers. She became an invaluable friend to Alfred North Whitehead, who allowed her to charm and inspire him while at the same time she remained close to his wife. Most of her friends now, though, were restricted to the clinic or to the few outside it who she felt would understand her relationship with Harry. Will remained in the Southwest for longer and longer periods, and on his return, when he felt well enough, busied himself with writing Jungian-oriented articles on aspects of Indian beliefs and religion. He made fewer and fewer demands on his wife. Both she and Murray continued their practice of analyzing and reanalyzing what their love meant. Murray would imbue their romance with almost archetypal grandeur, in an effort to increase its power over him. In spite of all this attention to the *history* of their love, Morgan was coming to realize that the reality was not far different from any man's relationship with his mistress. When they were together, their love flourished and was often filled with intense passion and drama, but it lacked consistency. The nature of their love and the amount of time they spent together changed with the tide of Murray's enthusiasms. His promises and commitments, though undoubtedly heartfelt, were seldom reliable, and Christiana, always preferring ecstatic intensity, grew to equate the strength of their brief peak moments and of her yearning loneliness with deepening love.

As the years sped by, the clinic, which had occupied so much of their time and mutual energy, often seemed to be spinning off in as many different directions as Murray's whims; the group's endeavors were tending to become more and more complicated and diffuse rather than solidly contained and publishable. Murray's book on Melville remained unwritten, his projected writing about Morgan's visions continually deferred. She saw their love becoming compartmentalized into rooms on Massachusetts Avenue or the property near Newburyport and restricted to the times that Murray chose. Though there were days and sometimes months of profound union, they increasingly encountered each other at the clinic like two strangers.

Perhaps the earliest threat to their union came from a research assistant who for a time enthralled Harry. In 1931, Eleanor Jones had come to the clinic through her friendship with Conrad Aiken's young second wife, Clarissa. Eleanor was different from Murray's other fleeting attractions, being far more intelligent and far more kind. Though she wrote darkly Gothic stories and was in the throes of a marital collapse, Eleanor was a warm, pretty woman with a disposition as sweet as Pierre's first love, Lucy, in the Melville tale. Like Lucy's, Eleanor's beauty reflected a profound goodness of heart, a giving, caring nature. These qualities combined with wit and intelligence to offer Harry the solace and mothering he had never experienced in a woman. While Christiana would prod, rage, compete, and demand the best from him, Eleanor Jones, her polar opposite, fell deeply in love with her charismatic, mercurial, and needy boss, and enfolded him with seemingly endless comfort.

Christiana called Eleanor "the witch"—albeit the white witch to her own dark passions—and endured for a while the torture of hearing Harry pass by her office door to visit Eleanor. "Struggling at the Clinic to deal with patients. Listening to M.'s step on the stair & hearing him go up to the witches' room on the third floor. Anguish & anguish. Stretched on the rack of racks. Was there ever such pain?"

The following spring, Morgan had what she termed a nervous breakdown, which she disguised from the others as a serious cold. She left her analysis with Sachs and went to see a motherly Jungian analyst, Frances Wickes, who had become her friend. When summer came, Morgan persuaded Wickes to come to York to continue the

208 analysis. Wickes advised Morgan to stay away from the clinic until things resolved themselves, and she did so for the four months from October 1931 through January 1932, fleeing to the comforts of nature, of her property near Newburyport, and of kindly "Mother Wickes," as Christiana's friend Jonah called her. The terse notations Morgan made in her diary during the crisis mark the history of her despair:

> Mar. 1931. During breakdown—letter [to Murray]: I didn't know how tired I was of myself with people—how tired I was of pulses and blood rhythms, attractions & repulsions. I see how you can lift us out of the bloodiness of things. I see that your rhythm has never had a chance to sweep clean through.
> Spring 1931: Will comforting me in his arms—trying to soothe my pain. My playing the Bach— Sudden strength in me—remembering what Jung had said—"He may not be good enough." Spring 1931. The witch at the Tower. Lunch at Topsfield [Jo's and Harry's country house, a fifteen-minute drive from Christiana's in Newbury-port]—Alfred Cohn there—Seeing M & witch in grave-yard. Picture Exhibit at Clinic. The *horrible* old dead glove that the witch exhibited—M laughing. My memory of the *living hand* of the trances— Horror and more horror—the trances still shining. Oh lost. Pain beyond all pain.
> Summer 1931: A horrible time in the summer at Rad-nor. M for dinner. My making a huge feast. Everything wrong. Mansol came to Property for an afternoon. Bleak & terrible. Told me when he died he wanted to die in my arms— But everything seemed lost.
> A terrible time with M at Radnor Wild with grief. Driving back to Frances [Wickes] at York. Her animad-versions against Jung. In spite of my terrible grief I rose up & said she was wrong—that in spite of everything the trances were the Way. Not Jung—but M was the failure. —Frances Wickes at York. —M. saying to Witch—"I have too much respect for Christiana to believe that she is jeal-ous." —Coming down from York to see M who had been away all summer. His telling me over the telephone that he had been to see the witch first.
> Aug. 1931 M spends week in hospital [for treatment of a kidney stone]. —Sept. "I am no longer leaning heavily on our continuity" [letter from Morgan to Murray].

Christiana, along with many of her iconoclastic generation and class, had felt free to take other lovers and experience other entanglements, but they had always been secondary to her love for Harry. She soon realized, however, that his affair with Eleanor was far more serious. Christiana and Mike Murray had continued to be close friends and occasional lovers, when they were both so disposed, as long as he was in Cambridge, and through his divorce and remarriage. After the breakup of his marriage, Mike had followed Christiana's and his brother's footsteps, going to Jung to be analyzed and becoming a psychoanalyst himself. Morgan and both Murray men proclaimed the new morality that extolled the senses, believing that they had the right to investigate the farthest boundaries of adult consensual sex. Neither Harry nor Christiana felt an excuse was needed for dalliances, although she derived perhaps as much rationale from his absence as from her freethinking. Morgan was left too often and too long alone, as Murray's duties toward his wife, the demands of his growing career, and society absorbed his time and energy.

In the final months of 1930, during a time when Will was in the Southwest and somewhat before Harry's infatuation with Eleanor, Christiana met another of the gentle boys who reminded her of her Bills—this time a young and gifted but unstable philosophy student, Ralph Eaton, who was a protégé of her neighbor and good friend, Alfred North Whitehead. Eaton admired Morgan with flamboyant exuberance and attracted her with his devotion; they soon became lovers, Eaton responding to the liaison with passionately single-minded intensity. The affair proved chaotic almost from the beginning, for Eaton insisted on Morgan's absolute fidelity to him, refusing to accept the centrality of Harry Murray in her life. His supposed gentleness shifted to wild ultimatums, heavy drinking, and suicidal threats and gestures. When he wouldn't or couldn't listen to her, Morgan and Murray succeeded in sending him off to Zurich for analysis in the fall of 1931.

Just when Eaton needed a tight rein on his growing hysteria, Jung, perceiving the richness of Eaton's unconscious, carried him off into archetypal realms that, alas, further unbalanced the young man. Eaton started to become delusional. He didn't remain in Zurich long enough for Jung to rectify his mistake, but panicked and fled. Jung wrote forebodingly to Murray: "He seems to be promising. If only America doesn't swallow him up and grind him to dust." But America and the psychosis did swallow him up; Eaton bolted back home to see Morgan in early spring of 1932. Alarmed at his incoherence, she refused to meet him, urging instead that he get psychiatric care. Eaton responded by drinking even more heavily and becoming increasingly manic. Murray and Morgan finally got him to a hospital, but the attendants did not heed their warning and left Eaton unguarded. Desperate, Ralph Eaton escaped and put an end to his life in the woods near Murray's house in Topsfield.

The tragedy was a further blow to Christiana; she felt responsible, having decided she had treated their affair too lightly. She may also have felt great empathy, Eaton's suicide being a response to the loss of love. From then on, suicide echoed in Christiana's research, as if she felt impelled to sound and re-sound the icy current of his death.

Harry, meanwhile, was falling more and more in love with Eleanor, thinking he might break up with both his wife and Christiana and marry Eleanor instead. The same winter that Jung analyzed Eaton, Murray traveled to Zurich to discuss the mess he had gotten himself into and this new form of his anima problem. By that time, Jung had received Morgan's three completed vision books and utilized them as the basis for his series of Visions Seminars. In a strange inversion, Jung used Morgan's material much as a Harvard Psychology Clinic subject would have used TAT pictures: he put himself, his method, and his own complexes into Christiana's visions, playing fast and loose with their reality. However, Jung's method proved ideal for teaching others about his own methodology, and the lectures attracted a growing audience. Morgan's images clearly excited and inspired Jung, who extended the seminars for four and a half years. But rather than examining what they said about her psychology and development, Jung appropriated them to animate and elucidate his theories. Ralph Eaton had also attended the seminars, and Christiana's exotic archetypal dramas further inflamed and unbalanced him. As Jung was mining Morgan's visions, Jung met with Murray and sided with him man to man, though he also criticized him for not having learned what he needed to from Morgan. The previous fall, Murray had written Jung requesting a visit and setting out his problem; Jung answered with an acerbic, even brutal letter about Christiana and Eleanor.

Küsnacht–Zurich
Seestrasse 228
21st of Sept
1931

Dear Dr. Murray,
I am sorry for Christiana, that she didn't succeed in whatever her quest was, or perhaps she succeeded and didn't
know it—which—alas—is a defeat just as well. I can't be
sorry for you, because you learn and experience, and you
got rid of a bother—a thing that became a nuisance— You
have not learned the one thing through Christiana, beyond
which there is no further experience, and therefore you
have to try the opposite. In the meantime the years are
hastening on and something in you slowly begins to orient
itself. If you know, you can share such consciousness, if
not, you get all the more entangled, which blind people
call liberation.

At all events, keep your eyes skinned and try to see
the symbol in this new reality.
My very best wishes!
Cordially yours C. G. Jung

P.S. Concerning Chr. There is nothing to be done, than
to tell the truth as plain as it is. A woman suffers a relationship to be and she also suffers it not to be. The deepest
nature in woman knows that things are and are not, and
both facts are equally good to her—or bad. That she went
to Fr. Wickes—well, all that is weak and infantile in her,
calls for the mother, all that is unconscious in her strives
back to the sea, whence it originated. I hope it will not
mean final dissolution.

Upon his return from Zurich, Harry continued to waver
among Jo, Christiana, and Eleanor. He delighted in the relief provided by Eleanor's sweet ease but recoiled from hurting any of
them; consequently, he profoundly wounded all three in his gyring
web of neediness and his desperately narcissistic love of each of
them. Christiana took him back as a lover and returned to her work
at the clinic, where Eleanor now no longer got all of Harry's devotion. It was Eleanor Jones, however, who finally solved Harry's
dilemma. In the summer of 1933, she confronted Harry in the clinic
one day upon his return from the country with Christiana and, after
an uncharacteristic scene, gave him an ultimatum to choose between
them. It was just what he preferred not to do. And so, unable to
tolerate her position or Harry's wild swings of feeling, Eleanor left
the clinic a year and half after their affair had begun. Harry wrote
to her and, a few years later, attempted to resume a closer connection
with her, under the pretext of looking over the writing she had

been doing. Her response exhibited a brilliant and hard-won comprehension of the dynamic behind Harry's problems with his work and with his co-workers, his friends, his students, and, most important, for her, the women he loved.

212

Eleanor wrote that she felt comforted and reassured by Harry's attempt to restore the current between them but that she didn't altogether trust it. She had been too burned to renew contact with him and feared that by exposing herself and her writing to his evaluation she would again become subject to the negative criticism that all too often followed Murray's overexuberant praise. She went on to tell him:

> Your over valuation of my gifts in this letter was a little frightening even when I understood it as the expression of impulsive warm feeling rather than a judgment. It remained frightening because of this tendency to over commit yourself and then the need to draw back afterward. I understand and love that out-rushing impulsiveness, and I understand I think how you must defend yourself afterwards from possible consequences—but I dread them none-the-less. . . .
>
> Maybe I'm all wrong but it seems like that reaction pattern that has troubled you so much—always your warm impetuous heart going all out and then coming to the next day and thinking "good god, what have I got into now"— and almost pretending you don't see the person, or maybe dropping some rebuff of some kind.
>
> So I want to tell you—thank you and its all right. You have renewed relationship—but don't, don't be frightened by having done so too impetuously. Like all the cruel things you say you don't mean—you don't entirely mean the other either.

Christiana, meanwhile, resumed her place in Harry's heart and sought her own precarious balance amid her lover's swerves between overvaluation and disgust. For a time Harry and Christiana became very close again; their relationship slowly healed as she sat beside him at their apartment in Fairfax Hall and sewed, while he wrote "for hours and hours—days & days—weeks & weeks." Harry, meanwhile, fantasized stopping his analysis with Alexander and being analyzed by Christiana instead.

In October of that same year, before her son went off to Exeter and while Will was still away, Christiana moved from her Memorial Drive apartment to the lower half of a house at 11 Hilliard Street;

between Brattle and Mount Auburn streets, it was a few blocks from the clinic. Christiana had the living room and entry-way painted a lacquered black enlivened with Chinese red trim and decorated them with Oriental pictures and furniture, some of which Harry bought or brought from his and Jo's house on Mount Vernon Street in Boston. Christiana entertained a variety of clinic people there as well as friends from her childhood and newer friends such as the Whiteheads and Sophie and Lewis Mumford. Harry visited circumspectly but preferred meeting at Fairfax or in the country.

Councie remembered Harry's visits and the strain of having to telephone his mother from Shady Hill before he came home in the afternoon, just in case her lover was there. Councie was happy to leave Cambridge for Exeter. He did very well, flourishing in the company of boys who valued him. The strain of always feeling last in his mother's heart and last among her interests ameliorated somewhat by their recognition.

Will's health continued to deteriorate. In late 1933, he finally had to give up his work with the Navajo and return to Cambridge, retiring to the dark and quietly opulent Hilliard Street house. He soon became bedridden, and he died of tuberculosis in May 1934, not yet forty years old. The disease had been contracted in the trenches of the Great War; he was one of its last casualties. His son declared that it was not the war but a broken heart that had killed him, for the only woman he had loved preferred another man.

A dream Will had a year or so before his death expressed some of the pain the lovers were causing the people around them, especially Jo Murray and himself:

> I was sitting in a restaurant—Josephine came in. She seemed drawn to me with the attitude that we were two together. She sat close to me with her head on my shoulder. Then she was sitting across the table. I said: "Well what do you make out of it?" With much vehemence she said: "It is not what we thought it might be. Harry is full of physical passion for her. He is never at rest. Even in my house he doesn't conceal his passion but storms around. Did you know they were married in a room upstairs in our house? When they are together he spends every minute of it in the bedroom." She implied that Christiana was not as bad. I was tempted to say, "Here are the conditions which are inherent in the situation. You cannot change

them" but refrained, fearing that she would reflect that I had quit.

Will Morgan published two monographs, "Navajo Dreams" and "Navajo Treatment of Sickness: Diagnosticians," in *The American Anthropologist*. Christiana went over other research material her husband had brought back with him, organizing and editing it for posthumous publication. The result was several substantial and well-researched monographs on aspects of Navajo culture, including a fascinating study entitled "Human-Wolves Among the Navajo"; an unpublished essay about a twenty-three-year-old Navajo woman, Yadiba, who had captured his imagination; and an unpublished study of Sioux culture, ritual, and healing. His undated article titled "Anthropology Today and Psychotherapy" credited Christiana Morgan for her "important contributions" and focused on his experience of the similarities between the Navajo nine-day healing ceremony of the Night Chant and Western psychotherapy and analysis. It seems that in the final years of his brief and tragic life, Will found a profession that engaged him. He applied his acute powers of observation, his Jungian interest in dreams, witchcraft, and shamanic healing, and his sensitive ability to feel his way into the Navajo's more gentle way of life, to describe a disintegrating world and vanishing way of life that in many ways echoed his own.

Christiana mourned her husband, recalling him as one of the amiable and gentle boys she liked to love and contrasting him with those who thrilled her and made her afraid, like Floyd Blair and Harry Murray. After Will's death, she kept up her work at the clinic, not without effort, writing in her diary of the final team meetings there before the summer break: "The terrible effort. Choking back the tears."

These years in the early and mid-thirties were as full of bereavement as they were of accomplishment. Christiana's father and mother had died within six months of each other, the year before Will's death; Mike Murray, who had recently become a psychoanalyst, died the year after, of Hodgkin's disease. These losses plus the pressure of Murray's and Morgan's partial and sporadic life exacted their toll.

A further upset had come in the spring of 1934, when Frances Wickes returned from a visit to Zurich and spoke of Carl Jung's handling of Christiana's visions; also, despite the stipulation of anonymity for Jung's use of her material, her identity had been guessed and was being whispered about by some of the participants in the seminars. Angry and upset, Morgan cabled Jung, insisting that he stop the seminars. Morgan objected not only because of his in- creasing disparagement of her as the material diverged more and more from the visions, but because she feared that her authorship would get back to Cambridge, implicating Murray and herself and hurting her tenuous professional and social life. Jung, having gone on far too long and strayed too far from her visions' substance, obliged, content to move the seminars on to Nietzsche's *Thus Spake Zarathustra* as a subject relevant to the ominous rise of National Socialism in Germany.

Morgan, somewhat relieved, turned back to her work at the clinic with renewed zeal and sought to solidify her position there as a psychoanalyst and an official member of the clinic. She labored for the next two years on the clinic's effort to complete the record of their work in *Explorations in Personality*. It was a monumental task. The invention of the various tests themselves were, as Robert White recalled, a heroic undertaking, but analyzing, codifying, and publishing their results was an even more daunting process. Mur- ray's exuberant enthusiasm and lack of knowledge in research design multiplied the material gathered, and before long the work reached Augean proportions.

In the middle of this, Morgan had found it difficult to seek external status for herself, because of her lack of academic degrees and because of her style: her instinct was that of a woman of her class—to be above it all and brush titles and tenure aside as nothing but Babbitry. She was of two minds, therefore, but also strength- ened, when in 1935 she was appointed a research fellow of Radcliffe College. This gave her some standing—even at a low rank—as an academic, and she maintained this title throughout her tenure at the clinic; her small salary, however, would always come out of the clinic's budget rather than the college's.

Morgan was relieved, too, when she and Jung patched up the breach between them. Jung came to Harvard to receive an honorary degree during its tercentenary celebration in 1936; Morgan and he had lunch and dinner together and took long walks in Harvard Yard. She presided at the clinic when he and other honorees, in- cluding Jung's mentor Pierre Janet came to lunch. Morgan seated Jung in the place of honor at her right, and he proceeded to scandalize some of his fellow dignitaries by spending more time flirting with his hostess than talking with them. During that same week, Jo

Murray met Jung for the first time over breakfast at the Faculty Club. Harry recalled that she had come wanting to reject Jung.
216 "But she was impressed by him. . . . She liked him. . . . She liked the cut of his jib." Jo has left no record of her feelings, but it seems as if her discretion as well as her good manners and good heart made the meeting pass uneventfully. By then Jo had become active in all sorts of social and charitable work, besides loving to travel and devoting herself to her daughter's education. She met her husband's continuing involvement with Christiana with outward acceptance but a pervasive inner sadness and private tears. There were rises and falls in Harry's attachment to her, as well as to Christiana and to other, less important, women in his life; Jo put on a brave front and made the best she could of their life together.

Christiana, however, was pressing for more time with Harry. After Will's death, she hoped, for a time, that they would be married. As she grew older, she had more and more difficulty accepting the ebb and flow of Murray's attention. In 1936, nearing forty, she wrote in her diary: "His way was to see her three or four times a week for three hours in the afternoon. He thought that this was a satisfactory form; and so she had to show him that longer and more consecutive periods were essential." She told him that their supposedly great love was nothing but "a provisional life." She wrote and spoke of how tired she was of the perpetual pendulum swing of his affection. Yet the very absences, the dizzying peaks and valleys of their affair, lent a frenzied intensity to their lives that both of them craved; they started to augment it, too, with Dionysian drinking and private ceremonies at Fairfax and at Newburyport.

Christiana's beauty, so lush in the early thirties, now took on a sterner, stormier quality, which the sculptor Gaston Lachaise captured as early as 1935. That winter he fashioned a torso of Morgan that emphasized her wildness and sexuality. When Alfred North Whitehead saw it, he exclaimed: "magnificent—absolutely magnificent. A great work. Not *you*—for you have a sense of humor. But very great. It is a primitive woman moving from one age to another. Terrible, magnificent,—a woman who would commit murder. A great primeval force. O, not you, not you at all as far as likeness goes. Good heavens! What have you inspired? Woman becoming, woman moving out of darkness into light. The most magnificent statue of a woman I have ever seen."

But it *was* very much her. The statue reflected an essential aspect of Christiana—a tumultuous energy—that would become ever more visible as the years progressed.

ELEVEN

Thunders
and Agitations

When . . . they enter
Into each others Bosom (which are universes of
     delight)
In mutual interchange . . . if they embrace &
     commingle
The Human Four-fold Forms mingle also in
     thunders of Intellect
But if the Emanations mingle not; with Storms
     & agitations
Of earthquakes & consuming fires they roll apart
     in fear

WILLIAM BLAKE,
Jerusalem

Though Christiana Morgan had known the Whiteheads ever since Altie, as she called him, started to drop by to visit her when they lived in the same building on Memorial Drive, their relationship deepened markedly during the menacing years just before World War II. Whitehead was a tall, gentle, yet dynamic man, thirty-six years older than Morgan. He had been in his early sixties and at the height of his intellectual stature when he left England to join Harvard's philosophy department. At first his wife's friend, Christiana soon became far more attached to Altie, finding an exciting reverberation between his ideas and her visions. Whitehead wrote most creatively when he had a beautiful, interested, and responsive listener to rouse and stimulate his thoughts. For many years his muse had been his wife, Evelyn, but now he found himself newly invigorated by Christiana.

Whitehead was secure enough to enjoy Morgan as his *femme inspiratrice* and to appreciate her strength. He had been a renowned mathematician in his youth at the University of Cambridge, then 217 a noted philosopher of physical sciences at the University of London; his work at Harvard opened new terrain. Enlivened by Morgan as well as by throngs of receptive students, he soon embarked on a new metaphysical philosophy concerning values, speculative cosmology, religious experience, and the historical relevance of metaphysical ideas in human experience. Whitehead had a lifelong interest in these subjects, as well as in history, education, poetry, and women's suffrage. He was an impassioned teacher and speaker, whose breadth of view and sensitivity to human values attracted Morgan's admiration and love. She delighted in stimulating her genius's imagination and responded to his appreciation by idolizing him, as she had her father, Chaim Weizmann, Carl Jung, and Harry Murray, and as she would, a few years later, yet another friend, Lewis Mumford.

At first, Christiana was put off by Altie, thinking him too brilliant and intellectual, but as they became more intimate, she understood how playful and childlike he could be; his freshness and lack of grandiosity appealed to her. Whitehead reciprocated, blossoming in her presence. They visited often in Cambridge and then in each other's summer houses, where even at breakfast, as Christiana put it, they would join in "delicious morning ruminations," playing with ideas and each other's imaginations as if they were toys. Morgan, in the same reminiscence, listed the things about Whitehead she prized: his kindness; his aesthetic sense and philosophy; his enjoyment of beauty and of others' talent; his appreciation of women; his simplicity, humor, expressiveness, loyalty, optimism; and his ability to evoke her love. She felt that Whitehead was in many ways similar to Jung; both men were her spiritual fathers and were powerful pioneers who, besides having deeply religious spirits, shared a zest and adventurousness that she prized highly. Both men also helped to give her the courage to lead her own unconventional life. Whitehead, though, held a closer place in her heart, because of his humility. Morgan faulted Jung in comparison, finding him, in spite of his protestations to the contrary, often arrogant and presumptuous about his Truth. Christiana, perhaps still smarting from Carl Jung's misreading of her in his seminars, criticized his sometimes authoritarian air of certainty, whereas "Altie conveys the pure joy in the living process of becoming conscious, the life joy in the formulation for its own sake. . . . He is simply speaking out of his own life and being" and not imposing it on others.

Whitehead combined in himself all the qualities that had drawn her to her Bills—humor, gentle sensitivity, and goodness—combined now with the electricity of Weizmann's brilliant mind and 219 worldly success. Unlike Harry, Altie was not competitive; he had the concentration to stay with one thing until he finished it, having no trouble developing his ideas into fully formed and published books. Altie's devotion and enduring loyalty to his very fragile wife also touched Christiana and made her love him all the more. As was true of all of Morgan's deepest attachments, it was not so much the physicality of the relationship that aroused her but the contact with his mind and the interplay with his spirit. They met most truly as lovers in this realm, and the children of their union leapt from his brain as ideas and books she helped him fertilize.

During the years of their friendship, Whitehead experienced a new surge of inspiration, writing nine books that probed the depths of his speculative mind. Among the ones she liked best were *Process and Reality, Adventures of Ideas,* and *Nature and Life,* all of which Whitehead discussed with Morgan, cherishing not so much her insights and comments but their power to engender his own. Morgan, in response, allowed him into her secret world; she showed him her vision books and revealed her relationship with Murray. This was something she had seldom risked before. Whitehead responded to her revelations with understanding, admiration, and support. In one of her letters to him, Christiana tried to put into words what his approval had meant to her: "How deeply you have influenced my life for you have fortified my purpose and had it not been for you I would have felt great loneliness on this journey."

After their meetings, Christiana would often make diary notes of their conversations, as if she were trying to understand the interplay of his genius and her muse.

Jan. 1940

Some very strange thing is happening between Altie and me. We were late arriving, & Evelyn told me that Altie had gone into a real depression for the moment because he thought I wasn't coming & didn't want to talk to him. When I did come and began to talk to him about all these articles he was just like a sky-rocket—& finally ended with the last two paragraphs he has been writing in his article. He kept looking at me all the evening when I was talking to Evelyn—so much so that it was really a pang to me. . . . Then we came to the subject of women—and

Altie said that the women he had taught were to him the most interesting students—as they always brought philosophy to a condition or situation in life—in which his strength as a philosopher was taxed. . . . Altie so precious and rare to my understanding tonight. I feel grateful that I have grown enough—not to know him—but find him—stir him—follow him—recognize him.

Jan. 19, 1941

Just home from Evelyn and Altie's. Evelyn wasn't feeling well, but Altie and I had a wonderful time together—I was so full of the theories & principles of democracy that I almost reduced him to a state of incoherence trying to keep up with me—which he loved. He is writing an article on Democracy & Religion. He is concerned with the pressing need for a religion & with the falsity of trying to make a religion out of Democracy. That religion must underlie all transitory social forms. I tried him out just a little on our relationship idea but he was so full of his own ideas that he had no ears—but we had a lovely time talking to each other with the minimum of communication but with a fine infection of mutual excitement. He looked happy and had such a light in his eye!

Oh dear—a sort of regression into my past which would depress me if it was anyone but Altie. But to make a light in *that* eye & excitement in *that* heart!

Whitehead and Morgan exulted in the vivacity each brought out in the other. Christiana also counted on Whitehead as she had her father—to be her ideal father/lover who would approve of her and whom she could please and inspire. In this role, the Whiteheads became exemplary parents, and her greatest feeling of family happened when she had the Whiteheads, Murray, her son, Councie, who was now at Harvard, and his girlfriend together for dinner in her kitchen at Hilliard Street. With Whitehead present as father and head, she felt her own outline no longer blurred or lost in Murray's shadow or in housewifely banalities. Harry, however, depreciated Christiana's deep love for Altie and his reciprocal devotion, putting it down to her "inclination and skill in drawing out the ideas of an older man, giving him the impression of his speaking beyond his usual level of expressiveness."

Morgan's ardent place in Whitehead's life and by his side was far more intense and reciprocal than Murray's laconic dismissal allowed. At Whitehead's eightieth birthday, Morgan was one of the few outsiders allowed at the celebration the Harvard philosophy department held. Whitehead insisted that she sit in the place of honor on his right and asked her help with the arrangements. Her diary entry about the party caught some of the depth of feeling between them.

> Feb. 15, 1941—Cambridge
>
> Tonight was Altie's 80th birthday dinner—given by his students—with a few friends & the faculty of philosophy dept. present. I spent the afternoon arranging the flowers. My great silver bowl was in the center & my candelabra on each side— Then at the end of the long table came the two low bowls filled with daffodils. It looked cool and gay and spring-like and I was well pleased.
>
> There were 38 people and I sat on Altie's right which touched me very much. Scheffer sat next to me & Ralph Barton Perry opposite. . . . Then Pickman, the toast master got up and made a little speech, very inadequate, I thought, emphasizing Altie's *charm*—that we would remember him for his truth, his wisdom, and his *charm*—which made me sick—because if anyone has ever had shining *beauty* it is Altie. I was so angry that when he sat down I said loudly "I don't agree with you. Altie has beauty!"
>
> Then George Morgan, one of Altie's beloved students stood up and made a most heartbreakingly loving and sincere speech— What Altie had meant to his students. I will long remember how that man stood there, sort of defenseless in his love—and spoke with utter simplicity. He talked of how Altie had stood for values of life, how inexorable and searching he always was in this respect. . . . Then they gave Altie a beautifully bound book—in which were inscribed the names of a vast number of his friends and pupils. And all kinds of telegrams were read—from Felix Frankfurter—and the one which pleased Altie the most—from Lord Halifax etc. etc.
>
> Perry gave the next speech. . . . Altie spoke after that and I was afraid I was going to be quite unhorsed. The tears kept coming up and I couldn't keep them back. I pinned my eye on a picture on the wall of a fisherman & tried to imagine what kind of fish he was catching. I never looked so hard at a picture in my life before or since.
>
> He began by saying that his mind was disrupted by the tensions of the times & that he could put nothing

together into any sequence. Then he said You have all been saying these things about *me*—but I want to say to you that in all of my work I have only been Evelyn's instrument—it is *her* voice that has talked through me—it is *her* understanding that I have spoken. We came together as two absolutely different people with two absolutely different backgrounds & inheritance. Out of this difference has come the fertilizing and creativity of my life—whereas in most cases it has led to strife. I know how rare and how precious this fortune is which has given to me the very center of my creativeness.

(The fisherman has on a red cap and a blue shirt. He is fishing in a stream so he must be fishing for trout—it can't be perch or flounder. There is a tree behind him. O dear Lord, don't let me break.) . . .

In what were to be storm-tossed years of agitation and loss, Morgan's friendship with Whitehead stood out as a firm beacon of support. She received limited comfort from Murray during these years. He stayed away from her for longer periods, while she in turn removed herself from active involvement with the clinic, seeing her patients, now, in an office at the back of her Hilliard Street house. Harry countered his absences with mercurial shifts back to intense attraction and passionate love. During early 1937 they entered one of these periods, brought close again by their plans to add a tower to Morgan's property near Newburyport.

Though Murray and Morgan saw each other at the clinic and at Fairfax, they had realized almost from the first that they needed more solid ground for their rendezvous; Christiana's country house seemed a freer and clearer place. She had found the land, above a tidal river in Rowley, Massachusetts, in 1927; it reminded her of her summer home at York. Harry had helped her buy the acreage, and on it she built a sturdy, single-room house with a loft for sleeping. After Harry visited Jung's towered retreat in Bollingen in the mid-1930s, he longed for a similar structure, and so Christiana and he started to design their own version of Jung's tower. Jung had used his—across Lake Zurich from the house where he lived with his wife and family—to rest, meditate, sculpt, carve, write, and be alone with his mistress, Toni Wolff. Christiana and Harry's tower was to stand as a similar affirmation of their union. A large enclosed porch, a kitchen, and a woodshed were added to the back of the house in early 1937, and an attached three-story tower overlooking the river was completed in the fall of the same year. What they had called the "property" now became the Tower on the Marsh.

Christiana's tower was to become the lovers' meeting place and her own retreat and summer home. After its completion, Harry spent a three-week interval there each year, as well as many long weekends and sporadic rests. It was here that he made at least some progress in his never-ending battle to complete his work. Here, also, the lovers established a secret life, rare in its creative intensity. Alone in their castle, they took on the identities of Wona and Mansol and invented laws, contracts, didactic formulations, rituals, celebrations, and feasts for a multilayered fantasy realm—a play world imbued with lusty eroticism. They recorded their secret life in diaries and journals, and in notes and drafts for the books they planned to write, Harry's on Melville and their joint meditations on their life together and the meaning of her trances. In an early draft of the collaborative book, Christiana described buying the land—"a great rock" set in "a jungle of scrub birches, broken down pine limbs, encroaching sumacs, [and] blackberry vines." Immediately, she went about finding a carpenter to help build her cabin and, later, the tower. He was a man of her own age, Kenneth Knight, who was son, grandson, and great-grandson of Newburyport carpenters. At first, there was no water and no electricity. All the building supplies had to be carried up in wheelbarrows until a road could be built. Knight, working as both carpenter and mason, constructed a house whose craftsmanship and solidity still amaze the visitor. Christiana Morgan worked beside him as often as she could and learned his craft.

> When she was around Knight, while he was building she always felt the simple goodness of the work,—the physical labor of a maker, which she experienced here for the first time,—clearing the ground, cutting down trees, pulling brush for the burning, tearing out stumps, hauling wood, digging the earth. This was the toil that took all her bodily strength. She learned what it was to be blinded by salt sweat running into her eyes, to be aware of every aching muscle, to lie down on the ground knowing that she had completely exhausted her strength, and that there was no more in her that she could summon to her will. And she learned the rich reward of inner peace and bodily serenity when, strength returned, at evening, she walked out to

see the new shape of the things which her labor had brought about. . . .

Knowing that she really cared, and was carving with wood, he would instruct her as to why a tool must be used this way and not that, how it should be sharpened, and he would tell her stories of his grandfather's experiences, the old ways with wood, the virtues and limitations of the old-fashioned tools. . . .

In Knight's hierarchy of values, patience seems to have had a high priority. . . . Through him she learned in media of wood, stone, cement, and brick, the virtue and satisfaction of work perfectly done all the way through, however long it takes, and however expensive of time and energy. She learned the vice of the quick effect, which may satisfy the eye, but because it is not structurally, integrally true, can never satisfy the heart, for it is without virtue. . . . And one of her deep sources of pride was when she heard that Knight had spoken of her as "a very good woman."

Even before the original part of the house was finished, Christiana started to craft shutters and decorate the place with wood and stone carvings from her visions. Meticulously translating these creative fantasies into three-dimensional reality bestowed a pleasure and peace she no longer felt in her work at the clinic. Forming her inner visions in this way, Christiana centered herself in a solitary ritual of creativity apart from Harry. Visions she had once rendered in small and beautifully crafted paintings were now amplified in her house and tower.

The small vestibule has a closet on one side, and on the other the plumbing. It was here on the pine paneling between the two doors that she made her first carving, the quotation from Dante.

Above the second door which opens into the room she set on one side of the door a crucifix, on the other a carved sunburst. Here she was representing the two opposites, and the hope for the New. She thought of this vestibule as a place of preparation where there could be no leak to sap any hardy virtues. Entering, from the sunlight outdoors, the big room has a stern look, with its small windows, red-tiled floor, and dark pine paneling on the walls. The opposite end is taken up by the seven foot fireplace, bricks which reach to the ceiling with no mantel to gentle it. At first glance it would seem to be a room where "savage fortunes half-imagined and half real" might play out their destinies.

Christiana continued to give minute attention to the construction of the Tower and planted and tended the land with the same pleasure her father had taken from his garden in Maine. She brought from York, or duplicated, the plants she had loved in her childhood: a sweet-smelling iris, Father Hugo Chinese roses, coral bells, old-fashioned Scottish roses, Congo lilacs and peonies, an enormous white-blossomed peony flecked with red and an old-fashioned red one from the house below her father's, "like the one which grew next to old Captain Sewall's doorstep. She wanted it here, because she can remember so well going to see him one day when she was about seven years old, and while waiting for him to open the door feeling for the first time that ecstasy, almost like pain, which can arise from beauty, in this instance the dark red cups of the peony."

After the Tower was completed, Christiana spent more and more time developing it as a sanctuary for herself and her art. Harry provided the money, but Christiana executed the project, becoming increasingly caught up in carving, sculpting, and decorating the place with private symbology.

The Tower possessed more comfort and elegance than Jung's primitive structure. It contained three large round rooms and a winding staircase. The bottom room, half underground below the level of the original house, was a mysterious bathysphere, where Christiana meditated and sometimes tranced and where some of the darker rituals she and Harry invented were enacted. Three long windows imbued the room with submarine light. Designed by Christiana in oiled and translucent paper, they formed a triptych that depicted high points of her visions. (The windows were finally executed in stained glass by Mary Leighton and installed in 1966.) Heavy beams resembling the mammoth spokes of a giant wheel radiated from the center of the white plastered celing. A thin-mattressed four-poster bed dominated the midpoint of the room, while an odd bishop's chair, a giant chest, and iron implements that looked both barbarous and liturgical surrounded it. The full-length torso Gaston Lachaise had sculpted of Morgan was transferred to this room from the garden to protect it from the weather.

Jung had written of his tower:

I had to make a confession of faith in stone. That was the beginning of the "Tower." . . . I wanted a room in this tower where I could exist for myself alone. . . . In the course of the years I have done paintings on the walls [there], and so have expressed all those things which have carried me out of time into seclusion, out of the present into timelessness. Thus the . . . tower became for me a place of spiritual concentration.

Revising Jung's concept into a more feminine form, Christiana set her meditation room partially into the ground, its buttressed entrance carved and incised as if it were part of a queen's crypt in an ancient Egyptian pyramid. The top room of the Tower contained a great plank of a desk set into the wall right below a semicircle of windows that overlooked the tidal river. In this airy, vaulted room Christiana wrote her diary, the chapters of her book, the record of her trances, and some articles for the Harvard Psychological Clinic. A built-in daybed adjoined the desk and lay beneath the third window. Harry, in his struggle to convert his tumultuous ideas into publishable form, sometimes insisted that Christiana sit or lie there as he wrote. Her purpose, as he interpreted it, was to inspire him and transfer the power of her visions into his books. Harry had always sought to commandeer the power of the visions to assist their love and energize his work, and Christiana outwardly concurred, willingly bending them to this service. Both seemed to want to concretize the subtle alchemy that sometimes plays between creator and inspiration, as if Harry's greatness were dependent on it.

Opposite the narrow bed where Christiana often sat or lay while Harry wrote was a wall of deep shelves. Though the living room below held the bulk of her books, here they kept poetry and English literature, Christiana's many books on women and women's psychology, and their collection of sexual arcana. A small wrought-iron ladder led to a trapdoor and the turreted rooftop, where they could sit and survey the Parker River as it bent again and again, reaching toward the sea beyond.

Between Christiana's claustrum and their aerie was the middle room of the Tower, the bedroom. Three wide French windows opened out over the gardens and the river below. A great bed commanded the room. Its sculpted headboard filled the whole wall, and behind it lay a hidden closet and dressing area, on whose door, disguised as a panel, Christiana carved "The Standard of Living is Ecstasy." The mahogany headboard holds concentric circles with joined hands centered on open tongues of fire; on the ceiling above the bed is a massive square of darker mahogany that looks as if it had survived many a ship's storm. On it is carved in a Celtic extravagance of designs: "AMOR FATI—Lead the Flown Away Virtue Back to the Earth. Yea, back to the Body and Life. There 227 is More Sagacity in the Body Than in the Cleverest Philosophy. What Am I but Love of You Made Flesh. Impart Thy Highest Aim Into the Heart of Thy Passions."

Christiana spent more and more time at the Tower, slowly adorning its rooms with idiosyncratic yet splendid icons; she created extraordinarily complex and moving panels, mandalas, carvings, and paintings. As Harry continued to absent himself, pursuing an increasingly busy life, he brought Christiana jewels, exotic Oriental costumes, and valuable artwork, as if to make up for his truancy. Christiana enjoyed toiling during the day and then walking around her castle in the evening dressed in luminescent saris with silver bracelets, anklets, and belled toe rings, tinkling as if she were a houri or a queen out of the *Arabian Nights*.

It was here, in the time she was alone, that Morgan's attention turned to women, especially to women writers and their views on women. In the fall and winter of 1938–39, she started an article on Margaret Sanger in which she considered the problems of dedicated and creative women and men's attitudes toward them. Perhaps remembering the intolerable meetings of the Boston Psychoanalytic Society and her impasse with Hanns Sachs, Morgan asserted that men, especially psychologists, tended to confuse a woman's dedication with neuroticism. The ensuing "vulgarity consists in not being able to distinguish between the *ardent* which is always outside the norm—and the *sick* which is also outside the norm." Morgan proceeded to examine the extra difficulties women have as professionals and the "difference between the great women with a cause and the great men with a cause"; she pondered the world's inequitable treatment of them. The notes are too fragmentary to discern anything but the framework of Morgan's article; however, its concern with gender disparity and the extra problems faced by a professional or creative person who is also female focuses on issues that are still alive in women's scholarship.

Morgan's work on Sanger was followed by two reviews, which were published in the *New York Herald Tribune*, one on Virginia Woolf's *Three Guineas*, the other on Frances Wickes's *The Inner World of Man*. The latter review wove dense congeries of interpenetrating interests, texts, and subtexts into a tiny frame, for Wickes had been inspired by Morgan's later trance drawings, some of which illustrated her book; Murray had written the introduction and lent a hand with the text. Titling the review "What to Do with Visions," Morgan used it as an opportunity to summarize her interests.

228

> Here is a book that has been needed ever since the hurricane of Jung, twenty years ago. His "Psychology of the Unconscious" was a great wind blowing through the mind's frail tenement of logic. Shutters of repression were wrenched off, furniture was overturned, pretty little fixings scattered, but the light of the sun and the moon streamed in. Was he a psychologist or a sorcerer? Physicians did not see how his ideas could be applied. But now Mrs. Wickes, a therapist of long standing, writes a book to harness the whirlwind, to illustrate his concepts with copious examples from her records and to demonstrate their usefulness in solving severe dilemmas. "The Inner World of Man" makes Jung concrete and by so doing to prove him.
>
> Of special interest are the drawings of typical fantasies and visions, taken in conjunction with Mrs. Wickes's clarifying comments. Most of these visions are consciously induced, but, because they consist of images that come unchosen, they may be viewed as signs of unconscious tendencies and insights. As Whitehead has said: "The ancient world takes its stand on the drama of the universe; the modern on the inward drama of the soul"; and for Mrs. Wickes the characters are archetypal images: the Terrible Mother, the Seer, the Martyr, the Vampire, the Hero, subjective facts of vital power. They are of the stuff that caused conversions such as Paul's, and led artists of Blake's temperament to their most moving compositions; but their use in health and sickness as guides to self-knowledge, well-being and inward evolution is one of Jung's particular contributions, which is now, for the first time, made clear in this absorbing book.

Harry Murray, after the gigantic effort of completing the clinic's 761-page report on their clinical and experimental study of personality, *Explorations in Personality*, took a two-year leave of absence from Harvard starting in the fall of 1939. He planned to spend the time completing the book on Melville he had begun in 1926 and see, in the process, if he could become the great writer he longed to be. Harry had so many skills and so many ideas that he could not stay put; he interrupted the work with trips all over the country, with lectures, with political maneuvering at Harvard, and with long stays in Europe with Jo. Most of the sabbatical was 229 soon frittered away. Murray returned to Melville and Morgan two months before he was due back at Harvard. With the urgency of a boy needing to cram for an exam, he demanded that Morgan work her magic on him. She wrote in her diary: "Mansol made me kneel down and three times made me repeat to him—'I give you my body and my spirit.' 'This is the year of my great sacrifice. . . . For a year I shall become Melville. I shall think, read, feel, know nothing but Melville. My God demands it.' "

Robert White, who served as head of the clinic while Harry was on sabbatical, recalled these crucial months. He believed that if Murray had completed the Melville book, he would have divorced his wife and married Morgan, embarking on the career he most coveted—that of a creative and potent writer. Murray had dreamed of going on from Melville to write a book on philosophy and passion, then one on Morgan's visions. Perhaps not by coincidence, his great friend Lewis Mumford published a book on Melville in 1929, Whitehead several on passionate philosophy in the 1930s and early 1940s, and Jung planned to make a book out of his four-and-a-half-year seminar on Christiana Morgan's visions. Murray's ambition was to outdo each of them. The writing of his own books and his commitment to Morgan seemed to go hand in hand. It was as if he felt he owned a goose capable of laying golden eggs: Morgan's visions had stimulated Jung to write and teach about women's psychology, and her subtle interchanges with Whitehead helped inspire his most original and profound books. With Morgan as his muse, he, too, would create a masterpiece. They remained in the country together for what was left of his sabbatical, and Murray tried to force two years' worth of work into the two months. Near the end of this time, he decided to show what he had produced to his close friend and drinking companion Conrad Aiken. Aiken's verdict was harsh: the text was a mess. Murray couldn't sustain a narrative form, and the best use of his manuscript would be to start fires in his fireplace!

Although too meanly worded, much of Aiken's criticism was just. Reading the chapters almost fifty years later, one finds that Murray was clearly unsuited for the solitary life a narrative form of this scope would have demanded, nor could he have answered Melville's riddles of infatuation, frenzy, and the ambiguities of re-

230 lationship without a sounder searching of his own depths. As it was, his biography of Melville trolled the shallows. Harry's talents lay elsewhere: in fireworks of ideas, wit, sparkling showers of brilliance, a genius for conversation and teaching. And Christiana could lend him neither her capacity for isolation nor her pearl diver's familiarity with the abyss.

Harry's literary frustration led him to ever more frantic juggling of his many lives and of Jo and Christiana. His pull toward the solitary life and then his recoil echoed in his treatment of Christiana. She found herself following Jung's and Sachs's mandate; believing it her duty to create and inspire Harry she felt his failure hers too. She tranced again in a forced and unsuccessful effort to help him, and she labored with all her heart to create the right setting for his work. Not only did Christiana blame herself for Harry's lack of success; Harry seemed to agree. During the years of his sabbatical, Christiana went through a stormy and agitated time; she turned more and more to her art and her diaries, planning various new "Propositions" for their life and work. She kept trying to persuade him to stay with her, to give them both the time to generate the kind of writing he longed to do. Christiana used her diaries now to voice the anguish of her love; she struggled to find a way to make Harry a literary genius. At the same time, she battled to understand where her roots were: what was hers and what of herself belonged, as Jung and Sachs would have it, more rightfully to Harry. And above all of this loomed the unarticulated need for a muse of her own.

Oct. 29. Mansol was full of suggestions for various pieces of research for me to undertake. As he talked my spirit grew heavy. Life fled from my body and waves of chill and loneliness came over me. Bits of research won't do. I must move toward the Proposition. I cannot wait upon him any longer. *I* must begin our true Proposition Life.

Feb. 1939. I sit here alone in our past and in the knowledge and flame of our future, my heart straining forward to *my* work and hate in me and upon me that the way should be so long and indirect.

Mar. 14, 1939. The knowledge of my spiritual loneliness is quite stark and terrible and brings with it fear. My daemon tells me that this shall only be found through my work. It is the long drawn out pain of the provisional life—not yet—not yet the trances made alive, not yet my true being said. Sometimes I feel that I come close to the verge of insanity. I feel unutterable terror, holding to this that is within me, terrified of its exposure to sickness, to time, to death.

May 25, 1939. Such a hard time we have been through and this diary long neglected. . . . But his life is positive, his life is strong. He is related to his work. I to our life. Is a new form necessary? We worked out a wonderful thesis about the "operationists." We laughed hard but it was grim. Our guts were depressed. Here is a historical outline of the past month. Alfred Cohn's dinner. Possibility of pregnancy and our relief. Our tree planting. My insistence that my love should stay until I started the wood carving. Pain and pain. My anguish. Sitting alone over the fire and knowing that a new form was necessary. Shocking pain fear struggle, and misery. My love coming and laughing about my symptoms. Enormous laughter, sadness underneath.

Dec. 15, 1939. How weary I am of this perpetual pendulum swing. . . .

April 19, 1940. We have had a long hard time together—Mansol's creative need cried out for separateness from me, for isolation and loneliness. There was something about the way he demanded it, some tearing up of our deep force of life that filled me with fear, sadness, and pain. I was terribly broken because I felt that in one wild exasperated frenzy he was casting off the last great step of our life—his recognition that I was the Creator of our life and that he was my disciple and instrument. And I was most miserably at fault because I had been without clarity as to the place in which our real life was. Without enough clarity as to the step we had taken. So for a time we were lost. And Oh God, what misery to be lost. All the fangs of the world which can only be warded off by good *positive* life come clawing in on me. . . .

So all the demons yelled, and I listened to them. All the time I had the feeling of being broken. I knew that if my Love failed me now that I was indeed broken for no anger was in me nor any further vision of a way. I knew that we had found it, that through him it would either live or die.

Where, before, the two had often mingled in a universe of delight, now they rolled away from each other in fear. Harry sought to close the gap by demanding that Christiana be as full of inflated pride as his dominating sister and as wounded as his syphilitic patient. Christiana now started to turn against herself, worrying that Sachs may have been right: her visions were unwomanly, denials of her true maternal function, while her love of ideas was perhaps nothing but false masculinity. Her and/or Harry's inability to sustain anything seemed a type of misplaced orgiastic pleasure; a pseudo penis that excited but then collapsed. Mixed in with the self-blame was immense but hidden rage, as she wrote that Harry's expectations of her were impossible for anyone to live out and made her feel sad, submerged, frightened, and broken.

His hopes dashed, Murray was unable to face the book or a further commitment to life at the Tower, and turned his energy from Morgan toward the clinic and his Harvard career. He persuaded Morgan to return to the clinic with him, promising that this would give them a chance to work together in renewed harmony. Both convinced themselves, at least in conversation with each other, that nothing really had gone awry, and Morgan, clinging to whatever kept Murray's love and interest flowing toward her, won herself over to the plan.

Murray had received a large Rockefeller grant to verify the clinic's original personality studies by repeating and expanding them with a new group of subjects. This intrigued Morgan because she had a personal interest in the study of values and motivation as well as creativity. In the fall of 1941, they returned to the clinic. Morgan started to work on an alternative series of TAT cards, which drew on many of her vision symbols; this version of the test was geared toward eliciting creatively imaginal themes. She helped test the new subjects and consulted with Whitehead who was also interested in the values underlying action. Morgan felt that it was an area vital in the study of personality but heretofore ignored. She also devised and administered one of the more valuable measurements in the new study, the Argument Completion Test, in which two people argued opposing viewpoints of various story situations, the subject being required to fill in both their dialogues.

As in the testing of the first group of Harvard students, on which *Explorations in Personality* was based, the tests multiplied. Murray kept generating ideas and, as with his accumulation of material for his own writing, never learned limits. Eleven subjects were finally tested and interviewed in a study of the individual's basic affective layer, his values, sentiments, and beliefs—an area that was left out of the earlier study. Morgan's and Murray's Thematic Apperception Test was again at the center of a test battery, in which twenty researchers administered over forty hours of tests to each of the eleven subjects over a period of two months. The study resulted in a second gargantuan accumulation of raw data, the responses being substantially influenced by the students' confrontation with America's entrance into World War II.

The war came just as Murray needed to withdraw from his failures at Christiana's Tower and from his growing dissatisfaction with his academic career. He left Harvard as soon as he could, this time to head the assessment staff at the Office of Strategic Services (OSS). Sent to Washington in late 1943, he was given the rank of major and a large estate for his work, the testing of men and women for their suitability for counterespionage and other top-secret work. The personality tests the Harvard Psychological Clinic had devised formed the core of his program, and many of the clinic staff accompanied Murray; his secretary, Marjorie Ingalls, came along, as did some of the key clinicians: Moses Stein, Nevitt Sanford, Elliot Jaques, and Don MacKinnon. Murray became part of the very center of the nation's war effort; he exulted in the urgent sense of mission, the frenetic activity, and the glamour of his top-secret job. Morgan stayed in Cambridge to write up the results of the study of sentiments.

Christiana wrote to a former graduate student she had worked with at the clinic and his wife, summing up her two years of work since her return to the clinic in 1941. Christiana declared how much she had been struck by the character of the students' responses to the war. It was as if she were contrasting them with what she, Will, and their friends had felt at the start of the First World War.

> Harry is working out a new theoretical consideration of sentiments, a subject which psychologists seem to have largely neglected. I have spent the whole winter writing up the sentiments of our eleven subjects (Harvard students) toward the war, religion, sex, and parents. It has been a fascinating and rewarding research. Particularly interesting to me, and I believe also of general interest, were the sentiments about war. We saw these boys two months after Pearl Harbor when they were still in a state of shock and before they had time to orient themselves to the almost overwhelming change that this would necessitate in their lives. It was a rare opportunity to study their ideas and

sentiments in this stage of transition. It was also, I may say, a very chastening experience for me being one of their parents' generation. Whatever we taught them was of no help to them whatever in their time of spiritual crisis. We had given them nothing, neither religion, nor world loyalty, nor love of country, nothing in fact to which they could dedicate themselves. There was nothing which they could not undermine with the youthful cynicism which we had allowed to go unchecked. It was pathetic to see how they floundered and how lost they were.

With Harry in Washington and Robert White still interim head of the clinic, Morgan was left with the task of producing the book. *A Clinical Study of Sentiments* was very much a product of that historical moment, and in it Morgan clearly reveals her political views. The tone of the book recalls her enormous surge of patriotism at the beginning of World War I and displays her impatience with young men who did not exhibit the same spirit.

After the book's general and very clear explanation of Jungian theory regarding the feeling function and the use of fantasy, Morgan emphasizes her subjects' conscious and unconscious attitudes toward war. She gives eighty pages to this discussion, while attitudes toward religion and parents receive about fifty pages each, and sex is disposed of in less than thirty. The book has an appealing earnestness and could well be a classic of the era; however, her arguments against her subjects' lack of commitment conflict with the neutrality such a text demands. Morgan's patriotic interpolations and asides overwhelm the book, and her judgments recall the jingoism of the time. The book rings with phrases reminiscent of her early letters to Will—"the right fighting spirit"; "zest [for] the destruction of Nazi tyranny"; "fighting morale"—including Morgan's very Bostonian epigraph for the book: "To ask for victory and not to feel like fighting, I consider that ill-bred."

Nevertheless, the case histories she and Murray worked on together reveal her subjects' inner turmoil with great clinical acuity, uncovering the unconscious fears, self-interest, and moral dilemmas that confronted men of fighting age at the start of war. The work makes perceptive evaluations of who would make the best fighters: those who were not neurotic and had a relatively low level of imagination, education, and fantasy. But Morgan's contemptuous comments on those who avoid war by entering such fields as medicine or the clergy contain a harsh judgment of Murray's similar avoidance of World War I.

Christiana's letters indicate that though she kept up her work at the clinic until the book was nearly completed, she tended to spend more and more time at her Tower on the Marsh and was 235 more frequently subject to depression, which she now tried to fend off with cigarettes and alcohol. In 1943, with Murray away and the pressure of finishing the *Clinical Study of Sentiments* weighing on her, Christiana Morgan's genetically high blood pressure escalated. Her father had died of hypertension, and it had been one of the factors that kept her out of the army nursing corps in World War I. When Murray later recollected her illness, he conflated his own emotions with hers, as if he had been the one who fell ill. He confused his pacifist detestation of war with Christiana's patriotic bellicosity, stating, in contrast to the words she had been writing at the time, that abhorrence of war was a significant trigger of her illness. He omitted her personal and professional stress and may not even have been aware of the anguish she experienced at her failure to inspire him to create his Melville book. With Murray's energies ebbing away from her, the pulse of their unlived life beat ever more harshly within her. Ignoring all this, Murray wrote:

> From the early nineteen-thirties the march of threatening events in Germany profoundly affected Christiana. With her, war had been a long abhorrence; not only World War I with husband at the front, but war anywhere anytime. The pervading anguish. The horrendous futility of it all. And now Pearl Harbor. A sneak attack; but something of that sort had been anticipated all along. What did surprise her was what her trusted physician had to tell: blood pressure escalating dangerously above 200, confirmed by signs of ominous retinal hemorrhages; life expectancy 1 year. Evil Fortune. But then, Good Fortune: the possibility of a better prognosis (5 years or maybe more) by suffering a very radical, two-stage surgical operation recently perfected by a Dr. Smithwick. Patients coming from around the globe to be cut up (in her native city of all places) Providential. But painful beyond words. Christiana's instant fearless choice at 46 was rewarded by as much as twenty-four more years of steadily productive living, despite smoking and drinking (so much enjoyed for a half-century).

The operation Christiana underwent, a radical sympathectomy, had side effects so severe that physicians abandoned the procedure soon thereafter. But it was the only solution available before the discovery of blood-pressure medications, and Christiana had little choice but to undergo the savage process. The surgeons severed part of Morgan's autonomic nervous system by cutting the nerves away, first down one side of the spine and then, about ten days later, down the other side. The effect was to stop Morgan's eyes from bleeding and prevent her nervous system from sending its destructive messages through her body. The operation probably saved her life. The messengers having been killed, or at least silenced, Morgan's arteries would remain unconstricted—no storms of agitation, stress, or passion could surge through Morgan now to pump her blood wildly, dilate her eyes, or lead to the injuries as well as the pleasures of vasoconstriction.

Josie Murray was at home in Boston when her father returned from visiting Christiana in the hospital. He told his daughter, then twenty-three, of the operation and confided his feelings of misery. She remembered that he was trembling and that his face was ashen, but she could not recall whether her mother comforted him in his distress. Harry stayed in Boston long enough to assure himself that even though she was in great pain and very ill, Christiana would recover. He then returned to his war work in Washington.

Morgan recuperated slowly and suffered a grim depression, due partly to her body's having ceased its self-regulation. She was bombarded with symptoms: her severe high blood pressure was succeeded by an equally severe low blood pressure; she endured tremendous sweats in her face and upper torso; pains seized her lower groin; she fainted if she sat or stood up too quickly. A consequence her doctor might neither have anticipated nor thought significant was how the operation would affect Morgan's smooth muscle responses, including her normal orgasmic cycle. There was little understanding of or interest in a woman's experience of her sexuality at that time (not until 1966, when Masters and Johnson mapped the role of the autonomic nervous system in women's sexual rhythm, were its dynamics portrayed), so it was left to Christiana to discover her new body, sundered from its warnings, responses, and desires. Like a man uninformed today about the effect of high-blood-pressure medication on his potency, she may well have blamed herself and her aging body for its inability to react.

To combat the now worrisome hypotension and her low spirits, she started to take the cocktail her physician recommended, but dosed herself with small drinks throughout the day. Christiana also discovered that smoking helped, and so she smoked more and drank more in an effort to self-regulate. By early 1945, her doctor, oblivious of her high-wire balancing act achieved through nicotine and alcohol, declared Christiana almost normal. The fainting, sweating, and groin pain had stopped, but her basal metabolism continued to fluctuate; it was sent into a further spin by the onset of menopause in late 1945. Murray's war duties kept him away during most of this desolate period. They met for weekends occasionally, mostly in Washington, Annapolis, or New York, but Morgan's body betrayed her, while Murray's interests and enthusiasm were often elsewhere; his pity acted as a whip to her pride. They exchanged long letters, as Christiana undertook the task of writing the history of their relationship as a way of keeping their love alive.

In Murray's absence, Morgan's energy turned further and further inward, and she sought refuge in her property. Her son had joined the armed forces but was released to attend medical school in New York. She felt close to Councie now and interested herself in his career. The letters she sent to him during this period were probably the most loving he ever received from her. As Morgan ornamented her Tower with her sculptures and carving, she slowly regained her health and started to look more to her family and friends for the companionship Murray had once proffered. But the loss and depression remained; she increasingly adopted Romantic longing for an absent lover as the true basis for her love, while her notes and meetings with Harry seemed tentative and formal in comparison.

A Clinical Study of Sentiments came out while Morgan recuperated; she had been unable to see the book through to publication. It was Murray's devoted new research assistant, Hansi Greer, not altogether trusted by Christiana, who wrote the book's conclusions and then oversaw its publication. Greer's excessive admiration for her boss led her to omit the names of nineteen of the twenty clinic psychologists who contributed to the work, and she gave Murray, who was absent during most of it, priority over Morgan as chief author. It made for a keen irony: Murray receiving pride of place as author of a book that jabbed at him for avoiding active duty in World War I. But the book received little attention. Interests after the war were elsewhere, and the book never underwent revisions for a more comprehensive edition that would have brought out its scientific value and perhaps allowed Morgan the credit she deserved.

With Murray away, her clinic work completed, and her health

improving, Christiana started taking patients again and also welcomed many more friends to her Tower. The only photograph of her from this time is a snapshot with her son in uniform, taken at the Tower. Christiana had lost weight, and strain blurred her face, but nearing fifty, she remained elegant, and her smile still drew the camera as it had when she was young. It was not for several more years that her beauty would reemerge, but the photograph makes it clear that her attractiveness lay in something far more profound than physical beauty.

Among her most valued friends now were two men, Ken Diven and Lewis Mumford, the gentle lad and the powerful man, one of them worshiping her as much as she worshiped the other. In each case there was a strong erotic component to the love, and at one point or another in the friendship, each seems to have become her lover.

Kenneth Diven, three years younger than Morgan, was a graduate student at the Harvard Psychological Clinic when they met in the mid-1930s. He had joined the clinic shortly after Will Morgan died and had reminded Christiana of her youth and of Will's devotion and gentleness. In her diary, Christiana described them both as sensitive sweet children who nourished her. Ken was not a typical psychology major; he not only carved and painted, like Christiana, but once had considered a concert career, having a beautiful baritone voice and a love of operatic arias. He was a good friend of Robert White's but somewhat distant from the rest of the clinic group, many of whom found him odd and arty, even effeminate. But Morgan reached out to him in the same way she had to the young Saul Rosenzweig, taking him under her wing as her knight; he responded at first with ardent devotion and gratitude.

Diven and Morgan found their tastes remarkably similar and shared a strong aesthetic sense; Diven was one of the few people from the clinic who visited her property, and they also started to travel together. After he earned his doctorate, Diven got a teaching job at nearby Pine Manor Junior College and then at Wellesley. Turned down for military service, he spent his summers and vacations with Morgan, carving and painting with her; he occupied a small guesthouse on the property. During 1945, he took a sabbatical and lived there full-time. Like Will Morgan, he comforted Christiana with a gently measured love she believed she could control. But Diven grew unsatisfied with courtly love and with Murray's continuing centrality in Morgan's life and, like Lancelot with Guinevere, sought to replace King Arthur. He began to believe that taking Christiana away from Harry would mean he had equaled or bettered Murray. Diven, androgynous and probably bisexual, loved Harry through making love to his woman. However, Diven failed to discern that although she loved the worshipful boy in him, Morgan kept Murray in a deeper and stronger place and was a more powerful woman than he imagined.

Ken Diven grew increasingly waspish and vindictive, and Christiana, alone with him at the Tower, started to taunt him for his unmanliness, as she had Will—possibly in order to challenge him, to rouse him, and make him prove himself her equal. He responded with loathing for her "monstrous" female power. Morgan and Diven worked side by side with growing tension; they bickered and drank and tried to wound each other in as many ways as they could. Where Morgan's challenges had roused Murray to meet her with combative joy, they drove Diven to sink into bitter and querulous hostility. He demonized his once shining queen, seeing her strength as threateningly abhorrent, and grew to hate what he could not master. Morgan became frightened of his stormy outbursts and his increasing references to *her* murderousness. She consulted her friend Frances Wickes and, unable to get Diven to go away, retreated from her property back to Cambridge. Diven remained at the Tower and started writing letters full of frenzied accusations to her and to Murray; then he blamed Morgan for Murray's rebuffs. Murray accused Diven of delusions both in his relationship with Morgan and in his now horrific view of her. Diven wrote back:

> Now then, in as few words as possible, I must say—not explain—with my own mouth why I exploded as I did. Last summer with true pseudo-objectification you said of Chris, "She is a powerful woman. She could commit murder." After the middle of July that is exactly what she did daily, from my point of view. Every day a stiletto in a new place or a new one in an old wound. I do not make a good slave. Insult and contempt are not instruments which foster friendship in me. Petty tyranny day in and day out cups the blood of creativity from my veins like a leech. When I have to sit and listen to a whole evening's enumeration of why she has "no respect from me" all I want is fresh air. I don't give a damn what she thinks of ME. What mattered was that she could make my work— for you both—next to impossible.
>
> She was really pleased when, at last, I began to fight

back. From then on it was dog eat dog. To me it was base and vile and evil. To me all strife is. I was bitter, frightened and full of hate; determined upon one thing only: to finish the ceiling and get out; for I saw plainly as I still do that I could never live, much less work, in the atmosphere she creates.

And then he wrote again:

Do not come expecting to sit down and adjudicate what you seem to think is a superficial misunderstanding. At numerous points in your letters you have chosen the word "delusion" to serve you in argument against my position: my delusion regarding this, my delusion regarding that and my delusion regarding something else with which you disagree. Using the word even less loosely than you have, I must point out that you have some delusions which you cannot escape by the very nature of things. The Chris you know is not the Chris I know. Poets have always sung that truth and I would never lift my voice in a single word, even if it is possible, to make it otherwise. It would be impossible for you, as one in love and utter devotion to her to know the Chris I know. My point is that we both are involved in a situation wherein no amount of logic can prevail against the difficulty. This is the prime characteristic of delusions.

Further, according to my view of my situation, you are entirely deluded about the cause of the summer's destruction. The whole situation did *not* build itself out of *my* reaction to Chris's remarks, as you try to explain it. But no amount of argument on my part would ever make you see that. Furthermore, I would honestly never want you to. So please, let us accept the psychological universe as it is and not try to change each other's words to fit our own perceptions. It is not a logical issue. If we realize that, we will hurt each other much less.

Morgan's and Diven's illusions crashed around them. Christiana's pull toward a fantasy of a nurturing, gentle lover once again found a man unequal to the challenge of her strength; and she proved incapable of playing the orthodox role he expected. She could not accept being the token of competition between the two men. She was not Harry's, not anyone's, little woman. After she left, Diven spent the next few months drowning his injured pride by emptying Morgan's wine cellar and, like an angered child, besmirched the house with dirt and trash before he finally departed. Morgan and Murray wrote long letters back and forth about the unfortunate affair and seemed to grow closer thereby. She returned to her prop- erty and reclaimed it gradually, purging it of this unhappy passage. This was the last of her significant involvements with a supposedly gentle man whom she could master. Her hopes of being nurtured by such a man had come to grief too many times.

During the same years, Christiana started a far more enduring friendship with Lewis Mumford, which deepened into love. Like Alfred North Whitehead, he was a man who could meet Morgan on her own level and rejoice in her strength and power. Ralph Eaton and Kenneth Diven had wanted Morgan to cater to their fragile sense of masculine superiority and, as confirmation, to claim her as their own. Whitehead and Mumford accepted and loved her as she was, each man honoring her relationship with Murray as he honored his own to his wife. Neither, though, believed in monogamy. In contrast to Whitehead, Lewis Mumford was Harry Murray's friend first; he had met Morgan at one of the Harvard Psychological Clinic's lunches in the late thirties and had grown to know and cherish her in large part through letters they exchanged. Born only two years before Morgan, in 1895, Mumford was an earnest, loving, brilliant man whose career was as wide and extraordinary as Whitehead's, though in less traditional spheres. During his long life he wrote on utopias, on architecture, on Melville, on the right size for human societies, on the history of towns and cities, on the environment, politics, and peace. He worked on newspapers, joined *The New Yorker* magazine as an art critic and became their columnist on architecture, taught at Dartmouth, Stanford, Harvard, and the University of Pennsylvania, was on a multitude of planning commissions, and was credited with saving New York City almost single-handedly from the misguided city planning of Robert Moses, all the while continuing to write wide-ranging and deeply humanistic books. Anti-imperialist and antiwar, he took an active part at age seventy in the Vietnam War protests. His biographer Donald L. Miller referred to Mumford as a humanist and as "one of America's last surviving men of letters. The author of some thirty books and over a thousand essays and reviews, he had supported himself entirely by his pen, producing a body of work almost unequaled in this century for its range and richness."

Mumford was an elegantly tall, shy man, with high temples and a receding hairline; his arresting, almost black, eyes matched

Christiana's for depth. Through a series of love affairs with three remarkable women when he was in his mid-thirties, Mumford had

242 become an accomplished and attentive lover: a fact he did not hesitate to disclose. Morgan and Mumford's correspondence began in the 1940s and lasted until her death. His letters grew in self-revelation and affection, while those he wrote to Murray grew chilly as he witnessed the ebb and flow of his interest in Morgan and what he took to be Murray's cruelty to her. Whereas some of Morgan's diary about Whitehead remains, no diary about her private feelings for Mumford has been found. Although Mumford and Morgan had the same habit of keeping everything and noting the most personal details of their lives in their journals and diaries, they were particularly circumspect about this relationship. Mumford's biographer tells nothing of their story and refers to Morgan only in passing, as Murray's mistress. In a chapter titled "Letters of Friendship" in Mumford's autobiography, however, it was not Murray but Morgan he cited as one of the three significant friendships of his life. Mumford cherished her letters, quoting or referring to many of them in his autobiography. In contrast to his frankness about three other women in his life, Mumford went out of his way to emphasize the platonic quality of their relationship; his friendship for Morgan, he said, "was part of a family friendship which included Sophia and our daughter Alison." He stressed Morgan's professional importance and reclaimed her coauthorship of the TAT:

> While a pale light from Christiana's special gifts is reflected in my letters to her, in conversation she betrayed, even more than in letters, some of the inarticulate passion of Mynheer Peeperkorn in "The Magic Mountain." But let me add here that Christiana, besides being a one-time disciple of Jung, skilled in the art of vision, collaborated in the design of the Murray-Morgan Thematic Apperception Test, and became a psychotherapist in her own right. Our personal contacts were sufficiently infrequent and aloof to permit an easy intellectual intimacy without any emotional complications.

Whereas the Whiteheads always lived nearby, the Mumfords seldom did. Lewis and Christiana forged their relationship through letters that were a true meeting of hearts and minds and recorded a remarkable friendship and love. Christiana inspired Mumford with her empathic comprehension of his work, but she also met him on a deeply feeling level. She was perhaps the closest person to him in the years when he mourned his son's death in the war.

In their first letter beyond formality, after an encounter in New York, Mumford made a special claim on Morgan. She replied: "I liked your idea of 'claim' but here I am going to break right down and refer you to my love." She went on to compliment him on his vitality, wisdom, and "personal art of living," and then continued a discussion of women and psychology they had been having. Morgan recommended that he read Margaret Mead, Melanie Klein, and, especially, Karen Horney. As the years progressed, Morgan wrote Mumford about women, Freud, Melville, her Irish cook, the weather, her garden, books, spirituality, Mumford's and her own work and life, family tirades, grandchildren, her efforts to write, and her life with Murray. It was to Mumford she revealed Murray's and her hopes and plans for marriage and then their collapse, and her valiant determination to adapt herself to the new form of their relationship.

In an uncanny way that both Mumford and Morgan acknowledged, their visions were often mirror images. The patterns of their lives also seemed synchronous, their various high and low points either occurring simultaneously or closely following one another. The most poignant of these was Morgan's brush with death, her operation, and her subsequent depression, which came at the same time as the death of Mumford's son and his own loss of hope. After his son, Geddes, was killed, Mumford wrote:

> Many things have made me think of you, dear Christiana. You were one of the few people with whom I could bear, even in imagination, to share my thoughts and feelings about our son's death. And now your letter shows that you alone have divined the inward change that follows death, or rather unfulfilled life, of one's son. There are sons who by circumstance or a natural disposition, inherit their father's position and carry on his work. But there was nothing in my experience or my reading to give me a clue to what is now happening to me: the desire to carry on young Geddes's work; to bring into the world, or if not into the world at least in my own work, the clear, unconditional self-reliance, the brooding intensity, the incorruptible firmness that showed even in the brief course of his life.

In her letters to Murray, Morgan often echoed Harry's operatic grandiloquence in a tone that is absent from her letters to Lewis

Mumford. The exaltations and depressions Mumford and she shared with each other, though extreme, appear far more grounded and sincere. The two friends tracked each other with a devoted attention that encompassed every part of their lives and knew no jealousy. Morgan was Murray's love and Mumford was his friend; therefore Mumford's letters to her and about her are far more circumspect than was usual for this frank and personal man. Like Murray, he had at least three muses who energized his work. The most notable of these, Catherine Bauer, he loved freely and openly for about five years. However, neither his wife, Sophia, nor his muse allowed him to juggle them in the way of Christiana and Jo with Harry; and so after the age of forty, Lewis turned to more transitory affairs. Part of Morgan's attraction for Mumford was that their relationship did not threaten his with his wife or hers with Murray; the two were friends above everything else, and both agreed to keep it so. The depth of their feeling for each other emerges from their letters. Mumford wrote:

> Your present image would enter my precincts as a comforting angel, bringing health to me! . . . We seem to take turns, dear Christiana, in giving each other lifts: your letter, your New York letter, in your veritable handwriting, came to me at the moment I needed it most; and the mere thought of your recovery was like the cup of water one needs to prime a pump. . . . I have read your letter at least seven times, dear Christiana. . . . Part of the miracle of our friendship is that we should be converging toward the same destination without having communicated a word to each other: both of us withdrawing, turning inward, digging into the compost of the past, preparing a bed for fresh seeds. . . . Your words on my book . . . the parts that you single out are precisely the places I am most satisfied with. . . . I am so glad you think so too. . . . One way or another, dear Christiana, our minds keep moving along parallel paths, toward a common destination.

In the middle of the war, Lewis wrote, signing off his letter with a tribute to the value of her love: "My love to you Christiana— Now is the time for the love of all lovers to cover the world."

At the end of the grief-tossed years after the death of his son, he started to flirt with her again, boasting: "You should see me at least once in the state I used to be between the ages of 35 & 40: just bursting with energy & glowing at both ends: It's such fun to feel that way again . . . with the sight of you, a flame within the charcoal bed of Hilliard Street. . . . How wonderful your letters are: 245 what sympathy, what understanding you've given me in the darkest days. Thank you for eternity."

Mumford filled letters with ideas for his books, descriptions of his moods, and of his struggles to write; Christiana kept pace with reactions, worries, and conjectures, but she spent far less time telling him about her own life than responding to his letters and supporting him. She did recount her constant delight in her affection for "dear Lewis," as well as some of the heartache of her struggle with Harry and her hopes for better things after the war years ended.

> You are indeed a joy Lewis—I have always told Harry that if I hadn't fallen in love with him I surely would with you! Now you know what you have escaped. . . . Together he [Murray] and I have been living through a tremendous upheaval with the prospect of the war, & then the living through it—we maintained a very firm inner shape for the long endurance test of the last years. Now an entirely new shape for our Synergy is in process of coming into being which taxes all my creative energies. 'Twill be good though— Oh dear Lewis—I do wish we lived so that we could just run in & see each other— And talk garden & books & have the lovely simple communication that friends should have.

Morgan's relationship to Murray during these years was far stormier and less comforting. Her letters to him during the war years reflect far more of her injury and loss of confidence than she exposed to Mumford. They make painful reading, as they arc between despair—especially about her creativity—and an abject, anima-like response to Murray, whom she started to refer to as her master, calling herself his slave. He seemed to like the idea and responded with masculine authority. Once more she evoked the large-eyed suffering woman in the hospital from Murray's past, once more she played the dark lady of sorrows who struck at Murray's tenderest emotions. He vacillated between pity and tender protestations of love and an almost sadistic response to her misery, demanding that they "go down to the roots of things in you, to dig below *pride* and unearth every source of *sorrow & inferiority & guilt & helplessness & defeatism, & passivity.*" He commanded her "complete obedience." At the same time, his letters were often

charming and filled with praise of her and their experiment in relationship, as well as fervent protestations of love and promises for
the future. But no sooner would he start his letters this way than he would attack Christiana for their failures. He hectored her to write their story and cajoled her about her inability to come up to his expectations, all the while bombarding her with unanswerable questions.

> Tuesday Dec. 18 [1944]
>
> O My Beautiful, My Darling. You are going through hell for our Synergy, for our Proposition, for the sake of our past & of our future. You are writing me amazing letters full of pith & substance, the material discovered along the floor of your ocean by repeated underwater swimmings. You are very brave, but you know that all this is *necessary* & so I push you deeper & deeper down— O my sweet, I'm not being sadistic; this is crucial, everything hangs on the sincerity & courage of your explorations. You know that *one* of the secrets of our Synergy, & this is very important, is *Exaggeration*. . . . According to my standards your search for your daemons, your precious pearls, has been prudent & rather prideful. You have not given a picture of the Unc[onscious] self—the daemon that resisted everything (repeated orgasms excluded). What did she want [in] that daemon? Just this? But she did not seek raw sex. She wanted it only from a creative man. She wanted to excite creation first—how important was it that creativeness should be destructive? Let us say she wanted mad destructive creativeness, a wild dance of Siva around her as the center. Now what was her role in this? Vicarious participation? To feel that she was being creative? To feel that she was impregnating the man? But yet she did not throw out ideas. She got hot when the man threw out ideas. He felt greatly excited by the fact that he could rouse her, animate her. She was the Sphinx. She could be stirred into life by creativeness that was abundant and sure of itself. And then why did she draw men with a broad strain of femininity—Jonah, Ken, Lewis, Ralph, Clyde, Mansol? How was masculinity operating? Was this shown in the impregnation process? And why was she disinterested in the *result* of the creative process? Was this like a man who delights in sex but shows no concern for the children that are born from it? . . . And if there was masculinity & aggressiveness unexpressed & desire for power, why did

the offering of power freeze her feelings? Was that because she wanted the Epiphany—complete worship without a word, or exertion, on her part? Did she conceive of making a man creative by the Epiphany alone, without a word—just beauty? And did she want Creativeness to be creativeness about her, not about psychology, or Melville, or general ideas? Was she all the time looking for a Painter or a Sculptor—a Lachaise of a sort? She would merely lie, sit or stand, & he would get excited & adorn her with clothes or portray her in paint, or bronze, or words? And when she had a man who worshiped her day in & day out, why did she weep every so often all through these years? What did she want that she didn't have? Closeness yes, but with closeness she allows she began to lose interest in Walpurgis. It became a kind of routine, & creativeness fell, & orgasms diminished. And then she has always been more interested in sights than words. She was more drawn to Jonah's and Ken's creativeness than to Mansol's. It is the Epiphany. She does not revel in books, in poetry, in passages as she does in visible objects. She reads but does not remember & does not reread. Well, *these* are some of the lines of inquiry, my precious. . . .

I hope you get this before you leave for New York. It brings *all my worship,* & my arms around you & *strong support* for you on all sides. And *great reserves* of *banked-up love & devotion.*

O Jesus, you are *my target of respect.*

M.

It was as if Harry had sat in his room in wartime Washington, creating a mask out of his own past wounds and sense of inferiority, which he then hung up on his wall as if it were his love. He blamed the figure for his failure to live up to his own grandly heroic expectations. He pounded at all that was feminine in himself, then blamed Christiana for it; he blamed her for his own lack of concentration, his own passivity, and his own sensitivities. Angry at the weak little boy within him, whom his strong sister had battered, he flagellated himself, dancing frantic apotropaic rings of words around the figure of Monstrous Woman, who from childhood had filled him with such fright. Christiana did not understand this for what it was. She grew confused, doubted her own judgment, became unable to make decisions and unable to continue her own intellectual work. Looking at Harry's mask of her, she lost herself and started to believe the mask instead. She took Harry's letters to heart and grew to feel that each way she turned was the wrong way, everything she did was valueless or not quite good enough, or had to be done again, in a different, impossible way. And she clung with desperation to her batterer, who all the while was declaring her a great and greatly talented woman, his beautiful magnificent love. She silenced the strong woman in herself through self-doubt and alcohol, sinking into passivity, battered by the onslaught of his ferocious words.

After their meetings now, Harry would be numbed by headaches, while Christiana fell into profound depressions. She came to doubt her whole life and wrote: "there is a lack of trust in me in our own shape against the world's shape." Their reality together felt like nothing but a great fantasy; she felt broken and old and unable to create in the vacuum of her loneliness. Murray's letters meanwhile vacillated between loving tenderness and shrewish hectoring in which he made further impossible research demands on Morgan or required her to do the kind of tightly controlled multipart analysis for which she had neither the gift nor the training. Her role of victim seemed to call up his of victimizer as well as savior, and their entanglement began to take on all the bizarre ambivalences of Nietzschean power. Christiana, weakened by her surgery and as if desperate to keep their relationship alive, donned the garb of scapegoat and masochist.

Murray's and Morgan's absences from each other increased, and their letters grew fewer. With this respite, Morgan slowly regained some strength and recollected herself in solitude. After many months alone or with friends at the Tower, Morgan traveled, after the war had ended, to Washington to confront Murray. He was to leave on a postwar mission to China, and they had a reunion marked by days of accusations and counteraccusations, as well as by some acknowledgment of their mutual faults. This time, Morgan stood up for herself and claimed power. She portrayed their history as one of repeated postponements and provisional living. She demanded what she needed: that Murray divorce his wife, end his work at the clinic, declare their union to his friends, and pledge himself wholeheartedly to her. Face to face with the real Morgan instead of the mirrored mask, Murray's erotic energy rushed to meet her spirited challenge.

In a collaborative document, Morgan takes on the role of Murray's dominatrix sister:

My first task will be to block the energy that flows toward the world. And here, Mansol, you will need utter trust because it will be for me to decide how you spend your time. I shall demand that you give less and less time to Jo, to Psychology, to the Clinic, to Science, to a hundred and one things which you suppose are duties. Eventually I shall demand that you separate yourself entirely from all these attachments. I have ceased to be interested in your successes in the world, in your speeches and writings. I have ceased to be interested in Melville. And what does not concern me must not concern you.

I shall ask for many courageous acts, major and minor. I shall ask that you prove your indifference to the world's judgments in small ways. I shall ask for gifts. . . . I shall call you "Instrument" for that will be your function. . . . You know I have *never* fully admired you. Now I am going to show you the way to my admiration. That is the mountain you will climb with me step by step. The summit of the mountain is my ideal for you, my standard of courage.

. . . On June 12 Mansol wrote that he had done all these things. He had added to the Testament, told Jo that the form of their life would be different after the war, and written to Lewis [Mumford]. The power that had been generated in Wona's soul had not been in vain. Her words effected the first step in Mansol's transformation. She had commanded and he had obeyed. . . .

Before leaving on his mission Mansol acted irrevocably and courageously in telling his colleagues that as soon as the war was over he will resign his professorship in Psychology.

And Wona wrote to him:

"Beautiful, powerful beyond all men in your obedience, your supreme honesty, and in the courage which is flowing into you. The *true*, the deep respect which you know that I have always withheld begins to stir. We face the very source and root of our highest powers and most creative energies. We can never, never, turn away from this. All the pent-up passion and power that is in me will create this step by step for us both, joyously, my Love. O so joyously."

Murray appeared delighted with the temporary shifting of dominance, their renewed pledge to each other, and this new staging of their refurbished passion. Yet when his China mission was finished, he returned to Washington. He stayed apart from her with government work and then extended their separation to take up new duties as well as dalliances. He did not divorce his wife. He spent three extra years away after the war, in order to finish a book he was coauthoring for the OSS, *The Assessment of Men*. Returning to New York to be with his wife and daughter while Josie went to medical school, Harry left Christiana to write about their relationship—the dyad, as he called it—alone.

TWELVE

The
Red and Gold
Diary

*I was now about to form another being, of whose
dispositions I was alike ignorant; she might become ten thousand times more malignant than
her mate, and delight, for its own sake, in murder
and wretchedness.*

MARY SHELLEY,
Frankenstein, Or the Modern Prometheus

In spite of their problems and increasingly long separations,
Christiana and Harry believed that their life together had great
significance and needed to be chronicled. Christiana put her
hand to it, but in a letter to Lewis Mumford, who was working
on his autobiography, she described her difficulty translating her
private symbols into common language and her wish to write an
honest book. Harry had criticized a chapter she called "What Joy"
for its too happy tone. She told Mumford about her planned book:

> One of H's complaints was that what I have written so
> far is a description of beautiful days—as though there were
> no such thing as wear and tear between us—and dark days
> indeed— One doesn't forget the horrors—but it is so hard
> to write about them. However—let's agree that we put
> no halos around our heads! *The* great thing—in our time—
> as we see it—is to be absolutely honest. The coming gen-
> erations need to see the worst & the best—and how we
> struggled to make the kind of life we have made.

Christiana wanted to write a history of the trances, as well as of her love for and relationship with Harry, and her Tower life. They both believed that their life together could be an exemplar for future generations; Harry claimed that they had found a way of individuation that surpassed Jung's because it involved *two* people evolving together. Creating the Tower and the book was intended to symbolize and define their joint venture. As such, the creation became a sacrament to replace and fortify their alliance. Harry could sally out on his worldly adventures, leaving Christiana to adorn the castle with their symbols.

One of the friends who became close to Christiana during the war years was Dona Louisa Coomaraswami, a widely read and cultured woman who had married the noted philosopher and expert on Hindu religion A. V. Coomaraswami. The two women had a friendship that was loving but stormy because of their similarities: each was strong, creative, and talented, yet attached to a more visible and successful man; neither woman had made as much of her life as she wished. After a visit to the Tower, Dona Louisa criticized Christiana and what she perceived as her friend's flagrant misuse of her creative energy. In June 1945 she wrote that she found far more of Christiana in her work in Cambridge than among her relics at the Tower. Questioning Christiana's myth-making as a waste of time, Coomaraswami added:

> You are capable of terrific work, and have enormous understanding but you will not do a stroke of it, you won't take the first step in chair-climbing until and unless you stop taking yourself seriously, and consider your Self, for what that is worth. . . . Most of the women I have known have had either hearts or minds: you have both but they are tangled up, get yourself untwisted, discard these objects like the chains on the hearth wall, these are not pleasant symbols. . . .

Dona Louisa realized her comments would upset her friend, but she recognized Christiana's problem to be, in many ways, similar to her own. She understood the root cause of what was to her an example of Christiana's misprized talent. "If you and I could have known how to put that 'passion' to a directed use, what could we not have made! Such vitality, such fire, such youth and beauty— pearls before the swine-of-anger! It beats all the waste, I could weep for the preciousness of a quality that was demolished."

Coomaraswami hated seeing her friend spending more and more of her time at the Tower and on her almost obsessively intricate carving. Christiana responded with anger. She must have felt that 253 her creating of myths and symbols at the Tower gave her life meaning and that by questioning them, her friend questioned the value of her life. Christiana sent Coomaraswami's letter to Lewis Mumford and asked for his opinion of the criticism. It must have been a difficult undertaking. Mumford, in a careful yet affectionate reply, both chided and supported Morgan but also asked her to examine the possibility that she had taken a wrong path in attempting to create a private world of representative objects. He felt that she still had not found a way to translate her experience so that it was accessible.

The question Mrs. Coomeraswamy raised about your carving is one that I first threshed out in relation to Blake's symbolism. Why is so much of Blake unintelligible? Why do his more formal poems, the very ones which one feels that his mature mind attempted to say most, actually convey so much less than he probably thought he had? The answer is that he was compelled to create a whole world by private fiat; and to understand these symbols one would have to be present at their genesis; for every verbal explanation would not suffice to recreate the experience out of which they grew.

The first purpose of art, I am sure, is to clarify something in oneself; and the only way to do this is to get it out of oneself. But the second purpose is to share it and test it with others; for this clarification is incomplete until others participate in it and thus assure one that the precious experience was not an hallucination or a form of self-indulgence. The artist today is fortunate, as the traditional artist was, when the audience is already half-way in on his secret; when he can devote himself to doing something with the symbol, exploring its further applications, not just inventing it or restating it. Lacking this, his works of art are tied to his own lifetime, almost to his own autobiography; and maybe without the biography they would not be self-sustaining.

As for the problem of symbolism in general, you have sought to convey, in the form of art, and even of decoration, that part of your experience which is unspeakable; yet the question remains whether the visual art can, in our time, do what music and literature do, or indeed, whether they have ever sought to do this in the past. New words can be coined by a poet; new rhythms created; even a new language and a new myth, up to a point, can be communicated by him; but it is precisely at the point where Blake begins to *portray* his new Gods, and where his poems pass into the realm of the visual, that he begins to be obscure and darkly undecipherable.

But Christiana and Harry believed that their myth could be created through willing it, and in spite of her friends' hints, she persisted in carving her icons and creating and naming her gods in a symbology that finally grew to resemble the necrology of the Egyptians during the years of their decline. Harry enjoyed the invention of their private universe as much as she and also was drawn to its endless elaboration, while Christiana's work at the Tower, as her work at the clinic, became in many ways a substitute for the daily life of a husband and wife. Harry abetted her, not only because he realized that all this carving, naming, drawing, planting, and construction kept Christiana busy with their myth of relationship but because when he entered their world at the Tower he entered wholeheartedly and delightedly in the fantasy. Thus their private world began to take on elements of a Romantic folie-à-deux pretend world, in which Christiana either dedicated herself to his comforts at the Tower or waited alone there for him to return. The reasons for this are complex and many-layered; most salient, perhaps, was the couple's shared grandiose delusion about their life together. Perhaps neither could bear the tawdry reality of being simply another married lover and his mistress, when by creating an ever-expanding story about themselves they could believe that their relationship carried a great myth of the future as well as a great new religion. In the same way that Harry, in opposition to Occham's theory, had sliced and multiplied his personality theory and the notes for his books into endlessly proliferating new categories, so he and Christiana filled their private world with a multiplicity of signs and symbols, each of which took on a significance intelligible only to themselves. The depictions of their life together, at least in the rough drafts of their book, read like minutely detailed yet plotless illustrations of the arcane practices of a lost religion whose central tenets elude the outsider. It is as if they were trying to describe some holy thing—like the Stations of the Cross—with much of the same lofty and intense religious tone but without getting at its substance. Or as if neither could allow their pillow talk simply to express the tenderness between two lovers but, lacking the sweet homeliness of daily love, forced it to assume the 255 grandiose importance of a new language full of relevance and universal validity and equal to the great religious symbolism of the past. However, as Mumford noted, this portentous mission was transmuted intelligibly neither in Morgan's carving, in their writing, nor in their lives.

Harry and Christiana occasionally experienced the numinosity they hoped their totems would bring, but nothing approached the power of her early vision quest, while the meaning of their lives seemed to disappear beneath the accretion of substitute theory and symbol. Perhaps the massing of detail and the multiplication of externals attempted to conceal the growing hollowness at the center of their lives. Their creation of an increasingly elaborate fantasy structure eventually replaced and masked the reality of what was happening between them. Rather than using the visions for her own inner work, as Dona Louisa Coomaraswami urged, or struggling to put them into her own words, as Lewis Mumford required, Christiana traded them to her lover and allowed him to appropriate them, in exchange for an inflated sense of their love. She and Harry both seemed to believe this carried out and extended Jung's teaching about Christiana's duty to inspire and create a man. Only a rare woman like Coomaraswami or a rarer man like Mumford accepted her as an equal who offered another view.

Harry seemed to have loved joining the drama when he visited Christiana at the Tower, but he left it up to her to compose it, in much the same way that mistresses, courtesans, and royal favorites have always invented ways to delight and inspire their lord while he contended with the demands of his worldly life. Harry's program for the lovers' book, on the other hand, involved an almost casuistic complexity. He drew up a plan in 1949 whose details matched Christiana's intricacy of carving:

> Here I am at the Tower on the Marsh, only now, at the age of 56, beginning to write the Proposition. Are we too late? Will the Sisters grant us time to finish? Perhaps we are too early, still too young to understand the intricate web of forces that made us grow and flower as we did. We shall see.
>
> Strictly speaking I shall not start with the proposition but with the scaffolding, or better still the blueprint, or

more precisely, the notes for the blueprint of the Proposition. The task I have set myself today is that of enumerating the pillars of the Proposition, of listing the facts & the determinants and consequences of the facts which are new and unusual in human history and which therefore are waiting to be said and heard. What is it that so urgently requires telling?

It is a practical imperative for us to do this now—previous to planning our research program at the Clinic—because, if we define the Points of the Proposition now, I can select topics for research which bear upon these points—supporting or correcting them and so we can proceed as one sympathy instead of playing two tunes at once.

Murray proceeded to analyze the proposition's central points and the determinants of their relationship, using the vocabulary of needs, presses, and determinants he employed for his Personology theory and for studies of individuals at the clinic. The major points of his somewhat grandiose proposition were that their union was the essence of romantic love and that there was no other union to compare with it "in the history of mankind." He attributed the success of their relationship to its endurance, its intensity, and its fecundity. Flagrantly disregarding its volatility, he described their relationship as stable, trustful, and serene, and claimed that it brought both of them contentment with "an absence of quarrels." Morgan's trances formed a major buttress for the relationship because they gave her a religious sense of vocation that Murray could believe in and trust. Through them, they were able to meet each other in their depths and be revitalized and renewed. The relationship fulfilled their basic needs, including succor, nurturance, religion, domination, submission, aggression, and, above all, erotic affection. Harry ended his list of major points by recalling that they had shared aims, tastes, values, and sentiments, and that each trusted the relationship in spite of the stresses on it and expected it to last and grow throughout their lives.

Murray went on to catalogue the chief determinants or underlying causes for the strength of their union: their religious commitment to the union's creativity; the trances; Carl Jung's example of his life with his wife and Toni Wolff; their use of psychoanalytic ideas, especially Jung's concept of animus and anima; their shared profession; their freedom from conventionality; their separation, which intensified their relationship and kept it fresh; Murray's wealth, which permitted their isolation and the building of the Tower property and their rental in Fairfax; and, finally, their ability to put their synergy first as their "highest philosophy."

With this for underpinning and preamble, Harry then proceeded to set forth the questions to which Christiana should apply herself in order to write their book. He created a didactic program of research for a Philosophy 1 course rather than a framework that could fire Christiana's poetical imagination or draw on the power of her experience. Instead of proceeding with a clear plan for a book, Harry led her away into multitudinous pedantic elaborations of philosophical generalities. Thus he succeeded in sabotaging the book he was ostensibly promoting, by making demands that were as impossible as his ever-proliferating testing programs at the clinic:

DYNAMICS OF INTERPERSONAL RELATIONS

1. What is the best conceptual scheme for formulating the history of a close interpersonal relationship (IR)—(a) anerotic, & (b) erotic? In less general terms we might ask: What has psychology to contribute to the understanding of successful & unsuccessful IRs? Building blocks for the construction of a conceptual scheme may be found in *The Clinical Study of Sentiments*.

2. In terms of what criteria may the value of IRs be assessed? (i.e. What are the properties of good & of bad IRs?)— For this we need real studies of numerous loves & friendships in (a) actual life; (b) fiction; (c) mythology.

3. What are the determinants (and the consequences) of good and bad IRs? Here we need longitudinal case studies to determine what background events and what personality variables are correlated with successful and unsuccessful IRs. These facts will help to answer the question: how can children be prepared for good IRs?

4. What *modes of behavior* facilitate and what modes impede the creation and preservation of good and bad IRs? Since *modes of behavior* are important determinants of good and bad IRs, this question might be subsumed under #3. It is given a separate heading, however, because of its peculiar importance: the answer to this question will carry us a long way towards the construction of a pragmatic system of morals. (Morality may be defined *positively* as a set of principles of conduct most conducive to the advancement of goodwill, fellowship, and love.)

For this it would be necessary to examine a large

collection of religious commandments and moral maxims & copy out those which deal with the production of good and bad human relations. Almost equally relevant would be a large collection of secular aphorisms defining conduct which leads to good and bad relations.

The boundlessness of this very grand, yet soul-killing, program of theory and research doomed it to failure. Similarly, Murray numbed Morgan by his inability to understand the very creativity that had given rise to her visions. Her source lay not in scholastics but in mysticism—the inner reality of her visions. Morgan dove for pearls, while Harry was their connoisseur; however, the connoisseur demanded that the diver use his science to describe her experiences of the deep. Christiana discovered but could not fully decipher, nor did she have the words to convey, a woman's psychological reality. It differed markedly from all the male myths already in place; to be understood, her visions depended not on research but on personal insight, self-examination, and her effort to translate what she had experienced. Jung had diverted Morgan away from this task and toward the supposedly more womanly one of inspiring Murray. Murray concurred, and Morgan listened to them both rather than to her visions, to her woman friends, or to Whitehead or Mumford. She tried to adapt herself to an alien task of writing the book about her visions and her life with Murray in the way that he proposed. She thereby betrayed both herself and her visions.

Murray put Morgan's mind, "her animus," to work in accordance with Jung's instructions to his handmaidens in Zurich. She was assigned an elaborate research program, as if this were the best way of developing and disciplining her mind and making use of her creativity. The program ignored the essential power of feminine creativity to find a voice in which to enunciate its new vision and new plot. Instead of plunging into the meaning of her visions, this good daughter of the fathers dutifully read what men had written about visions and about love. She compiled box after box of index cards on various religious commandments, moral maxims, and secular aphorisms about fantasy and relationship.

Morgan's initial approach to the planning of the book—which, unsupported, remained in note and outline form—had been more particular and realistic. If she had been able to hear her own voice and trust it, her work might have been as compelling and creative as her visions. Some of the early chapters, as well as Morgan's

scattered notes on her feelings about her relationship and the proposition, captured the essence of her different voice but also her lack
of confidence in it and her willingness to give it all away.   259

What a tremendous undertaking this of ours has been.
When *we* were unified *together* we had the knowledge and
feeling of the great religious perception—(Keats) For at
that time we had it all— Our destiny was laid— If I can
find the spiritual thread—Mansol will be able to embody
it all forth—fill it all out.

My unconsciousness lay in the fact that I thought this
was enough—this was all that was expected of me—Mansol recognized & knew better. He knew that the God was
in me and not in him—that he had a function to pursue
but that the Godhead was in me & out of me—

When I told Mansol the other night that my sin was
that of *unconsciousness* it was only a *half* sin—for without
the most painful and terrible consciousness I could not
have created our Synergy— We would both have broken
into two atoms a thousand times without my supreme
consciousness *here*—my sense of vocation, my loyalty—
which broke me (my feeling of vocation) during the war.

Numinous—I think this is a good and useful adjective
for us— It is like *mana* but *mana* suggests *power* whereas
numinous has the connotation of *holiness*. Good for the
trances and for the *Way* of Synergy.

Our Experience

My experience *with Mansol*

Pain. Separation from Mansol. Need for Synergy.
Hoarded heap of images used by the constructing imagination to create a new form for our life. Then the will to
actualize it. My creativity seems (with Mansol) to arise
from pain—separation. Here I have no feeling of zest only
pain & struggle until Mansol recognizes the new form
which I have come to out of pain. The process of creating
the new form is a creative act over which I have no control.
The *It* does the work & *I* am suddenly presented with it.
With Mansol's recognition I have the lofty feeling described by Rilke—the relief—the descent of the Holy
Ghost—the feeling of having given birth—the labor successfully completed. . . .

What about my *zest* Where? Seems as though my
zest comes with the Holy Ghost—the final phase—and
doesn't last very long—because life is always changing

and a new form being demanded— So I go back into *pain* to begin the whole process again.

Ecstasy— The *It* working through the *me* as instrument—cf. Rilke's perpetual struggle to get *pure* enough & far enough *in* & away from the world enough so this could happen— *Me & my trances*

Morgan never wrote her book, although various chapters and drafts of chapters and a multitude of notes remain; these rest side by side with the mass of Murray's incomplete projects. Individual passages compel interest, but taken all together, nothing works. Morgan's two chapters on finding her property and building the house generate interest and response because they are so specific; however, when the chapters follow Harry's grand program, especially on the universal and messianic meaning of their life together, they elude or irritate the reader with their inflated pomposity. The opus comes to life when it is personal and particular: when either of them struggled with what went wrong between them, or described what worked, or when they dared to explore the darker sides of their sexuality. But Morgan and Murray preferred to soar to Icarian heights rather than examine the ground of their reality, and they seldom wrote honestly enough to move the reader.

One could look at the life Christiana and Harry created at the Tower as the libretto of an opera, or as a kind of psychodrama through which they explored and lived out their fantasies. They were most honest, perhaps, in describing the most outlandish of the fantasies, and least successful in depicting the most sacred. Christiana had inaugurated cyclical days of prayer and recollection, for which they took turns making up the ceremonies. She created little prayerbooks, which she hand-printed and illuminated with the same care she had devoted to drawing her visions. The "Annuesta" (year celebration) booklets set out the bare bones of the various rituals, reading like a High Church service with poetry, antiphonal chants, hymns, offerings, and music, but honoring such things as masculine or feminine compassion, male or female beauty, atonement, and joy. Harry devised a "Fair of Goods," in which, before he departed on his many travels, he would present Christiana with valuable objects as troth of his love and safe return. In a courageous evening celebration Christiana called "Walpurgis," they set out to explore their sexuality with Dionysian excess. What keeps these recordings of private and personal rites from the ridiculous was their courage in facing what had been exiled or repressed in the culture of their time as well as what was most holy. In Walpurgis, they explored a trance where Christiana had seen behind the mask of goodness and then raised evil out of the darkness and into light. Both wanted to understand what it meant to raise evil and deal with it responsibly rather than through repression, and both liked to play with fire. The rituals they invented for this search condoned violence as well as excess.

261

Rituals usually bring people together to tame strong emotions by channeling them into ceremony and worship. They allow for and contain deep feeling and help unify a group with structured repetition. Christiana and Harry invented private rituals that united them in a way that pushed the limits of traditional rituals. They used ritual to enrich their life and to explore repressed wishes and desires. The two set out to confront what the superego abhorred— all the divine, dangerous, repressed, aggressive, sexual, perverse, and/or ecstatically religious impulses that were forbidden in their upbringing. They found a world of fascinating perversity, an infantile realm of pre-Oedipal and unbounded sensations—what Melanie Klein referred to as the infant's ecstasy of merger with the maternal and oceanic as well as its experience of murderous annihilation. Ritual provided Christiana and Harry with a formalized context in which they could play with, yet try to contain and regulate, the backwaters of the human psyche that fascinated and repelled them or drew their obeisance. In their secret explorations at the Tower, they discovered they needed to reverse roles, genders, and clothes, because whatever one created for the other they were really creating for themselves. Both had the courage to push their fantasies far enough and had imaginations large enough to risk experiencing the demonic side of their natures.

It would be a mistake to dismiss their whole experiment as either completely idiosyncratic or merely pornographic. Harry and Christiana attempted to imagine a post-Christian sphere where puritanical repression no longer locked up all vagrant and perverse imaginings. They chronicled their sexual psychodramas in a book called the "Red and Gold Diary," which Harry destroyed in the 1980s when he was going through his papers. Christiana had excerpted passages, which she kept in her files. The diary started as early as 1936, when Christiana recorded that Harry wore a green Hindu shirt and a black velvet skirt and whipped her before they made love. She justified her mistreatment as handing over her too threatening power and experiencing it through him:

My lover is myself explicit. My lover is all my past unconscious power made explicit. My life is like a deep pool
in a mountain stream. My life is like a field of wheat on
a windless day. My life is like the even tide without its
pain. Without its passionate ecstasy, craved for as lightening pain. This is the shape my lover has desired. Never
will my body know its delicious life without the touch of
my lover's strong whip. This is my body that speaks.

Their further experiments with sadomasochism seemed to take
place most often when Harry returned from some journey and may
have been a way for them not only to push the intensity of their
sexuality into pain but to suffer direct and swift retribution for
guilt. Harry became potent now not only when he wielded the
whip but also when he suffered from it:

Tonight Mansol returned from New Haven. . . . Tonight
my lover asked that I should have knowledge of my lust
& that my word should ask for it. I told my love that he
must wait patiently for my power to grow so that he would
at last feel *my* whip even as I had felt the lust of *his*. . . .
Mansol knew the rush of lust & asked for the final
assertion of the whip. Then Wona struck Mansol with her
black whip and it was good to her. . . . The old sun went
down to its death & Wona discovered a new land. "From
now on I shall care only for my nourishment." These were
the words of Wona. Wona was in black—black eye-
brows—black velvet dress & the strong turquoise ring on
her index finger. Her red nails transmitted power that was
irrevocable. And she said: "Again we are at the beginning
and again I shall trance. And I shall not care for any forces
that in the past have swayed you—your family, or any
demands from the world. I shall know my need and my
lust." Mansol's body knew that this was their truth. Here
they were at a new place—uncertain of fate. Mansol's lust
knew only obedience—ultimate, sensual submission.

Harry's and Christiana's erotic concentration on and use of
fabric, clothes, jewelry, and setting recalls fantasies more common
to Sacher-Masoch than to the Marquis de Sade. They excited each
other by describing their masturbations and their masturbatory fantasies and tried to reenact some of them together, each goading the
other a bit further to extremes. When Murray found himself unable
to write his Melville book, he started to dress more often in the

women's clothes that accompanied his sadist role; it was at this time that Christiana muted her power and played slave. The correlation of their actual violence to the excitation of the elaborate plans, equipment, and setting is hard to gauge. They possessed all the implements for their experiments—whips, chains, handcuffs, etc.— but there is never a diary entry about physical pain or wounds that needed healing, and both were busily at work the next day. But silence and absence of signs is typical of much family violence and part of its problem. Both Harry and Christiana sought and endured the swift "lightening" pain that seemed to take away and absolve the canker in their hearts.

The Red and Gold Diary and their sexual experiments lasted at least until the mid-1940s—enduring through a time when Christiana's visions focused on some personal acknowledgment of the devilish forces adrift in the world. With the war in Europe, the culture as a whole had immersed itself in a nightmarish outbreak of Nietzschean excess; Christiana and Harry echoed that spirit yet attempted to form a counterpart capable of containing some of the evil and understanding its hidden urges. Christiana, and then the two of them, invented rituals that explored their own particular and private evil—their shadow of the God of goodness they had been brought up to emulate—and so they struggled to express the demonic in a ritual form that could expose its built-in boundaries and limitations. This was dangerous work. Neither was aware of the parallels between their mediated investigations and the archetypal Dionysian frenzy of destructiveness loosed unconsciously in the world at large. Nor did they realize that venturing to mediate violence through direct experience opened them to all its dangers and to the very unleashing of what they were trying to contain.

They also invented more positive rituals, which continued throughout their lives and involved a tantric worship of the divine through varieties of sexual and spiritual union, or through sacred and formal ceremony. Other rituals necessitated cross-dressing or the making up of dramas, with roles each had to enact for the other. Still others had them, even in their sixties, improvising dances, in which one or both sported around the other like a faun or nymph, or danced lovingly, or reverently. They also played at being animals or gods. Some rituals enacted anger, the deadly sins, or acts of mercy; others returned to some of the more bizarre side streets of sexuality.

The sadomasochism they recorded in the Red and Gold Diary

recalled the sad old pattern of believing they were charting new reaches of sexuality when in fact they had returned to the basic ground of infancy's squirmy delights and nurses' or parents' retribution. Playing sadist or masochist, both were unaware how much the rituals connected with a child's polymorphously perverse needs and wounds. Their experiments re-created for Harry infantile memories not only of his dominating mother but of his treatment at the hands of his overstimulating and punishing sister; they reenacted his pleasure in the pain of his mother's, sister's, and nurse's little tortures and also his ambition to turn the tables on these overly powerful females. Christiana relived her early punishments for being too fiercely opinionated, too rebellious, and too strong; she reenacted her dark hours within the closet and her childhood religious ecstasies of atonement and relief. Each could be slave and dominator to the other in turn and thus, through repetition, try to master and heal the childhood assaults. The experiments also recalled Murray's doctor's prescription of fantasy for his impotence in the early years of his marriage. Harry had learned from this the potency of his imagination.

Elements of what Christiana and Harry were about lay unexamined while they studiously recorded everything that was happening on the surface of their lives. Yet few people seriously explore their sacred and profane fantasies, and fewer still leave records of them. Christiana and Harry risked exposing their "immoral, destructive, scary, immature, dirty, childish or sentimental" feelings in order to bring them into consciousness and deal with them objectively.

The problem was that they came to the enactment without fully understanding what they were doing. Neither was aware of one final element that played a pivotal role in Christiana's sexual fantasies. It had been part of her relationship with her husband and could have been so with Ken Diven if he had met her challenge. When Harry Murray no longer claimed Christiana's respect—when she could no longer honor him as he reneged on his promises and let her down time after time; when he never became the great writer and thinker she had hoped for; when he clung to his wife, his family, and his position as a noted Harvard professor at the Psychology Clinic; when again and again he talked his ideas away; when she let him use her as a common mistress rather than as the center of their spiritual and emotional life; and when she did not take on the responsibility of her own genius—then she tried to compensate by getting him to "thrill her and make her afraid," by mastering her with whips and chains. She had made these misguided attempts before, inciting men to do violence to her body, provoking them into being manly enough to conquer her strength. Thus did Harry and Christiana begin experimenting with violence as a way to bring some heat into a relationship that was growing increasingly empty and cold.

265

A good part of what remains of the Red and Gold Diary often sounds, to a modern eavesdropper, not like courageous exploration but like the futile self-stimulation of two naughty children seeking to thrill and shock each other. With childish grandiosity, they invented and described more than they probably ever acted out, but even for a modern taste it makes offensive reading.

> My love is my God and I have no other God but him. His word is the law, & for one year I shall obey it. My God will create from my blood. I will give all my substance to his best. Never will I disobey him. His word is my law. He will drink my blood, devour my flesh, ask for my last sacrifice, take all my spirit, possess me entirely. There is nothing he will demand that I will not give. . . . This is the year of my great sacrifice. I give up all my Gods for my *one* god. My blood, my thighs, my spirit—all that he demands. Every whim of his spirit to subdue me. I am mind for his impregnation. Glory to my Lord. For a year I shall become Melville. I shall think, read, feel, know nothing but Melville. My God demands it.

With the rituals, especially the Walpurgis evenings, and with Christiana's effort to regain her visions and Harry's to write his book, came a great deal of drinking. As Christiana's world dream narrowed down to the house and Tower, what had first been solace and inspiration now became habit and addiction; she used alcohol as she used their sadomasochistic rituals—to warm her glacial isolation and despair. At first during the war years, Christiana became a Walpurgis-evening alcoholic, well able to manage her clinic duties and private practice, to carve and garden, but then she started to have bouts of full-time drinking.

Harry meanwhile had started taking amphetamines to keep up with his war work, and the pills led him into furiously energetic explorations. In a moment of abject clarity, Murray descended from his Icarian height to realize he was unable to dedicate himself wholeheartedly to Christiana or anything else. He wrote: "I am second rate. My definition of someone who is second rate is Someone who hasn't dedicated himself to the vision he has recognized." Harry's solution was to literally whip Christiana, as the visioner, into providing more depth for him and to stimulate her into inspiring his Melville biography while Harry would write about her visions. And when this creativity through decree failed, his solution was to flee from her and spend more and more time away. Neither of them realized that each needed to take up his or her own task. Unable to make an inner marriage, they evaded their fate by projecting aspects of themselves on each other, each wanting the other to do the work and punishing the other for failing. Both, in their narcissism, forgot the sacred ecstasy they experienced in corporeal love. Harry ritualized his savage incantations to potency, but he veiled his little boy's fear, attraction, and repulsion toward the powerful female; he cloaked the violence in a transvestite surge of masturbatory sadomasochism. This met Christiana's own guilt for being a powerful female and her fantasies of finding a man who could master her. Both then looked back to Gothic Romanticism as their guide but found only its chiaroscuro, heroics, and langueurs, and its gruesome talent for making women into monsters and then torturing them.

One of the strangest testaments to their experiments was a long reverie of almost forty pages that Harry wrote on a trip West with his wife. In it, he looked back on his life with Christiana, composing the eerie scene from her point of view. It was almost as if he were giving Christiana stage directions for how she could become the image of his inner woman.

From Mansol's Tale of the Tower

Wona lifted a heavy log off the top of the pile, and dropped it on a bank of coals at the back of the fire. . . . It was five o'clock and she was alone, her beloved having left yesterday for the West. But she had warmed some cheese on crackers, mixed herself a Daiquiri and put on her brown and blue Indian Sari just as though Mansol were there to revel in it all. The entire rite had to be observed at a time like this when her destiny was threatened.

The feeling had grown in her, and now it could no longer be neglected, that there was something awry about the method of their life. She must brood on it, receptive to illumination. She poured a drink and lit a cigarette. . . .

Ah! the luxury of this moment. Only at such times, unmindful of all irrelevant considerations, would ideas flow out directly from the source of her trance life. Only these could be relied upon. With the records of her pioneering saga to aide her memory, she could review the steps that they had taken to reach their present place. . . .

"Do you favor Freud or Jung?" she had asked him the first time he dined with her, and he had no answer, having read neither. What life could she have made with him, if she had failed to excite his interest in psychology, if she had failed to convince him that psychology was the spearhead of modern thought, the science of the future? Her lover *had* to be a psychologist, a man whose conceptual powers could complement and order her estimates of life; and she had made no mistake in picking Mansol. It was chance perhaps that he received an appointment at Harvard giving him freedom in the afternoons, but it was due to her insistence that he rented a room where they could meet and have their life.

She thought with pain of the trysts of other lovers, of the thousands of young men and women who had to meet secretly and guiltily under the veil of night, on back alleys, dingy hotels, roadhouses, and parked motors. What if she had not built the Property? . . .

She remembered his proposing that they love each other without their body's rapture. What if she had yielded? Where would they be now if she had not ridiculed him when he said that he had formed a satisfying philosophy? Was it a philosophy to console his cowardice? She remembered how he used to cover his penis; she remembered his qualms and hesitations, his year or two of impotence. She had not been far wrong in giving him *The Temptations of St. Anthony* for Christmas. Only with difficulty and by degrees had she aroused him, made him unafraid, taken upon herself his load of guilt, taught him the beauties and the righteousness of lust, and ultimately made a complete male of him. How could she have flowered without his throbbing penis—the beginning and the goal of her bloody fantasies.

When she first met him he used to approach everything with his intellect, naming, classifying, cataloging, bearing down on people with his categories regardless of

267

their mood. All things were devoured, but the best—the core of what he touched escaped him. This habit of his had to be destroyed if they were to go on, and she had not hesitated to attack him with all the barbed strength of her outraged sensibilities. . . .

Another enemy to her spirit was Mansol's adherence to society, his loyalty to family, friends, clubs, and associations. There was a boyishness which annoyed her greatly. She remembered when she first asked him to throw his A.D. bull into the lake in Zurich, and he refused. It had taken her three years to get him to the point of the Great Conflagration when she asked him to burn pictures and symbols of every allegiance that had claims on him. She felt a wave of apprehension now—even now—as she thought of those years, those first three or four when she was laying the bare foundation of their future glory. Most of her energy had been devoted to destruction, breaking down interferences in him: his outmoded conscience, his deadening rationality, his affiliations, his scruples, his youthful sentiments. She was impatient to get on with her life, impatient of his caution, his cool reasonings, his impotence. It was all precarious. Any moment he might have taken flight, as he did do once, running to the arms of a woman who overflowed with honeyed flattery and pity. . . .

She had read him a few of her trances, but his blundering, commonplace remarks had chilled her to the bone. And she had been forced to admit to herself the disheartening fact that a vast distance in experience, in depth and sincerity of living separated them. A chasm of spiritual understanding lay between them, and she had no choice but to withdraw and bury her trance life in the sanctuary of her heart. She put away her books. They would have to wait. Her lover was hardly more than a boy, and she would have to move slowly, step by step. Her trances, in fact, had frightened him and she was forced to meet him on a simpler level. The space between them increased and the anguish and terror of her loneliness carrying the life force unaided, heightened the pain of her necessary ruthlessness, beating down obstructions, neglecting what others called her duties, tearing indignantly at the chains that bound her man. . . .

She had influenced him to push the work at the Clinic more and more in her direction, getting away from the old mechanical experiments, until he finally devised for her use the Thematic Apperception Test, his one contribution to methodology.

Just as it had been necessary for her to bring him to a realization of the flesh, so also did she have to teach him the significance and beauty of the earth. He knew nothing about the weather, never knew where the wind was from. He had never laid out a garden, transplanted a tree, or watched the ebb and flow of tides. . . .

She lifted up the silver mirror that Mansol loved, and looked into her face. Her lips were carmine at once passionate yet firm. Yes, LaChaise had seen them as they truly were. And her eyes—tightening the muscles around them as she looked—yes, they too were beautiful—and in them she could see the steady purpose of her heart. It was the purpose that had made this house, carved the shutters on the windows, picked the objects that were about, each of them compact with reminiscences of her endeavor, surrounding her at all times with memorials of lived experience. . . .

Her dwelling was built out of the tissues of their bodies. He could never break forth with these tokens of their enduring dedication. The forces that held other lovers were spider-threads that could be torn by any adverse wind of passion, but the links that her industry had forged were made of steel.

She threw her cigarette into the fireplace and contemplated the gilded chains strung across the chimney bricks. Life was so mysterious! One could never know or foretell what new requirements would arise. Here was Ken Diven who had entered her life, first as a warm admirer, then as a loyal slave, devoting his leisure to the gaiety and enchantment of her life and of her place. Once it was Ralph Eaton. "I need another man in my life," she had said to Mansol. But Mansol had told her that Ralph was not good enough to be admitted. And so it proved. Ken's fidelity, however, had been tested and Mansol accepted him. Ken belonged to her; he satisfied a lighter, minor side of her personality. Later she might need others, an artist or a young Prometheus like Lewis Mumford. Mansol was now far beyond jealousy. He was confident of his central place in the living pageant of her life and acknowledged without pain that she might need other men for her full flowering. . . .

She had never been so conscious as she was now of the method of their life. In simplest terms it had consisted of a long series of conversions, each stage of their pilgrimage having been a lesson she embedded in her lover's personality. At each victory she had rewarded him with beauty. In her body and clothes she had given him more splendors than any hungry eyes of man had ever gazed on—and she had given freely of her flesh for the joy of his bursting penis, his hand, his mouth, his skin—lying back to back for twelve hours of the night. *Inwardly,* during all these years she had not changed, but outwardly she was very different, for every step in Mansol's spiritual development had meant a confirmation and a re-enforcement of her Self. It had meant that one more fraction of her life could be shared with him and every sharing lessened her isolation. Thus she had become steadily more joyful and secure, less terrified and less inflammable. . . .

"The root sin," she said to herself as the issue suddenly sharpened in her mind, "was his habit of imposing programs for their life." It was his ego still bound to the world and its demands, that forced a schedule on her soul, just as if her spirit could be nailed down to a routine to satisfy a Department of Psychology. Did he not realize that their progress depended on the freedom, the vitality and sensitivity of her feeling? His way was the old way of life which she, long ago, had told him must not recur? She had let him go on confident that he would finish up with Melville. But experience had convinced her that his ego could not be trusted. This part of him was her adversary and she must beat it down and make it subservient forever to his penis. It must never be allowed to interfere again with the march of her long delayed quest. . . .

For twelve years—and it seemed hardly believable—she had made herself available to him at all hours, left her life open so that he could settle when they should meet, and where, and for how long. She had made no engagements—if so she had always been ready to break them at a moment's notice. She had been prepared to leave home with a bag in her hand for a day or for a week, whenever he was free. He had rarely consulted her; his power to decide had become a custom. However just this custom she now realized must change. The order of control must be reversed. She had no inclination to command. She detested power. It froze her body and put Eros to flight. . . .

She did not want to lead, she much preferred to rest in his domination. But, of late, the pace of his internal growth had been too slow and for the next eight months at least she would have to shape their course, taking charge of his becomingness. He was in a position to appreciate how much there was at stake. What did his untroubled ego know of the suffering out of which her visions had been born? Had he ever achieved such compelling concentration? Had he ever experienced the fearful forces that she had grappled with? Had he faced the revulsion, fright and pain of it; wrestled with his daemon; ventured alone regardless of consequences, to the outposts of sanity; persisted when all the world cried halt? And had he ever challenged his society; been faithful enough to an ideal to kick them in the guts? . . .

If only he had experienced what she had, stamping down her womanly tenderness in order that her visionary life might live! She had been tested in adversity and had worked through and finally found a way to shape their life according to her furthest hope. The torment, the anxiety, the burden, the huge trial of it all—this was why she loved her trances first and Mansol second. This was why she could not let them perish. This was why she must change Mansol to fit the vision, instead of changing the vision to fit him. . . .

But first she would demand the restoration of their lust. It seemed ages since she had seen his beauty, his red lips bending over her, his red fingers clutched about his cruel whip. Where was his massive power? To direct his life she needed his great penis very often. She was starved and sick. Did he think she could create a way for him without his penis? Where was his pride of manhood, his brutality, the savage lust that she craved? She took another drink and felt the hot blood run through her. Ah! This warmed her. This was what she required—drink and his penis and his fist and his iron heel. Her body tingled as she thought of it. Her power made her cold. His power made her hot. More wildness in him was what she wanted. She would have to include this as part of his morality. She would scorn him when his penis was small and glorify him when his penis was large. "Mansol," she would say, "I give you the morality of a large penis and an imperial authority. You are of no use to me with a small cowardly little penis. I want daring, my Mansol— Brutality! Show

me the animal in you, so that I can be proud of my lover.
I shall never take you as my instrument until you can hurt
me without pity. I detest your pity and your timorous
tame penis. Give me a hungry, swelling, piercing, insis-
tent, regal and demanding penis." . . .

She pictured Mansol back from the West sitting there
on the couch in his blue Navajo shirt. She lit a cigar, walked
to the hearth and with her back to the fire addressed him
thus:

Listen to me, my beloved, and let every word I speak
drop as a fruit-bearing seed into your heart. We have come
to a standstill. You have ceased developing and I am sad
and disquieted. . . .

I want assurances from you. I have a few troublesome
suspicions, my Mansol. Your ego has led us into barren
places and the provisional life stretches out too far. The
sand is passing through the hour-glass. Death is at my
shoulder. But I cannot admit you to the sealed hiding place
of my trance until you have moved ahead much further
than you are now. I cannot allow my trances to be diminished. You must grow in their stature before I can let
you see them again and you must grow rapidly. . . . Do
you understand, my beloved? Four things you must learn
from me before September. You must learn 1. the most
sensitive obedience; 2. the courage to acknowledge your
faith in my superiority; 3. my rhythm of creation; and 4.
savage manhood. . . .

Understand, my darling, I have no desire to exercise
authority. I am looking forward to the day when all the
power will be yours and I can rest in my submission. But
first I must teach you by example to lead precisely as I
wish. . . .

From now on I want you to center your life in me
and consider this place or wherever I happen to be your
home. I want this tower to be your base—the place where
you keep your things and do the main body of your work.
For after this you will visit your family when I choose to
let you go. I am the source of your well-being and of your
fruition. You are mine, not Jo's. I have not decided yet
what I shall do about your marriage, or when I shall have
you leave the Clinic permanently but I have made up my
mind that from now on I shall decide how much time you
will devote to your family and how much to the Clinic.
I have determined to advance the proposition at their ex-

pense. You have already given them more energy than they deserve. I do not want to hear one word from you on their behalf. . . .

Second, and this is most essential, you must learn boldness, the courage of the faith I have taught your penis. Mansol, my darling, I am distrustful of your daring. I am not certain yet—you have not shown me—that your courage is worthy of my trances. If I should admit you now to the sanctuary of my heart would you acknowledge me before the world? I am afraid not. I can almost hear you giving one of those nice, socially agreeable explanations of why you are not working at the Clinic. In the future many people will ask, "What are you doing?" "When is your next book coming?" What will you say? Will you deny me? . . .

I admit that you are my superior in science and the world, but that is not my path. I am wedded to the spirit and here, as your superior, I am determined to develop you to the utmost. . . .

And finally, Mansol, I want your full bodily life, your enormous penis, your utmost capacity of mastery. My need is vast and we cannot advance in our life until you have met my last demands. I want you to conquer all your fears of brutality. I need brutality. I want all the terrible cruelty of your nature. I want power such as no woman has ever known. I want to be humiliated physically just as I humiliate your ego spiritually. I want to be beaten and struck down and spat upon. I want your chains on my arms, the smoke from your cigar in my face. I want to be ordered and kicked about and prohibited and coerced. I want to be ground down and made to kiss your feet and eat my food from the floor. I want to slave for you and kneel before you and ask your favor and call you my master and my lord. And above all I want your savage penis, the whip in your hand, the burning blows upon my flesh. You shall know when I need this by my hands. Follow Eros as it appears on my finger nails. When my nails are orange, or blue, or imperial red you will know that my body is hungry for your penis, and when I make your fingers red you shall understand that I crave your supernal cruelty. I may want your body every day and I may want long periods of submission to your beautiful authority. Mansol, my beloved, I cannot admit you to my sanctuary until you have shown me that you are capable of prodigious cruelty. . . .

I do not want to frighten you. You must remember what you dare I have dared before you, that no matter how deep you go into life I have been there years ago. Remember that now I am beside you. You will be spared the uncertainty, the solitary vigil, the loneliness that I suffered at twenty-eight. You will never be without a guide for I include you, and my trances are beyond your reach, a track of light through darkness. . . .

You have asked me, "Where are we?" "What is our dilemma?" I can sum it all up for you. The slowness of your development is our dilemma. Therefore I intend to devote all my beauty, all my will, to its advance. I shall push my egotism to the limit. . . . I shall want the clearest proof: 1. that you have achieved the habit of unquestioning obedience to my word; 2. that you can happily neglect your family and your duties for my sake; 3. that you are proud to be my slave in public and proud to acknowledge my superiority before your friends; 4. that you have acquired my rhythm of creative work; and finally, that you can release your savagery and fill my cup of ecstasy.

But this was Harry writing, as if he were creating what he wanted Christiana to be and how he wanted his monster to respond. Christiana tried her best to fulfill Harry's need and his dark romantic fantasies. Her own guilt and early childhood complexes as well as her depressions and what she had learned about women from her culture conspired to desecrate her worship of a god of love. Instead of the convergence of equals they sought, they engaged in a power struggle, which Christiana lost because she began to punish herself for being as strong as or stronger than her man. She had written Harry letters during the war, calling him Master and referring to herself as his slave, while he in turn decreed who, what, why, and how she should be. He also demanded that she write their books *his* way, with his voice. And Christiana gave up her own instinct, intuition, and recognition of the divine—her way of envisioning— in a futile attempt to translate her experience into Harry's language. It didn't work.

At the same time that Christiana and Harry created their monster, she gained some rewards for giving up her independence and living in isolation. With Harry's support, she worked creatively in her Tower, with some of her patients at her home in Cambridge, and at the clinic. She could draw on Harry's love just as his woman patient had when he was a young medical resident—by arousing his pity. She also won his love by living like a romantic queen, alone, isolated, and captive in their Tower, nursing their hopes and dreams while he roamed the world, an errant knight. She secured time and space to be herself both out in the world and in her sanctuary, but ultimately she lost that self to Harry's vision of what he wanted her to be. And her love did fail her, as she gave herself over to Harry. Christiana forgot the summons her visions gave her to translate their meaning and she paid for her self-betrayal with the alcoholism of her later years.

Harry wanted her to remain in her place as a player on the stage of his Romantic fantasy. After the war had ended and his duties with the OSS were finished, he did none of the things he had promised her. Their relationship became a series of Wagnerian arias. She turned from her own power toward finding a perverse joy in her pain and, increasingly, toward drowning what might have been in drink.

THIRTEEN

The End
of the Chase

*It is the long drawn out pain of the provisional
life—not yet—not yet the trances made alive,
not yet my true being said—*

CHRISTIANA MORGAN

In the late 1940s, Harry completed his book *The Assessment of
Men,* and his energies returned once again to the clinic. His
continued good relationship with the Rockefeller Foundation
in New York resulted in a new Rockefeller grant for the clinic and
a plan for a longitudinal study of some of the clinic's earliest subjects. The clinic was renamed the Center for Personality Study and
separated from a psychology department that had grown even more
behavioristic. The center became part of Harvard's new Department of Social Relations, which joined personality study and abnormal psychology under Murray with sociology and anthropology
under his friends Gordon Allport and Clyde Kluckhohn, respectively, to create one of Harvard's first cross-disciplinary departments. This new configuration and the support these men gave each
other led to the professorship Murray had so long deserved.

The Plympton Street building now housed a clinical psychology program under Robert White and was no longer available to
Murray; with the help of the Rockefeller money, he bought the

house at 48 Mount Auburn Street for his group. Named the Annex (to Plympton Street) or, more commonly, the Baleen, in homage to Melville, the building remained empty for a time, for following Murray's return to Harvard, there was a hiatus before the new program began. This was partly owing to Murray's campaign to persuade Christiana Morgan to give up their dreams of a life together at the Tower and lure her back to the clinic. He had to convince her that they could write just as well at the new Annex as at the Tower and that the change in direction was not a renunciation of promises but a new passage, ever closer to their dream. Christiana let herself be persuaded.

It was not altogether a bad move for her. Christiana agreed to return with the proviso that she would work part-time on her own book. Harry also promised that the clinic would take up research questions revolving around her interests. She pulled herself together, stopped drinking, and focused on theoretical and practical psychology. Once again, Morgan designed another elegant sanctum for scholarship and comfort. Under the power of Murray's contagious enthusiasm and Morgan's inner spirit, the clinic crested in a brief renascence.

Robert White, who had known Christiana Morgan from the first years of the clinic, worried about her marked decline. Though Christiana was still beautiful and extraordinarily insightful, and she continued her role as the hidden soul of the place, serving as an invaluable part of a research team, White sensed a deterioration, which he attributed to her health problems, but even more to a real loss of heart. White decided, after her initial flush of renewal waned, that Christiana's hopes for a complete life with Murray had ebbed away for good.

Murray continued to be driven with a maelstrom's energy; his enthusiasms would sweep toward her and then just as suddenly sweep away. His inability to finish his Melville book put even more of a strain on their relationship, and she soon viewed the new grant and his eagerness to replicate the earlier studies with growing doubt. The shared dream ranged further and further away, and yet Morgan had staked her visions and her life on it, and so she willed herself to go on believing that following Harry's star was her fate. She had chased the vagrant whale too long and lost too much to that fatal goal to give it up now.

For a few years, though, Morgan played at her old role and involved herself in the clinic. Robert Holt, who was part of the

core postwar group that included White, David McClelland, Silvan Tompkins, and Fred Wyatt, regarded Morgan as a leading but enig-
278   matic member of the clinic—a patrician, elegant, unpretentious, and eminently unknowable colleague. He joined her research team, and although he was initially bothered by her lack of scientific training and knowledge of scientific research design, he soon learned to appreciate her skill in personality research and interviewing, and her grounded psychoanalytic contributions to the team's work. Holt considered her presence at case conferences very helpful; he felt she was thoroughly professional, paid close attention, and responded with informed and psychoanalytically acute questions, yet phrased them unobtrusively, saying, for example, "Do you think there may be another way of looking at this?" before presenting her own viewpoint.

Christiana worked for a time with her old effectiveness but found the clinic less and less congenial. She was no longer as essential to the organization as she once had been and felt pushed aside. Along with the grant money had come an excellent staff and a new and equally outstanding crop of graduate students, all of whom commandeered Murray's energy. David McClelland, who had been with Murray in Washington, took over Morgan's place as Murray's right hand, and with the increasing professionalism of the times, there were fewer tasks a lay psychologist could perform. And a new factor emerged—a growing prejudice, if not contempt, toward uncredentialed talent in a university setting.

Although men like White, Holt, and Murray accepted and even welcomed women colleagues, the end of the war brought a closing of the ranks against professional women in general throughout the United States, which was even more pronounced at Harvard. It was a period of severe setback for women, who, with the influx of returning war veterans, were often replaced or encouraged to re-sume their domestic roles. Along with that "climate of unexpec-tation" for women generally came a refractory hostility to women as academic peers. The new and pervasive arrogance made light of women or condescendingly ignored them except as lovers, mothers, daughters, or secretaries. Academia again became a club for men where women were outsiders—sexual objects first and creative workers second, if at all. Under this formula, female assistants and students were fair sexual game for the professors, but the double standard made Morgan's position as well as her free approach to sexuality and her liaison with Murray scandalous. Echoing the values of this censorious time, Wyatt, Tompkins, and others felt far less positive about Christiana Morgan than did her earlier colleagues. Some simply refused to acknowledge her; others, though usually outwardly polite, expressed their disdain in private. And because Harry's charisma induced an almost homoerotic intensity in even some of the most clublike men, Christiana's special relationship with him aroused envy and enmity. One noted colleague spurned her as nothing but a latter-day flapper, refusing to concede her any originality or talent; Wyatt made light of Christiana, yet pursued the fifty-year-old woman as fair game in corridors and the kitchen or at parties; and Tompkins disdained her so much that in the final years of his life, in the late 1980s, he refused to discuss her, dismissing her as a nymphomaniac.

During this time, Harvard, with Murray's concurrence, dropped Morgan's name from their best-selling Thematic Apperception Test, citing Henry Murray as its only author. Christiana may have pretended not to care as she brushed aside this rewriting of history as beneath her dignity, but it further eclipsed her value to the new department. This was only one sign of the hostile academic atmosphere that infected the clinic; though each woman at Harvard dealt with it differently, male chauvinism was so much a part of the time that its pervasive drag on women's energy went unremarked. Christiana had reveled once in the positive side of men's attraction to her, but as she aged she saw younger women take on the roles she used to play, sometimes even with Harry himself. Signs of her drinking could no longer be disguised, and clinic members started to consult with Murray about it.

During the late 1940s, Morgan did what work she could in the increasingly difficult professional climate and spent more and more time at the clinic working on the chapters for her book and concentrating on her patients. The support of her friends meant even more to her now. Lewis Mumford spent a year teaching at Harvard and provided a valuable and healing antidote to the regressive climate; he went so far as to claim Christiana as one of the three best minds at Harvard and preferred discussing his ideas with her than with a hundred professors. Morgan in response shared her ideas with him both in Cambridge and in long letters after he left Harvard. In one letter, she told him of the satisfaction she derived from her work with four new patients, all of them young; she codified her thoughts about analysis and mused on her creative and initiatory role. Morgan formed her ideas of analysis in a very different way from her former analyst Hanns Sachs; she found more of a basis in Jung's psychology but added a womanly tone of her own:

I find that I cannot deal with any of them according to the books—but must dare life face to face—and oh, what vigils and self-examinations this entails! . . .

Analysis necessitates a *creative* process on the part of the analyst. The patient appears. The analyst is the physician, the helper—so the transference at first is fairly established. Then the patient talks—strives to enlist the sympathy of the analyst—unconsciously tries to start up a response in the analyst. This [is] the basis of *all* human contact. Then suddenly a creative process is started in the analyst. This means that something in the unconscious of the patient has set fire to the unconscious of the analyst. The creative process implies this unconscious origin—for there is no creation without this. Then this process influences the patient— He thinks why this started up a creativeness in the other person (analyst)— It must be important—this has power—this created a contact—this was responded to—this made life happen. So he sees himself mirrored. Now as far as the analyst goes there can be no true creativeness which will have value for the patient unless the unconscious is developed—unless it is pure of personal problems—and further—unless it is a fiery nervous system—for the creative process starts from the unconscious response of the analyst—and it must be very delicate, highly tuned, impersonal— And it must further be formed in imaginative speech, in images—in words of symbolic meaning. So the instinct that no one should analyze until they themselves are highly developed is quite right—for the creative process must be separate from the individual—the child must be born separate—otherwise there is only an individual unconscious response to the patient—not a creative response— Then the patient would react to the analyst as an individual rather than reacting to or being inspired by the creative process. And as far as the analyst goes the patient can be a mirror for the creative thing. Its power, its timeliness, can only be known thru the patient. So the patient during analysis ought to be exalted, energized, animated as though he were in love— for indeed to start a creative process in an individual creates a new life and a new energy—but the erotic element will of course not be responded to by the analyst—so the obvious *sexual* element is of course left out. (Here is the secret of what we feel about I. [Irmirita Putnam] She is an uncreative person, and gives forth knowledge. So her patients lack the fire and the fury to carry ahead.)

Another thing— When emotion comes up in a patient—the patient may quickly see that it is unsuitable to the present situation or social order—& would therefore tend to repress it. Now what the analyst must do is to dignify it by stories of the past, for as Peirce says "it is antiquity which gives dishonour or dignity to an emotion." So by greatly dignifying a crude manifestation the patient can be made to feel that under no circumstances does he want to lose that emotion or to repress it. Hence it has sufficient energy for him to transform it—to change it—until it finds some suitable outlet in present circumstances. Thus the stories that Jung used to tell of the transformations & changes of emotional manifestation during the ages served a double purpose—that of dignifying the emotion & putting the idea of transformation into the unconscious.

Mumford and Morgan corresponded frequently during these years and drew strength from each other against what they perceived as an increasingly arid world. As the climate of the clinic grew less welcoming, Morgan developed more friendships with women, although her introversion and the awkwardness of her relationship to Harry still restricted the range of her companions. During these years, Christiana Morgan had few confidantes, but these tended to become lifelong friends; they had to pass the test of accepting Morgan's life without judging her by conventional morality. Christiana's old friend Sal Sherburne, now Putnam, continued as devoted confidante, not sharing Christiana's deepest experiences but accompanying her, laughing with her, and loving her as only a childhood intimate could do. Sal was joined by more strongly supportive and demanding friends—Morgan's onetime analyst Frances Wickes, and Cleome Wadsworth, whom Christiana had first met at the clinic but soon welcomed to her Tower. Morgan, in turn, visited Wadsworth at her house near Washington, D.C., and on her large property on Saint John in the Caribbean. Dona Louisa Coomaraswami and Christiana remained fast friends, taking perhaps as much pleasure in the fireworks of their intellectual arguments as in their mutual support. These women, all of them powerful in their own right, were able to meet Morgan with the intensity and verve she had loved in Lucia Howard, her friend of adolescence. They all shared books, philosophical and psychological discussions, and a deep interest in women's issues. Morgan also befriended Murray's research assistant Hansi Greer, who had typed some of their chapter drafts for them, but found her to be at once too impressed by Morgan's role in Murray's life and too much his slave. Irritated by Greer's treating her as if she were Murray's property, Morgan was relieved when the younger woman left the clinic for analysis with Barbara Hannah in Switzerland. The two became somewhat closer afterward, although both offered more allegiance to Murray than to each other.

Morgan's relationship with her own sisters was edgily friendly, while her love for her niece, Constance Wigglesworth, seemed freer and less problematical. Constance was awed by her glamorous aunt. The Wigglesworths often gave swimming parties, with everyone in bathing suits or shorts except Christiana, who, according to Connie, would arrive late, looking "divinely elegant." When Connie was ill, Christiana would bring her home to Hilliard Street, put her to bed, and take extravagant care of her. There were times also when Connie, almost frozen with shyness and fearing she would be a wallflower, would come in from the country to stay with Christiana before the various Boston and Cambridge dances. Christiana would discuss Connie's gown, let her try on some of her own dresses, loan her jewelry, make up her face, do her hair, and pull everything together for her; then, just before Connie left, Christiana would tell her she looked beautiful, give her a drink, and send her on her way in a rosy glow of anticipated success.

While Murray's daughter, Josie, was attending Radcliffe in the mid-1940s, Harry welcomed her into the Baleen and put her love of music and her knowledge of psychology to work to produce a musical association test. Josie and her friend Esmee Brooks, assigned rooms in the cellar of the Baleen, worked hard on their project but failed to produce a workable research design. Josie was remembered by Robert White and many others as being at that time a gentle, feminine version of her father—sharp, witty, and fun, but lacking her father's self-confidence. She combined her mother's gregarious generosity and goodness of heart with a beguiling shyness, and she labored valiantly to please Murray. He, alas, tended to be hypercritical of her and far less generous in his encouragement and praise than he was to others in the group. The young woman's tenure was awkward for both Christiana and Josie, and they generally kept their distance. Josie had learned of the Morgan-Murray relationship ten or more years before, when she and Councie had talked together after Will Morgan died. Christiana did reach out to her, however, over the question of clothes, much as she did to her niece. A short letter she wrote to Josie at this time showed Christiana's pleasure in helping the young woman.

> Josephine dear,
> What fun to participate in your "dressing up." Would that I could be a fly on the wall and see you there—the brightest and most beautiful of all stars.
>
> Now, dear, I want to *give* you the necklace and the scarf. There is little enough that I can do for you— So please accept these and the love and admiration that goes with them.
>
> > Christiana

Morgan rejoiced in and supported her son's fiancée, Hallee Perkins, in the same way and showed great relief upon Councie's marriage. It was as if she felt that he was finally in safe hands, as if only a lover could provide the comfort and nurturing he needed— a nurturing that might more naturally have characterized a mother-son relationship. Morgan had written Murray of her joy that her son had found such a warm, loving, open, and sensible wife, who was good fun besides. Christiana helped the young couple socially and practically and, after her own fashion, gave Hallee glorious lacy negligees, slips, and nightgowns. Councilman had finished medical school and was doing his internship in New York at the time of their marriage, and the young couple had little money. Christiana gave a huge cocktail party to introduce Hallee to as many friends and relatives in Boston as she could gather together and then took several trips to New York to help the couple choose and furnish their tiny apartment. The letters she wrote to Hallee were consistently warm and loving. Few letters survive from Christiana to her son, though it is clear that their relationship grew closer in these years. She wrote to Harry of her pleasure at being able to tell Councie, in his role of doctor, the essence of what she had learned about patient care as a nurse, psychologist, and patient herself.

> My beloved—
> Just one word on the telephone with you tonight told me how to write the letter to Counce— I said I was sure he was doing these things out of his own true instinct—but

that it might help him if he realized that there was a profound and ancient wisdom behind his natural instincts—which, in these hospitals—in his role of intern—he probably doesn't hear much about—but which should be as clear to them as therapy as any intravenous solution which they have to give.

I know that they are run ragged, and are most of the time worn out—so I tried to set it all forth for him very simply— I made four points and told him why I thought they were important—

I. Always call your patient by his name & make a point of repeating it—

II. Always tell your pt. what you are doing and why—(Otherwise you throw him to his *own* wolves of panic and the unconscious)

III. Always ask him about his pain—let him tell you—& promise to fix it— (Pain is a lonely business—& everyone—especially doctors—hate to hear about it— But they are in great need of understanding the psychology of the patient—and thus protecting themselves—)

IV. Always take the patients hand—or pat him on the shoulder after you have done what you have to do— (This is the ancient wisdom of the Laying on of Hands—)

So I took those four points—which are simple enough for any intern to carry out from bedside to bedside—and tried to tell Counce what was behind each one from our point of view— But at the same time I assumed that he knew them all— I feel that I wrote it all well enough to have added something to his depths—the first "personal" letter I have written to him since his marriage.

Like Leviathan I seem to breach for one project a day—and then sink back to the depths. But this is good. When I come to the surface now I bring the ocean floor with me—and feel absolutely unshakeable for the brief time in which I come up for air.

Again with Harry's financial help, Christiana built a summer cottage for her son, near to but out of sight of the Tower. Hallee and Counce began to use it for their vacations, and then, after their children were born, Hallee often spent summers there with their growing family. Christiana welcomed her grandchildren with no apparent qualm about aging. When she had one or another of them over for visits at her Tower, she taught enjoyment, faring much better at games, dances, and fantasy than at daily caretaking. Christiana did not hide the fact that she had favorites, nor did she ever try to balance out her favors equitably. She was especially fond of little Hallee, the eldest, who was enchanted by the magic of her visits alone with her grandmother. Morgan described a scene that captured some of the little girl's rapture at life in the Tower:

> One day this summer I took the babe—a city child—up to Magnolia Hill for a picnic lunch. For me this was the most charming moment of her visit and for her a great adventure. We sat on a rock looking down into the Philosophenweg. What delightful fantasies were induced by the awesome precipice, the huge trees, the darkness of the woods below us and around us. We were mountain climbers in dangerous territory, we were fearful of wild animals, we were squirrels gathering nuts, we were up in an aeroplane and could look on the house from on high.

At the Tower as well as at the Baleen during the 1950s, Morgan continued to work on the Thematic Apperception Test through its various revisions and additions. She returned to her earlier interest in creating a more fantastical series of pictures and redrew these, inserting many symbols from her visions into the mundane but still ambiguous settings. In one of these TAT cards, Morgan drew an intriguing picture that included a tower like Jung's in Bollingen but even more like her own. The tower dominates the center of Morgan's picture, a dark-haired woman (resembling Christiana Morgan) is in profile on the lower left, while a wise old man— reminiscent of both Jung and Chaim Weizmann—appears on the upper right. It was as much autobiographical statement of the puzzle of her own life as clue to draw others' imaginal response. Through its power to elicit fantasy material, Morgan's new version of the TAT was intended to help measure creativity for the clinic's new project on that subject. Christiana felt the new cards could also be useful in therapy, testing not only creativity but also whether or not a patient had the capacity for introspection and was ready to withstand probing into archetypal depths.

Dorothy Tobkin, who came to the Baleen in the fall of 1953, remembered Morgan working on these pictures and her occasionally vivid presence at the clinic. Tobkin had just received a summa cum laude from Radcliffe, having written a brilliant senior thesis in social relations, with Harry Murray as her professor. He hired her as a research assistant to work out a typology of the dramatic imagination. She had an office in the attic of the Baleen and slowly grew to know and admire Christiana; Tobkin occupied much the same role Saul Rosenzweig had in the early years of the clinic and like him became a loyal friend. A smart young woman from a middle-class Cleveland background, Tobkin confessed she was uncomfortable with anybody but a fellow Jew. Thus she was surprised that she felt completely at ease with Morgan; no one at Harvard had reached out to her as much, and Tobkin started to consider the older woman a mentor and substitute parent. Christiana's friendship and attention made these years some of the richest ones of Tobkin's life. She delighted in Morgan's interest and felt herself drawn into a better world, protected and secure. The women were mutually impressed: Morgan by Tobkin's intellectual brilliance and scholarly success; Tobkin by the depth of Morgan's knowledge of psychology and her rich and contemplative life. Like Saul Rosenzweig, as she grew fonder of Christiana Morgan and more taken by the solidity of her work, she was less impressed by Harry Murray. For the six years they knew each other, Tobkin occasionally heard rumors about Morgan's drinking but never saw signs of it. Perhaps Christiana was trying to live up to Dorothy Tobkin's admiration.

After they had become good friends at the clinic, Morgan invited Tobkin to dinner at Hilliard Street and then for visits to the Tower. When she learned that Tobkin planned to spend her summer in the airless little apartment she rented over a shop on Brattle Street, Morgan gave Tobkin her Hilliard Street house for the summer; Tobkin stayed there a subsequent summer, when she returned from a fellowship abroad. Tobkin loved the elegance and comfort of Morgan's house, from its sophisticated black living room to the huge and comfortable kitchen, with its ornate cast-iron wood-burning stove. She was moved by the closeness between Christiana and her longtime housekeeper, Isabella, and the care they took of each other. After one of her first visits to the house, Tobkin happened to tell Morgan how much she admired Morgan's vibrant dresses, with their daring mixture of bright-colored fabrics. Shortly thereafter she found a present of several bolts of the material at her door.

Tobkin's enchantment with Morgan grew to an open admiration of her range of talents. She described Morgan as a reserved, shy, intuitive, and glamorous older woman, whose strong feelings lay close to the surface. She was still very attractive, with a thin, somewhat lined face. She smoked a lot, was elegantly graceful and tall, with long legs that were a source of discomfort—the result,

Tobkin thought, of her surgery. The polite obliqueness of her manner reminded Tobkin of a Henry James heroine. Tobkin described Morgan's speech pattern as "a very relaxed, upper-class burbling meander, which required little of the listener. She talked a great deal in her own house but very little in meetings at the Annex. . . . She was herself unpretentious, but since she viewed HAM as like a god, she took *his* pretensions very seriously." When Morgan told Tobkin that she and Harry Murray were lovers, Tobkin began watching them closely. She found their relationship oddly formal and sensed the difficulty of Morgan's situation with Murray, concluding that Morgan had deluded herself about ever being able to spend her life with him. She noticed growing periods when Morgan appeared depressed. 287

They were on the same team for a while, reinterviewing original subjects in the personality study. Morgan showed Tobkin her vision books, in view of their connection with the TAT; she also spoke of the book she was trying to write about their connection with her artwork at the Tower.

Dorothy Tobkin once attended a dinner party given for clinic members at the Murrays' Mount Vernon Street house, on Beacon Hill. She found it old-fashioned, with a rather stiff and uncomfortable Victorian atmosphere. After dinner the men retired early to one parlor for cigars and brandy, and she, Mrs. Murray, and Josie retired to another, where they conversed about their common interests and experiences. Most exciting to Tobkin was sitting down with Christiana the next day and telling her everything. She marveled at the difference between the two houses and the two women's lives, far preferring the fluent comfort and aesthetic grace of Christiana's house, tower, and clinic to the grand correctness of Murray's real home.

Other graduate students either ignored Christiana or regarded her as an elegant but distant lady; a few remembered her as a great conversationalist. Morgan had interesting things to say to those who sought her out, and remained the consummate listener, with a knack for making others feel eloquent. Henry Riecken, who joined the clinic in the mid-fifties, saw that, for a time, Morgan was invaluable to Murray for her critically sympathetic responses and her core honesty. Riecken remembered her neither as an initiator of new work nor as a team member, but as a stimulus and an inspiration for Murray and his work.

Murray became increasingly difficult to work with and somewhat erratic in the late fifties and early sixties, partly because of his brief investigations of LSD with Timothy Leary, a young professor then in the psychology department, and because of Murray's continued use of amphetamines. The stimulants helped Murray get through his days and the enormous amount of work that multiplied around him, but benzedrine also fueled both its chaotic and its perfectionist character; projects proliferated into endless others, Sorcerer's Apprentice–like, each seeming to take on a life of its own. The effort to duplicate the initial studies foundered under a mammoth accumulation of material. Holt, Riecken, and other members of the clinic concurred with Rosenzweig's earlier observation that Murray was a great initiator, with marvelous ideas but little follow-through. Robert Holt concluded that it was only through Morgan's direct efforts that any of Murray's work got written.

Murray also had the habit of encouraging and praising clinic members to the skies initially, then switching them from one job to another before their work was done. When Murray did pay attention, his leadership had marvelous results. Person after person described being brought to life at the clinic, shining under Murray's charm, insight, sensitivity, associative connections, and support, and being enormously productive. But there were those, like Henry Riecken, who suffered when the current of Murray's interest abruptly shifted; they felt no longer valued, their research forgotten. Students who were only passing through claimed Murray's interest in just the right dose and time for them to finish their year, but the clinic's staff and Murray's own work were increasingly hampered.

Christiana Morgan experienced the same about-face with her projected book on their life as well as with her work on creativity. Her final contribution to psychology was an incomplete study based on her extended interviews of one of the creativity project's chief subjects, Merrill Moore. The records reveal that her analytic and interviewing skills remained superb. Merrill Moore was a psychiatrist who from 1930 through 1942 had been connected with Harvard (he worked at the clinic in 1937), as he made his way in neurology from teaching fellow and house officer to graduate assistant and research fellow in psychiatry at Harvard Medical School. Moore wrote extensively on alcoholism and suicide, and on the connection between them; he also published articles on syphilis, shell shock, and drug addiction, besides doing original research on various aspects of mental illness and neurology. Moore was also a poet, with a successful literary career. He was a member of the Fugitives, a respected and long-lived literary group that first formed at Black Mountain College in North Carolina.

Moore had become entranced with the sonnet form, and at the time he volunteered as a subject for the clinic's research on creativity, sonnets were fairly erupting from his fertile imagination. He wrote over fifty thousand of them, experiencing the same sudden up-welling of creativity that had given rise to Morgan's visions.

Besides conducting some of the other tests in the clinic's battery, Morgan recorded seventeen two-hour sessions with Moore from November 13, 1954 to January 28, 1955. She conducted the interviews with sensitive receptivity as if they were analytic sessions, and they remain the only primary source for measuring Morgan's therapeutic skill. In over twenty pages of text for each session, her comments fill about half a page. They are the comments of a good analyst: unobtrusive, supportive and/or probing, recalling Moore to his subject or repeating a key phrase to conduct him ever deeper into the heart of his material. Morgan was sometimes directive but always empathic and professional. At the very start, she facilitated his well-being and introduced him to the task ahead, paying close attention to the level at which they worked. In their third session, for instance, Moore skated self-consciously on the surface, saying a lot about nothing in particular; Morgan intervened, guiding him to an appropriate level so that he could get to the underlying unconscious elements in his poetry:

> Well look Merrill, I've got to stop you here because these are perfectly conscious things you could say when we come to each poem. You're saying something that you could perfectly well write down yourself. I mean there's no use having these millions of associations on this level. Do you see my point?

Because of the supportive feeling behind even this frank criticism, Moore and Morgan were soon in the normal psychoanalytic world of early-childhood memories, polymorphous perversity, and sexual fantasies. Christiana encouraged yet dignified Moore's possibly shame-filled material with her quiet interest and seriousness. Her brief comments brought him back to the subject when he wanted to flee, or invoked his affective reaction with the basic therapeutic question "Do you remember how it felt?" She urged him deeper with gently facilitating phrases, and when Moore deprecated himself, she was quick to reframe his self-denigration and return him to a sense of his own worth—perhaps the greatest gift an analyst can give a patient.

290

Both Morgan and Moore had been analyzed by Hanns Sachs, and they recalled for each other how much his reductionism had wounded each of them. Moore complained that his poetry was then the center of his life and that Sachs "never said one word about my poetry" and refused to discuss it. Christiana broke out of her objective analytic mode, without specificity, by responding: "Its interesting that you should say that because Sachs did just the same thing with me when I took him my material that was very important to me [her visions]. . . . He never touched it, just left it."

MM: What *we* are doing here is more like analysis—
but different—productive and cooperative.
CDM: Can't let it become analysis.
MM: What we're doing [has] a sense of pioneering,
& a certain excitement.
CDM: Well I feel just the same thing.

When Moore insisted that his work with Morgan seemed like a true analysis at its best, Morgan replied simply, "But of course we've got very deep," and steered him back to his associations to his poems. Morgan appeared skillful, sensitive, very present, yet in the background of each session, her attentive silence drawing the deepest confessions from her subject and resulting in his feeling heard and healed.

Morgan's interviews with Moore stand in marked contrast to the single one Murray conducted, in which Harry talked humorously and well for about two thirds of the record. Moore finally interrupted Murray toward the end of the session, in what analysts call a derivative response, reflecting his feeling about working with Morgan as compared to being talked at by Murray: "I only have one thing on my mind and that is this, that I'm enjoying this work very much, actually enjoying it. I'm learning a lot from it, myself, in all sorts of intangible ways. Working with Christiana is a real delight. She is a rare person, and I think we're getting spade work done."

Morgan worked on the results of her interviews and the other parts of the project, intending to produce a book; she did not complete her study, and it is impossible to decipher what in the remaining manuscript is hers, for Murray suddenly turned the project over to Hansi Greer who had returned from Switzerland. One could posit any number of reasons; the result, though, was that Morgan made no more original contributions at the clinic. A letter she wrote to Lewis and Sophie Mumford, which summarized Harry's work, hardly mentioned her own. She included her thoughts about women's psychology, choosing the single revolutionary book on the subject to emerge from Jungian theory at that time, *Amor and Psyche: The Psychic Development of the Feminine*. Its thesis, which she strongly supported, was that particular women were psychologically more advanced than men. These women, however, had sacrificed traditional female roles and traditional ways of being with men in order to pursue their own development. The book, a retelling and reinterpretation of the Eros and Psyche myth by the Jungian analyst Erich Neumann, demonstrated in theory what her own visions had revealed symbolically many years before. Neumann reinterpreted the myth in such a way that if Morgan could have but held on to it, his conceptualizations might have provided her with the key to a successful interpretation of her own parallel visions about a woman's solitary and heretofore untrodden path toward feminine individuation.

Feb. 18, 1957

Beloveds—

What joy to receive your letter— I was sitting in my kitchen rocking chair having a solitary drink of sherry and thinking how long it was since I had heard from you both—and how I missed you! The next morning your letter! Some good current always flows between us four! There is something about *me* when I get into that rocking chair. Maybe I will haul you right back from Rome—or wherever you may be. (Don't be too alarmed)

How wonderful, dear Lewis, that copiousness—freshets come to you in the dead of this dreadful winter. But I think maybe, something in us rises up to meet the death—and then comes to flower in the spring.

Harry is having a hard time—with the last effort to pull "psychology" & his own thoughts together— Something is working underneath— He lectures *beautifully*—without a note—which is something for the one time stammerer— He is hitting the deeps—and it seems that the young are catching on.

I had to laugh at your picture of old age—because I have been through that too—just recently— I had a skin infection on my face and hurried off to the hospital with the idea that I was growing old— All tests taken—I am *fine*— Watch out for me! Men beware! Why do we give up so soon? I suppose I have a horror of pretending that I am young—when I will be 60 in October—

The winter has been good at the Baleen— Five extraordinary PhD's have come to work with Harry—they are so good that they take a large part of our time, and challenge us to do our best for them— It is exciting to meet this challenge in possibly our last year at Baleen. (The great new Harvard *expansion program* is upon us— and the Bull dozers will probably tear our house and *lovely* garden into memory. Well we had it.)

One of our young men is a psychologist from Denmark. The first thing he did on arriving in the U.S. was to go see the United Nations building. He was stunned— I told him about your book. He bought it—and then took a *special* trip to N.Y. with your book in hand— He returned—one more of your passionate disciples— "Why," he asked, "could I have been so impressed by sheer height when I first saw it?— After reading Mumford's book that can never happen to me again. Now I know what to look for."

One of the things that I am engaged in is [to] read 27 autobiographies of Harvard Snrs. & Jrs.—students who offer themselves as subjects for our experiments. Their autobiographies are "free-floating"—no structure upon them whatever. They are extraordinarily candid—masturbation, sexual experimentation—the wildest phantasies—etc. etc.—not an inhibition. *But* out of the 16 that I have read so far—not one mentions an experience of beauty—aesthetic delight—as having had any effect upon them— I must say that if *I* had to sit down and write my autobiography I would begin with such experiences:

I remember seeing out my nursery window two dashing Arabian horses—pale yellow with streaming white tails and manes (driven by a man—my father took pains to tell me was "a scoundrel who made all his money in patent medicines")

The tall blue delphinium in the garden that towered over my head—unearthly beautiful—and found once again in the blue window of Chartres—

Well I could go on and on— Is this age? Perhaps one looks back on *those* experiences now as being more important than I would have thought them in the strain and stress of life at 22— But I doubt it—*These held.* It must have been the same with you—

Since I started this letter I have read "The Dark Edge of Africa" by van der Post. *Good*—to cut through the current mentality and to hit for the fundamentals—ie: the myth—

In the process of writing this I missed quite a day—(lunch) at the Baleen. Two physicists—Harry talked to them about the new myth—and they were terribly excited— They knew that they had pulled the house down— the myth of static matter— Now to build again— But that these bright young physicists should catch on!

Now this part of my letter is for my dear Sophia—

Isn't it annoying to have skin trouble? Can't tell you how much I sympathize with you— It seems to come and go like the plague— Do you suppose this means that we are trying to shed our old skins?

Now I want *you* to read something and tell me what you think about it.

This book is called *Amor & Psyche* by *Neumann*—Bollingen Series. Pantheon Press. I would definitely say that no woman could achieve a true relationship without having lived through these steps in her psyche. I really think that this is the only really sensible book I have read about woman in a long time—if ever. So much foolish talk on the *top* of everything— I regard this as the real *basic* myth of woman's development *toward*— I do wish you would read it and tell me what you think— I know you hate to write letters—but I love you as a woman and trust your judgment—This will be for us all— We women should get together and make sure that this is true. I think it is—

You don't tell me anything about Alison— I would love to have her address— My sister now belongs to the Cosmopolitan Club—so maybe, if I ever recover financially from my 5 days in the hospital—I will have a nice place to live in N.Y. for my infrequent visits.
So much love to you both—   C—

Any little snow drop or crocus shown its face yet? There seems to be a new feel in the air— That *spring* feel—ahead and all that—but still its there.

The Tower remained important to both Christiana and Harry, a respite from their work at the clinic; she still retreated there to write, garden, and do her carvings and paintings, he to be with her in their private world and to write. Another brief high tide in their love occurred after the Annex had closed. Murray would spend a month at a time at the Tower, and he completed what was to be the best of his psychological papers, as well as perhaps the most creative of his literary efforts—his Introduction to Melville's *Pierre*. A condensation of part of his uncompleted Melville book, it drew on Murray's knowledge of himself and Christiana as much as of Melville's Isabel and Pierre. Harry's profound analysis was a stunningly precise evocation of the four of them. Christiana sat by him again during its writing, and the two achieved a renewed harmony that needed neither alcohol nor sadomasochistic ritual to warm or counterfeit their closeness. Now, after a Walpurgis, they retired to bed—sometimes passionately, but more often keeping each other company, reading aloud from Pepys's *Diary* before they slept.

A charming picture of Christiana at this time shows her standing at the door of her Tower meditation room. Her hair is graying, and she is dressed in a long and graceful flowered skirt; elegantly slim, she welcomes her lover with a delightful come-hither look, part amorous and part mischievous. A formal portrait of her by her friend Mary Aiken, Conrad Aiken's third wife, painted three years before, in 1956, catches more of the strength of Christiana's beauty. The portrait recalls the clear gaze of Morgan in her first years at the clinic, but some of the confidence has disappeared; her expression is shadowed, her face is as weathered as that of a ship captain tracing his courses and remembering their progeny of griefs.

Christiana had seen the tides turn too many times. Whether the disappointment of her hope, her physical deterioration, or her self-medication came first or each contributed to the other, she continued to have periods of active alcoholism. After Dorothy Tobkin left the clinic and after the creativity project was taken out of her hands, Morgan appeared there less and less often, finally just coming in to do her own work and then leaving, with little interaction with other people. The clinic had moved for the fourth time, in the fall of 1958, to a house on Divinity Avenue; its work now revolved around Murray's classes, and the center engaged in increasingly professional and traditionally research-oriented matters. Morgan found herself part of a bygone time and increasingly passé. In the sixties, she used her clinic office simply as a haven in which to work on her own book about fantasies and the meaning of her trances and to maintain some contact with Murray's working life.

She continued to see a few patients, at both Hilliard Street and the clinic. Her patients remained devoted to her, a number of them becoming her friends after their analysis ended.

Harry Murray's wife died on January 14, 1962. Morgan may have revived her thoughts of marriage, expecting her life finally to change with Jo's death; there is little documentation of her feelings, although she wrote to Lewis Mumford about her surprise at her grief and how much Jo had become an integral and now missed part of her life. Mumford replied with heartfelt advice in two letters, a week apart.

> You have been very much with us, Christiana dear, ever since we came back here five days ago: for your three letters were here to greet us, and we'd have answered them with our voices had we not both come down with colds— in the aftermath of a long journey & grim rainy days in New York. —I am sure that you both are going through a shattering experience—of a freedom that may be almost a paralysis, because it leaves you, so to say, in the midst of open space, no longer confined by the circumspect ritual of your earlier life together. At this point Harry may feel more at loss than you do & even seem farther away: so don't be surprised if this new situation temporarily seems strange and queerly different to both of you. Forgive me for talking like an old uncle: but maybe that's what I am. There are a hundred other things to tell you about in the leisure of Amenia—as dear as ever!—but the only thing that needs saying now—is our love to you.
>
> Lewis
>
> Amenia, New York: 8 February 1962
> Your letter came this morning Christiana dear: and I have already—though with fear and trembling—written a brief word to Harry, mainly to remind him of Ignatius Loyola's great insight: "Make no important decisions in a period of desolation." In time, life will come right for both of you, I am sure: but you are wise to see that Harry must do nothing precipitate now: for he must *end* his old life before he can begin a new one; and that bringing of a relationship to an end, even with one who is dead—I might better say, "especially with one who has just died"—is never a quick or easy matter. One must stay with what one has lost before one can be fully released from the past and deal freshly and freely with the present—I know more

than one case where the impatience to cut all ties, beginning with the hasty sale of a house, resulted in a collapse of the whole structure of life. Harry doubtless knows all this; if so, my words will only re-enforce his better judgment. All this applies to you, too, Christiana dear: hold fast, have faith, and quietly wait! In some ways this is the greater ordeal than Harry's; but you will in the end share the same reward, all the more fully because you've not tried to snatch it.

Affectionately,
Lewis

Despite expectations that they would marry after this time of mourning, Harry came no nearer to Christiana than before. At sixty-nine, he was still a vigorous man and enjoyed attracting and being attracted by keen and admiring women—while Christiana Morgan, as a woman in her sixty-fifth year, did not have the same currency. Her culture preferred its women nubile and made little room for her professionally. When she was not drinking, Morgan retained her elegance and grace and did not look her age; her health was good aside from a shortness of breath from continued smoking. It may have been too late for anything much between Harry and Christiana but loyalty and companionship and the promise of their uncompleted book. At the end of the year she wrote Lewis Mumford about the book and about Harry's new house—he had moved to Cambridge, a few blocks from the Divinity Street Clinic.

Dec. 26, 62

Beloved Lewis—
How exciting to have achieved a granddaughter! You both have much to look forward to—especially after the infant stage is past and they become human. I know you and Sophie must be relieved that the accouchement is safely over and that both are thriving.

You neglected to mention the name. Do remember in your next.

Your brief word about your autobiography has whipped up our appetite to the greatest degree. I can't think of anything that I would rather read. Knowing you I know that it will be honest—with all the depth and passion and richness that is you. In this our day—I feel it is a terrible and serious obligation that is laid upon us in our declining years. One trembles at the task and is joyful at the same time.

Our autumn has been a hurly-burly while Harry has been settling the new house—carpenters, painters, masons all over the house—crates and crates to be unpacked. Now it is mostly completed and we will be able to resume work in peace and quiet. The house is really perfect for him and just as it should be. It is hard for me to get used to as in 35 years I have never seen him in any other place but here, at the Clinic or at the Tower. Strange to feel in any way strange with H. and only on account of *furniture!*

Aren't we going to see or hear bits and pieces of the work (autobiography) as it goes along—or must we wait for the full dress? Somehow the house won't feel right until you are in it with ms. tucked under your arm!

My love to Sophie—and to you as always dear Lewis—

Christiana

Christiana did not move into Harry's house. As for the clinic, whose identity she had done so much to create and whose work she had so furthered, she would never return. Of the clinic's three published books, *The Thematic Apperception Test Manual, A Clinical Study of Sentiments,* and *Explorations in Personality,* Morgan had been the first author of one, the main author of the second, and a valued contributor to the third. Morgan's other contributions to the clinic were her work on conceiving and drawing the TAT cards, in both their basic and their fantasy versions, her research on the claustrum, her uncompleted study for the creativity project, her in-depth interviewing of subjects, her career as an analyst, and the normal year-by-year research tasks of a member of the various clinic teams; Morgan's influence was also felt notably in and through Murray's work. Murray, interviewed by James Anderson at age ninety-four, said that Morgan was part of every paper he wrote and every lecture he gave, and that her very presence at the clinic raised the caliber of his thinking. He summed up his feelings of their synergy:

> The greater unifying idea included all of Jung and Freud and Adler. Christiana and I were the only ones who had that to that extent and reveled in it and got our nourishment from it and wrote about it and lectured about it. It's perfectly possible to go about your professional work and you get on all right with your wife, but if you hit the same way of looking at things, being in love with your work and your lover and the theories, it all goes together.

This, then, was the Eros that vivified the clinic and inspired its accomplishments. In a nine-page review of the clinic's work, in 1958, Murray gave one and a third pages to its successes, which, with typical exuberance, he then submerged under eight more pages of new ideas. The achievements were solid. The clinic as a whole had produced three books and many psychological papers; it introduced psychodynamic theory into academic psychology and developed a personality theory based on psychodynamics and the study of the individual over time. It developed a multiform method for investigating and comparing single personalities and developed multiple projection tests, the most important being the Thematic Apperception Test. It helped form a system to classify values and their determinants in a measurable way, it produced a novel typology and description of salient complexes for a new personality theory, and it made a comprehensive, though unpublished, study of the creative process.

What Murray did not write about in descriptions of the clinic's work, but what was perhaps as notable in both its positive and its negative elements, was his own character. He was an extraordinary teacher, and his enthusiasm for his subject, his charm, his wit, his intelligence, all kindled his students' interest and their desire to do their best for him. As a result of Murray's personal charisma, his broad view of psychology, and his colleagues' efforts, the clinic developed into a vigorous and exacting American Psychological Association–approved graduate program in clinical psychology— one of the few that remained humanistically diverse. It trained some of the most gifted, creative, and productive psychologists in the United States and overseas, who, in turn, created clinical psychology programs that also emphasized the importance of the psyche and the individual. The clinic's relative openness to women, its liberal attitudes, its concern with individual differences, its emphasis on values, all attracted women psychologists and produced the ground out of which feminist psychologists could and did emerge. As a significant member of the clinic, Morgan contributed to each of these spheres of success.

On the negative side, Murray's pattern at the clinic echoed in his life with Morgan and his work on Melville. Though there were sporadic fireworks of enthusiasm, little seemed to be brought to completion and less reached a permanent form. The clinic's glorious years from 1929 to 1939 and then again in the early and mid 1950s were as transient as those of other Camelots, leaving its followers nostalgically trying to recreate and recapture its golden moments. After an initial surge of productivity in the first ten years, and the landmark book *Explorations in Personality,* the clinic was a victim of Murray's increasingly elaborate plans for a comprehensive picture of individual personality, so that finally no one had a sense anymore of a job well done. As Murray extravagantly praised projects and clinic staff and then made impossible demands and/or changed course, the praise began to ring hollow. Toward the end of the clinic's productive life, Murray had at least eleven unfinished books he was planning alone or with coauthors. The people who labored with him started to count the cost of years sacrificed and careers hazarded to Harry's vagrant focus. And then Murray started to give away chapters and pieces of the work to new people who caught his fancy—work on which Morgan and other coauthors had staked the meaning of their lives.

During the late fifties and early sixties, Morgan experienced a sharp sense of loss: the clinic no longer reflected her views or her visions, and her inconstant life with Murray no longer nourished or sustained her. She grabbed at all too brief and transient epiphanies, whose passing added to her depression and to her drinking. Then, as in the summer they worked on *Pierre,* the current of Murray's attention would flow her way again and her enthusiasm would surge and her drinking would either stop or markedly decrease. Morgan's interests turned further and further inward, and her energy and time were spent more and more away from what had become primarily Murray's world and was no longer hers. During these difficult years, she turned for solace to the land and to her art at the Tower. Morgan's disillusionment grew, but she did not break away, claiming instead that giving everything for love had been her only choice.

From Mansol's Book

(WRITTEN BY HENRY A. MURRAY)

Mansol's Failure:

M has lacked moral courage. His actions have been determined by social pressures, tradition and convention, the needs of his wife and family, the claims of his profession, the dogmas of Science, habit, and his compulsion to work. In his behavior he has not heeded the voice of his spirit which tells him that Wona is the Creator of his life. . . . Mansol knows this, but yet he does not dare to put his whole trust in her and become obedient to her voice. Mansol has minor courage, Wona has major courage.

Wona in her spiritual pilgrimage has plunged down to the verge of sanity, daring to confront the irrational. Mansol fearing the irrational, has remained secure within the citadel of Reason.

Wona, in her social life has dared to go her solitary way, defiant of convention, undaunted by criticism. Mansol has never ventured to break connections, to leave the supporting structure of society, to confess his dedication to Wona. Mansol lacks Moral Courage. The gap in Wona's admiration for Mansol is the Gap of Courage.

Although M. devoted no time to *her* vision, the religion to which they were both committed, Wona devoted years in helping *him* at the Clinic, and ended by writing most of their monograph on Sentiments. In this way much enjoyable work was accomplished on the rational level, but it became perfectly clear to her that if they continued on this course her depths would never be touched, the trances would remain unspoken. This was not the passionate creativeness she had known, not the style of life which was conducive to upsurgings from the unconscious. Living under M's government meant work on a rational level, and the idea of writing the Trances on the rational level was abhorrent to her. Better not touch her vision, than perform a sacrilege.

Wona kept warning M. of the "Provisional Life"; and every so often his unconscious would respond with a clear recognition that the only way to escape from the treadmill of work on the rational level was to shift the power to plan their life from his hands to hers. He wrote a testament of absolute obedience, but nothing came of it. With him it was a constant conflict between religious recognition and ego demands. The ego won, and his sense of shame increased, shame because he knew she did not respect him for what he was doing. . . . In her heart the Proposition died, and she succumbed to her gravest depression, let her mind go to seed, and abandoned her destiny.

From Wona's Book

(WRITTEN BY CHRISTIANA MORGAN)

The usually inarticulate deep nature of woman had found a language. To deny it would be to deny herself—to be faithless to all women. In the beginning her visions made a deeper and more imperative demand than any *he* could make on her. . . .

She had already found out that no religious formula from the past could shield her and surround her . . . [and] that the new science of psychoanalysis couldn't shield her. The Old Man had told her to take her life in her hands. Some new hero-seed was in process of germination through her. Alone she would have to deal with the potency of her visions and endeavor to bring them into her life. Could she assimilate the visions or would she be forever divided between two worlds? . . .What was their purpose their meaning for life? How would they work, if at all, for her and M's life together? . . . What was the way to Synergy? Should she abandon all that she had been finding and experiencing and move to his rational world? Should he with his firm intellectual grasp try to diminish for her the visions which seemed to be separating her from him? . . . Gradually the visions began to incorporate their dual struggle. The dramatic form in which the early visions had been cast persisted but now it was *their own myth* which was being enacted. This was the living drama to which they were both sacrificing their blood and their individual structure in order that the show might go on. They were not just simply a man and a woman striving to love each other. For very slowly the sense of pilgrimage, of new creation, came to possess them both. . . . Was this the mystery play, the action of which gathering them up out of their individual pasts sweeping them forward beyond their full comprehension giving the general design for their mode of development together, to be fulfilled in actuality?

FOURTEEN

The Hidden
Last Act

Death is only a launching into the region of the strange Untried; it is but the first salutation to the possibilities of the immense Remote, the Wild, the Watery, the unshored; . . . and from the hearts of infinite Pacifics, the thousand mermaids sing to them. . . . Come hither! put up thy gravestone, too, within the churchyard, and come hither, till we marry thee!

HERMAN MELVILLE,
Moby Dick

Throughout their lives, Christiana Morgan and Harry Murray consciously sought a narrative form that would help structure their relationship and give it meaning. In chapters for their proposed book and in innumerable journal and diary entries, they kept returning to Morgan's visions as to a mother lode. In her visions, Morgan came upon, then discarded, the reality of her life's meaning: she had discovered the imagery and text for a woman hero's journey into strength, independence, and agency. The text was in a language still untranslated, but it appeared to contradict everything Christiana had been taught about women. In her search to translate the visions, she overvalued masculine authority and gave them to Jung and then to Murray to interpret for her. The visions inspired both men, yet each misread the text: Jung in a four-and-a-half-year battle to probe their meaning while bending them to his; Murray in a bid to conquer the visioner like a Caesar passionately seizing Cleopatra to expand his domain.

302   Because Morgan had nothing but her visions with which to

challenge the normal life of a woman of her class and era, because Jung taught her, and Freudian depth psychology seconded, that men act while women wait to *inspire* action in a man—and because 303 Morgan loved—she turned from her efforts to create her own self and her own mythic plot, ceding them to Murray's doomed quest. In order to gain closeness with another human being, she sacrificed her opportunity to define her own place and role. Morgan channeled her creativity into a relationship with a mercurial and inconstant though brilliant man and never developed her self-reliance or her inner resources. She expected, as his part of the bargain, to lean on Murray's strength and gain recognition, protection, and nurturance through his love. In her history of their union, Morgan wrote about this bargain and its costs:

> The citadel of her pride had to be broken. She had to accept her need for his hurturance [*sic*] which had always been there in her but which her pride had repressed. She had to learn to ask for it and she had to learn to submit to his authority to his generative power as creator.

In a classic Freudian slip, Morgan's unconscious revealed what her idealization of her love disguised—the "*h*urturance" of the time-worn bargain between the sexes and of Murray's individual style of demands, overpraise, dramatic reunions, and then neglect. Part of the problem was that the covenant they made could not be one between equals; when one class of human beings has to sacrifice itself for another, no one truly wins. Moreover, on a personal level, both Morgan and Murray did not rest strongly enough in their own center to form a true partnership. In response to the hazards of their upbringing, they attempted to maintain a sense of identity by gaining each other's admiration. Technically each had what psychologists once referred to as an "as-if" personality; this narcissistic personality disorder demanded that they pose as iconoclastic rebels in a grandiose drama of their own making.

Jung's and Murray's reliance on woman as mirroring anima—as the beloved who reflected, completed, and created the man—added to the fragility of Morgan's identity, dependent as it was now not on her visions but on an inconstant other. She who most needed accurate reflection of her female self now felt it her duty to reflect another. Playing an anima figure or *femme inspiratrice* precludes true pairing, for the woman behind the figure disappears beneath the role, while the man who loves his reflection feels he has the right to the reflector as part of his own imaginative property. So Murray, with Jung's blessing, took Morgan's visions and creativity to inspire him and complete his psyche. Morgan, who was still attempting to define herself through "the frail and tenuous scaffolding" of her visions, handed them, her power, and her psyche to Murray for his creative enlargement. She allowed herself to be further veiled by Murray's need for her at one and the same time to be a strong, magnificent anima—a superanima—and to reflect his own weak, wounded, and mistreated feminine aspect. Murray only took what he thought was his and responded with as much love, care, and affection as a tender conqueror could muster, but the woman in Morgan's visions, betrayed, slipped away into the hills, while Morgan tried to fit herself into one and then the other of her conqueror's Procrustean roles.

Murray imaginatively inhabited her and defined how she should be. He dressed in her clothes, and fantasized or wrote chapters of their book as if he were she, but what was reflected was himself and his own vividly animated style. More dramatic than Morgan's, it was also more sentimental, more histrionic, and more grand—a true picture of anima talents. Murray's style exemplified his unrealistic expectations and his narcissistic need to inflate Morgan to someone far beyond a real woman. At the same time, Murray crippled the very strength he cherished and perhaps feared in Morgan herself, silencing her attempt to develop her own style and voice, criticizing it as "commonplace" and unusable in contrast to the "great language" he preferred. Murray's chapters of their book, his letters, and his intellectual admonitions pinioned Morgan's attempts to write her life. In what was meant to be his deepest service to Morgan's visions and reality, he abrogated them to increase his own sense of himself, implying that without his input the trances would come to nothing.

> I conceive of our life, and I have no other life but ours, as being first an experience together to be lived, felt, formed and expressed, and that it depends for its structure and continuous evolution upon your trances. I think if we do not know what we are doing, if we are not self-conscious about what is evolving it will cease to evolve. It will be forever a chaos, mere sensations. As I see it the central problem is to fashion our feelings and sensations into meaningfulness. Your trances do that for us. *We must be forever outdoing outselves* until we have both achieved

successive insights, which become meaningful to us in terms of the trances. It is my complete conviction that these trances of yours must be worked over, and lived, and merged into our life, so that they are the reality and the essence of our tangible existence. They must be enriched by our blood and our thought. . . . Now comes a new awakening and renewal and more mountains ahead, always more, higher Everests of the spirit. Has there ever been anything like this in the whole history of mankind?

Murray coveted the visions and the visioner, and Morgan surrendered what she held most sacred and individual as if he were the way toward her self-knowledge. She puzzled, however, over Murray's demands that she be his powerful visioner and be ever outdoing herself; she fought his efforts to turn her into an impossibly one-sided ideal but at the same time adored his admiration of her, not understanding that its excess destroyed her own reality. She craved strength in him, perhaps taking his power, his money, his ability to advance her professionally, and his financial support of their fantasy as signs of his strength. She felt the withering blast of his competitive intellect as a destructive power, but she blamed herself when it robbed her of words. Looking back at her past, Morgan wrote:

> Throughout this period of creative trancing she had to contend against the destructiveness of M's intellect. On the one side was his imagination which would take fire from her and encompass her. On the other side he was capable of using his intellectual, analytical powers to protect himself from her,—and she knew this to be her enemy. This could lacerate her like sharp flint stones in her flesh. His analysis could tear down and seemingly demolish the delicate and fragile life of their first togetherness. She was fearful of that kind of sterile rationality which can be used to deny passion, to shrivel and emasculate. Too often M. sought to tear out the meaning and life of her visions and thus dispose of them.

Morgan silenced herself and began to react against her increasing autonomy as if it were a betrayal of Murray. Yet she accepted Murray's delusions as real—that the two were living one of the greatest love stories of all time, that they were discovering a spiritual path, that their myth would form a new religion for the world.

And so she allowed her betrayed self to be worshiped and condoned its punishment.

306   Morgan voluntarily submitted to Murray's double bind; he insisted that she abjure her passivity but remain his passive and mute anima image. He resisted her while demanding that she engulf and subjugate him; he ordered her to insist he choose between Melville and her, yet at the same time shape-shift him into a creative genius. Morgan felt the bind but allowed herself to be seduced by Murray's grand words of praise, which admiringly distorted and disguised her fragile self. Murray glorified himself in thinking his loved one so extraordinary. He fled self-doubt, writing "portentously" about themselves as two dramatic figures upon whose stage grand things transpired that "never in the whole course of human history" had befallen another man and woman. Lacking appreciation of the grounded dailiness of life, Murray assumed a lofty perch and contemplated Morgan's deficiencies. He blamed her failure as a *femme inspiratrice* rather than face his own defeat. And all the while he trained Morgan to embrace her own subordination.

They continually probed and assessed their relationship, sometimes alone and sometimes in a duet, sometimes honestly and sometimes in disguise, shielding their reality in images and words that, sooner or later, melted in the sun. Murray had the outer world to bask in, all the admiring and loving people his dynamic charisma drew to him, while Morgan remained more and more in the shade, her life finally narrowing down to the Tower, a few friends, and her pathetic role as the mistress of a busy man. The discrepancy between Murray's grandiose pronouncements and Morgan's lonely existence gnawed at her gut. As she grew older and more solitary, her need for Murray became greater, yet his response to it became rarer. In the end, she remained faithful to his idea of their love because she had sacrificed everything else for it. She may also have believed in it because Murray was one of the few people who *had* recognized the power of her visions and made a place in the world for them—even if, like caged birds, they had to live in his castle and under his command. Murray's acknowledgment of her power also weighed her down with its exaggerated notion that she could carry the entire archetype of the transformative feminine.

In a retrospective look at her life, Morgan considered some of this:

The easiest thing for her would have been to accept this idealization and picture herself in that role. If she took the other way and insisted upon the reality of her full nature as woman, she knew that she ran the risk of losing M's worshipful idealization and that sooner or later it would probably end in a debacle. Man could worship woman as image in a stained glass window, as a sovereign deity of Chartres. That was easy and required no change in his modus vivendi. The aim of man has always been to use woman for his own creativeness. But was it possible for M. to change his whole orientation so that his energies would be subordinate to hers. Could he permit himself to be used for *her* creativeness?

He could not. Morgan might have embarked on her new feminine hero's quest—what she and the world may have needed—through her own visions, but she could not accomplish this through her love for Murray. She ultimately deserted her visions, her talent, and her creativity, subordinating them to a Romantic yearning that took the place of love. It was the wrong historical moment for a woman to gain sovereignty while remaining romantically in love. Morgan's and Murray's culture and conditioning had created too much of a power disparity between them. Murray appreciated women and believed in egalitarian love; each time he loved, he chose a woman of character, exceptionally intelligent, and talented. But he could not help chipping away at these women's gifts and undermining the very strength that attracted him, loving them most when they were either gloriously strong or in tears. Possibly it wasn't misogyny but fear—as if their strength too potently recalled an all-powerful feminine. At any rate, he counted on Morgan's strength, for the development not of her own talents but of his. And Morgan accepted this role as the best one available to her.

The discrepancy between their dreams and their reality fed Morgan's depression. Jung had told her that a woman's glory lay in her ability to create a man; she accepted this idea but felt deficient when it emptied rather than fulfilled her, and in consequence she blamed herself. Lacking the partnership she had envisioned, Morgan tried to warm herself in the inconstant flames of Romanticism and sadomasochism. The first present Morgan gave to Murray, *The Trials of St. Anthony*—that great text of religious pain and ecstasy—signaled the perversions that lay behind much of their Romanticism.

Morgan and Murray took high romance as their sacred bailiwick and believed they could solve "the erotic problem in our civilization" in the context of their own lives. They did not realize that they were caught by the same regressive emotions that sent troubadours to sing of their desire, Kierkegaard's knight to prefer longing to any communion with a flesh-and-blood woman, or country-and-western singers to croon ballads of ill-fated love. But for all their idealization of an operatic kind of love, Morgan and Murray failed to articulate how this mainstay of nineteenth-century Romanticism would lead civilization into new territory.

308

The delusion trapped and wounded Morgan far more than Murray. In a 1946 letter urging her to research Romantic love rather than write her book, he asked her if Romantic love always "Has . . . death as its unconscious end." She took his request quite seriously. Her research led her to validation in de Rougemont's study *Love in the Western World* and in the connections it found between erotic love, mysticism, the search for emotional intensity, sadomasochism, and death.

> Passion means suffering, something undergone, fate's mastery over a free and responsible person. To love love more than the object of love, to love passion for its own sake, has been to love to suffer and to court suffering all the way from Augustine down to modern Romanticism. Passionate love, the longing for what sears us and anni-hilates us in its triumph—there is the secret which Europe has never allowed to be given away. . . . Western man . . . reaches self-awareness and tests himself only by risking his life—in suffering and on the verge of death. The third act of Wagner's drama [*Tristan und Isolde*] rep-resents far more than a romantic disaster; it represents the *essential* disaster of our sadistic genius—the repressed long-ing for death, for self-experience to the utmost, for the revealing shock.

In notes for a paper, "What Is the Origen [*sic*] of Death Wishes in Synergy?" Morgan traced this theme in her own life, concen-trating on the way passion, mysticism, ecstasy, and suffering com-bined to make death in love a higher goal than union with a fellow mortal. Her notes read like the description of a profoundly soul-destroying complex rather than the grand exaltation she may have imagined she was creating. In its most original section, Morgan demonstrates the guilt and vengefulness that come when Eros is spun away from a mother's world, rooted in marriage, children, and continuity, toward the Romantic agony of a father's world, where the *idea* of love is preferred to its actuality, the purifying *akesis* of desire rather than the risk of normal life between loving equals.

Toward the end of her life, Morgan worked on a longer project, probably with Murray and Hansi Greer, on the Byronic hero. Her section reads like the description of a negative animus, the inner masculine demon of her own psyche. She depicts this antihero as oppressed by a sense of original sin and guilt, accompanied by feelings of disillusionment, despair, melancholy, pessimism, and futility. A solitary outcast, egocentric, impulsive, sensitive, and proud, he is compelled to experiment with evil, shock the bourgeoisie, and continually seek out dreaded situations. Morgan concluded that the internal or external hero is drawn to women in distress, but in his effort to rescue her he fails, unable to free her from the despotic jailer. Morgan ended her notes: "*Death by water* is not uncommon."

Morgan's Gothic Romanticism echoed her profoundly destructive personal experience. She allowed, even sought, domination and abuse by Murray as punishment for her own rebellious, unfeminine self. It is the stuff of Gothic novels: a dark Byronic lord thrills the wild heroine, makes her afraid, and masters her; she, in turn, gains recognition by having inspired him. The heroine longs to be blindly ravished and spiritually adored at the same time.

Morgan, without a male companion who could cherish, love, and respect her without being terrified of her passion and her power, turned more and more to the harsh ironies of sadomasochism, sometimes exulting in, sometimes reviling her independent self as "a destroyer—a breaker of the structured life, an evil-doer."

Sadomasochism's twisted gender relations and its blend of religious, infantile, physical, and psychological elements placed it at the core of the Gothic Romanticism Morgan and Murray espoused. Both enjoyed living on the crest, for drama, intensity, and peak experiences, yet both had difficulty attaining this orgasmically—Murray having problems with potency and Morgan, after her sympathectomy, with normal sexual response. Sadomasochism offered them a ritualized way to intensify their excitement and obtain a release that compensated for their numbness. But their attraction to sadomasochism lay further back. Its roots can be discerned in Christiana's mother's diary, in which she records the punishments she visited on her daughter for her unladylike willfulness. Like all children, Christiana once felt herself the center of the world and,

309

310 for a time, considered herself omnipotent. Like all children, she also felt tiny, powerless, and subjugated by the huge figures of her father, mother, and nurse, each of whom held keys to intimacy and separation in their hands. Her struggle between domination and submission, omnipotence and insignificance, was exacerbated by her being locked away in the closet until she submitted—a profound abandonment. She learned what girls too often learn: that independence, self-assertion, and rebellion are wrong. Christiana mastered her forced submission by seeking it out. Then she learned to add to the punishment, hurting herself as others hurt her and castigating herself for her own pride.

In her closet as a child, Christiana had started to pray to a transcendent being; she learned to master her fear by voluntarily abandoning herself, not to the evil parent or nurse, but to an all-encompassing dark god. As she grew up in a harshly unmaternal world, the longings and yearnings of Romanticism took the place of a nurturing love. She replaced a natural need to care and be cared for with a need to worship, venerate, and surrender, no longer to the vengeful god of the closet but to a Byronic lover. She repeated her childhood ecstasies—mastering and transcending her punishment—by submitting willingly to Murray's iron fist and inviting its stigmata of physical and psychic abuse. The goal was the same: reunion and dissolution—not with a benevolent and nurturing mother, who would give her the recognition and love she needed, but with a male god, the idealized conqueror who would punish and annihilate that needy female in his rituals of ecstasy and pain. Despotism, submission, abandonment, shame, and release swirled unanalyzed in the adult woman's unconscious as they did, in different form, inside her male lover.

Murray was allowed more self-assertion as a boy. But he, too, experienced his mother as icily removed. It was his austere sister who instructed him in the discourse of humiliation and disgrace. From these infantile experiences, Murray brought with him into adulthood the desire of a man who, like Rousseau, longed "to be at the knee of an imperious mistress, to obey her orders, to have to ask her pardon . . . the proud scornful woman crushing him under her feet by weight of her royal wrath." He loved suffering. Yet he protected himself from it by focusing on his narcissistic sense of entitlement and injured pride and, though often tenderhearted, made others suffer in his stead. The repeated childhood humiliations at the hands of his mother and sister produced a reservoir of hostility mixed with arousal, and so the desire to punish, humiliate, hurt, and wound the female who had once so wounded him became part of his excitement as well. Murray's sexual violence may have derived from his effort to break out of the encased numbness he experienced as an unmothered child. As a civilized and caring adult, Murray sought to express this violence in a contained way. He yearned to experience both domination and submission, but he needed reassurance that whatever he did, the other side of him would remain intact. Thus he bounded violence with rituals wherein he demanded Christiana's imperious strength, then punished her for it by grinding her into abject servility. Their ritualized violence excited him as giver and receiver, for he could at one and the same time gain revenge for past wounds and expiate the omnipotent rage of his infancy. And so these infantile aspects of Murray and Morgan fused with daemonic bravado to explore the shadowy meridians of depth psychology—"the outward fringes of mind and life: the murky, dreadful zone of our being where sensuality becomes agony; pleasure, pain, and life, death . . . the terrifying forces of death and destruction that lurk in the depths of the erotic impulse."

When Christiana found that she could neither respect nor worship Harry and that he could no more match her inner Gothic lord than she could his sinister dominatrix anima, she tried to fan the flames by artificial means. Him who could not master her, she would make her master. And when Harry found he could neither write nor complete anything to his satisfaction, he sought to reenact the forms of his earliest sexuality with Christiana—to suffer and cause suffering, to wreak vengeance on the too powerful and make her pay for his failure, his inferiority, and his impotence. Armed with whips and chains, they took their turns, abetted by alcohol. She whipped the little boy, and he chained what he could not master. As each tried, through this devil's dance, to warm the arctic cold and bring fire and heat to the cold ashes of their hopes, they called it love.

The roles, alas, were never as equal or as much under their control as they presumed. Murray's sadism fused sulfurously with his culture's hostility to women. His childhood resentments erupted in a frightening rage against all women, which he normally kept in check by conscious attraction to, respect for, and promotion of that sex. But the Walpurgis and alcohol were a combustible pair; he beat Morgan, and his hatred and frustration broke through alongside his love. In bouts of excess and famine, he came to worship at her Tower and then escaped to resume his rational life, leaving Morgan behind to carry the burden of all the dark, depressed, alcoholic, perverted, and vagrant aspects of their souls alone. She took on the burden willingly. Their secret rites twinned and bonded them in ineffable proximity; nevertheless, Murray integrated neither Morgan nor this aspect of himself into his life but kept them safely apart, in the separate acts of their inconstant drama. He denied her through his failure to complete their life, complete his writing, and through his narcissistic destructiveness of Morgan's own career and work. How much he encouraged her drinking and how much it was her own revenge can only be surmised. Having left her to carry his darkness for him, he made a culturally reinforced attack on her in order to torment her for it and then to conquer her pride with ever-deeper humiliations and pain. Morgan denied him and annihilated herself in alcoholic stupors or submitted to the pain in masochistic subjugation, to delay or prevent what she most feared—his complete abandonment of her. He had refused her reason and control, ultimately making her pay the price for both of them. The end point of Romanticism and sadomasochism, as Morgan pointed out in her studies and then in her life, is the drama's final act—death.

The winter of 1966–67 buried the Northeast in glacial snow and severe cold. Harry Murray's winter, however, had been warmed by the charms of yet another vibrant woman with brains, character, and wit. Caroline (Nina) Chandler Fish was a graduate psychology student, about the same age as his daughter, Josie; she had raised five children and now was taking the opportunity to explore her own intellectual potentials with immense flair and vitality. When she and Murray met, their beguiling encounters brought him a feeling of early spring. Nina was almost twenty years younger than Christiana Morgan.

After his wife's death, Murray had proposed marriage to Morgan on the condition that she give up drinking; but as soon as Morgan stopped, he backed away from his promise. When he fled to another woman, Morgan tasted ashes in her mouth. Depleted and hopeless, she could not even turn to her Tower for consolation, held fast as it was by the deep of winter. The previous fall, Christiana had informed her son and daughter-in-law that she and Harry were to be married in six months, but when Harry pulled away, her pride flared; she declared that she had chosen not to marry him, telling her daughter-in-law, "What, and spend the rest of my life picking his dirty underwear off the floor?" After a long period of sobriety, Hallee Morgan's mother-in-law was drinking heavily again and becoming increasingly unpleasant to be around. 313

Christiana and Harry left New England for a late-winter vacation at their friend Cleome Wadsworth's Denis Bay Plantation on Saint John. The main house was on the north coast of the island, overlooking a wide point of land, where Cleome's husband had erected a giant statue of Christ surveying the waters below. On an enclosed bay to the side, about fifty feet from the sea, the Wadsworths had a small cottage, which they put at Morgan and Murray's disposal. Christiana planned to remain sober for the trip and hoped the two of them could re-create a passionate intimacy that would recall them to their love. After a rough journey and a brief stay on Anguilla, the austromancy of Saint John's moist and fragrant air seemed favorable at first, the climate recalling the halcyon moment in *Moby Dick* that augured its inevitable tragedy: "the eternal August of the Tropic. The warmly cool, clear, ringing, perfumed, overflowing, redundant days. . . . But all the witcheries of that unwaning weather did not merely lend new spells and potencies to the outward world. Inward they turned upon the soul, especially when the still mild hours of eve came on; then, memory shot her crystals as the clear ice most forms of noiseless twilights." The romance of Denis Bay—its turquoise sea, the soft wind amid the jacaranda, bougainvillea, and palms—affected the two differently. Harry's thoughts dwelt on Nina Fish, and he sent her flowers; Christiana suffered, sensing Harry's distance. The Tropic had rejuvenated him, filling him with a yearning for new love, but she felt ancient and spent, her isolation imploding on her. After a few days of Harry's inattention, the two fought again, and Christiana, cast adrift, started to drink. She woke early on the morning of March 14 with the taste of regurgitated food in her mouth. Drifting toward consciousness, she opened her eyes, to see Harry looking at her with unconcealed aversion. The first words she heard that morning from her lover were filled with hate. "You disgust me!" he said. She must have left the bed soon afterward, for when he got up, she had gone. Harry later found an open book on her dressing table. In it, a passage was marked: "To be read over my grave":

O sweet clean earth, from whom the green blade cometh!
When we are dead, my blest beloved and I,

Embrace us well, that we may rest forever,
Sending up grass and blossoms to the sky.

314

CONRAD AIKEN

Like a messenger in a Greek tragedy, Harry later announced
the death that nobody saw. Unlike that messenger, however, he
concealed what had happened. He offered different versions to different people. What is clear is that on that sweet and sun-drenched
morning, Christiana died. She had taken off the emerald ring Harry
had given her thirty years before, wrapped it in her little beach bag,
and placed it carefully on the sand. Then she had walked out into
the sea. She drowned in the lagoon just below their cottage, the
outline of her lifeless body floating unobscured in the tender ripples
of the waves.

"Death by report lends itself to conjecture vastly more than
does violence exposed to public view." Harry, according to some
letters he wrote, battered her body in trying to pump his breath
into her lungs; in a number of other letters, he wrote that they had
been contemplating marriage and had been swimming together as
usual when she fainted; in others that they always swam together
at that hour. Other letters stated that she never went near the beach
at that hour, which was what delayed his discovering her body; or
that for the first time in his life he'd been taking a morning nap.
Perhaps most revealing was a letter he sent to Saul Rosenzweig,
which conveyed some of the multiple meanings of the tragedy:
Christiana Morgan "feinted" [sic] dead in the water. To Robert Holt
and others he wrote that they had set their wedding day and were
on a pre-honeymoon trip, had gone for a morning swim, had just
gotten their feet wet when he had to go back inside. When he
returned, he found her floating face down in the water. Each message
overflowed with grief as their twinned life flooded back to embrace
him and he, whom she could not have in life, became hers in death.
And so the curtain fell on the last act of the drama. Yet even here,
Harry's ambivalences and his effort to save face obscured the true
horror of the tragedy: Christiana was robbed even in death, this
time by the muffled reports of her tragic statement. She had escaped
from the misfortune of her life into death—it was the expected
denouement for the heroine in a Gothic romance—but her last act
was made to seem confused, uncertain.

Harry had Christiana's body cremated and brought the ashes
back to the property. They were buried at the root of a newly

planted fir tree behind a granite pedestal from which Christiana's statue had once surveyed the tidal river below her Tower. Harry held a service attended by her family and a small group of her lovers, students, friends, and former patients. He penned a cardboard sign and nailed it to the tree:

315

CHRISTIANA D. MORGAN

Our Imponderable Superanima—Who was here at the laying of the Cornerstone and shared the dream; and while we fumbled for the way; and here through the steady years of diligent accumulation, a Part of all we did, the incalculable expenditure, and all that we experienced—the stress, the fury and the laughter, the repeated failures and renewals, the partial fruitions and the joy; and is here now. And what those with eyes can see is that every limb and branch of the Tree of Life that has taken root and grows bears the signature of her incorruptible integrity and love.

Cleome Wadsworth read the verses Morgan had left on the dresser, adding:

Life without love is load; and time stands still:
What we refuse to him, to death we give;
And then, then only, when we love, we live.

Lewis Mumford, perhaps as suspicious of Harry's treatment of Christiana in death as in life, refused to attend. Christiana's son, Councilman, a professor by then at the College of Physicians and Surgeons at Columbia University and as revered a teacher as his grandfather had been, also shrank back in dismay, finding the planned services a travesty. At the urgings of his wife, however, he relented and, with bitter heart and leaden voice, read passages Murray had picked from his condolence letters. None recalled the sharp tang of Morgan's demanding reality or her vivid creativity, nor listed her accomplishments. Instead each bland passage further veiled the woman by recollecting only Morgan's effect on others— her role as *femme inspiratrice*.

An accurate obituary would have mentioned Christiana Morgan's place in history and her contributions to psychology. Christiana Morgan lived a life that neither belonged to a tradition nor was part of a community, although she joined brave contemporaries in searching for ways to overthrow stultifying traditions and repression, seeking to replace them with a freer, more spontaneous, even hedonistic, but examined, private life. Morgan's most creative and lasting work remained the series of visionary images she had had when she was barely thirty. They pictured a feminine quest that prefigured women's search for self today and illustrated the many forces conspiring against women's development. Morgan envisioned a definition of a female self far different from the male-invented one. In her many years of collaboration with Murray, she was crucial in creating a setting, forming an atmosphere, and actively contributing to a clinic and a form of psychology that were potentially nonhierarchical and gender-blind, and that helped produce a third force in psychology between the Freudians and the behaviorists. It is from this third force that feminine psychology developed; many of its creators were trained at the Harvard Psychological Clinic or in university departments formed by its graduate students, with it as a model. In the clinic itself, Morgan contributed as a gifted analyst, an imaginative thinker, a tenacious researcher. She wrote most of *A Clinical Study of Sentiments*, one of the first efforts to pay attention to, examine, and categorize feelings and values. Her research contributed to many other areas of the clinic, most notably to its examination of needs and to its study on creativity. She built an amazing private world full of beautiful and intricate carvings, paintings, and symbols. She attempted to construct a new form for relationship that would give a woman more autonomy than what she found in the arrangements common to her Bostonian society. She kept diaries, journals, chapter drafts, and some short papers, in which she minutely examined the meaning of her life. She tried to live independently and productively while still maintaining an intensely demanding relationship with a man.

Yet Morgan betrayed herself. Her visions had combined the masculine and feminine sides of her personality to point to a new way of being a woman, but she failed to claim those visions for herself. Instead she sacrificed them to a doomed, romantic fantasy of relationship. She joined the male ranks against herself by choosing the male idea of love and putting that before her own needs. She avoided an honest commitment to her own life. Yet if she had stayed in touch with her visions, her body, and her myth, she would have lost Murray, for it was clear that their union was based on her suffering. She cheated herself, selling her soul for Murray and the roller coaster of his attention.

Christiana Morgan visioned a path to her own creativity, a Pilgrim's Way that found and reunited a womanly spiritual, dynamic, chthonic, and sensual self. She discovered a new form and territory in women's psychology and a new women's voice. Yet she could not hold on to them for herself but gave her visions first   317 to Jung and then to Murray. But what would she have gained if she had kept singly to the visions and given up Jung's and Murray's demands on her to live for and through a man, becoming their female impersonator? One of the ways in those days for a woman to have power and a chance to become more of herself was through alliance with a powerful man. Christiana was maimed, not as Sachs and contemporary psychology had told her—because she had no penis—but because she was not able fully to be who she could have been as a woman. Living as she was supposed to live, as a *femme inspiratrice* or an anima woman, destroyed the woman developing in her through her visions. A beautiful and intelligent woman trying to make her way in the man's world of Harvard in the late 1940s and the 1950s was in for a soul-killing experience. In order to survive the unremitting attacks on her integrity, she had to cut off, or pretend to cut off, every part of her that was unacceptable to that stultifyingly narrow environment or go underground. Morgan fled to her Tower, but even there her lover demanded that she amputate her own existence in order to facilitate his genius—a genius that could not be fertilized by an amputee.

The synergy that Morgan and Murray attempted had based itself on false premises. Synergy depends on a partnership of equals, and women were far from equal. Morgan not only carried the weight of an unlived creativity; she became a burden to her partner as well. She endured the social isolation of being the mistress of a married man—a kept woman. Their life together became virtually Morgan's whole life, while Murray could take or leave it. Morgan bore the dark, wounded, and evil parts of them both; she made it easy for Murray to blame her for them.

Their attempt at a creative relationship ended in a tragedy littered with corpses: Will Morgan, Jo Murray, other lovers, two abandoned children who suffered profoundly from the discord in their parents' lives. And, finally, Harry, an honest and creative man with eleven aborted books, and Christiana, her visions veiled and unlived, dead by drowning so Harry could try again with a younger, more rational, saltier woman.

Christiana Morgan tried to live her life free from the restrictions common to a woman of her generation and class; she attempted to invent a new way of being, in which she could be both creative and

318   free. Because she liked men and responded to them, she also sought
a life of relationship. She wanted work, love, career, marriage, and
achieved all but one of these with Murray, but she did so in a world
and a time that made her pay too high a price. She thought she
could be complete, not in herself, but only with a man, yet no man
allowed her sovereignty, so none could meet her as an equal. Her
Romantic quest ended in futility; her book was never written; her
visions remained untranslated; her relationship was one more triangle that primarily served the interests of a man.

Olive Schreiner wrote what would serve as a fitting obituary
for Morgan when, in "Women and Labour," she addressed the
women who would come after her:

> You will look back at us with astonishment! You will
> wonder at passionate struggles that accomplished so little;
> at the, to you, obvious paths to attain our ends which we
> did not take; at the intolerable evils before which it will
> seem to you we sat down passive; at the great truths staring
> us in the face, which we failed to see; at the truths we
> grasped at, but could never quite get our fingers round.
> You will marvel at the labour that ended in so little.

Yet Morgan and Murray loved each other as well as they knew
how. Morgan studied their relationship and herself for forty years.
Together they explored their feelings, inventing new ways to keep
the partnership alive; they also played with ideas and theories about
love and sex. Morgan opened herself to great joy and anguish, but
by choosing the grand gesture, the peak moment, she missed out
on the gentler and more constant warmth that might have accompanied a durable companionship. What would have stood her in
better stead was a man willing to be her equal in passionate intimacy
as well as in the daily exigencies of a lifelong collaborative partnership.

All great Romantic love stories end tragically. Their rigorously
restrictive script left Christiana Morgan's visions untranslated and
the walls of her life narrowed to the size of a closet. Death by
drowning released her from its painful enclosure into the total darkness of the abyss.

Acknowledgments

I am particularly grateful to the heirs of Christiana Morgan and Henry A. Murray as well as to Morgan's relatives, friends, and colleagues for their information, insight, and encouragement even when my research touched painful ground. In the first rank are Henry A. Murray, who first suggested I write this biography, and Councilman Morgan (they died in 1989 and 1990, respectively), and Hallee Morgan, Josephine L. Murray, and Caroline Murray, to each of whom I owe a special debt for their unqualified support. Then come Saul Rosenzweig, Eugene Taylor, and Robert White, who shared their recollections with utmost generosity. I would like to give pride of place also to Edwin S. Shneidman, a Melville and Murray enthusiast and a large and tenderhearted man, to whom I fear I've given much discomfort in my quest for Morgan's side of the story. To Richard and Elin Wolfe of the Countway Library, the best of archivists and librarians, who were always helpful and encouraging, as were Michael Raines of the Harvard Archives and Doris Albrecht of the Kristine Mann Library in New York. And to James W. Anderson, who put his biographical studies and interviews of Henry A. Murray at my disposal. My thanks to David Williams and the Governor Dummer Academy for the many days I spent at the Tower on the Marsh in Newburyport, Massachusetts.

Others who deserve my deepest gratitude are those I interviewed in person, by telephone, or who responded to my inquiries in writing. In

320 alphabetical order, they are: Leopold Bellack, Alan C. Elms, Risto Fried, Joseph Henderson, James Hillman, Constance Holden, Robert Holt, Goodhue Livingston, Earl Loran, Sophie Mumford, John H. Phillips, Henry W. Riecken, May Sarton, Sigmund Skard, Morris I. Stein, Dorothy Tobkin, Jane and Joseph Wheelwright, and Elizabeth Coolidge Winship.

I thank William Maxwell and John Beebe for their friendly support and their informal editorial suggestions. I am indebted to two other peerless editors: Marie Arana-Ward for her assistance during the book's gestation and Alice Mayhew for its final months and its delivery. Also to Leslie Ellen, who showed me that copyediting is an art as well as a craft, and for her and Elizabeth Schraft's eagle eyes. I am grateful to my agent, Lynn Nesbit, for her perceptive and nurturing foster care. I also thank my colleagues Barbara Koltuv, Geraldine Spare, and James Yandell for their presence and their comments at various crucial stages in the incubation of this book.

I thank the staff of these additional libraries and institutions for their assistance: The Library of Congress, manuscript division; The Henry A. Murray Research Center, Radcliffe College; Houghton Library, Harvard University; The New England Historic Genealogical Society; The Schlesinger Library on the History of Women in America; The Van Pelt Library, University of Pennsylvania; and, finally, The Winsor School and its Alumnae Office.

This book would not have been possible without a 1991–92 fellowship from the Bunting Institute. I would like to thank its director, Florence Ladd, as well as my sister fellows for their invaluable company, inspiration, and support; also to my research assistants, Betty Lou Marple and Zhiqi Yu.

Notes

The following abbreviations have been used throughout the Notes:

CDM: Christiana Drummond Morgan
HAM: Henry A. Murray
WOPM: William Otho Potwin Morgan
JRM: Josephine Rantoul Murray
JLM: Josephine L. Murray, M.D.
LM: Lewis Mumford
REJ: Robert Edmond Jones
CW: Jung's *Collected Works*
HA: Harvard Archives
CL: Francis A. Countway Library of Medicine, Harvard University
UMP: Unsorted Murray Papers

INTRODUCTION

page 11

"My dear Christiana Morgan": Gerhard Adler, ed., *C. G. Jung Letters* (Princeton: Princeton University Press, 1973), vol. 1, 48–49.

page 12

"Good heavens! What have you inspired?" Alfred North Whitehead,   321 as recorded in CDM diary, June 10, 1939, and in "Magnolia Hill," draft of chapter for uncompleted book (UMP/CL).

322   one of the three great minds: LM letter to CDM, 1947. Van Pelt Library, University of Pennsylvania.

"She illumined my life": HAM interview with author, 1987.

a problematical creativity: A common phenomenon in the early years of depth psychology, deriving from the link between repressed aspects of the feminine in both the woman and her male observer. The cultural unconscious in Europe and America had formed, glamorized, and empowered a creative, albeit wounded and deviant, feminine aspect. Some of the more famous duos resulted in studies of possession, multiple personalities, mediums, seers, hysterics, trance states, and hypnosis or self-hypnosis; among them were Pastor Blumhardt and Gottliebin Dittus (1815); Mesmer (1734–1815) and both Fräulein Oesterlin and Maria Theresa Paradis; Henri Puysegur (1850) and Victor Race (the only male in the group—a gentle, receptive, feeling young man); Justinus Kerner (1786–1862) and the Seer of Prevorst, Friederiche Hauffe; René Despine and Estelle (1836); René Charcot and his *grande hystérique,* Blanche Wittman (1882); Pierre Janet and Leonie (1886, 1887, 1888); Breuer and Anna O. (1895); Weir Mitchell and Miss Beauchamp (1898); Flournoy and Helene Smith (1899); Sigmund Freud and Elizabeth von R. (1895) and Dora (1900); Jung and Helene Preiswerk, Sabina Spielrein, Toni Wolff, and Christiana Morgan herself. Both Henri F. Ellenberger, in *The Discovery of the Unconscious* (New York: Basic Books, 1970), and James Hillman, in "Some Early Background to Jung's Ideas" (*Spring,* 1976), have noted this in the lives of these depth psychologists and its importance in the creation of theory. See also Sandra M. Gilbert and Susan Gubar's *The Madwoman in the Attic* (New Haven: Yale University Press, 1980) for another viewpoint.

Recently some of these women have found recognition: Lou Andreas-Salomé, in Rudolf Binion, *Frau Lou* (Princeton: Princeton University Press, 1968) and P. Roazen, *Freud and His Followers* (New York: New York University Press, 1984); Anaïs Nin, in Roazen and in Gunther Stuhlmann, *A Literate Passion* (San Diego: Harcourt Brace Jovanovich, 1987); Ruth Mack Brunswick, in Roazen; Beata (Tola) Rank, in Roazen; Toni Wolff, in Ferne Jensen, ed., *C. G. Jung, Emma Jung, Toni Wolff* (San Francisco: The Analytical Psychology Club, 1982); Sabina Spielrein, in Aldo Carotenuto, *A Secret Symmetry* (New York: Random House, 1982); and Christiana Morgan in C. G. Jung, *The Visions Seminars* (Zurich: Spring Publications, 1976); see also Nor Hall, *Those Women* (Dallas: Spring Publications, 1990).

page 13
"Conceptions of knowledge": Mary Belenky, Blythe Clinchy, Nancy Goldberger, and Jill Tarule, *Women's Ways of Knowing* (New York: Basic Books, 1986), p. 5.

page 14
"composed herself": Mary Bateson, *Composing a Life* (New York: Atlantic Monthly Press, 1989).

"It is possible for women": Simone de Beauvoir, *The Second Sex* (New York: Knopf, 1953).

page 15
her handwritten notes and research: Besides the two books and the articles directly credited to Morgan and discussed in my text, Christiana Morgan's research notes appear throughout the mass of unsorted material Henry Murray left to Harvard University and placed in the Harvard Archives, the Murray Research Center at Radcliffe, and the Francis A. Countway Library of Medicine at Harvard. See Bibliography.

ONE: FAMILY TREES AND THEIR FRUIT

page 19
On a spring day: CDM, Chapter 10, "Her Father," typescript (UMP/CL).

page 20
"wonderful and mysterious substance": Ibid.

allying herself with the beauty he loved: CDM diaries; "Her Father"; HAM interview with author, 1987; and notes for HAM's postscript to Spring edition of C. G. Jung's *The Visions Seminars* (UMP/CL).

"half convention and half lie": CDM, "Her Father."

page 21
"waging a mortal battle": Ibid.

The daughters: Constance Holden, CDM's niece, interviews with author 1989, 1990, 1992. Elizabeth Councilman Rogers, M.D., interview with Jeanette Bailey Cheek for Schlesinger Library Archives, Radcliffe College, Cambridge, Mass.

The father and the middle daughter: Councilman Morgan interview with author, summer 1989.

page 22
A rather complete genealogy: This information is to be found in the New England Historic Genealogical Society under the respective family names. Coolidge information primarily in Emma Downing Coolidge, *Descendants of John and Mary Coolidge of Watertown, Massachusetts, 1630* (Boston: Wright & Potter Printing Company, 1930).

Isaac Allerton: Information on Isaac Allerton's life comes from Walter S. Allerton, *History of the Allerton Family in the U.S., 1585–1885* (New York, 1888, 1900); and George Wilson, *Saints and Strangers: Being the Lives of The Pilgrim Fathers and Their Families and Their Friends and Foes; and an Account of Their Posthumous Wanderings in Limbo, Their Final Resurrection and Rise to Glory and the Strange Pilgrimages of Plymouth Rock* (New York: Reynal and Hitchcock, 1945).

324   By far the most colorful: Wilson, *Saints and Strangers,* p. 260.

Isaac Allerton's character: Ibid., p. 344.

page 23
"A change came over the young woman": Reminiscence by a grand-nephew, Benjamin Shurtleff, of Napa, California, in *The Descendants of William Shurtleff* (privately printed), pp. 43–47.

Susanna's friends were killed: Ibid., pp. 46–47.

Information on Hannah Dustan (also spelled Dustin and Duston) comes from E. M. Gagey, "Hannah Duston," in E. T. James, ed., *Notable American Women, 1607–1950,* vol. 1 (Cambridge: Belknap Press of Harvard University Press, 1971), pp. 535–36; and from Henry David Thoreau, *A Week on the Concord and Merrimack Rivers* (1847; reprint, New York: Viking Press, 1985 [The Library of America]), pp. 263–64.

page 24
"They escaped": Thoreau, *A Week,* p. 264.

Dustan's descendants still preserve: Candelabra shown to author by Constance Holden during 1990 interview.

page 25
Though Jung tended to consign: Jung, *Visions Seminars.*

Isabella herself: Information on Isabella Coolidge and her life from Isabella Councilman Wigglesworth, "A Club," typescript lecture (Holden family papers).

Saturday Morning Club: Founded by Julia Ward Howe and Katherine Peabody Loring (Alice James's friend and companion). It was at first a club for those who had graduated from the local girls' schools in Boston and derived partly from their interest in education for women. See Centennial Committee, *The Saturday Morning Club, 1871–1971.* Boston, 1971 (privately printed).

Isabella's letters: Isabella Coolidge–William Thayer correspondence (Morgan family papers).

page 26
The portrait: Probably by the Boston portrait painter Benjamin Curtis Porter (1845–1908), the painting was full-length but was cut to bust size by CDM in the 1950s and the painter's name lost. Painting now owned by Hallee Morgan.

Information on William Councilman's life comes from: Harvey Cushing, "William Thomas Councilman: 1854–1933," *Science* 77, no. 2009 (June 30, 1933): 613–18; reprinted in *National Academy Biographical Memoirs* XVIII: 157–74. William Henry Welch, "Remarks at Dinner in Honor of

William T. Councilman," in *Papers and Addresses by William Henry Welch in Three Volumes,* vol. 3. S. B. Wolbach, M.D., "Obituary: William T. Councilman 1854–1933," *Archives of Pathology* 16 (July 1933): 114; reprinted in *Harvard Medical Alumni Bulletin,* 1934. W. T. Councilman, "Autobiography," typescript (Holden family papers), 1918.

"a ground maker for creation": CDM, "Her Father."

page 27
"is representative": W. T. Councilman, "Autobiography."

William Councilman's reminiscences about farm: Ibid.

Information on Civil War: *Encyclopaedia Britannica,* 11th ed., vol. XXVII, 704–13, article on United States History by FJT (Frederick Jackson Turner).

page 28
"led an independent existence": W. T. Councilman, lecture delivered in Harvard Medical School, December 19, 1921 (privately printed).

page 29
Johns Hopkins Medical School: William Henry Welch, "Remarks," p. 423.

The Boston marriage register: New England Historic Genealogical Society, microfilms of Boston marriage registers, 1894.

page 30
This same interest: W. T. Councilman, "Diary of the Rice Expedition" (Morgan family papers and CDM journals and letters).

two years after his retirement: W. T. Councilman, "Travels in China," typescript (Holden family papers); CDM, "Her Father" (UMP/CL); and Morgan family letters (Morgan family papers).

This chapter also relied on supporting testimony from CDM diaries and unpublished papers; author's interviews with HAM, 1987, Councilman and Hallee Morgan, 1988–90, and Constance Holden, 1989, 1990, 1992; Benjamin V. White, M.D., *Stanley Cobb: A Builder of the Modern Neurosciences* (Boston: Countway Library of Medicine, 1984); and Saul Benson, A. C. Barger, and E. L. Wolfe, *Walter B. Cannon: The Life and Times of a Young Scientist* (Cambridge: Harvard University Press, 1987).

TWO: A TURN-OF-THE-CENTURY GIRL

page 31
A little before eight in the morning: Information on Christiana's infancy in Isabella Coolidge Councilman, "Christiana Drummond Councilman," handwritten birth book (Morgan family papers).

page 32

Christiana was singing: Ibid.

"habits are slowly improving": Ibid. Christiana's reenactment of her punishment would be recognized by a psychologist today as a child's effort to work through a trauma by acting it out on her dolls.

"Poor baby": Ibid.

page 33

The family remained: Description of the house and family life from Elizabeth Councilman Rogers, M.D., Cheek interview, and Isa Wigglesworth, "Boston—1895–1916" (Holden family papers).

"drawn by three galloping horses": Wigglesworth, "Boston."

page 35

a vengeful God: Ibid.

Father's reading and titles of books in CDM diaries.

page 36

The dollhouse now forms the central display on the second-floor left front room of the Manchester Historical Society, Manchester, Mass. It is described in Wigglesworth, "Boston."

dressmakers: Ibid.

On winter mornings: Ibid.

page 37

"hideous racket": Ibid.

The girls would have to sing songs: Wigglesworth, "A Club."

Christiana's godmother: Ibid.

page 38

"she was carried up and down": Isabella Councilman, birth book.

"All the women of the household": CDM notebook, undated (UMP/CL).

Miss Winsor's school: Information comes from the Winsor School catalogue, 1989–90, and from an afternoon I spent there in August 1989.

page 39

Christiana's favorite place: Constance Holden interview with author, 1990.

In art class: CDM diaries and papers.

Among Christiana's childhood papers: Drawings in Morgan family papers.

"To suffer was to come nearer": CDM, "Christ Shutter" draft of chapter for uncompleted book (UMP/CL).

THREE: "*GOD HELP ME, IS ALL I CAN SAY*"

This chapter is based on CDM's diaries, 1913–17 (Morgan family 327 papers).

page 40

"Real Life was singing": Edith Wharton, *A Backward Glance* (1933 MS), quoted in R. W. B. Lewis, *Edith Wharton: A Biography* (New York: Harper & Row, 1975), p. 25.

page 41

"big bribe she's paid": Edith Wharton, *The Custom of the Country* (New York: Charles Scribner's Sons, 1913), p. 207.

unsure of herself: CDM diary, frontispiece, 1913.

page 42

Billy Stearns: Ibid., February 1, 1913.

"Oh I wish I knew": Ibid., January 19, 1915.

Christiana's initial relationship with Billy Stearns: Ibid., as recounted throughout February 1913.

page 43

A photograph of him: Obituary notice, *Boston Herald,* September 18, 1917.

Christiana's feelings about Billy: CDM diary, March 2 and April 16, 1913.

"When the dance began": Ibid., March 8, 1913.

page 44

"The last dance": Ibid., May 31, 1913.

hopes for the school year: Ibid., September 28, 1913.

Wharton's memorable phrase: *The Custom,* p. 206.

Dr. Brigham "said": CDM diary, February 6, 1913.

"Honestly, I must pretend": Ibid., March 9, 1913.

page 45

to drop literature: Ibid., November 19, 1913.

"share in the real business of life": Wharton, *The Custom,* p. 206.

Overcome with shame: CDM diary, May 25, 1914.

page 46

"I lay almost absolutely flat": Ibid., June 27, 1914.

page 47

"I know that I have no right": Ibid., September 18, 1914.

page 48

from Dante's *Divine Comedy:* CDM adult notebooks on her early life (UMP/CL).

She studied the Old Testament: CDM, "Old Testament Shutters," draft of chapter for uncompleted book (UMP/CL).

"I have an awfully nice": CDM diary, February 22, 1914.

Dr. George Waterman: George A. Waterman (1872–1960) was a leading psychiatrist in Boston, who confined his practice to nonpsychotic upper-class patients. He studied under James Jackson Putnam and Morton Prince, whose celebrated patient, Sally Beauchamp, became Waterman's wife. Waterman used suggestion and hypnosis but primarily exhorted his patients to conform to society and its rules and to lead productive lives.

page 49

Throughout the rest of her adolescent years: CDM diary, October 11, 17, 30, and November 30, 1914.

"I am crazy to meet some older": Ibid., March 10, 1915.

page 50

"Hat said she thought I had changed": Ibid., May 28, 1915.

"Tonight I was reading": Ibid., May 20, 1915.

The change in Christiana after Farmington echoes and is an interesting cross-generational substantiation of Carol Gilligan's recent research on adolescent girls' loss of self-esteem and mastery. C. Gilligan, "Teaching Shakespeare's Sister: Notes from the Underground of Female Adolescence." In C. Gilligan et al., eds., *Making Connections* (Cambridge: Harvard University Press, 1990).

"It just came over me": CDM diary, May 30, 1915.

FOUR: LIKE A STAIN OF BLOOD

page 51

"White & cool & fresh": CDM diary (Morgan family papers), March 30, 1917.

"one of this season's most popular": Newspaper clipping in 1915 diary.

page 52

"too marvelous for words": CDM diary, December 3, 1915.

"stupidity and want": Jean Strouse, *Alice James: A Biography* (Boston: Houghton Mifflin, 1980), p. 86.

"I had to peg away": Ibid., p. 81.

page 53

letter she wrote to her aunt Alice: CDM letter in Holden family papers.

"Went to the last Saturday evening": CDM diary, March 25, 1916.

page 54

"I am so sick of thinking": Ibid., March 28, 1916.

"He agreed": Ibid., April 1, 1916.

page 55

"I knew I was playing with fire": Ibid., July 20, 1916.

page 56

"absolutely lacks poetry": Ibid., February 10, 1917.

"mastery always gives me": Ibid., July 23, 1916.

"I am so upset": Consecutive diary entries, January 23, 24, 1917.

"I don't think that I ever suffered": Ibid., February 11–12, 1917.

page 57

"In my diary this year": Ibid., frontispiece, 1916.

"I want to feel everything": Ibid., May 21, 1916.

Lucia Howard: Ibid., spring–summer 1916.

page 58

"These days in Barnstable": Ibid., May 18–19, 1916.

"Lucia has such a wonderful": Ibid., May 22, 1916.

page 59

"Thank God, I am beginning": Ibid., June 12, 1916.

Under her friend's tutelage: List of books on back pages of 1916 diary.

"I can't believe": CDM diary, June 14, 1916.

Lucia also shook: Ibid., August 16, 1916.

"Lately I have been getting": Ibid.

page 60

"Lucia rather irritated me": Ibid., April 3, 1917. If Lucia and Christiana had a lesbian relationship, this is the only—and vague—allusion to it. However, Christiana's curiosity and cultural outlook would make such sexual experimentation not unlikely.

"too tragic, too serious": Ibid., September 3, 1916.

"Be true to the highest": Ibid., August 16, 1916.

"Back to the whirling rush": Ibid., October 25, 1916.

page 61

"I still feel too wretchedly": Ibid., March 23–24, 1917.

FIVE: THE CLOUDS OF WAR

330   This chapter is based on letters between Christiana Councilman (CDM) and William Morgan (WOPM), 1917–19, and CDM's diaries, 1917–19, in the Morgan family papers.

page 62
"When I think": CDM diary, April 27, 1917.

page 63
"I have been seeing a lot": Ibid., May 10–11, 1917.

" 'Bill' Morgan . . . seems": Ibid., May 16–17, 1917.

page 65
William Otho Potwin Morgan biographical information from WOPM scrapbooks, diaries, letters (Morgan family papers).

cofounded the Chicago: Newspaper clippings; WOPM scrapbook (Morgan family papers).

Clara Marks: WOPM scrapbook (Morgan family papers).

Bill's father's illness and death: Newspaper obituary, "William Otho Morgan, 1865–1895," in WOPM scrapbook (Morgan family papers).

Bill grew up an overprotected: WOPM letters, 1921; WOPM three-page penciled notes of an autobiography, n.d. (Morgan family papers).

sent off to St. Paul's: St. Paul's School 1914 yearbook; various entries in WOPM scrapbook (Morgan family papers).

AD Club: Notes for the AD Club in the Harvard Archives. I am also grateful to George Plimpton for a masterly summary of the clubs and their membership: interview with author, 1991.

page 66
War notes from *AD Club 1914–1918* (Cambridge, Mass.: Riverside Press, 1923).

"spent all [his] life with fellows": WOPM letter to CDM, May 17, 1917.

"endure anything and everything": Ibid., May 15, 1917.

"I have wondered": Ibid. [early May, 1917].

"they are the kind of letters": CDM diary, May 25, 1917.

"I remember your saying": WOPM letter to CDM [early May, 1917].

page 67
"Imagine Chris": Ibid., August 13, 1917.

Bill Morgan's visit: CDM diary, August 22–24, 1917.

page 68
"Now I know": Ibid., August 26, 1917.

"It came as quite a shock": Ibid., September 1, 1917.

"the Babes in the Woods": Ibid.

Bill Meeker's death: *New York Times,* September 18, 1917 (Morgan family papers).

Christiana was overwhelmed: CDM diary, September 14, 1917.

fifty-one members: List of close friends who died in WWI is from the roll call that gradually accumulated in WOPM war diary and letters; CDM diaries and letters.

page 69
Because there was no clear route: See Carol Pearson and Katherine Pope, *The Woman Hero in American and British Literature* (New York: R. R. Bowker, 1981), for a discussion of the forces against women of CDM's generation playing a decisive role in the world.

She tried writing: CDM letter to WOPM, January 2, 1918.

page 70
"I find that I haven't written": CDM diary, December 31, 1917.

page 71
"I wish you could have seen me": CDM letter to WOPM, February 1, 1918.

page 72
"It is fundamentally *right*": Ibid., March 1, 1918.

"What a day": Ibid., March 6, 1918.

The Flower Hospital was replaced and rebuilt as part of New York Hospital.

page 73
men's gratitude: CDM letter to WOPM, April 3, 1918.

"This being a doctor's handmaiden": Ibid., May 24, 1918.

page 74
"I came out of the opera": Ibid., April 6, 1918.

"We get our diplomas": Ibid., May 29, 1918.

page 75
Her parents, meanwhile: Ibid., June 16, 1918.

"Pa is so amused": Ibid., July 15, 1918.

page 76
"It's the old awful feeling": Ibid., July 14, 1918.

page 77
The Spanish flu: My chief sources are: R. Collier, *The Plague of the*

Spanish Lady (New York: Atheneum, 1974); Alfred W. Crosby, Jr., *Epidemic and Peace 1918–* (Westport, Conn.: Greenwood, 1976); J. Fincher, "America's Deadly Rendezvous with the Spanish Lady," *Smithsonian* 10 (January 1989): 19; and E. D. Kilbourne, *Influenza* (New York: Plenum, 1987).

"Just at present I am writing": CDM letter to WOPM, September 18, 1918.

page 79

"Pa didn't know whether to laugh": Ibid., October 24, 1918.

"Our uniforms": Ibid., October 31, 1918.

SIX: MAYBE FOREVER

This chapter is based on letters between Christiana Councilman and William Morgan, October 1917–April 1919, in the Morgan family papers.

page 81

"Killed—but what matter?": WOPM letter to CDM, October 12, 1917.

"I must tell you of my wonderful Sunday": Ibid., October 23, 1917.

"A good keen officer": Morgan family papers.

page 82

"It is hard to keep new life": WOPM letter to CDM, November 18, 1917.

The Germans referred: Ibid., June 11, 1917; information on First Division from *New York Times,* February 2, 1919, clipping in Morgan scrapbook.

page 83

"We will set our gun up": WOPM letter to CDM, May 9, 1918.

page 84

citation for bravery: Special Order #49, Morgan family papers.

"this is such a beautiful little green wood": WOPM letter to CDM, May 19, 1918.

page 85

"You've got to have": Ibid., May 24, 1918.

George Haydock: Ibid., June 25, 1918.

The battle started during the night: Composite picture of Soissons gathered from WOPM letters, late July–August, 1918.

page 86

"Never shall I forget": WOPM letter to CDM, July 23, 1918.

page 87
Bill's condition: Ibid., August 15, 1918.

page 88
"Bill my own dearest": CDM letter to WOPM, November 6, 1918.

"I certainly am": WOPM letter to CDM, November 11, 1918.

"All I can say is Alf knew": Ibid., December 1, 1918.

page 89
"My darling, We have just heard": CDM letter to WOPM, November 7, 1918.

page 90
She wrote Bill . . . flirtatiously: Ibid., January 25, 1919.

What she didn't tell him: Constance Holden interview, 1990; verified by Hallee Morgan interviews, 1990, 1991.

She discussed where they would live: CDM letter to WOPM, November 24, 1918.

"I hate this place": Ibid., January 6, 1919.

page 91
"We had a wonder of a row": Ibid., December 27, 1918.

he had grown to approve: Ibid., December 22, 1918.

"disgusting and a waste": Ibid., December 26, 1918.

"I'm so thankful Bill": Ibid., November 24, 1918.

"no man's job": Ibid., November 25, 1918.

"I'm so glad dearest": Ibid., December 13, 1918.

page 92
"remember the first time": Ibid., March 3, 1919.

"Ideals, Bill": Ibid., January 4, 1919.

Christiana had insisted: Ibid., December 22 and 27, 1918.

Christiana chose the Arlington Street Church: Wedding description is from the *Boston Transcript,* May 9, 1919, clipping, and from the *Boston Herald,* May 10, 1919, WOPM scrapbook (Morgan family papers).

page 93
She also saw her faults: CDM letter to WOPM, March 16, 1919.

page 94
"I want to put all my energy": Ibid., December 13, 1918.

SEVEN: THE ORIGIN OF THE HERO

This chapter is based on letters between CDM and WOPM, 1918–1920 and on HAM, CDM, and WOPM diaries and notebooks, in UMP/CL; UMP/HA; and the Morgan family papers.

page 95

"In the spring evenings": CDM letter to WOPM, February 12, 1918.

page 96

He tried Harvard Law School: WOPM Harvard Class Notes, class of 1918, and Councilman Morgan interview, 1989.

"I guess you don't know Bill": CDM letter to WOPM, May 24, 1918.

page 97

different standard for women: For a fuller discussion of the problem of gender roles, sexuality, and the double standard, see Sandra M. Gilbert and Susan Gubar's masterly series, *The Madwoman in the Attic* (1980), *No Man's Land,* vol. 1 (1988), and *No Man's Land,* vol. 2 (1989), all New Haven: Yale University Press.

"I stopped at the hospital": CDM letter to WOPM, March 5, 1918.

page 98

Christiana's experience of childbirth: CDM notebooks, Councilman Morgan and HAM interviews with author, 1987, 1989; I have also used John B. Watson, *Psychological Care of Infant and Child* (New York: W. W. Norton, 1928), for his pronouncements on scientific childbirth and child rearing; Maternity Center of New York, *Handbook,* 1920. For a modern discussion of the deleterious effects of these practices, see Barbara Ehrenreich and Deirdre English, *Complaints and Disorders: The Sexual Politics of Sickness* (New York: The Feminist Press, 1973), and *For Her Own Good: 150 Years of the Experts' Advice to Women* (Garden City, N.Y.: Doubleday, 1979); for a description of an experience similar to CDM's, see Doris Lessing, *A Proper Marriage* (New York: New American Library, 1952).

Critics of childbirth customs: A. MacFarlane, *The Psychology of Childbirth* (Cambridge: Harvard University Press, 1977).

Waterman's beliefs about the postpartum period: See T. Lutz, *American Nervousness, 1903* (Ithaca, N.Y.: Cornell University Press, 1991). See also Henri F. Ellenberger, *The Discovery of the Unconscious* (New York: Basic Books, 1970), and Ehrenreich and English, *Complaints,* for a comparison of psychology's (especially Weir Mitchell's) treatment of women's neurosis and its parallels to Watson's treatment of childbirth and mothers.

page 99

The early perils: Constance Holden interview, 1990, 1992; CDM and HAM notes (UMP/CL).

Nine months after Peter's birth: CDM at back of I. C. Councilman, "Christiana Drummond Councilman," handwritten birth book.

William Peter Councilman Morgan: Ibid.

Watsonianism's chilling astringency: E.g., John B. Watson, in *Psychological Care of Infant and Child,* profoundly distrusted women's instincts and even wondered "whether there should be individual homes for children—or even whether children should know their own parents. There are undoubtedly more scientific ways of bringing up children which probably mean finer and happier children" (p. 82); and "If you expect a dog to grow up and be useful . . . you wouldn't dare treat it in the way you treat your child. When I hear a mother say Bless its little heart when it falls down, . . . or suffers some other ill, I usually have to walk a block or two to let off steam" (pp. 5–6). When Watson worked at Harvard, Cambridge was the center for behaviorism and the scientific training of children to mold them to the needs of a mechanical society.

"I think you get so little satisfaction": CDM letter to WOPM, February 22, 1918.

page 100

"Dearest Ma": CDM letter to Isabella Councilman, October 20, 1920.

page 101

Bill would sketch the outline: WOPM notebooks.

the small group of articles: See Bibliography.

Perhaps the most interesting: "An American Soldier in Vienna," in *The New Republic,* October 1, 1919, pp. 258–61.

page 102

Bolshevism, the great new bogey: See Frederick Lewis Allen, *Only Yesterday: An Informal History of the Nineteen Twenties* (New York: Harper and Brothers, 1931).

a hotheaded . . . defense: WOPM, "How Bolshevism Is Bred," letter in *The New Republic,* 1919.

"Chris has been much better": WOPM letter to William and Isabella Councilman, January 20, 1921.

page 103

Christiana started to spend: I am grateful to Earl Loran of the New York Art Students League for information about the League's early years and for looking up Christiana Morgan's class registrations, 1921–24. The Frick Art Reference Library provided examples of Frank DuMond's, Guy Pène du Bois's, and Leo Lentelli's work and "Fiftieth Anniversary of the Art Students League of New York," 215 West 57th St., Jan. 21–Feb. 2, 1925," exhibition catalogue. Also Marchal Landgren, *Years of Art: The Story of the Art Students League of New York* (New York: Art Students League, 1940).

page 104

C. G. Jung's *Psychology of the Unconscious:* Translated by Beatrice Hinkle (New York: Moffat, Yard & Co., 1916).

Christiana would be among the first to buy Jung's *Psychological Types:* HAM notes, metal box (UMP/HA).

page 105

Cecil Dunmore Murray: UMP/HA; HAM interview with author, 1987; JLM interview with author, 1991–92; JLM family scrapbook, family papers; Harvard Class of 1919 Class Notes and 25th Reunion Book (HA).

Christiana seemed another species: HAM interview, 1987; Caroline Murray (Mrs. Henry A. Murray) interviews with author, 1989–1992.

A far more powerful older man: Information on Weizmann and on CDM's relationship with him comes from: HAM interview, 1987; CDM, "Mr. Frankel," typescript, and various notations by CDM and HAM, especially in CDM's drafts for the chapter "The Fathers," (UMP/CL); and Norman Rose, *Chaim Weizmann* (New York: Penguin Books, 1986). Also Elizabeth Councilman Rogers, M.D., interview with Jeanette Bailey Cheek (Schlesinger Library).

page 106

"In her early twenties": CDM, "Mr. Frankel."

page 107

Christiana went so far: HAM, notes for postscript to Spring edition of Jung's *Visions Seminars* (UMP/CL).

Though they met again: CDM English notebook; HAM notes; and HAM interview with Gene Nameche, April 7, 1968 (C. G. Jung Biographical Archives, CL).

incorrigible flirt: Rose, *Weizmann.*

page 108

"Three times you have said": WOPM letter to CDM, November 26, 1920.

page 109

She wrote to him demanding: Ibid., February 16, 1921.

"My wonderful Christiana woman": Ibid., [May] 1920.

page 111

"My passion woman": Ibid., May 28, 1920.

page 112

enthusiasm for Nietzsche: Rose, *Weizmann,* p. 64.

page 113

Jung once had told a friend: Michael Fordham, "The Infant's Reach," in *Psychological Perspectives* 21 (1989).

page 114

In spite of . . . sophistication: HAM interview, 1987; Councilman Morgan interview, 1989.

captain of the Harvard varsity crew: Details of this scandal from HAM interview, 1987; Constance Holden interviews, 1989; JLM interviews, 1992.

Teddy Roosevelt's advice: Letter from Roosevelt to HAM (JLM family papers).

finished his surgical internship: HAM notes (UMP/CL); Harvard 337
Class Notes, class of 1915 (HA); James William Anderson, "The Life of
Henry A. Murray, 1893–1988," in Rabin, Zucker, Emmons, and Frank,
eds., *Studying Persons and Lives* (New York: Springer, 1990), pp. 304–34.

Josephine, née Rantoul: New England Genealogical Society and Rantoul papers; CDM diaries, 1916, 1917; Caroline Murray and Hallee Morgan interviews, 1989.

dying patient: Patient records and HAM's medical biographical write-up and photo (JLM family papers).

page 115
Jung's *Psychological Types:* C. G. Jung, *Collected Works,* vol. 6, Bollingen Series XX (Princeton: Princeton University Press, 1921/1971).

"For complete orientation": Ibid., p. 518.

page 116
Together, Christiana and the group: Allen, *Only Yesterday.*

Eight: Brother and Sister

page 117
L. J. Henderson: Henderson's work on the physiology of blood led
to the Henderson-Hasselbach equation concerning the balance of oxygen
in hemoglobin.

Though Morgan collaborated: L. J. Henderson, D. B. Dill, H. T.
Edwards, and William O. P. Morgan, "Blood as a Physicochemical System," *Journal of Biological Chemistry* XC, no. 3 (March 1931): 697–724
(received for publication December 22, 1930).

page 118
Lawden Cottage: CDM journal and photographs (Morgan family papers).

Malting House School: Malting House was a progressive and psychologically oriented Montessori school.

She saw Chaim Weizmann: CDM journal; Rose, *Weizmann;* HAM interview with author, 1987.

"a profoundly depressed woman": HAM Tower Journal (UMP/CL).

page 119
Virginia Woolf: *A Room of One's Own* (New York: Harcourt, Brace,
1929), from a series of lectures given in 1928.

page 120

journalism, the bank, and business: William T. Councilman letter from China, August 25, 1924 (Holden family papers).

Harry and Jo Murray seemed to thrive: This and what follows about the Murrays' life in England comes from the diary Jo kept of this year (property of JLM) and from JLM interviews, 1991–92.

page 122

Christiana realized from the first: CDM journal and "Annuesta" entry (UMP/CL and HA).

These women grappled: For a discussion of this problem, see e.g., A. Snitow, C. Stansell, and S. Thompson, eds., *Powers of Desire: The Politics of Sexuality* (New York: Monthly Review Press, 1983), especially Ellen Kay Trimberger, "Feminism, Men, and Modern Love: Greenwich Village, 1900–1925," pp. 131–53.

Mike, his brother: Author's interviews with Hallee Morgan and with Caroline Murray, 1990, corroborated by JLM, 1991.

page 123

Besides this, the profound effect: CDM analysis notes with Jung, 1926 (UMP/CL).

Though Murray in later years: HAM interview with Gene Nameche, 1968; James Anderson, "Henry A. Murray's Early Career: A Psychobiographical Exploration," *Journal of Personality* 56, no. 1 (March 1988): 139–171.

"certain ever recurring": C. G. Jung, *Psychological Types,* p. 44.

"Marriage as a Psychological Relationship": Jung, 1925, in *Collected Works,* vol. 17.

Jung defined: See Claire Douglas, *The Woman in the Mirror* (Boston: Sigo, 1990), for a further discussion of this thorny problem.

page 124

"Every man carries": Jung, "Marriage as a Psychological Relationship," *Collected Works,* vol. 17, p. 198.

"he is a hero": Jung, *The Visions Seminars* (Zurich: Spring Publications, 1976), p. 238.

page 125

Jung's typology: See also Jung's *Visions Seminars* and WOPM diary.

HAM's fascination with Christiana: CDM journal; JRM diary, 1925–1926.

page 126

fathoming her soul: See Gilbert and Gubar's *Madwoman in the Attic* for another view of this need in men in nineteenth-century English literature.

An anima figure: For a more complete explanation of the anima and its supposed counterpart, the animus, see Jung, *Collected Works,* especially vol. 7, "Anima and Animus," pp. 296–340; vol. 13, "Animus and Anima," pp. 57–63; and vol. 9ii, "The Syzygy: Anima and Animus," pp. 20–42. For this dynamic in Melville's life, see HAM notes on Melville's biography (UMP/HA).

"from the depths": D. H. Lawrence, *Twilight in Italy* (New York: Viking Press, 1958), pp. 83–84 (originally published 1916).

"What a villain": Ibid., pp. 83–84.

page 127

Harry's older sister, Virginia: I am grateful to Dr. Josephine L. Murray for extensive talks in 1991 and 1992 on the importance of HAM's sister in his development, verified by Caroline Murray, 1992. For sibling relationships' psychological permutations, see P. McDermott, *Brothers and Sisters* (Boston: Lowell House, 1992), and F. Klagsburn, *Mixed Feelings: Love, Hate, Rivalry and Reconciliation Among Brothers and Sisters* (New York: Bantam, 1992).

Harry . . . decided he would rescue her: Caroline Murray interview, 1990.

page 128

"grief, night, dark": HAM unpublished notecards for Melville's *Pierre* (UMP/HA).

"Why does Lucy not hold him": Ibid.

"read Pierre all afternoon": JRM diary, June 2, 1926.

page 129

Jung had been trained as a physician: For Jung's education and training, see Ellenberger, *Discovery of the Unconscious,* and Douglas, *Woman in the Mirror,* chaps. 1–3.

Jung had attracted the attention of Sigmund Freud: For further discussion of their Oedipal relationship and their break, see Ellenberger, *Discovery,* and Carotenuto, *A Secret Symmetry.*

page 130

Jung's probable liaison with a patient: Carotenuto, *A Secret Symmetry.*

"I still remember her": C. G. Jung, *Memories, Dreams, Reflections* (New York: Vintage Books, 1965), pp. 8–9.

"One cannot stress enough": Laurens van der Post, *Jung and the Story of Our Time* (New York: Random House, 1975), p. 91.

page 131

His wife, Emma: Douglas, *Woman in the Mirror,* chap. 1.

Jung first psychoanalyzed his wife: Of all the wives of the early psychoanalysts, Emma Jung was the only one to become an analyst herself. See Ellenberger, *Discovery*.

340   He found that his marriage: See Carotenuto, *A Secret Symmetry*.

"the prerequisite for a good marriage": William McGuire, ed., *The Freud–Jung Letters* (Princeton: Princeton University Press, 1974), p. 289.

"One could characterize": Adler, ed., *C. G. Jung Letters,* vol. 2, pp. 454–55.

Toni Wolff: Wolff elaborated on Jung's theory about the divisions of types in women's psychology. In her 1934 book, *Structural Forms of the Feminine Psyche,* she divided women into four types: the mother who nurtures men, the hetaira who is romantically involved with him and inspires him, the medium who accompanies him into the depths and opens this realm to him, the amazon who works beside him. She herself combined attributes of the hetaira and the medium, while Emma Jung was given (and fit) the mother-amazon role. Like Jung, Wolff defined each type primarily in relation to men, working out her psychology according to the basic template of Jung's experience of women. See Douglas, *Woman in the Mirror*.

page 132
In fact, the two women: This story is told by an early analyst, C. A. Meier, who trained under Jung at the same time as Wolff and Emma Jung. C. G. Jung Institute of Los Angeles, *Matter of Heart,* film directed by Mark Whitney (Los Angeles, 1983).

Friends of theirs noted: van der Post, *Jung;* Jane and Joseph Wheelwright interviews with author, 1985.

Within the first long session: HAM interview, 1989; also in HAM journal and notes (UMP/HA).

page 133
Harry left Zurich: JRM diary, April 1925 (JLM papers).

"Met H. at 2 o'clock train": Ibid., April 26, 1925.

"I wish that with Harry": CDM notebook, Cambridge, England, February 1925 (UMP/CL).

page 134
"He asks me, 'Do you remember' ": Ibid., June 1, 1925.

page 135
She felt even more left out: JRM diary, April–June entries. Also Caroline Murray interview, 1989.

"would not go an inch": JRM diary, April 1925.

Bill felt bitterly hurt: For his reaction, see CDM analysis notes (UMP/CL) and WOPM analysis notes (Morgan family papers).

"who could possibly think": Susan Isaacs, *The Malting House School: A Study of Its Students,* published in Cambridge, England, 1927. (The boy's identity was hidden under the name "Chris.") This book belonged to Councilman and Hallee Morgan and was discussed in interviews with them and the author in 1987 and 1988, and with Hallee Morgan in 1990 and 1992. It was mislaid circa 1989 and is out of print.

"There must have been awful things": Morgan family papers. Councilman and Hallee Morgan interviews, 1987.

page 136

"I knew that he would wake": CDM notebooks (UMP/CL).

Everything was out in the open: For itinerary of these few weeks, see JRM diary; CDM notebooks and "Annuesta" notes; Caroline Murray interviews, 1989, 1991.

"No; she is my sister": CDM "Annuesta" notes; HAM notes, 1926–1927 (UMP/HA).

"You must do what you think": CDM notebooks (UMP/CL) and WOPM notebooks (Morgan family papers).

page 137

"We spoke to each other through Melville": CDM notebooks (UMP/CL).

There are contradictory reports: HAM, in interviews in his later life with F. Robinson, *Love's Story Told,* seems to have told him CDM and HAM had sexual relations at this time and adds the "★" in an unreferenced notebook that must be in Robinson's private possession. CDM, in her analysis notes, discusses the problem of HAM's *not* having sex then and her later efforts to have him make love to her. Also in her notebooks, she refers to HAM's lack of physical passion. See note for p. 138 below.

"Then the thing broke": CDM "Annuesta" notes and journal, 1926 (UMP/HA; CL).

Jo had joined them: JRM diary, August 11, 1925.

page 138

"Chris and I ordered": Ibid., August 20, 1925.

"On our return": Ibid., August 30, 1925.

"I felt that—I was": CDM analytic-sessions notebook, p. 17 (UMP/CL).

Josie would wonder: JLM interview, 1991.

page 139

he was offered an appointment: HAM official letter of appointment, April 12, 1926 (UMP/HA).

Harry included plans for Christiana: HAM letter to CDM, 1926 (UMP/HA).

She included a brief life history: Handwritten notes dated 1925 before seeing Jung, found in "De Profundis" chapter of Morgan MS (UMP/CL).

342   "And now I want to write": CDM letter to HAM, September 24, 1925 (copy in Morgan family papers).

page 140
      "when they are one being": CDM letter to HAM, winter 1926 (UMP/CL).

During that long winter: CDM notebook, Cambridge, England, December 1925 (UMP/CL).

page 141
      odd series of letters: CDM letters to HAM, winter 1926 (Morgan family papers and UMP/HA).

"Oh, Harry, please": CDM letter to HAM, June 3, 1926 (UMP/HA).

NINE: THE WHALE

Wona and Mansol were the names Christiana (Wona) and Harry (Mansol) gave to each other in Germany in 1926. The names denoted:
Christiana as herself *and* as an anima figure for Harry;
Mansol as Harry and as an animus figure for Christiana.
Together they denoted the lovers' union.

page 145
      Herman Melville, *Moby Dick* (New York: Grosset & Dunlap, n.d.), p. 454.

page 146
      "very intelligent": Jung, *Visions Seminars,* p. 1.

"red-hot conflict": Ibid., p. 2.

"something fearfully strong": Ibid., p. 16.

She also had a father complex: Ibid., p. 2 and Murray, "Postscript," p. 518; Donald Sandner, "The Subjective Body in Clinical Practice," in *The Body in Analysis,* ed. M. Stein (Wilmette, Ill.: Chiron Publications, 1986), pp. 1–18.

Jung dealt with these issues: My discussion of Jung's analysis in this chapter comes from CDM notebook on her analytic sessions (UMP/CL).

page 147
      He also urged her: Ibid., June 8, 1926.

At the next visit: CDM letter to HAM, June 11, 1926 (UMP/CL).

She recorded that Jung: CDM analytic notebook, June 13, 1926.

"Dear Harry, You have spoken": CDM letter to HAM, June 17, 1926 (UMP/CL).

page 149

"Well now first comes": CDM analytic notebook, p. 21.

page 150

Jung understood: See Douglas, *Woman in the Mirror,* for further discussion of Jung's understanding of women's psychology.

"We all have to do": CDM analytic notebook, p. 21.

page 151

"You are a pioneer": Ibid.

"This relationship will be": Ibid., p. 59.

"This is what as a woman": Ibid., p. 98.

"Yes—I gave him": Ibid., June 28, 1926.

page 152

"Came home raging": Ibid., pp. 15–16.

"A strange oppression": Ibid., pp. 150–51.

"strange shapes": *Moby Dick.*

page 153

"only the beginning": CDM analytic notebook, June 28, 1926.

Though Jung did not show: Ibid.

Jung then asked him: REJ diary and letters to CDM, 1926 (Morgan family papers).

During the summer: Sources for Küsnacht in summer 1926 come from CDM, WOPM, REJ analysis notes; William McGuire, Introduction to C. G. Jung, *The Dream Seminars* (Princeton: Princeton University Press, 1984); Jung Archives; and Douglas, *Woman in the Mirror.*

page 155

It often seemed enough: CDM analytic notebook, June and July, 1926.

They were Jones's star pupils: WOPM diaries; REJ letter to WOPM (Morgan family papers).

"It must have more blood!": CDM analytic notebook, July 1926.

Active imagination: Information on its origins is taken from CDM, WOPM, REJ letters, diaries, and analysis notes; from Douglas, *Woman in the Mirror;* from author's interviews with Joseph Henderson, Jane and Joseph Wheelwright, and William McGuire in 1988 and 1989; from McGuire's Introduction to Jung's *Dream Seminars;* from Joseph Henderson, personal communication, 1988; and from REJ's conversations with Councilman and Hallee Morgan, relayed to author by the Morgans in 1989.

page 157

altered state of consciousness: See also Ellenberger, *Discovery of the Unconscious.*

perfect pitch: Sandner, "Subjective Body in Clinical Practice" and *Symbols of Feminine Development in Jung's Visions Seminars* (cassette recordings, C. J. Jung Institute of San Francisco, 1986).

"Now this is the way": CDM analytic notebook, July 8, 1926.

"I feel your greater calmness": Ibid., July 7, 1926.

"These are the origin of magic": Ibid., July 8, 1926.

page 158
"Yes, you can always do this": Ibid., July 7, 1926.

Jung remembered the rush of images: Jung, *Memories, Dreams, Reflections,* chap. 6, "Confrontation with the Unconscious."

page 159
"I should advise you": CDM analytic notebook, July 8, 1926.

A depressed American Indian: The story of the visions as retold in the following pages comes from CDM's *Visions Notebooks,* Houghton Library, Harvard University; visions notebooks in Countway Library and Morgan family papers; Jung, *Visions Seminars;* CDM analytic notebooks.

page 160
"beheld what no man": Jung, *Visions Seminars,* p. 62.

"I beheld a great Negro": CDM, entire text of July 26 vision.

page 161
snake, entered a church: For further discussion of the snake image, see Sandner, *Symbols of Feminine Development.*

"material for the next": CDM analytic notebook, July 8, 1926.

During the summer: Material about the trip comes from CDM "Annuesta" notes; CDM, "The Professor," journal chapter; WOPM journal; CDM–HAM correspondence; JLM interview, 1992; Alfred Cohn letters (UMP/HA).

page 163
She showed Jung the vision book: CDM analytic notebook, October 4, 1926.

"My Beloved": CDM letter to HAM, October 12, 1926.

The tragedy of what happened: See also Douglas, *Woman in the Mirror.*

page 164
"no longer law abiding": Jung, *Visions Seminars,* p. 438.

"Yes, the summer was": CDM analytic notebook, October 4, 1926.

Jung noted the change: CDM analytic notebook, morning and afternoon sessions, October 12, 1926.

page 165

"positive attitude": CDM analytic notebook, October 14, 1926.

"Of course you sweat": Ibid., October 18, 1926.

"The female thing": Ibid., October 20, 1926, A.M.

"but that whole relationship": Ibid.

page 166

"I felt very defiant": Ibid.

"My conscious attitude": Ibid., October 20, 1926, P.M.

Sabrina Spielrein . . . Siegfried: Aldo Carotenuto, *A Secret Symmetry;* McGuire, *Freud–Jung Letters.*

"I only say watch": CDM analytic notebook, October 20, 1926.

page 167

packet of correspondence: Referred to in Gerhard Adler–HAM letter, 1970s (UMP/HA).

"In passing let us note": Jung, *Visions Seminars,* p. 519.

"In early December": Adler, ed., *Jung Letters,* vol. 2, pp. 48–49.

page 168

urging his patient to leave analysis: CDM journal, late October 1926 (UMP/CL); also HAM Postscript to Jung, *Visions Seminars.*

"that is alien to man": Jung, "The Psychological Aspects of the Kore," *Collected Works* 9i, 1941 (Princeton: Princeton University Press, 1969), p. 203.

One trance started with a male: *Visions Notebooks,* vision 69.

page 169

"I came to a great river": Ibid., vision 72.

page 170

"The Gate of the Dark Will": Ibid., vision 74.

page 171

"day after day": Ibid., vision 81.

page 172

redeemed her . . . dragon: This image is similar to the vibrant goddess Inanna in Sylvia Perera, *Descent to the Goddess* (Toronto: Inner City Books, 1981).

She realized that a woman hero: See Nancy Chodorow, *The Reproduction of Mothering* (Berkeley: University of California Press, 1978) and Carol Gilligan, *In a Different Voice* (Cambridge: Harvard University Press, 1982), for some gender research on the difficulties of this; and Camille Paglia, *Sexual Personae* (New Haven: Yale University Press, 1990), for a chaotic literary embroilment in the same, but unmediated, chthonic female power.

discovered her own anima: See James Hillman, *Anima* (Dallas: Spring Publications, 1985); Edward C. Whitmont, "Reassessing Femininity and Masculinity," *Quadrant* 13, no. 2 (1980): 109–22, and *Return to the Goddess* (New York: Crossroad, 1982); and Douglas, *Woman in the Mirror,* for discussions of women's anima.

Satanic Christ: *Visions Notebooks,* vision 108.

"Answer to Job": in Jung, *Collected Works* 11, 1952 (Princeton: Princeton University Press, 1969), pp. 355–470.

Mysterium Coniunctionis: Jung, *Collected Works* 14, 1955–56/1970.

"I ascended the mountain": Trance notebook, May 1, 1927 (UMP/CL).

page 174

Inanna, Lilith, Hecate, and Kali: See Perera, *Descent to the Goddess;* Barbara Koltuv, *Lilith* (York Beach, Me.: Nicolas Hays, 1986); Betty Meador, *The Divine Feminine and Modern Women,* cassette recording (San Francisco: C. G. Jung Institute of San Francisco, 1984).

page 175

Will's dream of Toni Wolff: WOPM dream and analytic notebook, July 1926 (Morgan family papers).

"warning of coming DEATH": Ibid.

page 176

"His [Harry's] mother": Ibid., July 5, 1926.

"Dear Will": REJ–WOPM and REJ–CDM letters, October 1926 (Morgan family papers).

page 177

"Dear Christiana": Ibid.

SEGUE

page 178

From Mansol's Book, written by Harry Murray in August 1927 (UMP/CL).

page 181

From Wona's Book, written by Christiana Morgan. Part of typescript notes for a chapter, "Dissatisfactions with the Past," in CDM's book-in-progress, circa 1939 (UMP/HA).

TEN: LET'S DO IT, HARRY!

This chapter is based on CDM and HAM notebooks and on author's interviews with Robert White, Leopold Bellak, Robert Holt, Henry

Riecken, Saul Rosenzweig, et al.; also HAM, "The Harvard Psychological Clinic," *Harvard Alumni Bulletin,* October 25, 1935.

page 183
"The full philosophy remains": CDM letter to HAM, September 24, 1925.

When Christiana embarked: CDM, Chapter I, "The Voyage Home," typescript (UMP/CL).

page 184
"Why should I be pushed": Ibid., p. 7.

Councie attended Shady Hill: Elizabeth Coolidge Winship interview with author, 1992 (especially re her childhood crush on Councie); also May Sarton, *Plant Dreaming Deep* (New York: W. W. Norton, 1968), and interview with author, 1991.

"There is little of the grand scale": William James, *Principles of Psychology,* 1890 (New York: Dover, 1950), pp. 192–93.

page 185
"little inner life": HAM, *Harvard Psychological Clinic 1927–1937* (privately printed), p. 8; Robert White, *A Memoir: Seeking the Shape of Personality* (Marlborough, N.H.: The Homestead Press, 1987).

Miss Beauchamp: Morton Prince, *The Dissociation of Personality* (New York: Green & Co., 1906), and *The Unconscious* (New York: Macmillan, 1914).

He treated the young woman: More information on Morton Prince in Ellenberger, *Discovery of the Unconscious,* pp. 139–41.

Prince wanted to keep: Robert White interview with author, 1989.

"extracting from his enormously rich": HAM notes for postscript to Spring edition of Jung, *Visions Seminars* (UMP/CL).

page 186
"a lived-in atmosphere": HAM, *Harvard Psychological Clinic,* p. 16.

page 187
So that Morgan and Murray could meet: HAM letters to Maurice Firuski (UMP/HA).

Clarissa Lorenz: See her autobiography, *Lorelei Two* (privately printed, 1980).

upstairs room: My thanks to the manager at Leavitt and Pierce for showing me this area in 1992 (its door is now blocked off).

Jo, on good terms with the cook: JLM interview, 1991.

page 188
In August 1927: CDM and HAM, "Annuesta" notes, 1930.

Behind Murray's support: Ibid.

page 189
forum on the sexuality of women: "Annuesta" notes, 1934–35; Councilman and Hallee Morgan interview, 1987; Hallee Morgan interviews, 1989, 1990.

page 190
Karen Horney: "Annuesta" notes; Karen Horney, *Feminine Psychology* (New York: W. W. Norton, 1967); Merrill Moore notes (Library of Congress).

Morgan dreamed: CDM dream notebook, 1927 (UMP/CL).

"she would not disgrace": CDM, Chapter IV, "Hola," typescript (UMP/CL).

Her skill as an analyst: Robert White interview, 1988; Hallee Morgan interviews, 1988; Hansi Greer notes to HAM (UMP/HA).

From her writing about therapy: CDM letters to LM, 1947; CDM notebooks; CDM letters to HAM (UMP/HA).

page 191
Morgan's and Murray's erotic excitement: The personal material in this chapter, unless noted otherwise, comes from CDM "Annuesta" notes, diaries, and letters (UMP/HA).

page 192
Murray, probably unable to sire: Councilman Morgan interview, 1988; JLM interview, 1992.

The section on WOPM comes from Morgan family papers and from interviews with Councilman and Hallee Morgan, 1987, 1989.

Boston Psychoanalytic Society: Sanford Gifford, "Psychotherapy in Boston" in George E. Gifford, Jr., ed., *Psychoanalysis, Psychotherapy, and the New England Medical Scene, 1894–1949* (New York: Science History Publications, 1978).

page 193
To the public eye: HAM, in Sigmund Koch, ed., *Psychology: A Study of a Science* (New York: McGraw-Hill, 1959), p. 37.

The method behind their personality theory: Ibid.; White, *A Memoir;* Alan Elms, letter to author, 1990; R. Corsini, "Henry A. Murray's Needs-Press Theory," in R. Corsini, ed., *Current Personality Theory* (Itaska, Ill.: Peacock, 1977), pp. 408–10; HAM in, e.g., *Harvard Psychological Clinic,* p. 21.

These tests were grounded: Elms, letter to author, 1990.

page 194
"I was present as a graduate student": White, *A Memoir,* pp. 8–9.

"Working at the Harvard Psychological Clinic": White, quoted by HAM in "Supplement: Morsels of Information Regarding the Extraordinary Woman in Whose Psyche the Foregoing Visions Were Begot," unpublished notes (UMP/CL).

page 195
"Well, they had a little house": Cleome Wadsworth interview with Gene Nameche, pp. 12–16, Box 20, Jung Archives (CL).

page 196
"Lady Morgana's": I thank Saul Rosenzweig for linking Morgan to Morgana le Fay, letter to author, 1988.

such diverse people as: Edwin Shneidman, "A Life in Death," in C. Eugene Walker, ed., *The History of Clinical Psychology in Autobiography* (Pacific Grove, California: Brooks Cole, 1991), p. 251.

"with cuttings from [their] field": HAM, *Harvard Psychological Clinic,* p. 17.

It seemed that anyone of note: Loose mimeo calendar and announcement sheets, Harvard Psychological Clinic (UMP/HA).

page 197
"the most exciting place": Risto Fried letter to author, March 1989.

page 198
"the skill of women": HAM, *Harvard Psychological Clinic,* p. 16.

page 199
best interviewers: Robert Holt interview, 1990.

Skard's autobiography: Ase Gruda Skard, *Liv Laga: Ei Minnebok, 1905–1940* (Oslo: Gyldedal Norsk Forlag, 1985).

"the purely human values": Sigmund Skard letter to author, September 29, 1989.

Christiana's relationship with the staff: Leopold Bellak telephone interview with author, 1989, and "Preface to the First Edition," *The T.A.T., C.A.T. and S.A.T. in Clinical Use,* 4th ed. (Needham Heights, Mass.: Allyn & Bacon, 1986).

page 200
"The Signs": "Annuesta" notes, 1932 (UMP/HA).

"Winter 1934": Ibid., 1933–34.

"I am filled with pain": CDM letter to HAM, January 11, 1928 (UMP/HA).

page 201
Saul Rosenzweig: Rosenzweig interviews with author, 1989, and letters to author.

page 203

Murray . . . downplayed . . . Morgan's work: HAM interviews with James Anderson, 1987.

Morgan's most original contribution: Saul Rosenzweig interviews, 1989.

Morgan as the chief author: Saul Rosenzweig letter to CDM, 1930 (property of SR).

idea of the Thematic Apperception Test: See also HAM letter to Eugene Taylor; Taylor interview with author, 1992; and HAM, *Radcliffe Quarterly,* 1986.

page 204

remembered these games: Interviews with Councilman Morgan, 1988, and JLM, 1991, 1992.

Morgan played a main role: Interviews with White, Rosenzweig, Holt, Riecken, HAM (1986), Taylor, et al.; HAM, *Radcliffe Quarterly,* 1986.

first to utilize the test: HAM interview with James Anderson, 1987; Eugene Taylor interview, 1992; notes in CDM patient folder (UMP/HA).

In the final form: C. D. Morgan and H. A. Murray, "A Method for Investigating Fantasies: The Thematic Apperception Test," *Archives of Neurology and Psychiatry* 34 (1935): 290.

importance of the setting: Henry A. Murray, M.D., and the Staff of the Harvard Psychological Clinic, *The Thematic Apperception Test Manual* (Cambridge: Harvard University Press, 1971), p. 3.

Morgan's name was . . . dropped: HAM interview with James Anderson, 1987.

Morgan preferred not to be listed: HAM interview with author, 1987; HAM, *Radcliffe Quarterly.*

right to be cited as first author: Robert White interview, 1989; see also interviews with Rosenzweig, Holt, Riecken, HAM (1987), et al.

page 205

two further articles: Morgan and Murray, "A Method for Investigating Fantasies"; and *Explorations in Personality: A Clinical and Experimental Study of Fifty Men of College Age* (New York: Oxford University Press, 1938).

page 206

"Due to the resemblances": CDM manuscript, untitled, circa 1938, pp. 3–4 (UMP/HA).

page 207

Eleanor Jones: Information on Jones from Clarissa Lorenz, *Lorelei Two;* Conrad Aiken–HAM correspondence; Robert White interview, 1988; CDM notebooks and "Annuesta" notes; CDM and HAM letters;

JLM interview, 1991; Frances Wickes–CDM correspondence; Caroline Murray interviews, 1990, 1991; and Eleanor Jones letter to HAM, n.d. (UMP/HA).

"Struggling at the Clinic": "Annuesta" notes, October 1930–June 1931 (UMP/HA).

page 208

"Mother Wickes": REJ–Frances Wickes correspondence (Frances Wickes papers, Library of Congress).

"Mar. 31. During breakdown": CDM, "Annuesta" notes, March 1931–Winter 1932–33 (UMP/HA).

page 209

Christiana and Mike Murray: "Annuesta" notes (UMP/HA).

Ralph Eaton: Ibid., 1931–33.

"He seems to be promising": C. G. Jung letter to HAM, December 27, 1930 (UMP/HA).

page 210

suicide echoed: See especially CDM's work on Romanticism, on the claustral complex, and on suicide (UMP/HA and CL).

page 211

"Dear Dr. Murray, I am sorry": C. G. Jung letter to HAM, September 21, 1931 (UMP/HA).

page 212

"Your over valuation of my gifts": Eleanor Jones letter to HAM, n.d. (UMP/HA).

"for hours and hours": CDM, "Annuesta" notes, March 1931 (UMP/HA).

page 213

Councie remembered: Councilman Morgan interview with author, 1987.

Will's health: Councilman Morgan interview, 1988.

"I was sitting in a restaurant": WOPM dream notebook, circa 1927–1930 (Morgan family papers).

page 214

Will Morgan published two monographs: "Navajo Dreams," *The American Anthropologist* 34, no. 3 (July–September 1932): 390–405; and "Navajo Treatment of Sickness: Diagnosticians," *The American Anthropologist* 33, no. 3 (1931): 390–402.

See Bibliography for his further monographs and unpublished articles on Indian culture.

"The terrible effort": CDM, "Annuesta" notes, June 1932 (UMP/HA).

Wickes . . . spoke of . . . visions: Douglas, *Woman in the Mirror,* and CDM–Wickes correspondence; Wickes–REJ correspondence (Library of Congress); REJ–CDM correspondence (Morgan family papers).

page 215

standing . . . as an academic: Councilman and Hallee Morgan interviews, 1989, 1990; CDM–Hallee Morgan correspondence (Morgan family papers).

Jung came to Harvard: HAM, notes for "Supplement: Morsels of Information"; Morgan notebooks (UMP/CL).

Pierre Janet: Ellenberger, *Discovery of the Unconscious.*

Jo Murray met Jung: HAM interview with Gene Nameche, April 7, 1968; JLM interview with author, 1991.

page 216

outward acceptance: JLM interview, 1992.

"a provisional life": CDM diary, April 21, 1937 (UMP/CL).

"magnificent—absolutely magnificent": Alfred North Whitehead, as recorded in CDM diary, June 10, 1939, and in "Magnolia Hill," draft of chapter for uncompleted book (UMP/CL).

ELEVEN: THUNDERS AND AGITATIONS

page 217

Whitehead: Alfred North Whitehead (1861–1947); CDM "Annuesta" notes (UMP/HA); diary notes kept with drafts of chapter "The Fathers" (UMP/CL). Details of Whitehead's life and work from Victor Lowe, *Understanding Whitehead* (Baltimore: Johns Hopkins Press, 1962); and P. A. Schilpp, ed., *The Philosophy of Alfred North Whitehead* (New York: Tudor, 1951), esp. chap. 1, "Whitehead's Autobiography," pp. 1–14, and Victor Lowe, "The Development of Whitehead's Philosophy," pp. 15–125. HAM notes for "Supplement" (UMP/HA).

page 218

At first, Christiana was put off: First of three drafts of chapter "The Fathers" (UMP/CL).

"delicious morning ruminations": Ibid., loose page, undated.

"Altie conveys the pure joy": Ibid.

page 219

Altie's . . . very fragile wife: See Nicholas Griffin, ed., *Selected Letters of Bertrand Russell,* vol. 1 (New York: Houghton Mifflin, 1992), for more information on Evelyn Whitehead and her health (angina, etc.).

"How deeply you have influenced": CDM, Conclusion, "The Fathers" (UMP/CL).

"Some very strange thing": CDM diary, January 1940 (UMP/CL).

page 220
"Just home from Evelyn and Altie's": CDM diary, January 10 and 11, 1941 (UMP/CL).   353

Whiteheads became exemplary parents: CDM "Annuesta" notes, 1942 (UMP/HA); and CDM diary, February 18, 1942 (UMP/CL).

"inclination and skill": HAM notes for "Supplement."

page 221
"Tonight was Altie's 80th birthday": CDM diary, February 15, 1941 (UMP/CL).

page 222
During early 1937: CDM, Chapter IV, "Hola" (UMP/CL); and CDM notes (UMP/HA).

page 223
"a great rock": CDM, Chapter IV, "Hola."

"When she was around Knight": Ibid.

page 224
"The small vestibule": Ibid.

page 225
"like the one which grew": Ibid.

executed in stained glass: Mary Leighton, an American artist, worked in stained glass, especially for cathedrals. There was much controversy about ordering and installing the windows: see especially CDM five-year diary, 1960s, re their final arrival. Details of the Tower come from the author's numerous visits, 1987–92. The Lachaise sculpture has now been removed and a Murray portrait replaced by a companion one Aiken painted of Morgan.

"I had to make a confession of faith in stone": Jung, *Memories, Dreams, Reflections,* pp. 223–24.

page 226
Christiana sit or lie there: E.g., HAM diary, August 1927, and CDM diary, 1940s (UMP/CL).

page 227
"AMOR FATI": The inscriptions chosen were a mixture of phrases from Nietzsche and Blake with additions by Harry and Christiana.

"vulgarity consists": CDM, "Story of M. Sanger and Dr. Brill," unpublished notes (UMP/CL).

"difference between the great women": Ibid.

Wickes had been inspired: Original drawings by CDM reprinted in Wickes's book, gift of Caroline Murray to author, 1991.

page 228

Murray . . . lent a hand: In Morgan's diaries of that year, she noted that HAM and she wrote the review together (UMP/CL).

"Here is a book": "What to Do with Visions: The Inner World of Man by Frances G. Wickes," reviewed by Christiana D. Morgan, *New York Herald Tribune,*" [Fall] 1938. Copy of review, n.d., found in Frances Wickes's papers, Library of Congress, and in UMP/CL.

page 229

he demanded that Morgan work her magic: For this and further discussion of Murray's expectation that CDM could make him write, see CDM diary, April 1939, copied into notebook (UMP/CL); and CDM "Red and Gold Diary," January 25, 1938, as copied into "Annuesta" notes (UMP/HA).

"Mansol made me kneel down": CDM diary, April 1939.

Robert White . . . recalled: Robert White interview, 1989.

Aiken's verdict: Ibid.; verified by Eugene Taylor interview, 1991.

Reading the chapters: Melville boxes (UMP/HA).

page 230

"Oct. 29": CDM diary, 1939, excerpted in bound journal (UMP/HA).

page 231

"April 19, 1940": CDM "Annuesta" notes, 1940 (UMP/HA).

page 232

This intrigued Morgan: "Annuesta" notes, April 27, 1942 (UMP/HA). Information for Morgan's activities at the clinic at this time comes primarily from interviews with Robert White, his *A Memoir,* clinic files, and CDM–HAM correspondence.

alternative series of TAT cards: These have not been published. Originals found by author in unsorted Murray boxes at the Murray Research Center. To my knowledge, this form of the TAT was never used except in tests at the clinic.

page 233

He left Harvard: Robert White interview, 1989.

given the rank of major: Ibid. and Murray notes (UMP/HA and CL).

"Harry is working out": CDM letter to Ned and Elizabeth Handy, May 20, 1943 (UMP/HA).

page 234

left with the . . . book: Robert White interview, 1989.

product of that historical moment: H. A. Murray and C. D. Morgan,

A Clinical Study of Sentiments, published as a book and in *Genetic Psychology Monographs* 32 (1945): 3–149.

"the right fighting spirit": "A Clinical Study of Sentiments," p. 73,   355
the epigraph is from Charles Peguy.

the case histories: HAM letter to CDM, 1944 (Shneidman collection).

page 235

genetically high blood pressure: Murray, in various interviews, gave different dates for the operation: as early as 1938, often 1941, most reliably 1943, but as late as 1945; CDM letters to LM and Councilman Morgan interview set the operation in early 1943, as does JLM interview, 1992.

"From the early nineteen-thirties": HAM notes for "Supplement."

radical sympathectomy: I am grateful to the following sources of information on this operation: CDM Massachusetts General Hospital medical records; Countway Library Archives; Richard Wolfe of the Countway Library; Barbara Herbert, M.D., Josephine Murray, M.D.; plus conversation with an extremely helpful surgeon who told me of his work at Mass General with Smithwick and was trained in the procedure but wishes to remain anonymous.

page 236

Josie Murray was at home: JLM interview, 1992.

page 237

She felt close to Councie now: Councilman Morgan interview, 1987.

Hansi Greer: CDM notebooks and letters to HAM, 1943–45 (Shneidman collection). Both discuss Christiana's problematic relationship with Greer.

page 238

Kenneth Diven: CDM "Annuesta" notes, 1946 (UMP/HA). Interviews with Robert White, 1989; Councilman and Hallee Morgan, 1988, 1989; JLM, 1991, 1992. CDM and HAM diaries, notes, and letters (UMP/HA and CL).

page 239

"Now then, in as few words as possible": Kenneth Diven letter to HAM, February 8, 1945 (UMP/HA).

" 'She is a powerful woman. She could commit murder.' ": A reference to Whitehead's comment on the Lachaise sculpture, which Murray liked to quote.

page 240

"Do not come expecting": Kenneth Diven letter to HAM, March 2, 1945 (UMP/HA).

page 241

Lewis Mumford: Mumford (1895–1990) correspondence with CDM

and HAM (UMP/HA); Lewis Mumford, *My Work and Days: A Personal Chronicle* (New York: Harcourt Brace Jovanovich, 1979), and *Sketches from Life: The Autobiography of Lewis Mumford—Early Years* (New York: Dial Press, 1982); Donald L. Miller, *Lewis Mumford: A Life* (New York: Weidenfeld and Nicolson, 1989).

"one of America's last": Miller, *Lewis Mumford,* p. xiii.

page 242

three significant friendships: The indexer inexplicably omitted referencing the six pages in which Mumford celebrates Morgan, and so she disappears from the record again, except to the reader of the text itself. Mumford, *My Work and Days,* chap. 10, especially pp. 180–86.

Mumford cherished her letters: Ibid.

"was part of a family . . . While a pale light": Ibid., pp. 180–81.

page 243

"I liked your idea of 'claim' ": CDM letter to LM, 1938 (UMP/HA).

Morgan recommended that he read: Ibid., December 14, 1945 (UMP/HA).

"Many things have made me think of you": LM letter to CDM, December 4, 1944, in Mumford, *My Work and Days,* p. 402, and in UMP/HA.

page 244

"Your present image": LM letter to CDM, December 6, 1943 (UMP/HA).

"I have read your letter": Ibid., May 25, 1944 (UMP/HA).

"Your words on my book": Ibid., August 14, 1944 (UMP/HA).

"One way or another": Ibid., June 1945 (UMP/HA).

"My love to you": Ibid., July 13, 1945 (UMP/HA).

"You should see me at least once": Ibid., October 20, 1947 (UMP/HA).

page 245

"with the sight of you": Ibid., February 4, 1957 (UMP/HA).

"You are indeed a joy": CDM letter to LM, August 18, 1944 (UMP/HA).

"Together he and I": Ibid., December 14, 1945 (UMP/HA).

Morgan's relationship to Murray: My understanding of this during the war years derives mainly from the Morgan-Murray correspondence (Shneidman collection).

"go down to the roots": HAM letter to CDM, May 18, 1944 (Shneidman collection).

"complete obedience": Ibid.

page 246
"O My Beautiful": Ibid., December 18, 1944 (Shneidman collection).   357
The couple invented various rituals they named Epiphany, Walpurgis, and
also Manahatta.

page 248
"there is a lack of trust": CDM letter to HAM, 1945 (Shneidman
collection).

tightly controlled multipart analysis: HAM letters to CDM, 1941–45
(Shneidman collection).

page 249
"My first task": CDM and HAM untitled testament, 1944, loose
pages marked pp. 15 (43), 19 (49), 54 (UMP/CL).

page 250
finish a book: H. A. Murray et al., *The Assessment of Men* (New York:
Rinehart, 1948). The book was based on the tests Murray, Morgan, and
clinic members developed at the prewar Harvard Psychological Clinic and
then applied to screen men and women for espionage work.

Returning to New York: HAM, "Mansol's Notes on What Went
Wrong" (UMP/HA); and JLM interview, 1991.

TWELVE: THE RED AND GOLD DIARY

page 251
"What Joy": CDM typescript chapter for her unpublished book
(UMP/CL).

"One of H's complaints": CDM letter to LM (circa 1950) (UMP/
HA).

page 252
"You are capable of terrific work": Dona Louisa Coomaraswami
letter to CDM, June 6, 1945 (UMP/HA).

page 253
"The question Mrs. Coomeraswamy raised": LM letter to CDM,
July 13, 1945, in Mumford, *My Work and Days,* pp. 184–86.

page 255
"Here I am at the Tower": HAM handwritten foolscap, May 9, 1949
(UMP/HA).

page 256
"in the history of mankind": Ibid.

"an absence of quarrels": Ibid.

page 257

"highest philosophy": Ibid.

"Dynamics of Interpersonal Relations": Ibid.

page 258

box after box of index cards: File boxes of cards, some typed, some handwritten by CDM (UMP/HA).

page 259

"What a tremendous undertaking": CDM loose notes in "Annuesta" box (UMP/HA).

page 261

Rituals: I am indebted to Edward C. Whitmont, especially for his chapter on ritual, in *Return to the Goddess* (New York: Crossroad, 1982), which informs the following discussion.

infant's ecstasy of merger: Melanie Klein, *The Psychoanalysis of Children* (London: Hogarth Press, 1932).

"Red and Gold Diary": Eugene Taylor interview, 1989.

green Hindu shirt and a black velvet skirt: "Red and Gold Diary," November 18, 1936, excerpted in CDM, "Annuesta" notes (UMP/HA).

page 262

"My lover is myself explicit": Ibid., November 28, 1936.

"Tonight Mansol returned": Ibid., December 12, 1936.

"Mansol knew the rush of lust": Ibid., December 14 and 31, 1936.

page 264

prescription of fantasy: JLM interviews, 1992.

"immoral, destructive, scary": Whitmont, *Return to the Goddess,* p. 253.

page 265

"thrill her and make her afraid": CDM letter to WOPM, February 16, 1921. See p. 109.

"My love is my God": "Red and Gold Diary," January 25, 1938, excerpted in CDM, "Annuesta" notes (UMP/HA).

"I am second rate": HAM small loose-leaf notebook diary, "Written by Mansol," September 11, 1943 (UMP/CL).

page 266

"From Mansol's Tale of the Tower": HAM MS, February 4, 1940 (UMP/HA).

THIRTEEN: THE END OF THE CHASE

page 276

"It is the long drawn out pain": CDM diary, 1940s (UMP/CL).

The Plympton Street building: Robert White interview, 1989.

page 277

Harry also promised: CDM and HAM notebooks (UMP/HA).

White sensed a deterioration: Robert White interview, 1989.

page 278

"Do you think": Robert Holt interview, 1990.

closing of the ranks: This phenomenon and its toll on women has been studied by Barbara M. Solomon, *In the Company of Educated Women* (New Haven: Yale University Press, 1985); Wini Breines, *Young, White, and Miserable: Growing Up Female in the Fifties* (Boston: Beacon Press, 1992); Jessie Bernard, *Academic Women* (University Park, Pa.: Pennsylvania State University Press, 1964); and Mariam K. Chamberlain, ed., *Women in Academe: Progress and Prospects* (New York: Russell Sage Foundation, 1988), to all of whom I am indebted in writing this chapter.

"climate of unexpectation": Mary Bunting inaugural speech as Radcliffe president, 1961.

page 279

others felt far less positive: Henry Riecken interview, 1990; Silvan Tompkins letter to and telephone conversation with author, 1989; Edwin Shneidman interview with author, 1991; Forrest Robinson, *Love's Story Told*.

one of the three best minds at Harvard: LM letter to CDM (1947) (Mumford papers, University of Pennsylvania).

In one letter: CDM letter to LM, circa 1950 (UMP/HA).

page 280

"I find that I cannot deal": CDM letter to LM, March 8, 1948.

"Analysis necessitates a *creative* process": CDM letter to LM, circa 1950.

page 281

tended to become lifelong friends: Records of visits, CDM five-year diaries of this time (UMP/CL); and letters (UMP/HA).

page 282

Hansi Greer: Letters between CDM and HAM; HAM and Greer; Hannah and Greer (UMP/CL; HA).

love for her niece: Constance Holden interviews with author, 1989, 1990, 1992.

Josie, was attending Radcliffe: JLM interviews, 1991–92.

Josie was remembered by Robert White: Robert White interview, 1989; Henry Riecken interview, 1990; Eugene Taylor interview, 1991.

page 283

"Josephine dear, What fun": CDM letter to JLM, January 22 (circa 1948) (JLM family papers).

joy that her son had found: CDM letter to HAM, 1945 (Shneidman collection).

Christiana helped the young couple: Councilman and Hallee Morgan interviews, 1987, 1989; CDM–Hallee Morgan correspondence (Morgan family papers).

"My beloved— Just one word": CDM letter to HAM, January 1947 (Shneidman collection).

page 284

Hallee often spent summers: Dates of her visits are noted in CDM five-year diaries of this period (UMP/CL).

page 285

"One day this summer": CDM, "Magnolia Hill," draft of chapter for uncompleted book, 1952 (UMP/CL).

more fantastical series: UMP/Murray Research Center.

Christiana felt the new cards: CDM notebooks, n.d. (UMP/HA).

Dorothy Tobkin: I am indebted to Dorothy Tobkin for the vivid memories of her work at the Baleen with CDM, conveyed in letters and a telephone interview, 1991–92.

page 287

"relaxed, upper-class burbling meander": Tobkin letter to author, 1992.

Morgan showed Tobkin: Dorothy Tobkin interview, plus Tobkin letter, *Radcliffe Quarterly,* 1987.

Riecken remembered: Henry Riecken interview, 1990.

page 288

investigations of LSD . . . use of amphetamines: HAM letters; HAM, "Prospect for Psychology," Internat. Congress of Applied Psychology, Copenhagen, 1961; Caroline Murray interview, 1990; Henry Riecken interview, 1990; Leopold Bellak interview, 1990.

Morgan's direct efforts: Robert Holt interview, 1990; verified by Henry Riecken telephone interview, 1991.

Merrill Moore: Merrill Moore papers, Library of Congress, Manuscript Division. Container B, Box 47: Morgan, Christiana D., and Henry A. Murray, project of: Transcripts of Merrill Moore's interviews with, 1954–56.

page 289

Fugitives: "Introduction," *Merrill Moore: A Register of His Papers in the Library of Congress* (Washington, D.C.: Library of Congress Press, Manuscript Division).

seventeen two-hour sessions: Phonograph records and transcriptions,   361 Merrill Moore papers, Library of Congress, Manuscript Division.

"Well look Merrill": CDM interview with Merrill Moore, November 20, 1954, ibid.

page 290
"never said one word about my poetry": Ibid., November 27, 1954.

"I only have one thing": Ibid., January 18, 1955.

page 291
"Beloveds— What joy to receive": CDM letter to LM, February 18, 1957 (UMP/HA).

page 294
Introduction to Melville's *Pierre:* Henry A. Murray, ed., *Pierre, or the Ambiguities* (New York: Farrar, Straus/Hendricks House, 1949).

A condensation: HAM, Melville MS (UMP/HA).

Pepys's *Diary:* A full record of these days is in CDM's 1950s notebooks (UMP/CL).

A formal portrait: Notes on the date of its completion in CDM five-year diary, 1956 (UMP/CL).

page 295
"You have been very much with us": LM letter to CDM, February 1, 1962 (UMP/HA).

"Your letter came this morning": LM letter to CDM, February 8, 1962 (UMP/HA).

page 296
"Beloved Lewis— How exciting": CDM letter to LM, December 26, 1962 (UMP/HA).

page 297
"The greater unifying idea": James Anderson interview with HAM, October 1987. I am indebted to James Anderson for kindly Xeroxing these interviews for me and for his help and encouragement on this chapter.

page 298
In a nine-page review: HAM, "Secondary Spout Number 10: Review of Baleenian Endeavors," September 15, 1958 (UMP/Murray Research Center).

The achievements were solid: Ibid., and HAM, "Brief Summary of Researches at the Psychological Clinic Annex," Department of Social Relations, Harvard University, June 15, 1956.

362   *page 300*
From Mansol's Book: HAM handwritten document, circa 1945–46 (UMP/HA).

page 301
From Wona's Book: CDM, Chapter IV, "Hola," typescript (UMP/CL).

FOURTEEN: THE HIDDEN LAST ACT

page 302
"Death is only a launching": Herman Melville, *Moby Dick* (New York: Grosset & Dunlap, n.d.), pp. 527–28.

page 303
"The citadel of her pride": CDM, Chapter XII, "History of Their Synergy," typescript (UMP/CL).

"as-if" personality: See Karen Horney, *The Neurotic Personality of Our Time* (New York: W. W. Norton, 1967).

narcissistic personality disorder: American Psychiatric Association, *Diagnostic and Statistical Manual of Mental Disorders, Third Edition, Revised* (Washington, D.C.: American Psychiatric Association, 1987).

page 304
"the frail and tenuous scaffolding": CDM, Chapter XII, "History of Their Synergy."

Murray imaginatively inhabited her: Ibid.; also HAM, "Olenka," uncompleted chapter for their book (UMP/CL).

"commonplace" . . . "great language": Ibid.

"I conceive of our life": HAM quoted by CDM in Chapter XII, "History of Their Synergy."

page 305
"Throughout this period": Ibid.

page 306
"The easiest thing": CDM, "Gothic Shutters," unnumbered chapter, typescript (UMP/CL).

page 307
Morgan accepted this role: For an excellent analysis of similar situations and dilemmas among intellectual women, see Ellen Kay Trimberger, "Feminism, Men, and Modern Love: Greenwich Village, 1900–1925," in *Powers of Desire: The Politics of Sexuality,* eds. Ann Snitow, Christine Stansell, and Sharon Thompson (New York: Monthly Review Press, 1983), pp. 131–52. My thinking here is indebted to them.

page 308

Kierkegaard's knight: Søren Kierkegaard on the Knight of Infinite Resignation in *Fear and Trembling,* in *A Kierkegaard Anthology* (New York: The Modern Library, 1946), as well as his own life history.

"death as its unconscious end": HAM letter to CDM, February 20, 1946 (Shneidman collection).

Her research led her: CDM's notes, both typed and handwritten, on the interrelation of romance and death are found throughout her research boxes, especially in a metal box, under the heading "Transitions and Transformations" (UMP/HA).

de Rougemont's study: Denis de Rougemont, *Love in the Western World* (New York: Pantheon, 1940).

"Passion means suffering": Ibid., pp. 43–44.

In notes for a paper: "What Is the Origen [*sic*] of Death Wishes in Synergy?" circa 1946–50 (UMP/HA and CL).

page 309

Byronic hero: CDM et al., "The Byronic Hero," undated typescript, textual evidence and style of CDM, HAM, and a third person: Hansi Greer? See also Hansi Greer letters to Barbara Hannah for verification (UMP/HA).

"Death by water": Ibid.

Morgan's Gothic Romanticism: In this discussion, I am indebted especially to two writers who explore the gender politics in masochism and sadomasochism and view both as normal to neither sex and as aberrations that are self and ego alien: Jessica Benjamin, *The Bonds of Love: Psychoanalysis, Feminism, and the Problem of Domination* (New York: Pantheon, 1988), and Michelle A. Masse, *In the Name of Love: Women, Masochism and the Gothic* (Ithaca, N.Y.: Cornell University Press, 1992). Masse, in her masterly feminist and psychoanalytic study of female masochism, writes: "Girls who, seeking recognition and love, learn to forget or deny that they also want independence and agency, grow up to become women who are Gothic heroines" (p. 3). She studies the genre of Gothic fiction to understand "How and why women incorporate the expectations of their world so that they eventually hurt themselves as others once hurt them" (p. 5).

The heroine longs: For another, more political analysis of this syndrome see Ann Snitow, "Mass Market Romance: Pornography for Women Is Different," in *Powers of Desire: The Politics of Sexuality,* eds. Ann Snitow, Christine Stansell, and Sharon Thompson (New York: Monthly Review Press, 1983), pp. 245–63.

sadomasochism: For the discussion that follows, I have learned from and am indebted to Wilhelm Reich, *Character Analysis* (New York: Orgon Institute Press, 1945); Theodor Reik, "Masochism in Modern Man," Part

Two of *Of Love and Lust* (New York: Farrar, Straus, 1949), pp. 195–367; Richard von Krafft-Ebing, *Psychopathia Sexualis* (1886; reprint, New York: Bell, 1965); Nancy Chodorow, *The Reproduction of Mothering: Psychoanalysis and the Sociology of Gender* (Berkeley: University of California Press, 1978), and *Feminism and Psychoanalytic Theory* (New Haven: Yale University Press, 1989); Dorothy Dinnerstein, *The Mermaid and the Minotaur: Sexual Arrangements and Human Malaise* (New York: Harper & Row, 1976); Georges Battaille, *Death and Sexuality* (New York: Walker, 1962); Simone de Beauvoir, *The Second Sex* (New York: Vintage, 1974); Robert Stoller, *Sexual Excitement* (New York: Simon & Schuster, 1980); and, most especially, Jessica Benjamin, *The Bonds of Love: Psychoanalysis, Feminism, and the Problem of Domination* (New York: Pantheon, 1988), and "Master and Slave: The Fantasy of Erotic Domination," in *Powers of Desire: The Politics of Sexuality,* eds. Ann Snitow, Christine Stansell, and Sharon Thompson (New York: Monthly Review Press, 1983), pp. 280–99.

"a destroyer—a breaker": CDM, Chapter XII, "History of Their Synergy."

page 310
"to be at the knee": Jean-Jacques Rousseau, quoted in Krafft-Ebing, p. 112.

page 311
"the outward fringes of mind": F. Gonzalez-Crusso, *On the Nature of Things Erotic* (New York: Vintage, 1988), p. 186.

she could neither respect: CDM diary, December 19, 1930, "Annuesta" notes (UMP/HA).

dominatrix anima: In a passage in a draft of his uncompleted Melville book, Murray wrote with intimate understanding of this type of anima figure: "The incognito was a woman of the night, acquainted with the mysteries, revealer of the hidden soul of man, lustful, sinister in her strength. She came as the eruption of the dark side of Melville's spirit, standing for all the repressed: sorrow, sexuality, hate, egotism, power, and the *death wish*. . . . She opened the way to the unconscious, to the sharkish inner depth of mind. Queen Hautia he would call her: a witch who mocked conventional society, pure reason, innocent naive idealism." Melville typescript, box 3, Chapter XV, p. 23 (UMP/HA).

page 312
Caroline (Nina) Chandler Fish: Interviews with HAM, 1987; Caroline Murray, 1990, 1991; Eugene Taylor, 1989–92; JLM, 1992; Councilman and Hallee Morgan, 1988.

page 313
"What, and spend the rest of my life": Hallee Morgan interviews, 1988–92.

Denis Bay Plantation: Description from Cleome Wadsworth's various undated letters to CDM and HAM; and HAM letter to Lewis Mumford, March 17, 1967 (UMP/HA).

"the eternal August of the Tropic": Melville, *Moby Dick,* pp. 142–143.   365

"You disgust me!": JLM interview, 1991.

Harry later found: Murray's varying descriptions of Morgan's death come from interviews with Caroline Murray, 1990; Eugene Taylor, 1989–1992; JLM, 1992; Councilman and Hallee Morgan, 1988; Saul Rosenzweig, 1988; Joseph Wheelwright, 1988; Robert White, 1989; Robert Holt, 1990; Edwin Shneidman, 1991; and HAM letters to LM, March 17 and 20, 1967 (UMP/HA).

page 314

Harry later announced: I am indebted to Nicole Loraux, *Tragic Ways of Killing a Woman* (Cambridge: Harvard University Press, 1987), for a framework for understanding CDM's death as tragedy and the ways HAM's multiple versions of her death make her invisible.

"Death by report lends itself to conjecture": Ibid., p. x.

multiple meanings: Ibid.

Christiana Morgan "feinted": HAM letter, property of Saul Rosenzweig.

page 315

Harry held a service: The description of the service comes from "Order of Memorial Rite, At the Tower on the Marsh, Newbury, Massachusetts, May 21, 1967," typescript (UMP/CL).

"CHRISTIANA D. MORGAN Our Imponderable Superanima": HAM handwritten note in box of obituary notices (UMP/HA).

Lewis Mumford . . . refused to attend: LM letters to HAM, spring 1967 (UMP/HA). Councilman Morgan interview, 1987.

Councilman . . . shrank back: Councilman Morgan interviews, 1987, 1988.

page 318

"You will look back at us": Olive Schreiner, *Women and Labour* (London: Victor Gollancz, 1911).

Bibliography

The following abbreviations have been used throughout the Bibliography:

HA: Harvard University Archives, Pusey Library, Harvard University

CL: Francis A. Countway Library of Medicine, Harvard Medical School, Harvard University

UMP: Unsorted H. A. Murray Papers

MRC: Henry A. Murray Research Center, Radcliffe College

Houghton: Houghton Library, Harvard University

Schlesinger: Library on the History of Women in America, Radcliffe College

For other abbreviations see introductory paragraph to Notes.

CHRISTIANA MORGAN

PUBLISHED WORK

Morgan, Christiana D. What to Do with Visions: The Inner World of Man by Frances G. Wickes. Reviewed by Christiana D. Morgan. *New York Herald Tribune.* [Fall] 1938. Copies of review found in Frances Wickes Papers, Library of Congress and in UMP, CL.

————."Thematic Apperception Test" (in the Case of Ernest). In Henry A. Murray et al., *Explorations in Personality: A Clinical and Experimental Study of Fifty Men of College Age,* 673–80. New York: Oxford University Press, 1938.

————, and Henry A. Murray. "A Method for Investigating Fantasies: The Thematic Apperception Test." *Archives of Neurology and Psychiatry* 34 (1935): 289–306.

————, and Henry A. Murray. "Thematic Apperception Test." In Murray et al. *Explorations in Personality,* 530–45.

Murray, Henry A., and Christiana D. Morgan, "A Clinical Study of Sentiments." *Genetic Psychology Monographs* 32 (1945): 3–311.

Original drawings. In Frances Wickes. *The Inner World of Man.* New York: Henry Holt, 1938.

RESEARCH

Harvard Archives, UMP—162 boxes of unsorted papers:

"Annuesta Diary." 1926–40. Unnumbered metal file box.

"The Byronic Hero." Uncompleted typescript and handwritten notes. Parts of MS written by Hansi Greer (?) and HAM (?). Box 32.

Claustral Complex. Notes and uncompleted typescript. Box 143.

Clinic notebooks. Creativity Questionnaires; Experiments in Humor; The Philosophy of Aesthetic Criticism; Self-Knowledge; Variability (variability notes also by HAM). Notes. Box 67.

Clinic notebooks on clinic plans and experiments. Alternate pages written by CDM and HAM. Box 66.

Death wish. Notes for paper. Box 85.

Fantasy Inventory. Notes. Box 70.

"The Fathers." Typescript of a chapter of untitled book. Box 123.

Fuller, Margaret. Notes for article. Unnumbered metal file box.

Imagination & Fantasies, Dreams, Visions; relationship between Fantasy and Art, Fantasy and Religion, Fantasy and Science. Notes, typescripts, handwritten uncompleted papers. Box 106.

Melville; Emotions; Anima; Trances. Notes. Unnumbered metal file box. *Moby Dick,* mythology. Index cards and notes, some handwritten. Box 73.

Melville. Unfinished MS by HAM. Chapter annotations, marks, and extended comments by CDM, including extra pages of notes and questions. Especially interesting is Morgan's plea for a more integrated view of the feminine. She uses Melville's Hautia in *Mardi* to criticize Murray's idea that the feminine can be split into all-bad and all-good figures; Morgan argues for a more complex and integrated view of women combining Yillah and Hautia. She does the same with Murray's later treatment of Fayaway. Boxes 3–6.

Merrill Moore. Unfinished typescript by Hansi Greer. A large part of the material duplicates earlier work by CDM on Moore (Library of Congress). Box 2.

Needs. Notes, some handwritten. Box 62.

Needs. Notes. Boxes 146–47.

Needs. Notes with handwritten Proverbs pertaining to different needs. Box 113.

Patient files, including her notes on first administration of TAT. Box 102.

Quotations. Mostly typed; some handwritten. Index cards. Box 38.
Sex. Handwritten notes. Box 62.
"Story of M. Sanger and Dr. Brill." Notes for article on Margaret
Sanger: Unnumbered metal file box.
Suicide. Notes (1933). Box 122.
TAT (Thematic Apperception Test). Early forms, including photos
of CDM's paintings and some original drawings. Box 5.
Transitions, Transformations, *Moby Dick,* and Similes. Notes. Box
73.
Unconscious Psychic Processes. Notes (1930s). Box 102.
"What Is the Origen [sic] *of Death Wishes in Synergy?"* (circa 1946–50).
Notes and uncompleted typescript. Box 85.

Murray Research Center:

"Attributes and Vectors." Superiority (5 pages); Symbols; Attention
(4 pages); Cognizance; Possession; Construction; Security; Inviolacy
(bondage fantasies); Immaculacy; Association; Freedom; Destruction;
Submission (masochism); Novelty; Activity; Sameness; Sentience; Sex
(incl. rape fantasy); Succor; Object-Nurture; Rest; Elimination. Original
notes, handwritten and typed, on CDM's Tower notepaper. Dyads 6–10.
Box 2.
Drawings for Fantasy TAT.
Drawings for standard TAT.

UNPUBLISHED PAPERS

Analysis notebook, 1926. UMP, CL.
"Biography of a Trinity." Notes and outlines for a book. CL.
Chapters of unfinished book: Preface. *The Promise;* I. *The Voyage
Home;* II. *Finding of Sted;* III. *The Building;* IV. *Hola;* V. *Ru's Run;* VI.
Description of Lawn Garden; VII. *Coming Up the Turnpike;* VIII. *Old Tes-
tament Shutters;* IX. *Dialogue Points of Our Relationship;* X. *Pelionasa: Systole
Diastole;* XI. *Guardian Pine;* XII. *History of Synergy;* XIII. *Backward Look
at the Shutters;* XIV. *The Fathers;* XV. *Building of Tower;* XVI. *Arrival in
Spring;* XVII. *Conversation with Buddha;* XVIII. *Via Sacra;* XIX. *Dialogue
Points of Our Relationship.* 1961 additions: Chapters 5. *Reconsideration of
Promise;* 8. *The Neighbors;* 13. *The Road Up.* Loose and unnumbered: *Mr.
Frankel; De Profundis; The Professor; What Joy; Magnolia Hill; Christ Shutter;
Tribute to the Old Man; Dissatisfactions with the Past; Gothic Shutters.* Un-
published typescripts. UMP, CL.
Diaries, 1913–17. Morgan family papers.
Diary, April 1939. Copied into notebook. UMP, CL.
Diary, 1939. Excerpted in bound journal. UMP, HA.
Diary, 1940s. UMP, CL.
Diary, 1941. Unpaged. UMP, CL.
Diaries, five-year, 1950s, 1960s, and 1970s. UMP, CL.
"From Wona's Book" (circa 1955–65). Typescript draft. UMP, CL.
Interviews with Merrill Moore. In Container B., box 47: Morgan,

Christiana D., and Henry A. Murray, project of: Transcripts of Merrill Moore's Interviews with, 1954–56. *Merrill Moore: A Register of His Papers in The Library of Congress,* Washington, D.C., Library of Congress Press, Manuscript Division.

Lawden Cottage. Journal and photographs. Morgan family papers.

"Lilith." Notes, outlines, and typescript for a proposed book. Manuscript, untitled, circa 1938. Rough drafts and notes. UMP, HA.

Notebook, Cambridge, England, 1925–26. UMP, HA.

Red and Gold Diary, as copied into "Annuesta" notes. UMP, HA.

Trance notebook, 1926–27. Morgan family papers.

Untitled testament, by CDM and HAM, 1944. Loose pages numbered 15 (43), 19 (49), and 54. UMP, HA.

Visions Notebooks, Vols. I, III. Henry A. Murray listing. Paintings and text. Vellum pages, red leather bindings. Houghton, rare books section.

Visions notebooks. CL and Morgan family papers.

Whitehead, Alfred North. Diary notes on Whitehead. With 3 drafts for "The Fathers." UMP, CL.

CORRESPONDENCE

CDM–Coomaraswami. UMP, HA.

CDM–Hansi Greer. UMP, HA.

CDM–Ned and Elizabeth Handy. Letter, May 20, 1943. UMP, HA.

CDM–Robert Edmond Jones. Morgan family papers.

CDM–C. G. Jung. UMP, HA.

CDM–Councilman Morgan. Morgan family papers.

CDM–Hallee Morgan. Morgan family papers.

CDM–Hallee and Councilman Morgan. Morgan family papers.

CDM–William Otho Potwin Morgan. Morgan family papers.

CDM–Henry A. Murray, 1925–26. Mostly CDM copies. Morgan family papers.

CDM–Lewis Mumford. Lewis Mumford papers. Van Pelt Library, University of Pennsylvania.

CDM–Lewis Mumford, 1938–76. UMP, HA.

CDM–Henry A. Murray. UMP, HA.

CDM–Henry A. Murray, 1943–45. Edwin Shneidman family papers.

CDM–Josephine Murray. Letter, January 22 (circa 1948). JLM family papers.

CDM–Saul Rosenzweig. UMP, HA, and Rosenzweig family papers.

CDM–Cleome Wadsworth. UMP, HA.

CDM–Alfred North Whitehead. Copied by CDM in her diaries. UMP, CL.

CDM–Frances Wickes. Frances Wickes papers, Library of Congress.

CDM–Frances Wickes. UMP, HA.

Henry A. Murray

PUBLISHED WORK

370

"Autobiography." (The Case of Murr). In *History of Psychology in Autobiography,* vol. 5, edited by E. G. Boring and G. Lindsey. New York: Appleton-Century Crofts, 1967.

"Brief Summary of Researches at the Psychological Clinic Annex." Department of Social Relations, Harvard University, June 15, 1956.

Explorations in Personality, A Clinical and Experimental Study of Fifty Men of College Age. By the Workers at the Harvard Psychological Clinic. New York: Oxford University Press, 1938.

"Foreword." Frances G. Wickes. *The Inner World of Choice.* New York: Harper & Row, 1963.

"The Harvard Psychological Clinic." *Harvard Alumni Bulletin,* October 25, 1935.

Harvard Psychological Clinic 1927–1937. Privately printed.

"In Nomine Diaboli." *New England Quarterly* 24 (1951): 435–52.

"In Response to Tobkin." Letter to editor. *Radcliffe Quarterly,* 1986.

"Introduction." *Pierre, or the Ambiguities,* edited by Henry A. Murray. New York: Farrar Straus/Hendricks House, 1949.

"Postscript." In C. G. Jung, *The Visions Seminars.* Zurich: Spring Publications, 1976.

"Prospect for Psychology." *International Congress of Applied Psychology,* Copenhagen, 1961. Reprinted in *Science* 136 (1962): 483–88.

———, and Christiana D. Morgan. "A Clinical Study of Sentiments." *Genetic Psychology Monographs* 32 (1945): 3–311.

———, and Christiana D. Morgan. "A Method of Investigating Fantasies. *Arch. Neurol. Psychiat.* 34 (1935): 289–306.

———, et al. *The Assessment of Men.* New York: Rinehart, 1948.

———, and the Staff of the Harvard Psychological Clinic. *The Thematic Apperception Test Manual.* Cambridge: Harvard University Press, 1943.

MISCELLANEOUS

CDM biography. Handwritten notes for a postscript to *The Visions Seminars,* C. G. Jung. Zurich: Spring Publications, 1976. UMP, CL.

Diary, August 1927. UMP, HA.

Dream notebook, n.d. Box 46. UMP, HA.

"From Mansol's Book." Handwritten document. UMP, HA.

"From Mansol's Tale of the Tower," February 4, 1940. Typescript. UMP, HA.

Interview by Gene Nameche, April 7, 1968. C. G. Jung Biographical Archives. CL.

"Mansol's Notes on What Went Wrong," circa 1940s. Typescript. UMP, HA.

Melville's *Pierre.* Note cards. UMP, HA.

Melville. Uncompleted MS. Boxes 3–6. UMP, HA.

Obituary notice, CDM. Handwritten notes. UMP, HA.

Official letter of appointment, April 12, 1926, Harvard University. UMP, HA.

"Olenka." Typescript. UMP, CL.

"Order of Memorial Rite, At the Tower on the Marsh, Newbury, Massachusetts, May 21, 1967." Typescript. UMP, CL.

"Secondary Spout Number 10: Review of Baleenian Endeavors," September 15, 1958. UMP/Murray Research Center.

"Supplement: Morsels of Information Regarding the Extraordinary Woman in Whose Psyche the Foregoing Visions Were Begot." Notes on CDM. UMP, CL.

Tower journal. UMP, CL.

"What Questions Bear Upon the Proposition?" The Tower, May 9, 1949. Handwritten foolscap. UMP, HA.

"Written by Mansol," September 11, 1943. Loose-leaf notebook diary. UMP, CL.

CORRESPONDENCE

HAM–Gerhard Adler, 1970s. UMP, HA.

HAM–Conrad Aiken. UMP, HA.

HAM–Alfred Cohn. UMP, HA.

HAM–Kenneth Diven. UMP, HA.

HAM–Maurice Firuski. UMP, HA.

HAM–Hansi Greer. UMP, HA.

HAM–Eleanor Jones. UMP, HA.

HAM–C. G. Jung. UMP, HA.

HAM–Lewis Mumford, 1938–76. UMP, HA.

HAM–Cecil D. Murray. UMP, HA.

HAM–Saul Rosenzweig. Letter, March 1967. Saul Rosenzweig family papers.

HAM–Cleome Wadsworth. UMP, HA.

GENERAL BIBLIOGRAPHY

AD Club 1914–1918. Cambridge, Mass.: Riverside Press, 1923.

Adler, Gerhard, ed. C. G. Jung Letters. Princeton: Princeton University Press, 1973.

Allen, Frederick Lewis. Only Yesterday: An Informal History of the Nineteen Twenties. New York: Harper and Brothers, 1931.

Allerton, Walter S. History of the Allerton Family in the U.S., 1585–1885. New York, 1888, 1900.

American Psychiatric Association. Diagnostic and Statistical Manual of Mental Disorders, Third Edition, Revised. Washington, D.C.: American Psychiatric Association, 1987.

Anderson, James William. "The Life of Henry A. Murray, 1893–1988." In Studying Persons and Lives, edited by A. I. Rabin, Robert A. Zucker, Robert Emmons, and Susan Frank, 304–34. New York: Springer, 1990.

————. "Henry A. Murray's Early Career: A Psychobiographical Exploration." *Journal of Personality* 56, no. 1 (March 1988): 139–71.

————. Interview with HAM. October 1987. Xerox copy.

Art Students League. "Fiftieth Anniversary of the Art Students League of New York, 215 West 57th St., Jan. 21–Feb. 2, 1925." Exhibition catalogue, Frick Art Reference Library.

Barbach, Lonnie, ed. *Erotic Interludes*. New York: Harper & Row, 1987.

Bateson, Mary. *Composing a Life*. New York: Atlantic Monthly Press, 1989.

Battaille, Georges. *Death and Sexuality*. New York: Walker, 1962.

————. *The Tears of Eros*. San Francisco: City Lights, 1989.

Beauvoir, Simone de. *The Second Sex*. New York: Vintage, 1974.

Belenky, Mary, Blythe Clinchy, Nancy Goldberger, and Jill Tarule. *Women's Ways of Knowing*. New York: Basic Books, 1986.

Bellak, Leopold. "Preface to the First Edition." *The T.A.T., C.A.T., and S.A.T. in Clinical Use*. 4th ed. Needham Heights, Mass: Allyn & Bacon, 1986.

Benjamin, Jessica. *The Bonds of Love: Psychoanalysis, Feminism, and the Problem of Domination*. New York: Pantheon, 1988.

————. "Master and Slave: The Fantasy of Erotic Domination." In *Powers of Desire: The Politics of Sexuality,* edited by Ann Snitow, Christine Stansell, and Sharon Thompson, 280–99. New York: Monthly Review Press, 1983.

Benson, Saul, A. C. Barger, and E. L. Wolfe. *Walter B. Cannon: The Life and Times of a Young Scientist*. Cambridge: Harvard University Press, 1987.

Bernard, Jessie. *Academic Women*. University Park, Pa.: Pennsylvania State University Press, 1964.

Binion, Rudolf. *Frau Lou*. Princeton: Princeton University Press, 1968.

Blake, William. *Jerusalem*. In *The Portable Blake,* edited by Alfred Kazin, 445–96. New York: Viking, 1946.

Boston Herald. May 10, 1919. Society page. Clipping in William Morgan scrapbook.

Boston marriage register. New England Historic Genealogical Society, microfilms of *Boston Marriage Registers,* 1894.

Boston Transcript. May 9, 1919. Society page. Clipping in CDM Diary, 1919.

Breines, Wini. *Young, White, and Miserable: Growing Up Female in the Fifties*. Boston: Beacon Press, 1992.

Brittain, Vera. *A Testament of Youth*. 1933. Reprint. London: Virago Press, 1978.

Brown, Lyn M., and Carol Gilligan. *Meeting at the Crossroads: Women's Psychology and Girls Development*. Cambridge: Harvard University Press, 1992.

Bunting, Mary. Inaugural speech as Radcliffe president. 1961.

Carotenuto, Aldo. *A Secret Symmetry*. New York: Random House, 1982.

372

Centennial Committee. *The Saturday Morning Club, 1871–1971*. Boston, 1971 (privately printed).

Chamberlain, Mariam K., ed. *Women in Academe: Progress and Prospects*. New York: Russell Sage Foundation, 1988.

Chernier, Kim. "An American in Paris." In Lonnie Barbach, ed. *Erotic Interludes*, 66–77. New York: Harper & Row, 1987.

Chodorow, Nancy. *Feminism and Psychoanalytic Theory*. New Haven: Yale University Press, 1989.

————. *The Reproduction of Mothering: Psychoanalysis and the Sociology of Gender*. Berkeley: University of California Press, 1978.

Collier, Robert. *The Plague of the Spanish Lady*. New York: Atheneum, 1974.

Coolidge, Emma Downing. *Descendants of John and Mary Coolidge of Watertown, Massachusetts, 1630*. Boston: Wright & Potter Printing Company, 1930.

Coolidge, Isabella–William Thayer correspondence. Morgan family papers.

Corsini, Raymond J. "Henry A. Murray's Needs-Press Theory." In *Current Personality Theory*, edited by Raymond J. Corsini, 408–10. Itaska, Ill.: Peacock, 1977.

Councilman, Isabella Coolidge. "Christiana Drummond Councilman." Handwritten birth book. Morgan family papers.

Councilman, William T. "Autobiography." Typescript, 1918. Holden family papers.

————. "Diary of the Rice Expedition." Morgan family papers.

————. Lecture in pathology delivered to second-year class of Harvard Medical School. December 19, 1921. Privately printed. Morgan family papers.

————. Letters from China, 1924. Holden family papers.

————. "The Relation Between the Roots of Plants and Fungi." *Proc. Soc. Exper. Biol. & Med.* 21 (1923–24): 361–63.

————. "Travels in China." Typescript. Morgan family papers.

Crosby, Alfred W., Jr. *Epidemic and Peace, 1918–*. Westport, Conn.: Greenwood, 1976.

Cushing, Harvey. "William Thomas Councilman: 1854–1933." *Science* 77, no. 2009 (June 30, 1933); reprinted in *National Academy Biographical Memoirs* XVIII: 157–74.

Dante Alighieri. *The Divine Comedy*. 3 vol. Translated by Dorothy Sayers. Baltimore: Penguin, 1968.

Dinnerstein, Dorothy. *The Mermaid and the Minotaur: Sexual Arrangements and Human Malaise*. New York: Harper & Row, 1976.

Douglas, Claire. *The Woman in the Mirror*. Boston: Sigo, 1990.

————. "Christiana Morgan's Visions Reconsidered," *SFJILJ*, 8, 4, (1989): No 1–21.

Duras, Marguerite. "Smothered Creativity." Reprinted in E. Marks and I. de Courtivron, eds. *New French Feminism*. New York: Schocken Books, 1975.

Edel, Leon, ed. *The Diary of Alice James*. New York: Penguin Books, 1964.

Ehrenreich, Barbara, and Deirdre English. *Complaints and Disorders: The Sexual Politics of Sickness.* New York: The Feminist Press, 1973.

374 ————. *For Her Own Good: 150 Years of the Experts' Advice to Women.* Garden City, N.Y.: Doubleday, 1979.

Ellenberger, Henri F. *The Discovery of the Unconscious: The History and Evolution of Dynamic Psychiatry.* New York: Basic Books, 1970.

Elms, Alan C. "The Personalities of Henry A. Murray." *Perspectives in Personality* 2 (1987): 1–14.

Encyclopaedia Britannica. 11th ed., Vol. XXVII, 704–13. Article on United States History by FJT (Frederick Jackson Turner).

Fincher, J. "America's Deadly Rendezvous with the Spanish Lady." *Smithsonian* 10 (January 1989): 19.

Fordham, Michael. "The Infant's Reach." *Psychological Perspectives* 21 (1989): 58–91.

Frick Art Reference Library. Photographic files. Works of art by Frank DuMond, Guy Pène du Bois, and Leo Lentelli.

Gagey, Edmond M. "Hannah Duston." In *Notable American Women, 1607–1950.* Vol. 1, edited by Edward T. James, 535–36. Cambridge: Belknap Press of Harvard University Press, 1971.

Gifford, Sanford. "Psychotherapy in Boston." In George E. Gifford, Jr., ed., *Psychoanalysis, Psychotherapy and the New England Medical Scene, 1894–1949.* New York: Science History Publications—USA, 1978.

Gilbert, Sandra M., and Susan Gubar. *The Madwoman in the Attic.* New Haven: Yale University Press, 1980.

————. *No Man's Land.* 2 vols. New Haven: Yale University Press, 1988–89.

Gilligan, Carol. *In a Different Voice: Psychological Theory and Women's Development.* Cambridge: Harvard University Press, 1982.

————. "Teaching Shakespeare's Sister." In C. Gilligan, N. Lyons, and T. Hanmer, eds. *Making Connections.* Cambridge: Harvard University Press, 1990.

————, J. V. Ward, and J. M. Taylor, eds. *Mapping the Moral Domain.* Cambridge: Harvard University Press, 1988.

Gonzalez-Crusso, F. *On the Nature of Things Erotic.* New York: Vintage Books, 1988.

Greer, Hansi–Barbara Hannah correspondence. UMP, HA.

Greer, S., and E. Myers. *Adult Sibling Rivalry: Understanding the Legacy of Childhood.* New York: Crown, 1992.

Griffin, Nicholas, ed. *Selected Letters of Bertrand Russell.* Vol. I. New York: Houghton Mifflin, 1992.

Hall, Nor. *Those Women.* Dallas: Spring Publications, 1990.

Harvard 1917. Class Book. HA.

Henderson, L. J., D. B. Dill, H. T. Edwards, and William O. P. Morgan. "Blood as a Physicochemical System." *Journal of Biological Chemistry* XC, no. 3 (March 1931): 697–724.

Hillman, James. *Anima.* Dallas: Spring Publications, 1985.

————. "Some Early Background to Jung's Ideas." *Spring,* 1976: 128–36.

Horney, Karen. *Feminine Psychology*. Edited by Harold Kelman. New York: W. W. Norton, 1967.

———. *The Neurotic Personality of Our Time*. New York: W. W. Norton, 1967.

375

Isaacs, Susan. *The Malting House School: A Study of Its Students*. Cambridge, England: Privately printed, 1927.

James, Henry. *The Bostonians*. New York Edition. New York: Scribner, 1907–9.

James, William. *The Principles of Psychology*. 2 vols. New York: Dover, 1950.

Jensen, Ferne, ed. *C. G. Jung, Emma Jung, Toni Wolff*. San Francisco: The Analytical Psychology Club, 1982.

Jones, Robert Edmond. Analysis notes. Morgan family papers.

———. Diary, 1925–26. Morgan family papers.

———–CDM–William Morgan correspondence. Morgan family papers.

———–Frances Wickes correspondence. Frances Wickes papers. Library of Congress.

Jung, C. G. "Anima and Animus." (The Relations Between the Ego and the Unconscious, Part Two, II). In *Collected Works* 7. Translated by R. F. C. Hull. Princeton: Princeton University Press, 1928.

———. "Answer to Job." In *Collected Works* 11. Translated by R. F. C. Hull. Princeton: Princeton University Press, 1952.

———. "Commentary on *The Secret of the Golden Flower.*" In *Collected Works* 13. Translated by R. F. C. Hull. Princeton: Princeton University Press, 1929.

———. *Dream Analysis: Notes of the Seminar Given in 1928–1930*. Edited by W. McGuire. Princeton: Princeton University Press, 1984.

———. *Interpretation of Visions: Notes on the Seminar Given by Dr. C. G. Jung*. Edited by Mary Foote. Multigraphed for private distribution. Zurich, 1930–34.

———. "Marriage as a Psychological Relationship." In *Collected Works* 17. Translated by R. F. C. Hull. Princeton: Princeton University Press, 1925.

———. *Memories, Dreams, Reflections*. New York: Vintage Books, 1965.

———. *Mysterium Coniunctionis: An Inquiry into the Separation and Synthesis of Psychic Opposites in Alchemy*. *Collected Works* 14. Translated by R. F. C. Hull. Princeton: Princeton University Press, 1955–56.

———. "The Psychological Aspects of the Kore." In *Collected Works* 9i, 1941. Translated by R. F. C. Hull. Princeton: Princeton University Press, 1969.

———. *Psychological Types*. In *Collected Works* 6. Translated by R. F. C. Hull. Princeton: Princeton University Press, 1921.

———. *Psychology of the Unconscious: A Study of the Transformation and Symbolism of the Libido. A Contribution to the Evolution of Thought*. Translated by Beatrice Hinkle. New York: Moffat, Yard & Co., 1916.

———. *Symbols of Transformation*. In *Collected Works* 5. Translated by R. F. C. Hull. Princeton: Princeton University Press, 1952.

——. "The Syzygy: Anima and Animus." In *Collected Works* 9ii. Translated by R. F. C. Hull. Princeton: Princeton University Press, 1951.

——. *The Visions Seminars*. From the notes of Mary Foote. Zurich: Spring Publications, 1976.

C. G. Jung Institute of Los Angeles. *Matter of Heart*. Film directed by Mark Whitney. Los Angeles, 1983.

Kierkegaard, Søren. *Fear and Trembling*. In *A Kierkegaard Anthology*. New York: The Modern Library, 1946.

Kilbourne, E. D. *Influenza*. New York: Plenum, 1987.

Killoran, J., ed. *Selected Letters of Conrad Aiken*. New Haven: Yale University Press, 1978.

Klagsburn, Francine. *Mixed Feelings: Love, Hate, Rivalry and Reconciliation Among Brothers and Sisters*. New York: Bantam, 1992.

Klein, Melanie. *The Psychoanalysis of Children*. London: Hogarth Press, 1932.

Koch, Sigmund, ed. *Psychology: A Study of a Science*. New York: McGraw-Hill, 1959.

Koltuv, Barbara. *Lilith*. York Beach, Maine: Nicolas Hays, 1986.

Krafft-Ebing, Richard von. *Psychopathia Sexualis*. 1886. Reprint. New York: Bell, 1965.

Landgren, Marchal. *Years of Art: The Story of the Art Students League of New York*. New York: Art Students League, 1940.

Lawrence, D. H. *Twilight in Italy*. 1916. Reprint. New York: Viking Press, 1958.

——. *Women in Love*. 1920. Reprint. New York: Viking Press, 1960.

Leeners, A. A. *Suicide Notes: Predictive Clues and Patterns*. New York: Human Sciences Press, 1988.

Lessing, Doris. *A Proper Marriage*. New York: New American Library, 1952.

Lewis, R. W. B. *Edith Wharton: A Biography*. New York: Harper & Row, 1975.

Loraux, Nicole. *Tragic Ways of Killing a Woman*. Cambridge: Harvard University Press, 1987.

Lorenz, Clarissa. *Lorelei Two*. Privately printed, 1980.

Lowe, Victor. "The Development of Whitehead's Philosophy." In *The Philosophy of Alfred North Whitehead*, edited by P. A. Schilpp. New York: Tudor, 1951.

——. *Understanding Whitehead*. Baltimore: Johns Hopkins Press, 1962.

Lutz, T. *American Nervousness, 1903*. Ithaca, N.Y.: Cornell University Press, 1991.

McDermott, Patti. *Brothers and Sisters: Resolving Adult Sibling Relationships*. Boston: Lowell House, 1992.

MacFarlane, Alison. *The Psychology of Childbirth*. Cambridge: Harvard University Press, 1977.

McGuire, William. *Bolligen: An Adventure in Collecting the Past*. Princeton: Princeton University Press, 1989.

———, ed. "Introduction." C. G. Jung, *The Dream Seminars*. Princeton: Princeton University Press, 1984.

———, ed. *The Freud–Jung Letters*. Princeton: Princeton University Press, 1974.

Masse, Michelle A. *In the Name of Love: Women, Masochism and the Gothic*. Ithaca, N.Y.: Cornell University Press, 1992.

Maternity Center of New York. *Handbook*. 1920.

Meador, Betty. *The Divine Feminine and Modern Women*. Cassette recording. C. G. Jung Institute of San Francisco, 1984.

Melville, Herman. *Moby Dick*. New York: Grosset & Dunlap, n.d.

———. *Pierre, or the Ambiguities*. Edited and with an introduction by H. A. Murray. New York: Hendricks House, 1949.

Miller, Donald L. *Lewis Mumford: A Life*. New York: Weidenfeld and Nicolson, 1989.

Moore, Merrill. *Merrill Moore: A Register of His Papers in the Library of Congress*. Washington, D.C.: Library of Congress Press, Manuscript Division. Container B, Box 47: Morgan, Christiana D., and Henry A. Murray, project of: Transcripts of Merrill Moore's interviews with, 1954–56. The Library of Congress, Manuscript Division. Morgan interview with Merrill Moore, Nov. 20, 1954, Session 3, record 1.

Moore, Thomas. *Dark Eros: The Imagination of Sadism*. Dallas: Spring Publications, 1990.

Morgan, William Otho Potwin. "An American Soldier in Vienna." *New Republic,* October 1, 1919.

———. "Anthropology Today and Psychotherapy." In Roheim, ed. "Psychoanalysis of Primitive Cultural Types." *International Journal of Psychoanalysis* XIII (January–April 1932).

———. "Austria's Agricultural Schools." 4-page typescript, n.d. Morgan family papers.

———. "Austria's Farm-lands." 5-page typescript. October 28, 1922. Morgan family papers.

———. Biographical entry. In Harvard class notes, class of 1918. HA.

———. "How Bolshevism Is Bred." 3-page typescript, n.d. Morgan family papers.

———. "In Transylvania—Huts and Plains." 5-page typescript, n.d. Morgan family papers.

———. "Human-Wolves Among the Navajo." Yale University Publications in Anthropology, no. 11. 43 pages. New Haven: Yale University Press, 1936.

———. "Lapford, Devon, England." 7-page typescript. September 1922. Morgan family papers.

———. "Navajo Dreams." *The American Anthropologist* 34, no. 3 (July–September 1932): 390–405.

———. "Navajo Treatment of Sickness: Diagnosticians." *The American Anthropologist* 33, no. 3 (1931): 390–402.

———. "Notes on Cross-Cultural Needs Press as Seen in Native American Ritual." 29-page typescript, n.d. Morgan family papers.

———. "Notes on Land Settlements—Austria." 17-page typescript. October 31, 1922. Morgan family papers.

378 ———. "Peace Treaty and Peace Commission." 9-page typescript. April 1919. Morgan family papers.

———. "A Preliminary Report on Navajo Treatment of Sickness." 70-page typescript, n.d. (Title page hand-printed by CDM). Morgan family papers.

———. "Rehabilitating Austria's Livestock." 9-page typescript. October 24, 1922. Morgan family papers.

———. "Sioux Culture." 80-page typescript, n.d. Morgan family papers.

———. Analysis and dream notebooks, autobiographical notes, diaries, scrapbooks, letters, newspaper clippings, and notebooks. Morgan family papers.

———–CDM correspondence. Morgan family papers.

———–HAM correspondence. Morgan family papers.

———–Robert Edmund Jones correspondence. Morgan family papers.

Moseley, Eva. "Reading Other People's Mail: Sisters in the Schlesinger Library." *The Radcliffe Quarterly,* March 1990.

Mumford, Lewis. *In the Name of Sanity.* New York: Harcourt Brace, 1954.

———. *My Work and Days: A Personal Chronicle.* New York: Harcourt Brace Jovanovich, 1979.

———. *Sketches from Life: The Autobiography of Lewis Mumford—Early Years.* New York: Dial Press, 1982.

———–CDM correspondence. Lewis Mumford papers. Special Collections. Van Pelt Library, University of Pennsylvania.

Murray, Cecil Dunmore. Biographical note. Harvard Class of 1919. HA.

———. Biographical note. Harvard Class of 1919, 25th Reunion book. HA.

———. Clippings and photos. JLM family scrapbook.

Murray, Josephine Rantoul. Diary, 1924–1926. JLM family papers.

Neumann, Erich. *Amor and Psyche: The Psychic Development of the Feminine.* New York: Harper, 1962.

New England Historic Genealogical Society files: Coolidge, Dustan, Allerton, Shurtleff, Councilman, Rantoul genealogies.

Paglia, Camille. *Sexual Personae.* New Haven: Yale University Press, 1990.

Pearson, Carol, and Katherine Pope. *The Woman Hero in American and British Literature.* New York: R. R. Bowker, 1981.

Perera, Sylvia. *Descent to the Goddess.* Toronto: Inner City Books, 1981.

Polster, Miriam. *Eve's Daughters: The Forbidden Heroism of Women.* San Francisco: Jossey-Bass, 1992.

Post, Laurens van der. *Jung and the Story of Our Time.* New York: Random House, 1975.

Prince, Morton. *The Dissociation of Personality*. New York: Green & Co., 1906.

———. *The Unconscious*. New York: Macmillan, 1914.

Reich, Wilhelm. *Character Analysis*. New York: Orgon Institute Press, 1945.

Reik, Theodor. *Of Love and Lust*. New York: Farrar Straus, 1949.

Reinharz, Jehuda. *Chaim Weizmann: The Making of a Zionist Leader*. New York: Oxford University Press, 1985.

Roazen, Paul. *Freud and His Followers*. New York: New York University Press, 1984.

Robinson, Forrest. *Love's Story Told*. Cambridge: Harvard University Press, 1992.

Rogers, Elizabeth Councilman, M.D. Interview recorded for the Schlesinger Library Archives. Dr. Elizabeth Councilman Rogers interviewed by Jeanette Bailey Cheek. Interview notes at Schlesinger Library, Radcliffe College. Cambridge, Mass. (OH-37).

Roosevelt, Theodore. Letter to HAM. JLM family papers.

Rose, Norman. *Chaim Weizmann*. New York: Penguin Books, 1986.

Rosenzweig, Saul. "The Experimental Measurement of Types of Reaction to Frustration." In *Explorations in Personality,* edited by Henry A. Murray. New York: Oxford University Press, 1938.

———. "The Experimental Study of Repression." In *Explorations in Personality.*

———. *Freud, Jung and Hall The King-Maker: The Historic Expedition to America (1909)*. St. Louis: Rana House, and Kirkland, Wash.: Hogrefe & Huber, 1992.

———–CDM correspondence. Saul Rosenzweig papers.

Rougemont, Denis de. *Love in the Western World*. New York: Pantheon, 1940.

Ruemann, G., and W. Robinson, eds. *The Romantic Spirit: German Drawings, 1780–1850*. New York: Oxford University Press, 1988.

St. Paul's School. Yearbook. 1914.

Sandner, Donald. "The Subjective Body in Clinical Practice." In *The Body in Analysis,* edited by Murray Stein. Willmette, Ill.: Chiron Publications, 1986.

———. *Symbols of Feminine Development in Jung's Visions Seminars*. Cassette recordings. C. G. Jung Institute of San Francisco, 1986.

Sarton, May. *Plant Dreaming Deep*. New York: W. W. Norton, 1968.

———. *A World of Light: Portraits and Celebrations*. New York: W. W. Norton, 1976.

Schilpp, P. A., ed. *The Philosophy of Alfred North Whitehead*. New York: Tudor, 1951.

Schreiner, Olive. *Women and Labour*. London: Victor Gollancz, 1911.

Serrano, Miguel. Interview by Gene Nameche. Box 17, C. G. Jung Biographical Archives. CL.

Shneidman, Edwin. "A Life in Death." In *The History of Clinical Psychology in Autobiography,* edited by C. Eugene Walker. Pacific Grove, Calif.: Brooks Cole, 1991.

Shurtleff, Benjamin. *The Descendants of William Shurtleff.* Privately printed, n.d.

380 Skard, Ase Gruda. *Liv Laga: Ei Minnebok, 1905–1940.* Oslo: Gyldedal Norsk Forlag, 1985.

Snitow, Ann. "Mass Market Romance: Pornography for Women Is Different." In *Powers of Desire: The Politics of Sexuality,* edited by Ann Snitow, Christine Stansell, and Sharon Thompson. New York: Monthly Review Press, 1983.

Solomon, Barbara M. *In the Company of Educated Women.* New Haven: Yale University Press, 1985.

Steele, Valerie. *Paris Fashion: A Cultural History.* New York: Oxford University Press, 1988.

Stoller, Robert. *Sexual Excitement.* New York: Simon & Schuster, 1980.

Strouse, Jean. *Alice James: A Biography.* Boston: Houghton Mifflin, 1980.

Stuhlmann, Gunther. *A Literate Passion.* San Diego: Harcourt Brace Jovanovich, 1987.

Thoreau, Henry David. *A Week on the Concord and Merrimack Rivers.* 1847. The Library of America. New York: Viking Press, 1985.

Tobkin, Dorothy. Correspondence with author, 1991–92.

———. Letter to editor. *Radcliffe Quarterly,* 1987.

Trimberger, Ellen Kay. "Feminism, Men, and Modern Love: Greenwich Village, 1900–1925." In *Powers of Desire: The Politics of Sexuality,* edited by Ann Snitow, Christine Stansell, and Sharon Thompson. New York: Monthly Review Press, 1983.

Triplet, R. G. "Henry A. Murray and the Harvard Psychological Clinic, 1926–1938: A Struggle to Expand the Disciplinary Boundaries of Academic Psychology." Ph.D. diss., University of New Hampshire, 1983.

U.S. Department of Labor, Bureau of Labor Statistics. *Consumer Price Index—Urban Consumers.* 1990.

Vance, Carole S., ed. *Pleasures and Dangers: Exploring Female Sexuality.* Boston: Routledge & Kegan Paul, 1984.

Wadsworth, Cleome. Interviewed by Gene Nameche. C. G. Jung Biographical Archives, Box 20, CL.

Watson, John B. *Psychological Care of Infant and Child.* New York: W. W. Norton, 1928.

West, Morris. *The World Is Made of Glass.* New York: William Morrow, 1988.

Wharton, Edith. *The Custom of the Country.* New York: Charles Scribner's Sons, 1913.

White, Benjamin V., M.D. *Stanley Cobb: A Builder of the Modern Neurosciences.* Boston: Countway Library of Medicine, 1984.

White, Robert. *A Memoir: Seeking the Shape of Personality.* Marlborough, N.H.: The Homestead Press, 1987.

Whitehead, Alfred North. *Adventures of Ideas.* New York: Macmillan, 1933.

———. *The Aims of Education and Other Essays.* New York: Macmillan, 1929.

———. *Process and Reality*. New York: Macmillan, 1929.

Whitmont, Edward C. "Reassessing Femininity and Masculinity." *Quadrant* 13, no. 2 (1980): 109–22.

———. *Return to the Goddess*. New York: Crossroad, 1982.

Wickes, Frances. *The Inner World of Man*. New York: Henry Holt, 1938.

———–Robert Edmond Jones correspondence. Frances Wickes papers. Library of Congress.

Wigglesworth, Isabella Councilman. "Boston—1895–1916." Typescript lecture prepared for the Saturday Morning Club, n.d. Holden family papers.

———. "A Club." Typescript lecture prepared for the Saturday Morning Club, n.d., Holden family papers.

Wigglesworth, Isabella Councilman. By her children. "My 70 Years with Isabella." Typescript play. Holden family papers.

Wilson, George. *Saints and Strangers: Being the Lives of the Pilgrim Fathers and Their Families and Their Friends and Foes; and an Account of Their Posthumous Wanderings in Limbo, Their Final Resurrection and Rise to Glory and the Strange Pilgrimages of Plymouth Rock*. New York: Reynal and Hitchcock, 1945.

The Winsor Club. Graduate Bulletin, 1940. Class of 1915 entry.

The Winsor School Catalogue, 1989–90.

Wittig, Monique. *Les Guerilleres*. Boston: Beacon Press, 1971.

Wolbach, S. B., M.D. "Obituary: William T. Councilman 1854–1933." *Archives of Pathology* 16 (July 1933): 114. (Reprinted in *Harvard Medical Alumni Bulletin*, 1934.)

Wolff, Toni. *Structural Forms of the Feminine Psyche*. 1934. Zurich: Spring Publications, 1973.

Woolf, Virginia. *A Room of One's Own*. New York: Harcourt, Brace, 1929.

381

Index